ENCHANTED EVENINGS

ENCHANTED EVENINGS

The Broadway Musical from
Show Boat to Sondheim

Geoffrey Block

OXFORD
UNIVERSITY PRESS

OXFORD
UNIVERSITY PRESS

Oxford   New York
Auckland   Bangkok
Buenos Aires   Cape Town   Chennai   Dar es Salaam
Delhi   Hong Kong   Istanbul   Karachi   Kolkata
Kuala Lumpur   Madrid   Melbourne
Mexico City   Nairobi   São Paulo   Shanghai
Taipei   Tokyo   Toronto

Library of Congress Cataloging-in-Publication Data
Block, Geoffrey Holden.
Enchanted evenings: the Broadway musical from
Show Boat to Sondheim / Geoffrey Block.
p.   cm.
Includes discography (p.), bibliographical references
(p.), and index.
ISBN 0-19-510791-8 (cloth)   ISBN 0-19-516730-9 (pbk.)
1. Musicals—New York (State)—New York—
History and criticism.
I. Title.
ML1711.8.N3B56   1997
782.1'4'097471—dc21   96-53477

1   3   5   7   9   8   6   4   2

Printed in the United States of America
on acid-free paper

To the beloved memory of

JOHN EASTBURN BOSWELL ("JEB"), 1947–1994

Best friend, best man,
Godfather to Jessamyn and (in spirit) to Eliza

CONTENTS

Contents

Act II: The Broadway Musical After Oklahoma!

Contents

PREFACE

I n many ways the preparation of this book brings me back to my childhood, where Rodgers and Hammerstein as well as Bach and Beethoven were frequent and compatible visitors. I cannot remember a time when my father, a professional jazz violinist and part-time lawyer (before he metamorphosed into a full-time attorney and part-time classical violinist), was not playing Cole Porter's "Anything Goes" on the piano, invariably in the key of E♭. Like many Americans in the 1950s, our family record library included the heavy shellac 78 R.P.M. boxed album of *South Pacific* with Mary Martin and Ezio Pinza and the lighter 33 R.P.M. cast album of *Carousel* with Jan Clayton and John Raitt. A major event was the arrival of Rodgers and Hammerstein's *Oklahoma!* and *South Pacific* in their newly released film versions. Keeping in tune with Rodgers and Hammerstein mania, I played every note and memorized many words of the songs contained in *The Rodgers and Hammerstein Song Book* and read Hammerstein's librettos in the (then) readily obtainable Modern Library edition of *Six Plays by Rodgers & Hammerstein*.[1]

My family was one of the eighteen million to purchase the cast album of *My Fair Lady*, and my sister quickly mastered the dialect and memorized the lyrics for all the roles. With the dawn of the stereo era in the late 1950s, we purchased *The Music Man* to test out our new portable KLH record player.[2] My parents, transplanted New Yorkers who settled near San Francisco, would see the traveling versions of Broadway shows, and by the early 1960s they began to take their offspring along.

Musicals created before the era of Rodgers and Hammerstein and Lerner and Loewe were less known. Only Gilbert and Sullivan and the occasional 1920s operetta were presented as dramatic entities. The songs, however, of many musicals from the 1920s and '30s were heard and played regularly in our community as well as in our home, especially those from *Porgy and Bess*. A memorable event occurred in the sixth grade when a dear family friend from Boston came to visit, sang and played Kern and Hammerstein's "Make Believe," and assisted me in my efforts to compose a small musical of three songs as a creative arts project. Earlier that year I had written a short term paper, "Rodgers and Hammerstein II with Lorenz Hart."

By the time I entered high school I had churlishly abandoned Broadway in favor of Bach, Beethoven, and Ives. As a sophomore I somewhat grudgingly served as rehearsal pianist for *South Pacific* and the following year still more grudgingly played the saxophone and clarinet in the *Guys and Dolls* pit band. Soon even Gershwin was suspect. I had not yet read the philosopher and sociologist Theodor Adorno and the highly acclaimed but decidedly unpopular composer Arnold Schoenberg, both of whom vigorously championed and successfully promoted the view that great art was rightfully destined to be unpopular. Only in retrospect did I realize that an ideological and elitist component was somehow connected to my genuine love of classical or "serious" music. Disdain for the music of the masses followed, including hit Broadway musicals, until and unless this repertory could earn endorsements from respectable sources, such as when Leonard Bernstein compared the Beatles' "She's Leaving Home" from *Sergeant Pepper's Lonely Hearts Club Band* favorably with Schubert.

In the early 1970s graduate students in historical musicology in many programs were strongly discouraged from studying American music of any kind. Instead, my colleagues and I at Harvard dutifully learned to decipher medieval notation and researched such topics as the life and works of King Henry VIII's Flemish-born court composer Philip van Wilder, Haydn's *opera seria,* and what really happened at the first performance of *Rite of Spring*. A research paper on the chronology and compositional process of Beethoven's piano concertos evolved into a dissertation and inaugurated my lifetime desire to understand how compositions of all types initially take shape and the practical as well as artistic reasons behind their revision.

These activities did not prevent me from stumbling on a free ticket to *Kiss Me, Kate*, which to my surprise I enjoyed immensely, despite a negative predisposition. My dormant love for Broadway musicals would receive additional rekindling when, several years later, I found myself the musical director in a private secondary school in Ojai, California, selecting a musical to produce and choosing *Kiss Me, Kate* to everyone's enjoyment and delight, including mine. In my second year at The Thacher School I anticipated *Crazy for You*, the 1992 musical based on *Girl Crazy*, with my own assemblage of freely interpolated Gershwin songs mixed with songs from the "dated" 1930 show—a triumph of accessibility over authenticity. By the end of that year I completed my doctorate, a milestone that somehow liberated me to explore American popular music of all types.

By then I had witnessed a broadcast in which Stephen Sondheim and conductor André Previn conversed with extraordinary articulateness about what a musical can accomplish.[3] Increasingly, stage and film musicals of both recent and ancient vintage occupied a major and passionate role in my life. After teaching a sequence of one-month "winterim" courses on American musical theater at the University of Puget Sound, including one in which students collaborated to create an original musical, I began to teach a Survey of American Musical Theater course first during alternate years and later annually. When faced with the dearth of usable textbooks, I began writing one of my own in the late 1980s. The book would, of course, correspond to what I had been teaching, a musical-by-musical study beginning with *Show Boat* that focused on the so-called Golden Era from the 1930s to the late 1950s, with a survey of Sondheim to round out the semester. You are now holding this book.

Before the 1990s, books on Broadway musicals were almost without exception written by theater historians and critics. For the most part these journalistic accounts typically covered a large number of musicals somewhat briefly and offered a useful and entertaining mixture of facts, gossip, and criticism. What they did not try to do is address what happens *musically* or how songs interact with lyrics within a dramatic context.[4]

Most books on the Broadway musical provided biographical profiles of principal composers and lyricists and plot summaries of popular musicals or those judged artistically significant. Some authors went considerably beyond these parameters, for example, Gerald Bordman by his comprehensiveness and Lehman Engel by focusing more selectively on critical topics and other issues such as adaptation of literary sources.[5] Two of the musicals surveyed in the present volume, *Show Boat* and *Porgy and Bess*, have inspired book-length monographs, and several musicals and their creators have received rigorously thoughtful scholarly, bibliographic, and critical attention. The fruits of this activity will be duly acknowledged in what follows.[6]

With few exceptions the musicological community studiously ignored the Broadway terrain. In the 1990s two important books emphasized (or "privileged") music for the first time: Joseph P. Swain's *The Broadway Musical: A Critical and Musical Survey* (1990), a study of selected musicals from *Show Boat* to *Sweeney Todd*, and Stephen Banfield's more specialized study, *Sondheim's Broadway Musicals* (1993).[7] Swain's valuable survey contains a great deal of perceptive musical and dramatic criticism and analysis. Nevertheless, Swain only rarely tries to place the discussion in a historical, social, or political context, he presents virtually no documentary history of a musical, and he does not address the questions of how and why musicals evolved as they did, either before opening night or in revival. Most general readers will also find Swain's analysis, which deals primarily with harmony, too technical to be easily understood. In contrast to Swain, Banfield, who focuses on a body of work by one significant composer-lyricist, does address compositional history and offers a multivalent and less autonomous approach; additionally, his sophisticated and frequently dense musical and dramatic analysis successfully incorporates techniques borrowed from literary criticism. Building on the solid edifices constructed by Swain and Banfield, the present book attempts to offer a musical and dramatic discussion more accessible to readers unfamiliar with analytical terminology.

Two important books on European opera have influenced the ensuing discussion of American musicals and merit special mention and gratitude here: Joseph Kerman's *Opera as Drama* and Paul Robinson's *Opera & Ideas*.[8] Kerman's unflinching insistence on music's primary role in defining character, generating action, and establishing atmosphere results in a somewhat sparse assemblage of canonic masterpieces. However, his brilliant overview of opera with its powerful guiding principle, "the dramatist is the composer," can be fruitfully applied to Broadway, even to those works that resolutely reject Kerman's model of a major operatic musical masterpiece. Robinson's accessible yet subtle survey of six operas (one each by Mozart, Rossini, Berlioz, Verdi, Wagner, and Strauss) and of dramatic meaning in the two Schubert song cycles offers imaginative and convincing insights on the power of texted music to express emotional and intellectual nuance. Both studies display a standard of excellence that might serve and inspire nearly any serious study of dramatic music, including the Broadway musical.

A third book on opera, Peter Kivy's *Osmin's Rage,* supplies valuable philosophical underpinning for a discussion on music and text.[9] Kivy's distinctions between the opposite principles of "textual realism" (music that "sets meanings, not words") and "opulent adornment" (music that "sets words, not meanings") are particularly helpful. The tensions between these two principles are embodied in the "song and dance" musicals (composed mainly but by no means exclusively in the 1920s and '30s) that feature "opulent adornment," and the so-called "integrated" musicals, the Rodgers and Hammerstein models of "textual realism" that gained commercial success, critical stature, and cultural hegemony beginning in the 1940s.

In the recent past intense ideological differences have been solidified. In one camp are those who argue that musicals are at their best when fully integrated and aspiring towards nineteenth-century European tragic opera; in another are those who relish nonintegrated and nonoperatic musical comedies. The contrasting perspectives of Swain and Banfield offer strong advocates for each side. Swain, who claims to disparage the taxonomic differences between opera and Broadway shows, nonetheless invariably places the latter, especially musicals that eschew their tragic potential, on a lower echelon. Thus for Swain, "though a number of its best plots have offered opportunities for tragic composition," the Broadway musical provides a litany of "missed chances and unanswered challenges."[10] Even *West Side Story*, the only musical that Swain unhesitatingly designates a masterpiece (in part because a central character achieves the heights of tragedy when he dies singing), falls short of operatic tragedy when Maria speaks rather than sings her response to the death of her beloved Tony.

Banfield, sympathetic to a subject (Sondheim) who is rarely "trying to challenge opera on its own territory," argues that in musicals, in contrast to operas that are through-sung, music "can often not just move in and out of the drama but in and out of itself, and is more dramatically agile ... than in most opera."[11] For Banfield, *West Side Story* keeps faith with Bernstein's desire to avoid "falling into the 'operatic trap,' " and Maria's final speech works perfectly.[12]

Among other juicy bones of contention are the conflicts between popularity and critical acclaim, authenticity and accessibility, opulent adornment and textual realism, artistic autonomy and social and political contextuality, and nonintegrated versus integrated musical ideals. This preface has introduced some of these issues and critical quagmires that will be reintroduced in chapter 1 and developed in subsequent chapters. Neutrality is neither always possible nor always desirable to achieve, especially on the subject of critical relationships between music and text and music and drama. My general intent, however, is to articulate the merits as well as the flaws of opposing arguments. In the court of free intellectual inquiry, more frequently than not, at least two sides are competent to withstand scrutiny and trial.

Tacoma, Wash.   G. B.
January 1997

ACKNOWLEDGMENTS

Without more than a little help from parents, family, friends, teachers and professors, colleagues, students, readers and editors, librarians and archivists and the collections they serve, and copyright owners and their assistants and lawyers, this book could not have been written. I am glad for this opportunity to thank some of the institutions and people that contributed to this collaborative process.

Collections in the New York Public Library (Loesser), Yale University (Porter, Weill), the State Historical Society of Wisconsin (Blitzstein, Moss Hart, Sondheim), the Kurt Weill Foundation (Weill), and the Library of Congress (Gershwin, Kern, Loewe, Porter, Rodgers, and Weill) were indispensable in my research. Of the many who facilitated my use of these priceless holdings I would like to thank individually Harold L. Miller of the State Historical Society of Wisconsin, David Farneth and Joanna C. Lee of The Kurt Weill Foundation, Victor Cardell and Kendall Crilly of Yale University, and especially Raymond A. White of the Library of Congress, for sharing his time and knowledge so generously.

For special kindnesses I would like to identify and thank the following: Louis H. Aborn, President, Tams-Witmark; Tom Briggs, Director, The Rodgers and Hammerstein Theatre Library; Tom Creamer, Dramaturg, The Goodman Theater; Marty Jacobs and Marguerite Lavin of the Museum of the City of New York; David Leopold, Al Hirschfeld's representative at the Margo Feiden Galleries; and Roberta Staats and Robert H. Montgomery of the Cole Porter Musical and Literary Property Trusts. A grant from the National Endowment for the Humanities in 1990 enabled me to research and draft several chapters, and the University of Puget Sound provided generous financial and other assistance at several stages over the past decade. I am also grateful for the expertise and helpfulness of Oxford University Press, especially my editor, Maribeth Payne, her assistant, Soo Mee Kwon, production editor Joellyn M. Ausanka, and copy editor Paul Schlotthauer.

Jacqueline Block, Andrew Buchman, and Richard Lewis read portions of various early drafts, offered useful advice and encouragement, and helped me to consolidate central ideas as well as many details. In later stages several reviewers offered valuable suggestions both large and small that I was able to incorporate into the final draft. Throughout I was guided by the wise counsel of my friend, colleague, and "ideal reader" (i.e., intelligent, curious, and challenging, but not necessarily a musician), Michael Veseth, Professor of Economics.

The following people also provided much-needed information, services, or support: Marcie Bates, Ronald L. Blanc, Abba Bogin, John E. Boswell, J. Peter Burkholder, Theodore S. Chapin, Tara Corcoran, Christopher Davis, Lee Davis, Denise Dumke, Sarah Dunlop, Arthur Elias, Hugh Fordin, April Franks, Peter P. Mc.N. Gates, Rosemarie Gawelko, Peter Greenfield, David Grossberg, John L Hughes, Judy Hulbert, Autumn Inglin, Caroline Kane, Andrew King, Al Kohn, Frank Korach, Deann Kreutzer, Arthur Laurents, Florence Leeds, bruce d. mcclung, Anne McCormick, Judith McCulloh, Kathy McCullough, Paul McKibbins, Zoraya Mendez, Betty Kern Miller, Jeremy Nussbaum, Leonard Pailet, Harriet F. Pilpel, Mitchell Salem, Evelyn Sasko, Joan Schulman, Larry Starr, Jo Sullivan, Hope H. Taylor, Andrea N. Van Kampen, and Robin Walton.

Finally, I would like to thank my family and friends. My parents and my sister, Norma, introduced me to the joy of musicals when I was a child, and the senior Blocks have unceasingly nurtured my intellectual and aesthetic growth ever since. My friends shared and profoundly enriched my processes of discovery. My wife, Jacqueline, was my friendliest and most helpful critic. My daughters, Jessamyn and Eliza, not only inspired me to organize my time more efficiently but gave perspective and meaning to this and all my other work.

ENCHANTED
EVENINGS

OVERTURE

CHAPTER ONE

INTRODUCTION

Setting the Stage

T he central subjects in this book are fourteen "book" musicals that premiered on Broadway between the late 1920s and the late 1950s, beginning with *Show Boat* (1927) and ending with *West Side Story* (1957).[1] All of these shows—most for several generations—have demonstrated a measure of popularity and critical approbation. They also offer an array of fascinating critical, analytical, social, and historical issues. Perhaps more important, the musicals surveyed here continue to move us to applaud and cheer (and sometimes hiss), to sing their songs, follow their stories, and make us laugh and cry. In short, they entertain us. Forty, fifty, sixty, even seventy years later we eagerly revisit these shows, not only on Broadway, but in high school and college productions and amateur and professional regional theaters of all shapes and sizes, artistic aims, audiences, and budgets.

In this selective (and to some degree idiosyncratic) survey I do not presume to develop a theory of permanent or ephemeral values or to unravel the mysteries of either artistic merit or popular success. I do, however, attempt to establish a critical and analytical framework that might contribute to an understanding, appreciation, and enjoyment of the selected musicals. The purpose of this introduction is to present recurring topics and issues, to encapsulate the approach to the subject this book will take, and to explain—and sometimes defend—the choices.

Why start with *Show Boat*? Certainly, other American musicals that premiered before December 27, 1927 are still successfully revived. Nevertheless, although the choice of where to begin a survey of Broadway is by nature somewhat arbitrary and destined to generate controversy, Broadway historians and critics with surprising unanimity subscribe to the view espoused by the admittedly biased judgment of *Show Boat* enthusiast Miles Kreuger: "The history of the American Musical Theatre, quite simply, is divided into two eras—everything before *Show Boat* and everything after *Show Boat*."[2] *Show Boat* not only opened up a world of possibilities for what an ambitious American musical on an American theme could accomplish, it remains firmly anchored as the first made-in-America musical to achieve a secure place in the core repertory of Broadway musicals.

Before *Show Boat* the Broadway shows that created their greatest initial and most lasting imprints were often British and Viennese imports such as William S. Gilbert's and Arthur Sullivan's *H.M.S. Pinafore* (1879) and Franz Lehár's *The Merry Widow* (1907), respectively. Earlier shows that displayed unequivocally American themes, for example the so-called Mulligan shows of Edward Harrigan and Tony Hart between 1879 and 1883, Percy Gaunt's and Charles H. Hoyt's phenomenally successful *A Trip to Chinatown* in 1891 (657 performances), and George M. Cohan's *Little Johnny Jones* in 1904, are today remembered for their songs.[3] The latter show is perhaps best known from its partly staged reincarnation in film (the 1942 classic film biography of Cohan, *Yankee Doodle Dandy*, starring James Cagney) or the musical biography *George M!* (1968), which features a potpourri of memorable Cohan songs. Victor Herbert's *Naughty Marietta* (1910), Jerome Kern's so-called Princess Theatre Shows (1915–1918) with books and lyrics by P. G. Wodehouse and Guy Bolton (especially *Very Good Eddie* and *Leave It To Jane*), Harry Tierney's and Joseph McCarthy's *Irene* (1919), Sigmund Romberg's *The Student Prince in Heidelberg* (1924), Vincent Youmans's and Irving Caesar's *No, No, Nanette* (1925), and *The Desert Song* (1926) (music by Romberg, lyrics by Otto Harbach and Oscar Hammerstein II) are occasionally revived and singled out as outstanding exponents of the American musical before *Show Boat*.[4] But unlike Gilbert and Sullivan and Lehár's imported classics, these stageworthy as well as melodious musical comedies are not widely known, and the Herbert and Romberg operettas are mainly familiar to the Broadway-attending public primarily in greatly altered MGM film versions.[5] The unfairly neglected musicals before *Show Boat* certainly merit a book of their own.

By 1927 the early masters of the American Broadway musical, Herbert, Cohan, Romberg, and Rudolf Friml, either had completed or were nearing the end of their numerous, lucrative, and—for their era—long-lived Broadway runs. Joining Kern, a new generation of Broadway composers and lyricists—Irving Berlin, Cole Porter, Oscar Hammerstein, George and Ira Gershwin, Richard Rodgers, Lorenz Hart, and, in Germany, Kurt Weill (all but Hammerstein and Weill are featured in Al Hirschfeld's drawing "American Popular Song: Great American Songwriters") had already launched their Broadway careers by 1927.[6] But despite their auspicious opening salvos, the greatest triumphs for this illustrious list, with the exception of Kern, would arrive after *Show Boat* in the 1930s and 1940s.

Critical Issues

Although the present survey will offer biographical profiles of the composers, lyricists, librettists, and other key players in order to place their careers in the context of a particular musical, critical and analytical concerns will receive primary attention. In fact, each of the fourteen musicals explored in the main body of the text and the career of Stephen Sondheim in chapter 13 demonstrate critical issues of enduring interest. Two issues in particular emerge as central themes and will occur repeatedly throughout this survey: the tension between two ideological approaches—song and dance versus integrated—to the Broadway musical, and the alleged conflict between temporal popularity and lasting value and the selling out, again alleged, not of tickets but of artistic integrity.

Acute manifestations of the latter conflict have been attributed to the careers of Gershwin, Rodgers, Weill, Frank Loesser, Leonard Bernstein, and Sondheim. The former issue is embodied in (but by no means confined to) the differences between the Rodgers and Hart and the Rodgers and Hammerstein shows; the career of Porter, who, after a string of hits (and then some flops) in musicals modeled after *Anything Goes*, responded in *Kiss Me, Kate* to the "anxiety of influence" generated by Rodgers and Hammerstein; and the controversial but frequently alleged schism between the European and the American musicals of Weill.[7] At the risk of giving away the plot, the view espoused here is that the song and dance musical comedies that prevailed in the 1920s and '30s and the integrated musicals that became more influential in the 1940s and '50s both allow a meaningful dramatic relationship between songs and their shows. A subtext of the ensuing discussion is that selling tickets does not necessarily mean selling out artistic integrity.

In each chapter readers will hear again from opening-night theater (and occasionally music) critics. These critics were usually the first to offer prophetic pontifications for Broadway audiences eager to discover whether or

"American Popular Song: Great American Songwriters" (clockwise from left): Richard Rodgers, Lorenz Hart, Cole Porter, Harold Arlen, Dorothy Fields, Jerome Kern, Johnny Mercer, Ira Gershwin, Irving Berlin, Hoagy Carmichael, George Gershwin, and Duke Ellington. 1983. © Al Hirschfeld. Drawing reproduced by special arrangement with Hirschfeld's exclusive representative, The Margo Feiden Galleries Ltd. New York.

not they should feel smug or inadequate in their appreciation or rejection of a show. The critics (again, mostly theater critics) can be reviled but they cannot be ignored, especially since, despite their lack of specialized musical training, they have consistently demonstrated remarkable precognition (or inspired self-fulfilling prophecies) regarding the critical as well as the popular fate of Broadway shows. Although they must produce their work under enormous pressure and seemingly against all odds, receiving little sympathy in the process, opening-night critics frequently call attention to issues that will reappear to haunt a show. Such early perceived problems and issues as *Show Boat*'s second act or the jarring stylistic heterogeneity of *Porgy and Bess* or *The Most Happy Fella* do not go away but remain to be reassessed and reinterpreted by future generations.

The degree to which the stage works we love should be performed in authentic versions has been a source of debate in America for more than two centuries. Writing about nineteenth-century American approaches to European opera, Richard Crawford defines accessibility as "the tailoring of the music to suit particular audiences and circumstances" and authenticity "as an ideal countering the marketplaces's devotion to accessibility."[8] According to Crawford, accessibility "privileges occasions over works" and "*invests ultimate authority in the present-day audiences.*" "Authenticity privileges works over occasions" and "*invests ultimate authority in works and the traditions within which they are composed.*" The desirability of—or resistance to—establishing an authentic musical and literary text for a show and the struggle between authenticity and accessibility will loom as a major issue in several chapters of this survey, in particular those on *Show Boat, Anything Goes, On Your Toes, Porgy and Bess*, and the Goldman-Sondheim-Prince-Bennett *Follies.*[9] Kern and Hammerstein, the principal creators of *Show Boat*, themselves produced a second "authentic" version that would be more "accessible" to audiences desiring the newer Rodgers and Hammerstein model. *Anything Goes* revivals in 1962 and 1987 would be equipped with a new book and many songs interpolated from other Porter shows. The 1983 *On Your Toes* would match a new book with the original score (albeit somewhat rearranged).

The original "operatic" sung form (emphasizing authenticity) of *Porgy and Bess* has clearly prevailed in recent years over its "Broadway" form with spoken dialogue (emphasizing accessibility). Nevertheless, considerable debate continues to rage over what constitutes an authentic text for this work. Charles Hamm has argued that the cuts made by the creators in its original Theatre Guild production are justifiable for artistic as well as for commercial reasons and that the current urge to restore these cuts creates a historically and aesthetically untenable reconstruction.[10] With the purpose of shedding some light on this heated subject, the chapter on *Porgy and Bess* will treat at length the historical background and aesthetic problems posed by one such cut, the "Buzzard Song."

The starting point for contemplating the "text" of a musical is almost invariably a vocal score rather than a full orchestral score, and later—after the release of *Oklahoma!* in 1943—the cast recording in various states of completion. It is therefore not surprising that Broadway musicals as a genre have been unusually susceptible to identity crises. Although some musicals after *Oklahoma!* were considerably reworked in future productions, musicals prior to this landmark show typically have been treated as less fixed and therefore more subject to revision and interpolation. The first part of this survey will trace how several shows have evolved in response to the competing interests of accessiblity or authenticity and what these responses tell us about changing social and aesthetic tastes and values.

Analytical Issues

The principal analytical question raised in this survey is how music and lyrics serve, ignore, or contradict dramatic themes and ideas, both in specific scenes and in the shows as a whole. Although this study will only infrequently treat music autonomously, a major factor behind the selection of the shows surveyed is the widely appreciated musical richness and enduring appeal of their scores. In contrast to most previous surveys, in which music is neglected beyond unhelpful generalities about its power to convey mood, music in this study will emerge as an equal (and occasionally more than equal) partner to the other components of a show, including lyrics, librettos, choreography, and stage direction.

Even when a musical is seemingly distinguished more by self-contained rather than integrated songs, the relationship of music and lyrics and music's power to express dramatic themes will be a central aesthetic issue for each musical. While some admiration will be reserved for those musicals that approximate Joseph Kerman's criteria for European operatic excellence, using music to define character and generate action as espoused in his *Opera as Drama,* other musicals considered with equal favor here do not accomplish this at all.[11]

The philosophical distinctions regarding text setting expressed by Peter Kivy apply also to the disparate approaches of Broadway musicals. As noted in the Preface, Kivy contrasts "the *principle of textual realism,*" in which the meanings of words are "interpreted" musically, "with another approach to the setting of texts . . . the *principle of opulent adornment,*" in which texts are set like precious jewels "hindered neither by the meaning nor the intelligibility of what he [the composer] 'sets.' "[12] The contrasting careers of Rodgers and Hart and Rodgers and Hammerstein embody these different approaches. Comparisons might suggest that something was lost as well as gained by the abandonment of cleverness, wit, and autonomous memorable tunes (Kivy's "opulent adornment" of words) in favor of integrated and more operatically constructed musicals filled with such techniques such as leitmotivs, foreshadowing, thematic transformation, and classical borrowings, however convincingly employed for various dramatic purposes (Kivy's "textual realism").

The language of the analysis is intended to be accessible to readers unversed in musical vocabulary. For this reason harmonic details will receive less emphasis than melodic and rhythmic aspects. Some of the shows discussed here adopt techniques analogous to those practiced in the operas of Mozart, Verdi, and Wagner, and the book is based on the premises that for some musicals, melodic and rhythmic connections and imaginative use of classical borrowings (for a striking example of the latter see *West Side Story*) audibly enrich the dramatic fabric, and that some knowledge of these connections might contribute to the appreciation and enjoyment of these works.

For readers who neither read music nor profess any musical discernment beyond a knowledge of what they like, the intent here is that the lyrics which accompany most of the musical examples will provide an aid in figuring out the point and purpose of the analytical discussion without undue discomfort. Since for many, negotiating musical terminology of any kind is an ordeal, occasionally even rudimentary concepts such as intervals, rhythmic note values, and the idea of central and hierarchical key relationships will need to be explained. Although the attempt to create a text suitable for a "Broadway audience" unaccustomed to musical terminology may inevitably lead to some oversimplication from the perspective of theorists and musicologists, it is nevertheless the goal that something meaningful and new can be gained for this audience as well. In nearly all cases the focus will be on those musical features which can actually be heard, and on the musical expression of dramatic meanings and dramatic context.

The Making of a Musical, Adaptation, and Social Issues

How is a musical created and how does knowledge of compositional process, including the revisions made during out-of-town tryouts, lead to a better understanding and appreciation of the works we see and hear today? How were the composers, lyricists, and librettists, our principal subjects, influenced by directors, choreographers, producers, and audiences? How did the creators of these shows achieve a balance between artistic and commercial control of their work?

Although a knowledge of a musical's compositional process can provide partial answers to these questions, the study of how a musical evolves from precompositional discussions, early sketches, and drafts to opening night and subsequent revivals has not been widely explored in the literature on

Broadway.[13] Sometimes the creative problems posed by musicals seem to find solutions by opening night or shortly thereafter; other problems remain for the life (and afterlife) of the show. When source materials permit this type of an inquiry—and some musicals were selected for this survey in part because they left conspicuous paper trails—the present study will examine how unpublished compositional materials (such as, early libretto and lyric drafts, musical sketches, and letters), support or contradict more widely available published memoirs, interviews, and retrospective panels of creative participants.

One common denominator that links most of the musicals discussed in this survey is the practice, ubiquitous after *Oklahoma!*, of adapting a literary source for the musical stage (Appendix A). Three adaptations that contend with formidable antecedents are explored at some length. The chapters on these shows will examine how and why these famous plays were adapted for new audiences in a new medium and how they preserved (*Kiss Me, Kate* and *West Side Story*) or distorted (*My Fair Lady*) the fundamental dramatic meanings of their sources in their musical reincarnations.

More specifically, the chapter on *Kiss Me, Kate* (chapter 9) will compare Sam and Bella Spewack's original libretto with the final Broadway version as well as with Shakespeare's *The Taming of the Shrew*, and in the process suggest that Porter may have learned as much from his own *Anything Goes* as he did from Rodgers and Hammerstein about how to relate music to character. In *My Fair Lady* (chapter 11) Lerner and Loewe departed significantly from Shaw's ending to *Pygmalion*. After giving the mean-spirited Professor Henry Higgins a more humane face (intentionally denied by Shaw) by the end of act I, the Broadway team, in their second act, made explicit, mainly through the songs, what Shaw implies or omits. Ironically, although they romanticized—and thereby misrepresented—Shaw's intentions, Lerner and Loewe managed to convey Eliza Doolittle's metamorphosis as Higgin's equal, through both Lerner's lyrics and Loewe's reversal of their musical roles, more clearly than either Shaw's play or director Gabriel Pascal's 1938 film, upon which *My Fair Lady* was based.

When discussing *West Side Story* (chapter 12) the point argued is not simply that the Broadway collaboration more closely approximates the spirit of Shakespeare's *Romeo and Juliet* than earlier operatic adaptations (or some films) that retain the Bard's namesakes and setting, but that Bernstein—with considerable help from Sondheim (lyrics), Arthur Laurents (libretto), and Jerome Robbins (choreography and conception)—found a musical solution to convey the dramatic meaning of Shakepeare through the use of leitmotivs and their transformations in combination with a jazz American vernacular.

10

The present survey will only occasionally emphasize social history. That is another book that very much needs to be written. Nevertheless, the study of a musical most often leads to political and cultural issues, even if it was the expressed intent of its creators to escape from meaning. For many of the musicals discussed in Act I especially, the changes that went into their revivals over the decades offer a valuable tool to measure changing social as well as artistic concerns. Some musicals, such as *Show Boat, Porgy and Bess,* and *West Side Story* are overtly concerned with racial conflicts; others, such as *Anything Goes, On Your Toes, One Touch of Venus,* and *My Fair Lady* explore class differences. All musicals discussed here either directly or inadvertently make powerful statements about what James Thurber called The War Between Men and Women.[14]

The Cradle Will Rock serves as a worthy representative to show both the wisdom and futility of the didactic political musical. Two songs from this "avant-garde" musical will be discussed from this perspective. The first is "Croon– Spoon," which satirizes the vapidity of ephemeral popular music, and the second is "Art for Art's Sake," which from Marc Blitzstein's perspective indicts the equally vapid messages of so-called high art, the purposes to which art is used, and the blatant hypocrisy of some artists.

Not surprisingly, few musicals measure up to evolving sensibilities. The disparity between these shows and feminist values will be given special attention in interpreting *Anything Goes, Lady in the Dark, One Touch of Venus, Carousel, Kiss Me, Kate, Guys and Dolls,* and *My Fair Lady,* all of which provide gender issues of unusual interest. Some musicals fare better than others from the vantage point of the late 1990s, but no musical surveyed here can fully escape the assumptions and collective values of their era.

1
Why These Musicals?

The present selection makes an effort to include representative musicals from *Show Boat* to *West Side Story* that pose intriguing critical, analytical, aesthetic, and political issues as well as musicals which engage the enthusiasm of the selector. No attempt was made either to be comprehensive or to discuss only the very most popular musicals of the era, but Appendixes B and C will provide useful reference points for measuring and interpreting the degree of popularity these musicals enjoyed. Despite the above disclaimer, a few words should be said about the degree to which popularity governed the present selections.

Ten of the fourteen Broadway musicals receiving top billing here were also among the most popular of their respective decades. *Show Boat* was the third longest running musical of the 1920s, *Anything Goes* and *On Your Toes* ranked second and eighth respectively in the 1930s, and in the 1940s and '50s *Kiss Me, Kate, Carousel, One Touch of Venus, My Fair Lady, Guys and Dolls, West Side Story,* and *The Most Happy Fella* all fall within the top fifteen longest runs. Eight of these musicals are among the top thirty-four musicals spanning these four decades; three rank in the top ten.[15]

While one measure of a show's popularity and its even more important correlate, commercial success, is the length of its initial run, the revivability of a show arguably constitutes a more compelling measure of its success. Many musicals, even blockbusters of their day, never manage to regain their hit status and acquire a place in the Broadway repertory despite rigorous marketing or a lustrous star. For example, despite its many merits, *Of Thee I Sing* (1931), the longest-running book musical of the 1930s and the recipient of the first Pulitzer Prize for drama, has disappeared as a staged work on Broadway after its disappointing seventy-two performance revival in 1952. Two of the musicals under scrutiny here, *Lady in the Dark* (1941) and *One Touch of Venus* (1943), both enormous hits in their time, still await a staged New York revival. The chapter devoted to these last mentioned shows (chapter 7) will offer the view that the absence of *One Touch of Venus* is especially lamentable.

The remaining twelve musicals, ten since 1980, have resurfaced in at least one popular Broadway, Off-Broadway, or other prominent New York revival.[16] By 1960 New York audiences had had the opportunity to see *Show Boat* 1,344 times, a total that more than doubled its original run and was surpassed only by five continuous running musicals in the top forty. *The Cradle Will Rock,* something of a cult musical, admittedly remains an idiosyncratic choice for a selective survey. Nevertheless, this controversial and sometimes alienating show has been revived in New York City no less than four times since its original short but historic run in 1937. Although these *Cradle* revivals may have been generated out of political sympathy, the present study will make a case for the work's still unacknowledged and unappreciated artistic merits.

If popularity in absolute numbers is the ticket for admittance, what then are *Pal Joey* (1940), *Lady in the Dark* (1941), and *Porgy and Bess* (1935), three shows that were neither in the top forty nor among the top ten or fifteen musicals of their decades, doing in a survey of popular Broadway musicals? To answer this question, it might be helpful to consider a musical's popularity by the standards of its immediate predecessors. Although it may not have enjoyed a major New York revival in more than fifty years, *Lady in the Dark* at 467 performances would surpass even the longest run of the 1930s, *Of Thee I Sing*.[17] *Pal Joey* (374 performances) would rank as the fifth-longest-running show of the 1930s had it premiered one year earlier.[18] More significantly, in contrast to nearly every other musical *comedy* before *Guys and Dolls*, including *Anything Goes* and *On Your Toes*, revivals of *Pal Joey* for the most part retain the original book without fear of ridicule or loss of accessibility.

The inclusion of *Porgy and Bess* on popular grounds requires some spin control. Because it lost money, it is fair to judge its initial total of 124 performances as a relatively poor showing—even in a decade when 200 performances could constitute a hit. As a musical in the commercial marketplace, *Porgy and Bess* failed; as an opera, arguably a more accurate taxonomic classification, it can be interpreted as a phenomenal success. No other American opera of its (or any) generation comes close.[19]

In contrast to his musical comedies and operettas, Gershwin's only Broadway opera returned a few years later in 1942, albeit more like a conventional musical with spoken dialogue replacing sung recitative—favoring accessibility over authenticity—and became a modest commercial success at 286 performances. Within seven years New York audiences thus were able to see Gershwin's opera (or a reasonable facsimile) 410 times before the arrival of *Oklahoma!*, thirty performances less than *Of Thee I Sing*, the biggest hit of the 1930s and of Gershwin's career. And in contrast to Gershwin shows that, in revival, have been transformed into barely recognizable but highly accessible and commercially successful adaptations (*My One and Only* [1983], *Oh, Kay!* [1990], and *Crazy For You* [1992]) revivals of *Porgy and Bess*, at least since the mid-1970s, often go to great lengths to restore Gershwin's opera to prevailing notions of authenticity.

The willingness to eschew comprehensiveness leads to inevitable omissions. In addition to Styne's four top forty musicals the most conspicuous absentees are Berlin, whose *Annie Get Your Gun* (ranked eighth) has for many years earned an enduring place in the core repertory despite the relative absence of major New York revivals since 1966, and the team of Richard Adler and Jerry Ross, the composer-lyricists who in 1954 and 1955 produced two of the most successful musicals of their era, *Pajama Game* (tenth) and *Damn Yankees* (eleventh), before Ross's premature death in 1955 at the age of twenty-nine. Some readers may lament the absence of lyricist E. Y. ("Yip") Harburg's collaborations with composers Harold Arlen and Burton Lane, or of composer-lyricists Harold Rome and Robert Wright and George Forrest.[20]

Despite these omissions, the present representative survey includes at least one musical selected from the work of those composers, lyricists, and librettists responsible for many of the top forty musicals shown in Appendix C. The most popular creators of each decade are also well represented. In the 1920s six of the eleven longest runs had either a score by Kern or lyrics or a libretto by Hammerstein. In the 1930s only two musicals of the twelve longest runs did not feature a score by Rodgers and Hart, Kern, Porter, or the Gershwins (who provided four, three, two, and one, respectively), and one of these consisted of recycled music by Johann Strauss, Jr. By the 1940s and '50s, Rodgers, now teamed with Hammerstein, dominated the musical marketplace with no less than five of the ten longest runs of those years.[21]

Coda

In *The American Musical Theater* noted Broadway conductor and educator Lehman Engel offered the following list of fifteen Broadway "models of excellence" that "represent that theater in its most complete and mature state": *Pal Joey, Oklahoma!, Carousel, Annie Get Your Gun, Brigadoon, Kiss Me, Kate, South Pacific, Guys and Dolls, The King and I, My Fair Lady, West Side Story, Gypsy, Fiddler on the Roof, Company,* and *A Little Night Music.*[22] The first twelve of Engel's list fall within the focus period of this study, and six of these will be explored. In his pioneering volume Engel is primarily concerned with the "working principles" that govern "excellent" musicals. In another chapter he singles out four Broadway operas that also embody these principles—*Porgy and Bess, The Cradle Will Rock, The Consul* (Gian-Carlo Menotti), and *The Most Happy Fella* (three of which will be featured in the present volume).

All the musicals in Engel's list of fifteen turned a profit and nearly all had long runs, including seven of the ten longest runs between *Oklahoma!* and *The Sound of Music.* Engel's most conspicuous omission is without a doubt *Show Boat,* a musical almost invariably honored by subsequent list-makers and Broadway historians and critics as the first major musical on a uniquely American theme, one of the first to thoroughly integrate music and drama, and the first American musical to firmly enter the Broadway repertory. Although subsequent lists added a few scattered musical comedies from the 1930s and the musicals of Weill, all of which Engel excludes, the spirit of Engel's list is echoed in nearly all those that followed.[23] With virtually no exceptions the musicals on these lists enjoyed long initial runs and critical acclaim, and usually received one or more major New York revivals.[24]

Within a few years after *West Side Story* the age of Porter, Lerner and

14

lin, and Rodgers and Hammer-
masters of the 1930s, '40s, and
of popularity and critical acclaim
ratic and instrumental predeces-
differences between this incom-
, exemplified by the contrasting
Sondheim, and few musicals by
uld earn the combination of love
and critically acclaimed musicals

take a look at the career of the
ized as a central artistic figure on
here is that Sondheim's modern-
is an extension and reinterpreta-
del rather than a rebellion from
ondheim has vigorously denied
he pressure to compromise faced
those faced by Sondheim himself
essures of commercial theater.
sonal fictive level, Sondheim, in
We Roll Along and *Sunday in the*
issue of artistic compromise in
ced more obliquely by several of
his spiritual Broadway ancestors surveyed here who experienced similar
creative crises in their effort to simultaneously transcend the conventions
of their genre and retain their audiences. The last chapter will acknowledge
Sondheim's attempt to move beyond the integrated action model to the
concept (or thematic) musical and his ability to convey the nuances of his
increasingly complex characters and musically capture the meaning of his
dramatic subjects. It will additionally emphasize how Sondheim's musicals
can be viewed as the proud inheritance of the great traditional musicals
from *Show Boat* to *West Side Story*.

As revivals continue to demonstrate, many musicals between *Show Boat*
and *Gypsy* (1927–1959), as well as another group created in the 1960s by
several relatively new Broadway artists (perhaps most notably Jerry Bock's
and Sheldon Harnick's *Fiddler on the Roof* [1964] and John Kander's and
Fred Ebb's *Cabaret* [1966]), have not simply disappeared. Although the verdict for these more recent musicals is still inconclusive, it is not too soon
to notice the spectacularly long runs and endless tours of Webber musicals
and the revivals of Sondheim's earlier shows in the 1970s, '80s, and '90s.

If it does not seem politically correct these days to speak of a Broadway canon, few would deny the presence of a core repertory of Broadway musicals for the period of this study and considerably beyond. While the term "core repertory" avoids cultural bias and has the benefit of inclusiveness—in the core repertory there is a place somewhere for both Webber and Sondheim—the idea of a canon, or nucleus of works within a genre perceived as models of excellence, remains a useful if somewhat unpalatable construct. In any event, it is ironic that the deconstruction and even demolition of canons, including the venerable and unassailable eighteenth- and nineteenth-century European classical repertory, has become fashionable just as a firm foundation for canonization has begun to emerge in the genre of Broadway musicals.

While it is still permissible to say that some musicals are more popular than others, most critics and historians are loath to argue that some are actually more worthy of canonical status.[25] Northrop Frye, perhaps wisely (or least safely), chastized advocates of both "popular" and "art for art's sake" camps, when he wrote in his *Anatomy of Criticism* that "the fallacy common to both attitudes is that of a rough correlation between the merit of art and the degree of public response to it, though the correlation assumed is direct in one case and inverse in the other."[26]

The stance of the present volume is that "popularity" and "art for art's sake" are not mutually exclusive values, that writing for a commercial market can lead to inspiration as well as compromise. Perhaps we cannot explain or tell why this is so, but we can nonetheless revel in the many enchanted evenings (and some matinees) that these musicals continue to provide.

BEFORE RODGERS AND HAMMERSTEIN

CHAPTER TWO

SHOW BOAT

In the Beginning

T he *New Grove Dictionary of Music and Musicians* informed its readers in 1980 without exaggeration or understatement that *Show Boat* is "perhaps the most successful and influential Broadway musical play ever written."[1] For the authors of *New Grove* the impact of *Show Boat* has been "inestimable, particularly in that it impelled composers of Broadway musicals to concern themselves with the whole production as opposed to writing Tin Pan Alley songs for interpolation."[2] For the many who judge a show by how many songs they can hum or whistle when they leave (or enter) the theater, *Show Boat* offered "at least" an unprecedented six song hits for the ages; moreover, nearly all of these songs, according to *Grove*, "are integral to the characterization and story." And the many who place opera on a more elevated plane than Broadway musicals could be impressed by the knowledge that *Show Boat*, when it entered the repertory of the New York City Opera in 1954, was the first Broadway show to attain operatic stature.[3] By virtually any criteria, *Show Boat* marks a major milestone in the history of the American musical and has long since become the first Broadway show to be enshrined in the musical theater museum.

Show Boat gained recognition in the scholarly world too when in 1977 it became the first Broadway musical to receive book-length attention in Miles Kreuger's thorough and authoritative *"Show Boat": The Story of a Classic American Musical.*[4] Five years later, manuscript material for the musical numbers, discarded during the tryout months prior to the December

1927 premiere, was discovered in the Warner Brothers Warehouse in Secaucus, New Jersey.[5] By April 1983 the Houston Opera Company—which
had in the late 1970s presented and recorded a *Porgy and Bess* that restored
material cut from its pre-Broadway tryouts—arrived in New York with a
version of *Show Boat* that used Robert Russell Bennett's original orchestrations (rediscovered in 1978) and most of the previously discarded tryout
material.

In 1988 John McGlinn, who had served as a music editor for the Houston Opera, conducted a recording of *Show Boat* on EMI/Angel that incorporated Bennett's 1927 orchestrations and restored tryout material.
McGlinn's recording offered a significant amount of dialogue with musical
underscoring. It even included an appendix containing longer versions of
several scenes (shortened for the New York opening) and songs that Kern
composed for the 1928 London engagement, the 1936 Universal film (with
a screenplay by Hammerstein and new songs by Kern), and the New York
revival in 1946.[6]

Critics who attended the opening night on December 27, 1927, at the Ziegfeld sensed that *Show Boat* was not only a hit but a show of originality and
significance. Robert Coleman, for example, described *Show Boat* in the *Daily
Mirror* as "a work of genius" and a show which demonstrated the sad fact
that "managers have not until now realized the tremendous possibilities
of the musical comedy as an art form."[7] Coleman's review is also representative in its praise of the original run's exceptional production values,
including "fourteen glorious settings" and a superb cast. Although *Show
Boat*, in contrast to other Ziegfeld productions, did not open with a lineup
of scantily clad chorus girls, Coleman thought he saw "a chorus of 150 of
the most beautiful girls ever glorified by Mr. Ziegfeld."[8]

Within a few days after its opening Percy Hammond wrote that *Show
Boat* was "the most distinguished light opera of its generation," and Brooks
Atkinson described it as "one of those epochal works about which garru-
lous old men gabble for twenty-five years after the scenery has rattled off
to the storehouse."[9] Nearly every critic described Kern's score either as his
best or at least his recent best. Surveys of the American musical as far back
as Cecil Smith's *Musical Comedy in America* (1950) support these original
assessments and single out *Show Boat* as the only musical of its time "to
achieve a dramatic verisimilitude that seemed comparable to that of the
speaking stage."[10] Beginning in the late 1960s historians would almost invariably emphasize *Show Boat*'s unprecedented integration of music and

drama, its three-dimensional characters, and its bold and serious subject matter, including miscegenation and unhappy marriages.

Although critics for the most part found silver linings nearly everywhere, they also freely voiced their discontent with one aspect of the work: the libretto. *Show Boat* might give the highly respected (albeit somewhat curmudgeonly) critic George Jean Nathan "a welcome holiday from the usual grumbling," but most critics felt that the libretto, while vastly superior to other books of the time, did not demonstrate the same perfection as Kern's music and Florenz Ziegfeld's production.[11] In particular, critics voiced their displeasure with the final scene. Robert Garland, who described *Show Boat* as "an American masterpiece," noted some "faltering, like many another offering, only when it approaches the end," and Alexander Woollcott wrote that "until the last scene, when it all goes gaudy and empty and routine, it is a fine and distinguished achievement."[12]

More recent historians continued to view *Show Boat* as a refreshing but flawed departure from other shows of its day. Richard Traubner, for example, who praised *Show Boat* as "the greatest of all American operettas," attributed this greatness to its triumph over "libretto problems."[13] Even *Show Boat* aficionado Kreuger corroborates the verdict of earlier complaints: "As a concession to theatrical conventions of the time, Hammerstein kept everyone alive to the end and even arranged a happy reunion for the long-parted lovers, decisions, he revealed to this writer, that he came to regret."[14]

Despite these reservations, only Lehman Engel, the distinguished Broadway conductor and the first writer to establish canonical criteria for the American musical (chapter 1), would banish *Show Boat* from this elite group. Although Engel acknowledges that *Show Boat*'s "score and lyrics are among the best ever written in our theater," he tempers this praise by his assessment of "serious weaknesses."[15] For Engel, *Show Boat*'s "characters are two-dimensional, its proportions are outrageous, its plot development predictable and corny, and its ending unbearably sweet."[16] Engel is particularly perturbed by six "not only silly but sloppy" coincidences that take place in Chicago within a three-week period in 1904 (significantly all in the second act), coincidences that are comically improbable, even in a city with half its present population.[17]

Of the two principal collaborators, Hammerstein (1895–1960) had far more experience with operetta-type musicals as well as recent successes. *Wildflower* (1923), created with co-librettist Otto Harbach and composers Herbert Stothart and Vincent Youmans, launched a phenomenally successful decade for Hammerstein as librettist, lyricist, and director for many of Broadway's most popular operettas and musical comedies: *Rose-Marie* (1924) and *The Wild Rose* (1926) with Rudolf Friml and Stothart; *Song of the Flame* (1925) with George Gershwin and Stothart; and the still-revived *The Desert Song* (1926) with Sigmund Romberg. Two years before *Show Boat* Hammerstein had also collaborated with Harbach and Kern on the latter's most recent success, *Sunny*.

Kern (1885–1945), whose mother was a musician, "had some European training in a small town outside of Heidelberg" when he was seventeen and studied piano, counterpoint, harmony, and composition the following year at the New York College of Music.[18] Ten years before *Show Boat* Kern stated in interviews that "songs must be suited to the action and the mood of the play."[19] At the same time he also considered devoting his full attention to composing symphonies.

Although there is no reason to doubt Kern's aspiration "to apply modern art to light music as Debussy and those men have done to more serious work,"[20] it was not until *Show Boat* that Kern was able to fully realize these goals. Kern had, of course, previously created complete scores for an impressive series of precocious integrated musicals during the Princess Theatre years (1915–1918), at least two of which, *Very Good Eddie* and *Leave It to Jane*, have been successfully revived in recent decades. For the earlier years of his career, however, Kern had been confined mainly to composing interpolated songs to augment the music of others. Two of these, "How'd You Like to Spoon With Me?" interpolated into *The Earl and the Girl* (1905), and "They Didn't Believe Me" from *The Girl from Utah* (1914), remain among his best known. Similarly, *Sally* (1920) and *Sunny* (1925), two vehicles for the superstar Marilyn Miller and his most popular shows composed during the years between the intimate Princess Theatre productions and the grandiose *Show Boat*, are remembered primarily for their respective songs "Look for the Silver Lining" and "Who?" and have not fared well in staged revivals.

Before 1924 Edna Ferber had never even heard of the once-popular traveling river productions that made their home on show boats. By the following summer she had begun the novel *Show Boat*, which was published serially in *Woman's Home Companion* between April and September 1926 and in its entirety in August by Doubleday. Early in October, Kern, who had read half of Ferber's new book, phoned Woollcott to ask for a letter of introduction to its author and met her at a performance of Kern's latest musical, *Criss Cross,* that same evening. Even before Ferber had signed a contract on November 17 giving Kern and Hammerstein "dramatico-musical" rights to her hot property, the co-conspirators had already completed enough material to impress *Follies* impresario Ziegfeld nine days later.[21] On December 11 Kern and Hammerstein signed their contracts, according to which a script was to be delivered by January 1 and the play was to appear "on or before the first day of April 1927."[22]

By 1927, Kern had long since earned the mantle allegedly bestowed on him by Victor Herbert (1859–1924), the composer of *Naughty Marietta* (1910) and dozens of other Broadway shows, as the most distinguished American-born theater composer. For more than a decade Kern had been the model and envy of Porter, Gershwin, and Rodgers, who were embarking on their careers during the Princess Theatre years. But it was not until *Show Boat* that Kern had the opportunity to create a more ambitious species of Broadway musical. The care which he lavished on the score is conspicuously evident from the numerous extant pre-tryout drafts on deposit at the Library of Congress (Appendix D, p. 321, no. 1) and by an unprecedentedly long gestation period from November 1926 to November 1927 that included numerous and lengthy discussions with librettist and lyricist Hammerstein. Many other changes were made during the out-of-town tryouts.

Reconstructing Show Boat *(1927–1994)*

In order to provide a framework for discussing *Show Boat* it will be useful to distinguish among its various stage and film versions. Although the vocal score of the 1927 production, published by T. B. Harms in April 1928, has been out of print for decades, much of this original Broadway version was retained in the still-available London vocal score published by Chappell & Co. (also 1928). It is also fortunate that much of the Convent Scene and two brief passages absent from the Chappell score—the parade music in act I, scene 1, and the "Happy New Year" music ("Hot Time in the Old Town Tonight") in act II, scene 6—can be found in a third vocal score, published by The Welk Music Group, that also corresponds reasonably well to the 1946 touring production.[23]

McGlinn's 1988 recording is an indispensable starting point for anyone interested in exploring a compendium of the versions produced between 1927 and 1946 (as well as the 1936 film).[24] All of these versions incorporate new ideas and usually new songs by the original creators. Even if one does not agree with all of McGlinn's artistic and editorial decisions, especially his decision to include in the main body of the recording (rather than in the appendix) material that Kern and Hammerstein had agreed to cut from the production during tryouts, the performances are impressive and the notes by Kreuger and McGlinn carefully researched.

In the introduction to his monograph Kreuger notes that "one fascinating aspect of *Show Boat* is that, unlike most major musicals, it has never had an official script or score."[25] The lack of the former did not pose a problem to Kreuger, who had obtained the 1927 libretto directly from Hammerstein himself a few days before his death in August 1960.[26] Its absence has proven, however, to be an enormous headache for historians and, conversely, a source of opportunity for some directors (for example, Hal Prince), who have been given a free hand to decipher and interpret the complicated evolution and varied documentary legacy of this musical according to their personal visions.

One extended number published by Harms, "Mis'ry's Comin' Aroun'," had been dropped from the production in Washington, D.C., as early as November 15 after the very first evening of the tryouts. Because Kern "insisted that the number be published in the complete vocal score," McGlinn argued, not without justification, that Kern "hoped the sequence would have an afterlife in a more enlightened theatrical world."[27] For this reason McGlinn includes "Mis'ry" into the body of his recording rather than in an appendix.

McGlinn's other "restorations and re-evaluations" are less convincing on historical grounds. Dropped from both the Harms score and the 1927 production were two numbers, "I Would Like to Play a Lover's Part" (originally placed at the beginning of act I, scene 5) and "It's Getting Hotter in the North" (act II, scene 9). The latter song was replaced by a reprise of "Why Do I Love You?" called "Kim's Imitations," performed by the original Magnolia, Norma Terris, who was made up to look like her daughter Kim and performed impressions of famous vaudeville stars. Since Kern did not wish to include this discarded material in the vocal score (and it was in response to Kern's wishes that McGlinn reinserted "Mis'ry"), its presence in the body of McGlinn's recording is questionable. One other number deleted before the December premiere, "Trocadero Opening Chorus" (at one time in act II, scene 6), was placed in the main portion of McGlinn's recording for "technical reasons."[28]

For the first London production in 1928—which premiered after the New York version had been playing for a little more than four months—Kern and Hammerstein wrote "Dance Away the Night" (replacing Kim's reprise of "Why Do I Love You?," itself a replacement of "Kim's Imitations"). Also in this production Kern's 1905 London hit, "How'd You Like to Spoon with Me?," replaced the non-Kern interpolation, "Good-bye, Ma Lady Love." Two scenes were entirely omitted, the Convent Scene (act II, scene 4) and the scene in the Sherman Hotel Lobby (act II, scene 5), along with the song, "Hey, Feller!" (act II, scene 7). Another song, "Me and My

Show Boat, the marriage of Magnolia and Ravenal at the end of act I (1946). Photograph: Graphic House. Museum of the City of New York. Gift of Harold Friedlander.

Boss," composed especially for Paul Robeson, who sang the role of Joe, was not used and is presumed lost.[29]

The next major Broadway revival, with extensive changes by Kern and Hammerstein, arrived on January 5, 1946.[30] Even the overture was new, a more traditional medley-type version to replace the "Mis'ry"-dominated overture of the 1927 production. The first word heard in the original 1927 New York production, "niggers," had already been replaced by "coloured folks" in the 1928 London production. For the 1946 revival Hammerstein removed other references to this offensive word and rewrote a quatrain in the opening chorus in which "Coal Black Rose or High Brown Sal" was replaced by the less racially tinted phrase in dialect, "Y'work all day, y'git no fun."

Other changes in 1946 included a new emphasis on dance numbers, the composition of yet another song for Kim in the final scene, "Nobody Else But Me" (Kern's final song before he died on November 11, 1945 during auditions), three major deletions ("Till Good Luck Comes My Way," "I Might Fall Back on You," and "Hey, Feller!" [dropped in London 1928]), an abbreviation ("C'Mon Folks"), a repositioning ("Life Upon the Wicked Stage"), the deletion of two scenes (act I, scene 3, and act II, scene 5), and the rewriting of a third (act II, scene 7).[31] Kreuger, who briefly discusses these changes, does not mention the elimination of local color (including

banjos and tubas) and comedic elements such as Captain Andy's introduction of Rubber-Face Smith in the opening scene. Although Kreuger regretted the absence of style in the stage performances, he unhesitatingly
supported these revisions as improvements.[32]

Theater historian and critic Ethan Mordden in a *New Yorker* essay on
Show Boat published one year after the McGlinn reconstruction assesses the
1946 version far less favorably. Although, like Kreuger, Mordden recognizes the incalculable influence of *Oklahoma!* and *Carousel,* he regrets the
alterations which "homogenized a timeless, diverse piece into a document
of a specific place and time: Broadway mid-nineteen-forties."[33] Mordden
continues:

> In 1927, "Ol' Man River" and the miscegenation scene and "Bill"
> derived their power partly from a comparison with the musical-
> comedy elements dancing around them. Take the fun away, the
> apparently aimless vitality, and "Show Boat" loses its transcen-
> dence. The 1946 "Show Boat" is dated now, too consistent, too
> much of its day. The 1927 "Show Boat" is eclectic, of many days.
> Nevertheless, the revisions were locked in. American "Show
> Boat" revivals honored the 1946 version without question, and it
> became standard.[34]

In contrast to most of the musicals discussed in subsequent chapters,
Show Boat directors and their public can choose among two authentic
stageworthy versions and one film version (considerably fewer, for instance, than the possibilities extant for Handel's *Messiah*). More commonly
they have chosen to assemble a version of their own. Just as conductors
have for two hundred years created their own *Messiah* hybrids, the 1971
London and 1994 Broadway revivals presented provocative conflations of
several staged versions of *Show Boat* as well as the 1936 film.[35] For example, two songs from the 1971 London revival that were part of the 1928
London version did not appear in the original 1927 New York production.[36] Kern's swan song and last attempt at a final song for the show,
"Nobody Else But Me," introduced in the 1946 New York revival (but not
in the touring production), also appears, albeit sung out of context in 1971
by superstar Cleo Laine, who refused the role of Julie unless she was assigned a third song. From the 1936 Universal film the 1971 London revival recycled two of its three new songs, "Ah Still Suits Me" (for Paul
Robeson's Joe) and "I Have the Room Above Her" (for Allan Jones's Ravenal), sung by their rightful characters but in newly conceived dramatic
contexts.[37] Although critical assessments may vary, the 1971 London pro-

duction provides an unmistakable example of the triumph of accessibility over authenticity.

In director Hal Prince's revival of Show Boat in 1994 (the first Broadway production to take full advantage of McGlinn's research) "brothers" and later "coloreds" "all work on the Mississippi" and racial prejudice is acknowledged on stage throughout the evening.[38] Blacks move scenery and pick up messes left by whites, whites steal the Charleston dance steps from black originators, and an endlessly reprised "Ol' Man River" sung by Michel Bell looms larger than ever. In scenes depicting 1927 as well as the late 1880s audiences could see conspicuous signs over drinking fountains and elsewhere marked "White Only" and "Colored Only."[39]

Prince and production designer Eugene Lee employed modern stagecraft "to create montages which integrate a leap of years, restore serious incidents and clarify plot and character motivations."[40] From the 1928 London version Prince borrowed "Dance Away the Night" when he needed some music for the radio. From the 1936 film he used Ravenal's suggestive song, "I Have the Room Above Her" and, more pervasively, "motion picture techniques such as cross-fades, dissolves and even close-ups."[41] As in the 1946 Broadway production, Frank and Ellie's "I Might Fall Back On You" was dropped (although used as underscoring) and dance assumed a still more important role, especially in the montages staged by choreographer Susan Stroman.[42] The powerful "Mis'ry's Comin' Aroun'," restored for the Houston Opera production on Broadway in 1983, was again featured.

In earlier productions act II opened with a crowd scene at the 1893 World's Fair in Chicago. Prince drops this scene along with its two songs ("At the Fair" and "In Dahomey") and takes the duet between Magnolia and Ravenal, "Why Do I Love You?", which was sandwiched between these songs, and gives it to the otherwise songless Parthy (Elaine Strich) to sing to her granddaughter. Perhaps inspired by the 1936 film, which, unlike the stage version, shows the birth of Kim and Parthy rocking her, the effect of this change is enormous. With this one gesture, the shrewish, bigoted, and largely unsympathetic Parthy gains a humanity denied in all previous staged versions.

Musical Symbolism and Dramatic Meaning

In an article that appeared in Modern Music during Show Boat's initial New York run, Robert Simon, a staff writer for the New Yorker and an opera librettist, wrote about what he perceived as Kern's operatic predilections:

In *Show Boat*, Kern has an opportunity to make much of his dramatic gift. The action is accompanied by a great deal of incidental music—although "incidental" is a misleading trade term, for Kern's music heightens immeasurably the emotional value of the situation. . . . Themes are quoted and even developed in almost Wagnerian fashion.[43]

Without further elaboration Simon suggests that Kern, like Wagner and several of the Broadway theater composers considered in this study, embraces his principal dramatic themes within a family of leitmotivs.[44] All of these motives in Kern and Hammerstein's "leit-opera" (a term perhaps coined by Simon) can be seen against the backdrop of the Mississippi, arguably the principal protagonist of the drama, much as the "folk" form the heart and center of Musorgsky's *Boris Godunov* and Gershwin's *Porgy and Bess*.

In its purest form, closest to nature, like Mahler's cuckoos in his First Symphony (1888), Kern has chosen to represent the river by the interval of a perfect fourth (the same interval that begins "Taps" and "Reveille"). As shown in Example 2.1a, "Fish got to swim [B♭-E♭], and birds got to fly" [E♭-B♭]), Kern uses this perfect fourth to connect the force of the natural world with the central human theme of the work embodied in "Can't Help Lovin' Dat Man": a woman in love is destined to love her man forever, even when he abandons her. The theme first appears early in the work as underscoring for the dialogue in which the unrequited lover Pete questions Queenie about how she acquired the brooch he had given Julie. Since audiences have not yet heard the words to this song, its meaning cannot be fully grasped during the exchange between Pete and Queenie that interrupts choruses of "Cotton Blossom." But with Example 2.1a, the lyrical version of Julie's song that whites would not know (it was sung by her African-American mother when Julie was a child), Kern and Hammerstein have successfully connected Queenie and Julie from the outset of the show. Julie's identity as a mulatto otherwise remains undisclosed until two scenes later, when the meaning and impact of her assocation with Queenie's race will be clarified.

Significantly, the five three-note *Show Boat* themes shown in Example 2.2 are sung by and to people–or in one case to an anthromorphized boat— who are part of the river and close to nature.[45] The largest group of these "river" motives, nearly all introduced in *Show Boat*'s opening scene, consist of short musical figures, in which Kern fills in the perfect fourth of "Can't Help Lovin' Dat Man" with a single additional note. The four notes of the

Example 2.1. "Can't Help Lovin' Dat Man"
(a) original form
(b) transformation into a rag

"Cotton Blossom" (Example 2.2a) when reversed provides the opening musical material for the main chorus of Joe's "Ol' Man River" (Example 2.2b) and, when reshuffled, Captain Andy's theme (Example 2.2c).[46] Additional transformations of these three notes encompassed within a perfect fourth can be found in the opening of "Queenie's Ballyhoo" (Example 2.2d) and in a prominent segment of "Mis'ry's Comin' Aroun'" (Example 2.2e), included in all three published vocal scores. Although Kern never acknowledged a source, all of these themes might be traced, appropriately enough, to Dvořák's contemporaneously composed "New World" Symphony (1893) (Example 2.2f).[47]

Parthy and Sheriff Vallon also lead their lives along the river. In contrast to the characters who are in sympathy with this life force, however (Captain Andy and his *Cotton Blossom*, Joe, Queenie, the black laborers, and the women of any race who can't help loving their men), Parthy and Vallon demonstrate their intrinsic antipathy to the river with subtle alterations that intrude on the simplicity and perfection of the perfect fourth. Audiences first meet Parthy and her theme (Example 2.3) after the climax of the song "Cotton Blossom" as underscoring to her yelling "Andy!!!! Drat that

29

(a)

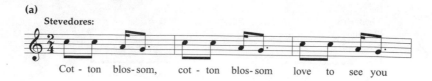

Stevedores:

Cot - ton blos-som, cot - ton blos- som love to see you

(b)

Joe:

Ol' man Riv - er, dat ol' man Riv - er, He

(c)

Ensemble:

Cap - tain An - dy, Cap - tain An - dy,

(d)

Queenie:

Hey!——————— Where yo' think yo' go - in'?

(e)

(f)

Example 2.2. "River Family" of motives (transposed to the key of C Major)
(a) "Cotton Blossom"
(b) "Ol' Man River"
(c) "Captain Andy's theme"
(d) "Queenie's Ballyhoo"
(e) "Mis'ry" theme
(f) from Dvořák's "New World" Symphony

Parthy Ann appears. "Andy!!!! Drat that man, he's never around!"

Example 2.3. Parthy's theme

man, he's never around!" moments before we hear Magnolia's piano theme (Example 2.4).

The first two notes of Parthy's theme are a descending perfect fourth (D-A). But although Parthy may lead a life along the river, Captain Andy cannot and Kern will not make her drink in its physical beauty and spiritual richness. Consequently, after this perfect fourth, Kern has Parthy introduce a B♭, only a half-step up from the A but a giant step removed from the natural world of the river. The B♭ and its following note G combine with the still-held D above to produce a G-minor triad, significantly the same chord that generates and supports Magnolia's inhibition and lament later in the scene in section 4 of "Make Believe" ("Though the cold and brutal fact is"). By the second measure of her theme Parthy has moved below the descending fourth of the "Cotton Blossom" (to an F♯). In the third and fourth measures—a repetition of the first two but transposed up a sinister augmented fourth or tritone (D to G♯), the tense and dissonant interval that will figure so prominently in the music of Sporting Life (*Porgy and Bess*) and the Jets (*West Side Story*)—Parthy's theme has moved radically from G minor to C♯ minor (also a tritone) where it will remain for the duration of its remaining four measures. Perhaps in her musical resistance to the river Parthy is expressing a longing for her home state of Massachusetts, where "no decent body'd touch this show boat riffraff with a ten foot pole."[48]

Once he has established musical equivalents for his characters and their world, Kern transforms and links these themes melodically and rhythmi-

(a)

Piano (*off stage*). Ravenal listens.

(b)

Andante moderato

Example 2.4. Magnolia's piano theme and "Where's the Mate for Me?"
(a) Magnolia's piano theme
(b) "Where's the Mate for Me?" (B section, or release)

cally to make his (and Hammerstein's) dramatic points, as, for example, the transformation of Captain Andy's theme into a wedding march at the end of act I and then into a processional and hymn in Kim's convent school.[49] Perhaps the clearest example of this technique can be observed in the evolution of "Can't Help Lovin' That Man." In the late 1880s the song is introduced in its lyrical form by Julie (Example 2.1a) followed immediately by an accelerated version sung by Queenie, Joe, the black chorus, and Magnolia (act I, scene 2); in the second act (scene 4) the song undergoes further transformation into a rag tune in 1904, when the Trocadero pianist Jake encourages Magnolia to sing a more animated modern version in order to get her act into the Trocadero production (Example 2.1b).

Magnolia's piano theme (Example 2.4), one of the most ubiquitous themes of the show, will also undergo various transformations after its introduction in the opening scene. These include a reharmonized statement that underscores Captain Andy's announcement of Magnolia's wedding to Ravenal near the end of act I and a jazzy version, "It's Getting Hotter in the North" (the original finale dropped after the Washington, D.C. tryouts), sung by Magnolia's daughter, Kim, in 1927. It is also possible that Kern intended audiences to hear a musical connection between Magnolia's piano theme and the opening fragment of the verse to "Ol' Man River"—a verse that not incidentally also begins the show opener, "Cotton Blossom"—when he decided to adopt it almost unchanged from *The Beauty Prize* (1923).[50] In any event, Kern's decision to join the second measure of Magnolia's theme with the central theme of the all-knowing and timeless river is more than a detail. Not only does this touch provide another dramatically strong musical linkage, it also bonds Ravenal to his future bride and all she represents. Her theme immediately enters his consciousness (even before they meet) and takes over the B section of his song, "Where's the Mate for Me?"[51]

The vast network of thematic foreshadowings and reminiscences introduced here rarely fail to credibly unite the present with the past. One such example of Kern's ability to make a dramatic point through a musical reference is his use of the "Mis'ry" theme (from the discarded song), which underscores Julie's lecture to Magnolia about men, immediately after the impressionable younger woman has met Ravenal (at which point such a lecture is, of course, already too late). The presence of "Mis'ry'" here anticipates Julie's misery two scenes later, when her partially black heritage is exposed and she and her blood partner Steve are exiled from the *Cotton Blossom*. It also prepares listeners for Julie's and Magnolia's eventual misery in act II when both will lose the men they love.[52] A rhythmic connection that might also suggest a dramatic interpretation is the similarity between the prevalent long-short-short rhythm of this "Mis'ry" theme and the opening two measures of Ravenal's "Where's the Mate for Me?" (Example 2.5).[53] In any event Ravenal's musical remembrance of the waltz portion (section 2) of "Make Believe," when he sings "I let fate decide if I walk or ride" in "Till Good Luck Comes My Way" (the latter unfortunately dropped from the 1946 revival), reveals more clearly than anything he could say or do that Ravenal's own destiny is to love Magnolia even as he will one day abandon her.[54]

Ravenal's Entrance and Meeting with Magnolia

An exceptionally powerful example of what Kern and Hammerstein were able to achieve with their second collaboration can be found in *Show Boat*'s expansive, intricate, and brilliantly conceived opening scene (act I, scene 1). After the opening chorus, "Cotton Blossom," and Captain Andy Hawks's "Ballyhoo," we meet the river gambler Gaylord Ravenal, he meets his future bride Magnolia Hawks (Andy's daughter), and the two fall in love at first sight. In addition to its classic status as the quintessential Broadway "boy meets girl" scene, Ravenal's entrance and meeting with Magnolia offers two major songs, "Where's the Mate for Me?" and "Make Believe," as well as a continuous scene in which all actions and dialogue are underscored.

Ravenal's meeting with Magnolia also provides an example of how perceptively Kern and Hammerstein understood the dramatic potential of Ferber's narrative. In the novel Ravenal notices Magnolia on the deck of the *Cotton Blossom* at the same moment Captain Andy offers him the leading romantic role in their troupe. When Ravenal finds out that she will be his dramatic counterpart, he unhesitatingly accepts the challenge even though he has no experience (but of course he will not actually need to act). Ferber then tells her readers of Ravenal's and Magnolia's destiny, an "inevitable" and "cosmic course."[55] After describing this silent meeting Ferber conspires with her character Parthy and does not allow the future lovers to speak to one another again for another twelve pages—and then not alone. Although Kern and Hammerstein made many revisions in this portion of scene 1 during the 1927 tryouts (Appendix D, p. 321), only relatively minor changes differentiate the original New York and London books from the 1946 revival and the three published scores for this scene.[56]

From the moment audiences first glimpse the future hero, Kern estab-

Example 2.5. "Where's the Mate for Me?" (opening and "fancy" harmonizations)
(a) "Who cares if my boat goes up stream"
(b) "I drift along with my fancy"
(c) "I drift along with my fancy"

lishes the connection between Ravenal and his theme, capturing his aim-lessness with a harmonically ambiguous accompaniment that refuses to find a tonal harbor. The theme continues to underscore Ellie May Chipley, the leading female comic with the *Show Boat* troupe, in her endeavor to attract Ravenal's attention. Ellie drops her handkerchief, Ravenal picks it up—but not her cue—"hands it to her with courtesy," and graciously ac-knowledges her gratitude before leaving the embarrassed comedian to fall back on her stage partner, Frank Schultz. After Sheriff Vallon's appearance interrupts what would have been a harmonic resting point on D major, Kern foreshadows Ravenal's song from scene 3, "Till Good Luck Comes My Way," to underscore the remaining dialogue in which Vallon and Rav-enal reflect on the drifter's bachelorhood.

In the thrice-repeated opening phrase of "Where's the Mate for Me?" the first shown in Example 2.5a ("Who cares if my boat goes up stream" and two statements of "I drift along with my fancy") Kern ingeniously varies the harmony of the final melodic note D (Example 2.5b and c). Its first appearance on the words "up stream" (the third measure) is para-doxically and perhaps unintentionally the *lowest* note of the phrase—after all, the point is that Ravenal does not care whether he is going upstream or downstream. Here Kern harmonizes the tonic or central key, D, with a conventional tonic D-major triad. Although Kern's music initially *preceded* Hammerstein's lyrics here and elsewhere in *Show Boat*, one nonetheless suspects that Kern may have occasionally altered his harmonies to corre-spond to the musical potential of Hammerstein's lyrics. A major candidate for this creative scenario occurs in the third measure of the opening phrase of "Where's the Mate" (Example 2.5b), where Kern sets the word "fancy" with a fancy (and deceptive) resolution to a minor triad on the sixth degree of the scale.[57] On the final statement of this phrase (Example 2.5c), mo-ments before Ravenal hears Magnolia's piano theme, and Kern displays his fanciest chord, again on the word "fancy."[58] Ravenal is now as far adrift as Broadway harmony can take him.

To depict his speechlessness (or songlessness) upon seeing Magnolia, Ravenal stops abruptly before the music moves toward a conclusion on the expected tonal center. But "Where's the Mate for Me?," in contrast to most Broadway songs, remains incomplete. Instead, Ravenal's unasked fi-nal musical question is answered by the mere presence of Magnolia. For such a special occasion Kern and Hammerstein were willing to deprive audiences of the opportunity to disturb dramatic continuity with applause. Even before Magnolia's physical presence interrupts the final statement of the A section, however, Ravenal had already become subliminally aware of the answer to his question "Where's the mate?" In what is clearly a case of love at first sound as well as first sight, Magnolia's music (her piano theme shown in Example 2.4) becomes immediately and completely absorbed into the B section of Ravenal's song.

In "Make Believe," the ensuing duet between Magnolia and Ravenal (thankfully, in contrast to the Ferber novel they are allowed to speak and sing), Kern connects no less than four individual melodies and distinguishes each by metrical or key changes. As in Ravenal's "Where's the Mate for Me?" Kern's purpose here is to provide a musical narrative that accurately reflects the psychological progression of a budding romance. By the end of the first section Ravenal has already admitted that his love for Magnolia is not a pretense ("For, to tell the truth, I do"). On the word "do" the music responds by becoming a waltz, which as far back as Franz Lehár's *The Merry Widow* and Johann Strauss Jr.'s *Die Fledermaus* had come to represent the language of love for American as well as European audiences.[59] Ravenal apologizes for "the words that betray my heart," but Magnolia, who has in fact betrayed her heart by joining Ravenal's waltz, is not quite ready to abandon the "game of just supposing" when she sings, "we only pretend." Although Magnolia wants to pretend that Ravenal is only "playing a lover's part," Kern's music belies Hammerstein's words.

The third section of "Make Believe" leaves the tonic D major and modulates four notes above to the subdominant (G major) with another metrical change, this time from triple (waltz time) back to duple meter. Now Magnolia plays her game with a new level of flirtation accompanied by appropriate melodic playfulness ("The game of just supposing"). Following Ravenal's reply to this flirtation, Magnolia introduces a fourth section in the parallel minor mode (G minor, foreshadowed in Parthy's theme), a response to her sobering realization that "the cold and brutal fact is" they have never met before. But the pessimism of the minor mode disappears after only four measures when Magnolia states her rationale: since they are only playing a lover's part, they "need not mind convention's P's and Q's." Clearly, imagination that "can banish all regret" can also banish minor modes.[60]

Magnolia, a bystander in the first section and half of the second, has now dominated all but eight measures since she first pointed out to Ravenal that they are only pretending, after all. Most significantly, Magnolia introduces the return of the central "Make Believe" melody more intensely than Ravenal's opening gambit, and to match this intensity the music escalates a half-step higher (E♭ major) from the original tonic D. When Ravenal joins her on the words "others find peace of mind in pretending," it is by now unequivocally clear that Ravenal and Magnolia are not like these others. Their love is real.

The distribution between Magnolia and Ravenal during this return of the main tune underwent several changes between the tryouts and the New York premiere, and there remains some lingering ambiguity about who should sing what after the first two lines (invariably given to Magnolia). For example, according to the libretto typescript in the Library of Congress's Jerome Kern Collection (Appendix D, p. 321, no. 1), Kern and Hammerstein had once indicated that Magnolia alone should sing the next lines ("Others find peace of mind in pretending—/ Couldn't you, / Couldn't I? / Couldn't we?") before they conclude their duet. The evolution of the final line is especially intricate.

Hammerstein remained unsatisfied by his decision to have both principals sing the last line ("For, to tell the truth,—I do"). Was Magnolia ready to admit the truth of her love to Ravenal? In a pencilled change Hammerstein has Ravenal sing the "I do" without Magnolia. In the New York Public Library libretto typescript (Appendix D, p. 321, no. 2) the entire last line is given to Ravenal alone but placed in brackets. In the New York production libretto published with the McGlinn recording (no. 3) Ravenal sings the final line (without brackets), and this version is preserved in the published London libretto of 1934 (no. 4), the 1936 screenplay (no. 5), and the 1946 New York revival (no. 6).[61] Further contributing to the ambiguity and confusion is the lack of correspondence between these text versions and the piano-vocal drafts and published scores, none of which specifies that Ravenal profess his love alone until the Welk score (which corresponds to the 1946 production), where Magnolia's "For, to tell the truth,—I do" is placed in brackets.[62]

Perhaps most revelatory about these manuscripts are Kern and Hammerstein's gradual realization that this portion of the scene needed to focus more exclusively on Ravenal and Magnolia. The New York Public Library and Library of Congress typescripts, for example, present two versions of a conversation between Ellie and Frank that would be discarded by the December premiere.[63] Hammerstein eventually concluded that this exchange slowed down the action and distracted audiences from their focus on Ravenal.[64]

A second interruption, also eventually discarded, occurred after the B section of Ravenal's song "Where's the Mate for Me?" (based on Magnolia's piano theme, Example 2.4). Both the Library of Congress and New York Public Library typescripts present some dialogue and stage action during the twenty-six measures of underscoring that have survived in Draft 2: Parthy's theme (Example 2.3), Captain Andy's theme minus its six opening measures (Example 2.2c), and Ravenal's theme (Example 2.5).[65] Moments later Parthy intrudes once again, shouting "Nola!," and Hammerstein provides the following comment: "Magnolia looks down on this splendid fellow, Ravenal. Her maidenly heart flutters. She really should go in and answer mother—but she stays."[66]

Like the brief dialogue between Ellie and Frank that intrudes on this moment in the 1936 film, the appearance of Parthy here and after the B section of "Where's the Mate for Me?" interrupts the focus on the soon-to-be-lovers. Parthy, while always unwelcome, is also unnecessary during this portion of the scene, particularly since she had made a prominent exit shortly before we met Ravenal. Wisely, Kern and Hammerstein in 1927 allowed Parthy's music to prompt Magnolia to tell Ravenal she "must go now" and avoided the reality of Parthy's intrusion on the young couple's private moment before "Make Believe."[67]

After *Show Boat* Kern and Hammerstein would collaborate on three of the composer's remaining five Broadway shows, two with respectable runs, *Sweet Adeline* (1929) and *Music in the Air* (1932), and a disappointing *Very Warm for May* (1939). Despite their considerable merits, none of these shows have entered the repertory. Less than a year after *Show Boat* Hammerstein collaborated with Romberg on *The New Moon*, a show that went on for an impressive 509 performances. Then, despite the success of individual songs, including "All the Things You Are" from his final collaboration with Kern, a series of unwise choices (both in dramatic material and collaborators) and hurried work resulted in eleven years of Broadway failures for Hammerstein.

Similarly, his Hollywood years in the 1930s and early 1940s yielded no original musical films of lasting acclaim, although here, too, a considerable number of songs with Hammerstein's lyrics have become standards.[68] Hammerstein also adapted the screenplay for the penultimate Fred Astaire and Ginger Rogers film, *The Story of Vernon and Irene Castle* (1939).[69] In the next decade Hammerstein began his historic collaboration with Rodgers, and by the time *Show Boat* was revived in 1946, they had already written two of their five major hit musicals, *Oklahoma!* and *Carousel* (the latter the subject of chapter 8).[70]

In addition to his subsequent work with Hammerstein, Kern created two successful musicals with Harbach, the unfortunately overlooked *The Cat and the Fiddle* (1931) and *Roberta* (1933), the latter best known in its greatly altered 1935 film version. In fact, most of Kern's career after *Show Boat* was occupied with the creation of twenty-two full or partial film scores—thirteen original and nine adapted from Broadway—including several with lyrics by Hammerstein and the Astaire and Rogers classic,

Swing Time (1936), with lyrics by Dorothy Fields. Unfortunately, Kern never had the opportunity even to begin a new musical in the Rodgers and Hammerstein era, since he died shortly after Rodgers, who was producing a musical based on the life of Annie Oakley, had asked him to write the music.[71]

Kern and Hammerstein's inability to produce another *Show Boat* in the 1930s enhances the significance of their earlier achievement. Although its ending did not embrace Ferber's darker version, *Show Boat*, "the first truly, totally American operetta" had dared to present an American epic with a credible story, three-dimensional characters, a convincing use of American vernacular appropriate to the changing world (including the African-Americanization of culture) from the late 1880s to 1927, and a sensitive portrayal of race relations that ranged from the plight of the black underclass to miscegenation.[72] As the first Broadway musical to keep rolling along in the repertory from its time to ours, while at the same time enjoying the critical respect of musical-theater historians for more than seventy years, *Show Boat*, the musical "that demanded a new maturity from musical theatre and from its audience,"[73] has long since earned its coveted historical position as the foundation of the modern American musical.

CHAPTER THREE

ANYTHING GOES

Songs Ten, Book Three

Before the curtain rose on the 1987 revival of *Anything Goes* at Lincoln Center's Vivian Beaumont Theater, audiences heard the strains of Cole Porter's own rendition of the title song recorded in 1934. At the conclusion of this critically well-received and popularly successful show a large silkscreen photograph of Porter (1891–1964) appeared behind a scrim to cast a literal as well as metaphoric shadow over the cast. More than fifty years after its premiere the message was clear: the real star of *Anything Goes* was its composer-lyricist, the creator of such timeless song classics as "I Get a Kick Out of You," "You're the Top," "Blow, Gabriel, Blow," "All Through the Night," "Easy to Love," "Friendship," "It's De-Lovely," and the title song. Readers familiar with *Anything Goes* from various amateur and semiprofessional productions over the past thirty years may scarcely notice that the last three songs named were taken from other Porter shows.

Anything Goes, after the Gershwins' Pulitzer Prize–winning *Of Thee I Sing* the longest-running book musical of the 1930s and almost certainly the most frequently revived musical of its time (in one form or another), was Porter's first major hit. Otherwise virtually forgotten, each of Porter's five musicals preceding *Anything Goes* introduced at least one song that would rank a ten in almost anyone's book: "What Is This Thing Called Love?" in *Wake Up and Dream* (1929), "You Do Something to Me" in *Fifty Million Frenchmen* (1929), "Love for Sale" in *The New Yorkers* (1930), and

Anything Goes, act II, finale (1987). Photograph: Brigitte Lacombe. Museum of the City of New York.

"Night and Day" in *Gay Divorce* (1932). The Porter shows that debuted in the years between *Anything Goes* and *Kiss Me, Kate* (1948) are similarly remembered mainly because they contain one or more hit songs.

In the unlikely midwestern town of Peru, Indiana, Porter's mother, appropriately named Kate, arranged to have Cole's first song published at her own expense in 1902 (he was eleven at the time). Three years later Porter entered the exclusive Worcester Academy in Massachusetts. Upon his graduation from Yale in 1913, where he had delighted his fellow students with fraternity shows and football songs, Porter endured an unhappy year at Harvard Law School. Against his grandfather's wishes and in spite of financial threats, Porter enrolled in Harvard's music department for the 1914–1915 academic year. In 1917 he furthered his musical training

with private studies in New York City with Pietro Yon, the musical director and organist at Saint Patrick's Cathedral; in 1919–1920 the future Broadway composer continued his studies in composition, counterpoint,
harmony, and orchestration with Vincent D'Indy at the Schola Cantorum
in Paris.

Although his first success, *Paris*, would not arrive for another twelve
years, Porter had already produced a musical on Broadway, *See America
First* (1916), before Gershwin or Rodgers had begun their Broadway careers
and only one year after Kern had inaugurated his series of distinctive musicals at the Princess Theatre. The years between the failure of his Broadway debut after fifteen performances (inspiring the famous quip from
Variety, "*See America First* last!") and the success of Irene Bordoni's singing
"Let's Do It" in *Paris* were largely dormant ones for Porter. In fact, the
sum total of his Broadway work other than *See America First* was one song
interpolation for Kern's *Miss Information* in 1915 and approximately ten
songs each in *Hitchy-Koo of 1919* and the *Greenwich Village Follies* in 1924.
During these years the already wealthy Porter—despite his profligacy an
heir to his grandfather's fortune—grew still wealthier when he married
the socialite and famous beauty Linda Lee Thomas in 1919. In 1924 the
Porters moved to Italy where they would soon launch three years of lavish
party-throwing and party-going in their Venetian palazzos. On numerous
such occasions the expatriate songwriter would entertain his friends with
his witty lyrics and melodies. Near the end of this partying Porter in 1927
auditioned unsuccessfully for Vinton Freedley and Alex Aarons, the producers of several Gershwin hit musicals and the future producers of four
Porter shows starting with *Anything Goes*. When the following year Rodgers and Hart were preoccupied with *A Connecticut Yankee*, Porter was
easily persuaded to leave Europe and bring *Paris* to New York. *Anything
Goes* would arrive six years and many perennial song favorites later.

The Changing Times of Anything Goes

Most accounts of the genesis of *Anything Goes* attribute the disastrous fire
that took between 125 and 180 passengers' lives on the pleasure ship *Morro
Castle* off the coast at Asbury Park, New Jersey, on September 8, 1934 as
the catalyst that led to the revised book by Howard Lindsay and Russel
Crouse. According to conventional wisdom, the earlier libretto about a
shipwreck could not be used any more than Porter could use his line about
Mrs. Lindbergh in "I Get a Kick Out of You" after the kidnapping and
murder of the Lindbergh baby.[1] But at least two sources, George Eells's

biography of Porter and Miles Kreuger's introductory notes to conductor John McGlinn's reconstructed recording, report that producer Freedley was dissatisfied by the Guy Bolton–P. G. Wodehouse book when he received it on August 15 and that the *Morro* disaster served mainly as a convenient explanation.

According to Eells, Freedley thought there was "a tastelessness about this piece of work that no amount of rewriting would eradicate," a view echoed by both Kreuger and Bolton-Wodehouse biographer Lee Davis. Kreuger writes, "Freedley was fearful that the rather derisive attitude toward Hollywood might ruin chances of a film sale." Davis goes further: "The first script was rejected by Freedley for its Hollywood treatment, not its similarity to the tragic fire at sea of the liner *Morro Castle,* as has been historically accepted. Nor would he blanch at the second version because of its continued treatment of a catastrophe at sea. It would be because the second version was a hopeless mess."[2]

In an interview with Richard Hubler published in 1965, one year after Porter's death, the composer-lyricist anticipated the future conclusions of Eells, Kreuger, and Davis. Porter recalled that the *Morro Castle* tragedy provided an excuse to scrap a Wodehouse-Bolton book whose quality was "so bad that it was obvious that the work was completely inadequate."[3] The synopsis included in this book is of course based on the revised *Anything Goes* book (the Lindsay and Crouse book based in part on the rejected and now-lost second draft by Bolton and Wodehouse).

Since it is possible Lindsay and Crouse retained relatively little of the Bolton-Wodehouse second draft—although the new book may have contained more than an alleged five lines—it is not surprising that the inexperienced collaborators would be able to complete only a few scenes from act I and nothing of act II before rehearsals began on October 8. In contrast to the painstaking work and lengthy gestation period of most of the musicals surveyed in this volume, *Anything Goes* was hastily, perhaps even frantically, put together.

But Freedley, Lindsay, Crouse, and Porter had other objectives than to create an epic book musical along the lines of *Show Boat.* Their main objective was to produce a comic hit and to provide dramatic and musical opportunities to suit their outstanding preassembled cast. In particular they needed a vehicle to display William Gaxton's (Billy) proven flair for multifarious disguises and to exploit the inspired silliness of comedian Victor Moore's incongruous casting as a notorious gangster (Moon). The result was enough to prompt Brooks Atkinson to exclaim that "comedy is the most satisfying invention of the human race."[4] Atkinson could not ask anything more of a show that exuded such refreshing topicality and personality, a show for the moment, if not for the ages. If one or two songs stuck around for awhile, so much the better.

Although McGlinn later proclaimed the 1934 *Anything Goes* as "one of the most perfect farces ever written," most producers and directors for the past thirty years have been trying to solve the perceived disparity in quality between the book and the songs by altering the former and interpolating more of the latter.[5] The 1987 Lincoln Center revival was not the first time audiences found themselves leaving a production of *Anything Goes* humming or whistling songs from other Porter shows. In the 1962 revival, the only version distributed by Tams-Witmark for the next twenty-five years, still other songs from other Porter shows had been interpolated. The lyricist-composer's own reputed cavalier attitude toward his books and song interpolations prompted Broadway and Hollywood historian Gerald Mast to state erroneously that Porter's last will and testament "granted explicit permission to take any Porter song from any Porter show and use it in any other."[6] The commercial success of McGlinn's recorded enterprise may encourage future producers and directors to consider reviving the 1934 *Anything Goes*, but this is by no means certain.

Appendix E presents an outline of the scenes and songs of the *Anything Goes* that audiences would have heard during most of the initial run of the show that opened on November 21, 1934. As in the case of most musicals from any period (as well as many eighteenth-century operas), additional songs were tried and then discarded during tryouts or during the early weeks of the New York run. In act I, scene 2, "Bon Voyage" was originally juxtaposed, then ingeniously combined, with another song, "There's No Cure Like Travel," a song which interestingly contains the main musical material of "Bon Voyage."[7] Just as Mozart composed the easier-to-sing aria "Dalla sua pace" to accommodate the Viennese singer in *Don Giovanni* who was unable to negotiate the demands of the aria from the original Prague production ("Il mio tesoro"), Porter composed "All Through the Night" in this scene for Gaxton (Billy Crocker) to replace the difficult-to-sing "Easy to Love."

Another song intended for this scene, "Kate the Great," was, according to the recollection of *Anything Goes* orchestrator Hans Spialek, rejected by Ethel Merman who "vouldn't sing it" because it was a *"durr-ty* song!"[8] A song planned as a tongue-in-cheek romantic duet in act I, scene 6, between Hope and Billy, "Waltz Down the Aisle" (which bears striking melodic and rhythmic similarities as well as a similar dramatic purpose to "Wunderbar" from Porter's *Kiss Me, Kate*) was also dropped from *Anything Goes*. A song for Hope in act II, scene 1, "What a Joy to Be Young," was deleted before the Broadway premiere.[9]

One song in the beginning of the Broadway run, "Buddie, Beware," was replaced by a reprise of "I Get a Kick Out of You" within a few weeks. In order to understand the artistic implications of this change it is necessary to recall Porter's original motivation. Composers of musicals before (or after) the Rodgers and Hammerstein era could not, of course, always predict which song would become a hit, but they nevertheless almost invariably tried to place their best bets sometime *after* an opening number (usually for chorus). In *Anything Goes* Porter tried something more unusual. Instead of opening with a chorus, Porter decided to begin less conventionally with a potential hit song for Ethel Merman five minutes into the show, "I Get a Kick Out of You."

Porter's reasons for beginning with what he felt would be the hit of the show may have been somewhat perverse. According to Kreuger, Porter's "society friends thought it was amusing to drift into the theatre fifteen or twenty minutes after the curtain had gone up, so that all their friends could observe what they were wearing."[10] Porter therefore "warned his friends for weeks before the opening that they had better arrive on time or they would miss the big song."[11] There is no record that Merman objected to "Buddie, Beware" in act II, scene 2 for the same reason she objected to a song about the sexual exploits of Catherine (Kate) the Great. Her objections in this case were practical rather than moral: the show needed a reprise of "I Get a Kick Out of You" "for the benefit of those who had arrived late!"[12] If this undocumented anecdote is to be believed, Porter, who had earlier agreed to cut "Kate the Great," was again willing to accommodate his star and cut "Buddie, Beware."[13]

The history of *Anything Goes* after its premiere in 1934 differs markedly from the fate of *Show Boat* discussed in the previous chapter. The original 1927 Broadway version of *Show Boat* was superseded by Kern and Hammerstein's own rethinking of the work in the 1946 revival that included a reworked book, several deleted songs and a brand new one, and new orchestrations. As we have seen, after Hammerstein's death in 1960, the 1971 London and 1994 Broadway *Show Boat* revivals presented conflated versions of the musical that included songs from various earlier stage productions (New York, 1927; London, 1928; New York, 1946) and also songs from the 1936 film classic. Some of the original as well as interpolated songs were also either placed in different contexts or distributed to different characters.

Despite these liberties, both the 1971 London and 1994 Broadway revivals contained interpolated songs that had been associated with one version or another of this musical ("How'd You Like to Spoon With Me?" from the 1971 London production is an isolated exception). In contrast, the *Any-*

thing Goes revival in 1962, the version distributed to prospective producers until replaced by the 1987 revival, incorporated no less than six songs out of a total of fourteen from *other* Porter shows ("It's De-Lovely," "Heaven Hop," "Friendship," "Let's Step Out," "Let's Misbehave," and "Take Me Back to Manhattan"). Also, in 1962 the order of several songs was rearranged and, ironically, a thoroughly revised book was written by Guy Bolton, who with P. G. Wodehouse had submitted the rejected 1934 book.

The 1987 revival contained yet another new book, this time by Russel Crouse's son Timothy and John Weidman.[14] This book retained two of the interpolations from 1962 ("It's De-Lovely" and "Friendship"), and added two other Porter tunes from shows that had not even appeared on Broadway, "Goodbye, Little Dream, Goodbye" from *O Mistress Mine*, a 1936 musical produced in London, and "I Want to Row on the Crew," from the Yale fraternity show *Paranoia* of 1914. The 1987 production also rearranged the order and dramatic context of several other songs from the original 1934 Broadway run. Most strikingly, the 1987 revision resurrected three songs that had appeared at various phases of the 1934 tryouts and initial run: "There's No Cure Like Travel," "Easy to Love," and "Buddie, Beware." Appendix E outlines the scenes and songs of the 1962 and 1987 revivals along with the sources of the interpolated songs.

One year before criticizing the undramatic use of recitative in the Theatre Guild production of *Porgy and Bess*, Brooks Atkinson reviewed the Broadway premiere of *Anything Goes*. The review is an unequivocal rave of "a thundering good musical show" with "a rag, tag and bobtail of comic situations and of music sung in the spots when it is most exhilarating."[15] Most surprisingly from a 1990s perspective is the fact that Atkinson praises the book, not as a work of art, perhaps, but as a well-crafted vehicle to set off William Gaxton's talent for wearing disguises and the comic characterization of Victor Moore's Moon, "the quintessence of musical comedy humor." Atkinson does not feel the need to consider *Anything Goes* as anything other than the "thundering good song-and-dance show" it purports to be.[16] Another reviewer, Franklin P. Adams, lambasted the *songs* from *Anything Goes* (because they were difficult to remember or whistle), but offered no negative remarks about the book.[17]

Like Atkinson's new-found distaste for *On Your Toes* upon its ill-fated 1954 revival (discussed in chapter 5), the *New York Times* review of the 1962 Off-Broadway revival, twenty-eight years after *Anything Goes* made its debut, demonstrates that a new standard for musical theater had evolved during the intervening years. In contrast to Atkinson's appreciation of the original book, Lewis Funke wrote that "if you can get by the deserts that lurk in the libretto, knowing that there always will be that oasis of a Cole Porter tune waiting at the end of each rugged journey, you may find yourself enjoying the revival of *Anything Goes*."[18] In Funke's account "only some of the lines retain their mirth" and the encapsulated plot summary that he offers serves merely to remind sophisticated 1960s audiences that "those were simple days in musical comedy."[19] What Funke neglects to report is that the book he is criticizing is *not* the 1934 book by Lindsay and Crouse but a version rewritten in 1962 by Bolton.

In his autobiography director and librettist George Abbott (1887–1995), who authored or coauthored books for an impressive array of musicals, including *On Your Toes, The Boys from Syracuse, Where's Charley?", A Tree Grows in Brooklyn, The Pajama Game, Damn Yankees,* and *Fiorello!,* discusses a review of a 1963 Off-Broadway revival directed by Richard York of the 1938 Rodgers and Hart classic *The Boys from Syracuse:*

> I was delighted to read of its outstanding success, and distressed that some of the reviewers referred to the old-fashioned jokes in the book. But I was puzzled when one of the reviewers cited one of these jokes, a corny pun: "Dozens of men are at my feet." "Yes, I know, chiropodists." This kind of humor is so alien to me that I knew I could never have written it; and when I got back to New York I found that the "old jokes" in the revival were new jokes inserted by Mr. [Richard] York to "modernize" the script. I took out some of these gags, but because the production as a whole was so delightful, I couldn't get very angry.[20]

It has become a commonplace almost universally shared by writers on Broadway musicals—along with directors and producers—that weak books are the main reason for the neglect of most musicals before *Oklahoma!* and *Carousel.* For this reason, after Rodgers and Hammerstein began an irreversible vogue for integrated book musicals, revivals of musicals were almost invariably accompanied by a team of doctors performing major surgery that included the reordering of songs and interpolations from other musicals of the same composer.

This type of surgical procedure begs several questions that merit further exploration. Is the idea of the integrated musical heralded by Rodgers and Hammerstein in the 1940s intrinsically superior to a musical with an anachronistic book and timeless songs? Are the books of the 1930s as weak as later critics make them out to be? Can some of the alleged weaknesses be attributed to the modernized books rather than to the originals? If the books of 1930s musicals are weak, why are they weak, and can they be salvaged by revisions and interpolations? Is it really a good idea to strip the original books down to their underwear and then dress them up again with as many songs as possible from other shows? Or can reasonable men and women provide an acceptable modern alternative? Are modern actors unable to successfully recapture and convey an older brand of comedy? Might the problem with *Anything Goes* stem more from an incongruity between music and text than from a diseased book?

Part of the answer to these questions might be traced to evolving social concerns rather than aesthetic considerations. Our current sensitivities and our understanding of topical issues are no longer what they were in 1934. As Porter would say, "times have changed." The following chapter will suggest that much of the criticism of *Porgy and Bess*, which followed the Porter hit one year later, was due (especially after the civil rights movement of the 1950s and '60s) less to its artistic qualities than to its perceived perpetuation of negative black stereotypes and Heyward's and Gershwin's presumption to speak for blacks. In *Show Boat* changing sensitivities made it necessary for Hammerstein to alter offending references, and later versions, especially the 1951 MGM film and the 1966 Lincoln Center production, tried to deflect criticism by minimizing the miscegenation scene and the role of blacks in general. Most musicals suffer, some irreparably, when their depiction of women is judged by feminist standards that emerged in the 1970s (see the discussion of *Kiss Me, Kate* in chapter 9).

Although a new sensitivity to ethnic minority groups or to women is probably not the major obstacle to the revivability of *Anything Goes*, the stereotypic depiction of Reverend Dobson's Chinese converts to Christianity, Ching and Ling (and the pidgin English adopted by Billy and Reno when they put on Ching's and Ling's costumes), were subsequently considered to be racially insensitive. In act I, scene 6 of the 1934 libretto, Moon refers to the converts as "Chinamen"; in the analogous place in 1962 he refers to them as Chinese.[21] In 1987 Reverend Dobson was still accompanied by two Chinese converts, but their names have been changed to the more biblical John and Luke. The new authors also took care "to give them independent comic personas and not base the humor on the fact that they're Chinese."[22]

In response to dated slang Crouse (the younger) and Weidman removed some "terrible words in the language like, 'wacky' and 'zany'" and other topical words and phrases that required a 1930s cultural literacy alien to later audiences.[23] But since the lyrics to the musical numbers were considered untouchable, the removal of "wacky" and "zany" do not fully solve the problems of topicality. In the preface to his essay "The Annotated 'Anything Goes'" that accompanies McGlinn's reconstructed recording, Kreuger describes the audiences for this and other 1930s shows as a "constricted group of *cognoscenti,* who went to the same night spots, read the same newpaper columns, and spent weekends at the same estates," and were therefore "swift to pick up even the most obscure references in all the lyrics."[24] Kreuger goes on to explain the meaning of seven references in the title song and no less than thirty-eight topical references in "You're the Top."[25]

Although this level of topicality is problematic to modern audiences who have neither lived through the 1930s nor had the opportunity to study Kreuger's annotated guide, it might also be said that Porter's lyrics presented problems to his British neighbors in his own time. In fact, in preparing for the London opening of June 14, 1935, Porter was asked by producer C. B. Cochran to remove several incomprehensible Americanisms when he took his show across the Atlantic. Eells mentions a few of these changes: "Cole agreed and set about converting the Bendel bonnet into an Ascot bonnet; a dress by Saks into one by Patous; and the eyes of Irene Bordoni into those of Tallulah Bankhead."[26] Nevertheless, in contrast to audiences who attended the 1962 and 1987 productions, most 1930s audiences, both in New York and London, would have recognized the parodistic parallels between Reno Sweeney, the evangelist who became a singer, and the then-famous evangelist Aimée Semple McPherson.[27] What about audiences in 1962 or 1987 and beyond? And does it matter?

In a *New York Times* interview that appeared shortly before the 1987 revival, the younger Crouse and Weidman admit to adding even more "swashbuckling slapstick gags" to their updated version, although they quickly add that none of these new gags were "gratuitous," and that they are "all closely tied to the plot."[28] Crouse and Weidman also express their intention to take their characters "more seriously" and to make them three-dimensional (or "maybe two and two-thirds").[29] In a feature story on *Anything Goes* that also appeared several days before the premiere of the 1987 revival, director, editor, and dramaturg Jerry Zaks discusses his search for a theme ("people dealing with the ramifications of trying to fall in love") and explains his intention "to ground everything in a recognizable reality," i.e., to remake the book in a post–Rodgers and Hammerstein image. He continues with a telling example: "In previous versions of the show, Lord Evelyn Oakleigh, with whom Reno Sweeney falls in love, is someone so totally foppish and out of touch with his sexuality that she ends up looking stupid for having fallen for him. Both in the book and the casting we tried to suggest the potential for a real relationship between them."[30]

Zaks makes a good point. When Sir Evelyn is introduced in 1934 (scene 2) his masculine identity is immediately called into question:

REPORTER: Sir Oakleigh, you and Miss Harcourt. Right here, please.
(SIR EVELYN OAKLEIGH *and* HOPE HARCOURT *are pushed into focus*)
Society stuff.
CAMERA MAN: What are their names? Who are they?
REPORTER: Sir—what's your first name?
OAKLEIGH: Evelyn.
1ST CAMERA MAN: Not her first name—your first name!

When in act II, scene 1, Sir Evelyn relates that he "had an unpremeditated roll in the rice and enjoyed it very much" with a Chinese maiden named Plum Blossom, his admission may be taken more as a boast of his full-blooded heterosexuality than the confession of a sin. And Reno, who has experienced chagrin that Evelyn has been treating her every inch a lady and is much relieved by this welcome revelation, immediately responds accordingly: "Brother, I've been worried about you but I feel better now."[31] Reno will repeat this sentiment both in 1962 and 1987.

The main reason that the generally stiff and staid Sir Evelyn provides a less-than-perfect match for the exuberant Reno in the original *Anything Goes* is more substantive than his androgynous first name and questionable heterosexuality: the Englishman is never allowed to sing. Although his sexual identity is eventually resolved to the satisfaction of a 1930s audience, his nonsinging status significantly reduces his dramatic identity. In a musical (or opera) a character who does not sing—for example, Parthy before the 1994 *Show Boat* revival (discussed in chapter 2)—proceeds at his or her own peril.

Apparently, future book doctors saw this as an illness that needed a cure. Thus in the 1962 revival Bolton celebrates Sir Evelyn's emergence as a regular fellow in act II, scene 1 by letting him sing an innocuously risqué interpolated duet with Reno, "Let's Misbehave." In 1987 Sir Evelyn remains musically silent in his stateroom scene with Reno but eventually emerges in act II, scene 3 with his own song for the first time, "The Gypsy in Me," a song that Hope sang in the 1934 original and no one sang in 1962.[32]

Extending the premise that a musical comedy character will be denied three-dimensionality or identity if he or she is not allowed to sing, even Billy's boss, Elisha J. Whitney, is given a brief interpolated song to open act I, scene 4 in 1987. On this occasion he sings "I Want to Row on the Crew," borrowed not from Broadway but from one of Porter's fraternity shows at Yale. The ship's deck becomes even more crowded when Moon's female accomplice, Bonnie, is given two interpolated numbers in 1962

("Heaven Hop" in act I and "Let's Step Out" in act II). In 1987 Crouse and Weidman discard these interpolations and in act II give Bonnie (now named Erma) "Buddie, Beware," the tune sung briefly by Ethel Merman as Reno in the original Broadway production before she persuaded Porter to give his late-arriving friends an opportunity to hear a reprise of "I Get a Kick Out of You."

In the 1987 revival words such as "wacky" and "zany" had been replaced, offending ethnic stereotypes were removed, and all the important characters were dramatically enhanced and, more important, allowed to sing. But do these changes make the 1987 *Anything Goes* superior to the original? Is it any funnier to hear a new set of topical jibes at Yale, Porter's alma mater, in a libretto created by two former Harvard roommates? Is it an improvement that Reno in 1934 is asked by Billy to seduce Sir Evelyn while in 1987 Reno meets and falls in love with the Englishman on her own?

What is lost and gained by this book surgery? Gone from latter-day versions of *Anything Goes*, for example, is much of the Marx Brothers humor built on puns and misunderstandings. Note the following exchange between Mrs. Wentworth (a humorless society matron not unlike Groucho's Margaret Dumont) and Moon, an exchange missing from the 1962 and 1987 revivals. Are modern audiences better or worse off for its absence?

MRS. WENTWORTH: We have a great deal to talk about. You see, I'm honorary president of the Texas Epworth League.

MOON: Oh, the Texas League—you must know the Dean Boys.

MRS. WENTWORTH: The Dean boys?

MOON: Yes, Dizzy and Daffy.

MRS. WENTWORTH: No, I don't remember them—

MOON: Well, you ask the Detroit Tigers about them. They remember them.

MRS. WENTWORTH: The Detroit Tigers? I know a family in Detroit named Lyons.

MOON: Lyons? Well, I know Maxie Baer [the boxing champion], but he's from San Francisco.

MRS. WENTWORTH: Ah, San Francisco. Have you ever been there?

MOON: I summered a few years at San Quentin.

MRS. WENTWORTH: San Quentin . . . Is that near Santa Clara?

MOON: Clara wasn't there when I was there. I wonder what ever became of Clara?

MRS. WENTWORTH: I'm not sure I understood what you just said.
MOON: Well, I wasn't listening.[33]

Some things about the evolving *Anything Goes* books stay the same the more they change. In 1987 Billy still has the opportunity to reply when asked his nationality that he is Pomeranian—the beard he is wearing was taken from a dog of that breed—even though Reno no longer notices that Billy is "putting on the dog."[34] Although many of the original puns and gags had disappeared by 1987, one 1934 line, "calling all pants," remained a part of *Anything Goes* scripture because it always got a laugh, even though to this day no one seems to be able to explain why it was so funny or even precisely what it meant.

This survey of the reworked books for *Anything Goes* in 1962 and 1987 evokes a paradox: comedy seems especially susceptible to becoming dated, yet many of the plays that have survived from the 1930s are comedies rather than serious dramas. Revivals of George S. Kaufman's and Moss Hart's comedies *You Can't Take It with You* (1936) and *The Man Who Came to Dinner* (1939) or Noël Coward's British import *Private Lives* (1930) are frequent guests on modern stages, yet audiences may have to wait a lifetime before getting an opportunity to see Clifford Odets's *Waiting for Lefty* (1935). Theater historian Gerald Bordman, who plays an active role in the resurrection of unjustifiably forgotten musicals, concedes "that some older musicals seem old-fashioned," but is quick to point out that "so are gingerbread houses, Charles Dickens, and Mozart symphonies."[35]

Dramatic and Musical Meaning

Is it fair to ask of *Anything Goes* what we ask of some of the other musicals featured in this volume? What dramatic meaning does the work possess, and how is this meaning conveyed through Porter's music? What, if anything, goes? In fact, *Anything Goes* is about many things, including the wrong-headedness of disguises and pretenses of various kinds and the unthinking attraction that common folk have for celebrities, even celebrity criminals.

Perhaps the central dramatic moral of *Anything Goes* is that sexual attraction and the desire for wealth exert a power superior to friendship and camaraderie in determining longterm partnerships. A few minutes into the play, for example, we learn that Reno has a romantic interest—or, as Sir Evelyn will later declare in his typical malapropian American English, "hot pants"—for Billy that has gone unreciprocated for years. In any event, although Billy thinks Reno is the "top" as well, he nevertheless enlists her help to wean Sir Evelyn from Hope, Evelyn's fiancée at the beginning of the musical.

The final pairing of Hope with Billy and Reno with Sir Evelyn has some satisfying aspects to it. Billy brings out the "gypsy" in Hope and, because he stays on board the ship, he is eventually able to extricate Hope and her family from a bad marriage and financial ruin. For her part Hope proves a positive influence in Billy's life when she persuades him to drop his pretenses and confess that he is not the celebrity criminal Snake Eyes Johnson, even though he will be penalized by the rest of the ship, even temporarily imprisoned, for his newfound integrity. Reno rekindles Sir Evelyn's dormant masculinity; Sir Evelyn will continue to entertain his future bride by his quaint Britishisms and distortions of American vernacular and, not incidentally, make an excellent provider for the lifestyle to which Reno would like to become accustomed.

But there is a darker side to the happily-ever-after denouement in this rags-to-riches Depression fantasy. Even though Hope appreciates Billy's persistence and joie de vivre, she berates him for being a clown and will not speak to him until he confesses (at her insistence) that he is not Snake Eyes Johnson. More significantly, the main reason Reno rather than Hope remains "the top" is because Porter's music for Reno is the top. For all his wealth, the non-singing Sir Evelyn might be considered the consolation prize.

Porter certainly cannot be faulted for giving nearly all his best songs in the show—"I Get a Kick Out of You," "You're the Top," "Anything Goes," and "Blow, Gabriel, Blow"—to Reno as played by Merman, a singer-actress of true star quality. As the curtain opens, Reno sings the first two of these songs to Billy, the man she supposedly loves, before he asks her to seduce Sir Evelyn so that Billy can successfully woo Hope. The degree to which Reno expresses her admiration for Billy in "I Get a Kick Out of You" and the mutual admiration expressed between Billy and Reno in "You're the Top" might prompt some in the audience to ask why the creators of *Anything Goes* could not bring themselves to "make two lovers of friends."[36]

In *Anything Goes* Porter does not attempt the variety of musical and dramatic connections that will mark his relatively more integrated classic fourteen years later, *Kiss Me, Kate* (discussed in chapter 9). But Porter does pay attention to nuances in characterization and to the symbiotic relationship between music and words. To cite three examples, the sailor song, "They'll Always Be a Lady Fair," sounds appropriately like a sea chantey, the chorus of "Public Enemy No. 1" is a parodistic hymn of praise, and Moon's song, "Be Like the Bluebird," makes a credible pseudo-Australian folk song (at least for those unfamiliar with "authentic" Australian folk songs).

More significantly, Reno's music, as befitting her persona, is rhythmically intricate, ubiquitously syncopated, and harmonically straightforward. It is also equally meaningful that in "You're the Top" Billy adopts Reno's musical language as his own but changes his tune and his personality when he sings the more lugubrious "All Through the Night" with Hope. But even this song, dominated by descending half steps and long held notes, exhibits Reno's influence with the syncopations on alternate measures in the A section of the chorus and especially in the release when Billy laments the daylight reality (Hope does not sing this portion). Billy's syncopated reality partially supplants the long held notes: "When dawn comes to waken me, / You're never there at all. / I know you've forsaken me / Till the shadows fall."

Although rarely faithfully executed in performance, Porter's score also gives Reno an idiosyncratic and persistent rhythmic figure in "I Get a Kick Out of You," quarter-note triplets in the verse ("sad to be" and "leaves me totally") and half-note triplets in the chorus ("kick from cham-[pagne]", "[alco]-hol doesn't thrill me at," and "tell me why should it be"), the latter group shown in Example 3.1a. Because they occupy more than one beat, quarter-note and half-note triplets are generally perceived as more rhythmically disruptive than eighth-note triplets.[37] Consequently, Reno's half-note triplets shown in Example 3.1a, like the quarter-note triplets that open the main chorus of Tony's "Maria" ("I just met a girl named Maria" [Example 12.2b, p. 251]), are experienced as rhythmically out of phase with the prevailing duple framework. A good Broadway example of the conventional and nondisruptive eighth-note triplet rhythm (one beat for each triplet) can be observed at the beginning of every phrase in Laurey's "Many a New Day" from *Oklahoma!* (Example 3.1b). Broadway composers have never to my knowledge articulated the intentionality or metaphoric meaning behind this practice. Nevertheless, with striking consistency, more than a few songs featured in this survey employ quarter-note and half-note triplets in duple meter (where triplets stretch in syncopated fashion over three beats instead of two) to musically depict characters who are temporarily or permanently removed from conventional social norms and expectations: Venus in *One Touch of Venus*, Julie Jordan in *Carousel*, Tony in *West Side Story*.[38] In *Guys and Dolls* rhythms are

Example 3.1. Triplet rhythms
(a) "I Get a Kick Out of You" (*Anything Goes*)
(b) "Many a New Day" (*Oklahoma!*)
(c) "Gypsy in Me" (*Anything Goes*)

employed or avoided to distinguish one character type from another. The tinhorn gamblers and Adelaide freqently use quarter-note triplets, while Sarah Brown and her Salvation Army cohorts do not.

Porter's use of Reno's rhythm in the chorus of "I Get a Kick Out of You" constitutes perhaps his most consistent attempt to create meaning from his musical language. Half-note triplets dominate Reno's explication of all the things in life that do not give her a kick; they disappear when (with continued syncopation, however) she informs Billy that she does get a kick out of him. Reno will also sing her quarter-note triplets briefly in the release of "Blow, Gabriel, Blow" (not shown), when she is ready to fly higher and higher.[39] By the time Hope loses some of her in-hibitions and finds the gypsy in herself ("Gypsy In Me") in act II, she too will adopt this rhythmic figure on "hiding a-[way]," "never been," and "waiting its" (Example 3.1c). By usurping Reno's rhythm, Hope will become more like the former evangelist and, ironically, a more suitable partner for Billy.[40]

The verse of the title song shown in Example 3.2 offers a striking ex-ample of Porter's "word painting," Kivy's "textual realism" introduced in chapter 1. Even if a listener remains unconvinced that the gradually rising half-steps in the bass line between measures 3 and 7 (C-D♭-D) depict the winding and consequently faster ticking of a clock, Porter unmistakably captures the changing times in his title song. He does this by contrasting the descending C-minor arpeggiated triad (C-G-E♭-C) that opens the song on the words "Times have changed" with a descending C-major arpeg-giated triad (C-G-E-C) on the words "If today."[41] The topsy-turvy Depres-sion-tinted world of 1934 is indeed different from the world of our Puritan ancestors. Porter makes this change known to us musically as well as in his text.

In the chorus of "Anything Goes" Porter abandons "textual realism" in favor of a jazzy "opulent adornment" and does not attempt to convey nuances and distinctions between "olden days," a time when "a glimpse of stocking was looked on as something shocking," and the present day when "anything goes." Much has changed between 1934 and today and the chorus of "Anything Goes" remains one of the most memorable of its time or ours. Nevertheless, it is difficult to argue that this central portion of the song possesses (or attempts to convey) a dramatic equivalence with its text, even if it brilliantly captures an accepting attitude to a syncopated world "gone mad." Similarly, in "You're the Top" Porter does not capi-talize on the text's potential for realism and opts for inspired opulent adornment instead. Thus, although the "I" always appears in the bottom throughout most of the song, the "you" blithely moves back and forth from top to bottom."[42] The upward leaping orchestral figure anticipates the word, "top," but the sung line does not, and at the punchline, "But if Baby I'm the bottom, / You're the top," both Billy and Reno ("I'm" and "You're") share a melodic line at the top of their respective ranges.[43]

In the end a search for an underlying theme in *Anything Goes* yields more fun than profundity. An Englishman is good-naturedly spoofed for speak-ing a quaint "foreign" language and for his slowness in understanding American vernacular, and the celebrity status of religious entertainers like Aimée Semple McPherson and public criminals like Baby Face Nelson are caricatured by evangelist-singer Reno Sweeney and Public Enemy No. 1.

Example 3.2. "Anything Goes" (verse)

On a somewhat deeper level, the music suggests that the friendship between Reno and Billy has more vitality and perhaps greater substance than the eventual romantic pairings of Billy and Hope and Reno and Sir Evelyn. Not only does Porter demonstrate their compatibility by having Billy and Reno share quarter- and half-note triplet rhythms, he shows his affection for them by giving them his most memorable songs. By the end of *Anything Goes* some may wonder how a person who cannot even sing could deserve a gem like Reno who sings nothing but hits.

Anything Goes does not conform to the organic "Wagnerian" model of some pre- and post-Rodgers and Hammerstein musicals beginning with *Show Boat*. Instead it presents a striking parallel with the generally less ostentatiously organic world of Baroque opera, in which great stars and show-stopping arias can ensure at least short-term success (which is all that is required). In any of its forms, including the 1962 *Anything Goes* that held the stage for almost three decades and the 1987 reincarnation with its new book and numerous interpolated songs, *Anything Goes* still works. And even if the book that changes with the times falls short of the integrated ideal, it continues to provide marvelous vehicles to drive and showcase a parade of timeless hit songs. Times have changed, but *Anything Goes* is apparently here to stay.

CHAPTER FOUR

PORGY AND BESS

Broadway Opera

P*orgy and Bess,* described by its composer George Gershwin (1898–1937) as "a serious attempt to put in operatic form a purely American theme" and "a new form, which combines opera with theatre," began its public life in 1935 before a Broadway audience.[1] While the possibilities of a Metropolitan Opera production had been explored, a Theatre Guild production offered a more extended rehearsal schedule (six weeks), many more performances, and fewer logistical problems in assembling a large cast of operatically trained African-American singers.[2] Six years earlier the Met had signed a contract with Gershwin to produce an opera based on Sholem Ansky's version of the Jewish folktale "The Dybbuk," but abandoned the project after Gershwin was denied musical rights to this property.[3]

After a disappointing initial Broadway run of 124 performances, *Porgy and Bess* achieved a wider audience seven years later in the most successful Broadway revival up to that time. But in contrast to the 1935 operatic form, the 1942 revival presented a Broadway opera shorn of its operatic accoutrements, i.e., without recitatives (sung dialogue). Although some spoken dialogue replaced Gershwin's recitative, in the 1950s *Porgy and Bess* regained more of its operatic form as it toured opera houses all over the world (including La Scala).

In 1976 the work gained additional acceptance as an authentic as well as an accessible operatic classic when the Houston Opera performed the first largely uncut stage version since the Boston tryouts in 1935. By 1980 two competing unexpurgated recordings, one by the Houston Opera and another by the Cleveland Orchestra and Chorus, had appeared. Then, after fifty years of negotiations, *Porgy and Bess* appeared at the Met in 1985.[4] Nevertheless, despite its newfound popularity and acclaim among opera audiences, *Porgy and Bess* remains best known to the general public today as a collection of Broadway show tunes including "Summertime," "I Got Plenty o' Nuttin'," and "Bess, You Is My Woman Now," sung, played, and recorded by jazz and popular artists as diverse as Ella Fitzgerald and Louis Armstrong, Sammy Davis, Jr. and Diahann Carroll, Harry Belafonte and Lena Horne, Mel Tormé and Frances Faye, and Miles Davis.

Gershwin's exposure to the European classical tradition began two years after he started to play the piano at the relatively late age of twelve in 1910, when his teacher Charles Hambitzer introduced him to the music of Debussy and Ravel. Following his apprenticeship as a popular song "plugger" for the publishing house Remick & Company and some modest success in his own right as a songwriter for various revues between 1919 and 1921, Gershwin studied theory, composition, and orchestration with Edward Kilenyi. For more than a decade before completing *Porgy and Bess* Gershwin had composed a small body of jazz-influenced classical instrumental works including *Rhapsody in Blue* (1924), *Concerto in F* (1925), and *An American in Paris* (1928) that earned the respect, or at least the attention, of composers as diverse as Ravel, Prokofiev, and Berg. Between 1932 and 1936, partly in preparation for his first opera, Gershwin continued his studies in composition with Joseph Schillinger, a theorist who possessed a teachable system of melodic composition (including some techniques that Gershwin was able to incorporate in *Porgy and Bess*).

For the revue *George White Scandals of 1922*, Gershwin created an unusual work that revealed an interest in opera parallel to his interest in instrumental music, a work that similarly combined the cultivated European tradition with the American vernacular. This modest first effort, *Blue Monday*, a one-act verismo opera about blacks in Harlem, was dropped after opening night. For the next thirteen years Gershwin would undergo a rigorous Broadway apprenticeship that eventually gave him the technique and the experience he needed to attempt a full-length opera in the European tradition, again using the black experience for subject matter.

By 1924, with *Lady, Be Good!*, George had found a first-rate lyricist in his brother Ira (1896–1983), and over the next decade the Gershwins pro-

George and Ira Gershwin. © Al Hirschfeld. Drawing reproduced by special arrangement with Hirschfeld's exclusive representative, The Margo Feiden Galleries Ltd. New York.

duced mostly successful musical comedies filled with great songs and great stars such as *Tip-Toes* (1925) with Queenie Smith, *Oh, Kay!* (1926) with Gertrude Lawrence, *Funny Face* (1927) with *Lady, Be Good!* leads Fred and Adele Astaire, and *Girl Crazy* (1930) with new stars Ethel Merman and Ginger Rogers. All of these shows were produced by Alex Aarons (who had independently presented George's first book musical *La La Lucille* in 1919) and Vinton Freedley.[5] From 1930–1933 the Gershwins created a trilogy of musicals that satirized contemporary politics: *Strike Up the Band* (1930), *Of Thee I Sing* (1931), and *Let 'Em Eat Cake* (1933). In addition to the opportunities they provided for musical humor and wit, these political musicals allowed Gershwin to continue the practice he started in *Oh, Kay!*, in which extended ensemble finales are presented continuously with a minimum of intervening dialogue.

The act I Finale to *Of Thee I Sing* also displays a substantial passage of accompanied recitative or arioso (a singing style between recitative and aria). This passage is sung by Diana Devereaux, the character who, by winning first prize in a national beauty contest, was entitled to become the First Lady but was passed over in favor of Mary Turner because the latter could make irresistible corn muffins. When instead of muffins Diana serves President Wintergreen a summons for breach of promise, Gershwin gives the jilted Southerner a blues-inflected musical line in recitative that would not be out of place in *Porgy and Bess.*

When Gershwin finished reading the novel *Porgy* (1925) by DuBose Heyward (1885–1940) after a sleepless night in October 1926, he wrote a letter to the author, a leading Southern novelist and poet, informing him that he wanted to use the novel as the basis for an opera. Nine years later *Porgy and Bess* appeared on Broadway, a delay that can be contributed both to the successful run of the Theatre Guild production of the play *Porgy* in 1927 and to Gershwin's many commitments and excuses and his sense that he needed more experience before tackling a full-scale opera.

Since several Gershwin biographies offer detailed surveys of *Porgy and Bess*'s pre-history, the events leading to the premiere need only be encapsulated here.[6] The summer after he had first written Heyward, Gershwin met the author for the first time, and they agreed to collaborate on an opera based on *Porgy.* DuBose's wife, Dorothy, who had coauthored the play, recalled years later that Gershwin informed her husband that he "wanted to spend years in study before composing his opera."[7] Although by March 1932 he wrote Heyward to express a continued interest in composing the opera, two months later Gershwin hedged again when he informed DuBose that "there is no possibility of the operatic version's being written before January 1933."[8] The two men met in New York City even as plans were brewing for a *Porgy* that would feature the popular entertainer Al Jolson in blackface with lyrics and music by *Show Boat* collaborators Hammerstein and Kern. The Jolson project was not abandoned until September 1934, long after Gershwin and Heyward had begun their version.

By November 1933, Gershwin had experienced two successive Broadway flops, *Pardon My English* and *Let 'Em Eat Cake,* the latter a bitter sequel to the relatively less acerbic Pulitzer Prize–winning *Of Thee I Sing.* Despite these setbacks the Theatre Guild, which had produced the popular play *Porgy* six years earlier, announced that Gershwin and Heyward had signed a contract to produce a musical version. On November 12 Heyward sent Gershwin a typescript of the first scene, and in December and again the following January the composer visited the librettist in Charleston, South Carolina.

On February 6, 1934, Heyward mailed Gershwin a typescript of act II, scenes 1 and 2. Several weeks later (February 26) Gershwin informed Heyward that he had begun to compose the music for the first act and that he was relieved to learn their work would not suffer in comparison with the all-black opera by Virgil Thomson and Gertrude Stein, *Four Saints in Three Acts,* that had recently premiered on Broadway (February 20). On March 2 Heyward sent the composer a typescript of act II, scene 3, and six days later Gershwin wrote that Ira was working on lyrics for the opening of the opera.[9] By the end of March Heyward had sent act II, scene 4, and completed a draft for act III. In April Heyward travelled to New York to meet with the Gershwins and together they created "I Got Plenty o' Nuttin'," one of the few numbers in the opera in which the music preceded the lyrics.

Gershwin completed the music for act I, scene 1, before the end of May. In the summer he worked on the opera in Charleston (June 16 to July 21). In a letter to Heyward dated November 5 Gershwin announced that he had completed act II and begun act III, scene 2. On December 17 he reported to Heyward that he had heard a singer, Todd Duncan, who would make "a superb Crown and, I think, just as good a Porgy," and several weeks later he wrote to Todd Duncan (who would in fact be cast as Porgy) that he had just completed the trio in act III, scene 3 ("Oh, Bess, Oh Where's My Bess"), and was about to orchestrate his opera. The arduous task of orchestration occupied Gershwin until three days before rehearsals began August 26.[10] The Boston tryouts began on September 30 and the Broadway premiere took place October 10 at the Alvin Theatre.

Questions of Genre, Authenticity, and Race

Prior to its eventual acceptance into the operatic community reviewers and historians alike were uncertain how to classify *Porgy and Bess.* At its premiere the *New York Times* did not know whether to approach the work as a dramatic event or a musical event, and assigned first-string reviewers in both camps, drama critic Brooks Atkinson and music critic Olin Downes, to review the work in adjacent columns.[11] Most subsequent accounts of these reviews conclude that Atkinson, who praised Gershwin for establishing "a personal voice that was inarticulate in the original play," appreciated the work more fully than Downes.[12] It is true that Downes, in contrast to Atkinson, expressed reservations about the stylistic disparities in the work when he wrote that Gershwin "has not completely formed his style as an opera composer" and that "the style is at one moment of opera and another of operetta or sheer Broadway entertainment."[13] Nevertheless, Downes found much to praise in Gershwin's melody, harmony, vocal writing, and the "elements of a more organic kind," especially the "flashes of real contrapuntal ingenuity."

Atkinson, who had nothing but praise for *Anything Goes* the previous year, put his cards on the table when he now wrote that "what a theatre critic probably wants is a musical show with songs that evoke the emotion of situations and make no further pretensions."[14] It is not surprising then that he expressed such distaste for the convention of recitative, which he, like Gershwin, designated as "operatic form." Atkinson also questioned "why commonplace remarks that carry no emotion have to be made in a chanting monotone."[15] Playing from the same deck, Downes lamented that a composer like Gershwin, "with a true lyrical gift and with original and racy things to say, has turned with his score of 'Porgy and Bess' to the more pretentious ways of musical theatre."[16] For Downes as well as for Atkinson, a composer who can "go upstairs and write a Gershwin tune" but whose "treatment of passages of recitative is seldom significant," should know his place and stick to writing great but unpretentious tunes.[17]

The question of genre and "operatic form" raised by Atkinson and Downes can be traced to the earliest stages in the collaboration of Gershwin and Heyward. In fact, the issue of recitatives was their principal source of artistic disagreement. As early as November 12, 1933, when he sent the first scene, Heyward offered the following suggestion: "I feel more and more that all dialogue should be spoken. It is fast moving, and we will cut it to the bone, but this will give the opera speed and tempo."[18] Gershwin differed strongly and overruled his librettist.

For the first decades of its history a critical consensus supported Heyward's original conviction. In his review of the Theatre Guild production in 1935 Virgil Thomson writes critically of Gershwin's recitative as "vocally uneasy and dramatically cumbersome" and concludes that "it would have been better if he had stuck to [spoken dialogue] . . . all the time."[19] Part of Thomson's subsequent praise in 1941 for the Cheryl Crawford revival in Maplewood, New Jersey, can be attributed to her practice "of eliminating, where possible, the embarrassment due to Gershwin's incredibly amateurish way of writing recitative."[20]

Vernon Duke—like Gershwin a hybrid classical-popular composer but unlike Gershwin a man sharply divided between his two artistic personalities, Duke and Dukelsky—was similarly critical. In their precompositional discussions about *Porgy and Bess* he recalled that "George was still under the sway of the Wagnerian formula," which Duke believed to be "anti-theatrical," and wrote somewhat smugly that "it is generally acknowledged that the separate numbers are superior to the somewhat amorphous stretches of music that hold them together," i.e., the recitatives.[21] Less surprisingly, Richard Rodgers, who rarely abandoned the Broadway convention of spoken dialogue, also believed that Gershwin had made "a mistake in writing *Porgy and Bess* as an opera."[22] According to Rodgers, "the *recitative* device was an unfamiliar and difficult one for Broadway audiences, and it didn't sustain the story." Consequently, it was only "when Cheryl Crawford revived it later as a musical play that it gained such overwhelming success and universal acceptance."[23] More recently Gershwin biographer Charles Schwartz concurred with the above-mentioned composers that the Crawford revival "vindicated" Heyward's original conception of the work, "for as he had argued, Gershwin's recitatives impeded the pacing of the original production."[24]

In addition to his controversial decision to give his work operatic form by connecting his musical numbers with recitatives, the composer had the audacity to load his score with hit songs, which makes the distinction between aria and recitative more glaring than in most hitless operatic works (see Appendix F). Clearly this issue was a sensitive one for Gershwin, who felt the need to publicly defend the presence of songs in *Porgy and Bess*:

> It is true that I have written songs for "Porgy and Bess." I am not ashamed of writing songs at any time so long as they are good songs. In "Porgy and Bess" I realized I was writing an opera for the theatre and without songs it could be neither of the theatre nor entertaining from my viewpoint. But songs are entirely within the operatic tradition. Many of the most successful operas of the past have had songs. Nearly all of Verdi's operas contain what are known as "song hits." "Carmen" [then performed with Ernest Guiraud's added recitatives] is almost a collection of song hits.[25]

In his overview of Gershwin's posthumous reputation Richard Crawford offers an insightful summary of several seemingly insurmountable criticisms that made Gershwin so defensive about inserting popular songs in a serious work that in the composer's words "used sustained symphonic music to unify entire scenes."[26] Crawford writes:

> We see Gershwin as a great natural talent, to be sure, but technically suspect, and working in a commercial realm quite separate

from the neighborhood in which true art is created. So there sits Gershwin, as Virgil Thomson once wrote, "between two stools," vastly appealing to the mass audience and hence a bit raffish, not quite deserving of serious academic scrutiny: a man without a category.[27]

Somewhat related to the problems of genre definition is another controversy surrounding *Porgy and Bess:* how to determine an authentic performing version. To place this debate in perspective it may be helpful to recall the difficulties in establishing a text for *Show Boat* (discussed in chapter 2). Since Kern and Hammerstein themselves revised their work nineteen years after its original Broadway run for the 1946 Broadway revival, it is arguable that this later version represents the final intentions of the creators. Despite its claim to legitimacy, however, revisionists such as John McGlinn rejected the 1946 version as an impure mutation of original authorial intent. Further, the Houston Opera (1983), McGlinn (1988), and Prince (for the 1994 Broadway revival) restored material that had been discarded—presumably with the consent of Kern and Hammerstein—in the pre-Broadway tryouts. The appearance of the dropped "Mis'ry's Comin' Aroun' " in the first published vocal score provides fuel for the idea that Kern really wanted this music in the show but capitulated to external pressures. Other reinsertions were not supported by equally compelling evidence.

The authenticity problems associated with *Porgy and Bess* (and many European operas in the core repertory) differ from those posed by the performance history of *Show Boat.* For example, in contrast to the *Show Boat* score, which was published four months into the original Broadway run, by which time the cuts had been stabilized, the *Porgy and Bess* vocal score was published as a rehearsal score prior to the Boston tryouts on September 30, 1935, and therefore includes most of the music that was later cut in the Boston tryouts. For good or ill, the Gershwin score, unlike the first published *Show Boat* score (with the exception of "Mis'ry's Comin' Aroun' "), is not a score that accurately represents what New York audiences actually heard on opening night ten days later. Thanks to the work of Charles Hamm it is now possible to reconstruct what audiences did hear on the opening night of *Porgy and Bess* (October 10, 1935) down to the last measure.[28] But the question remains: Were these cuts made for artistic or for practical or commercial considerations?

Hamm argues that "most cuts made for apparently practical reasons were of passages already questioned on artistic grounds," and that "the composer's mastery of technique, his critical judgement, his imagination, and his taste come as much in play in the process of final revisions as in the first stages of composition." In addition to the relatively modest "cuts to tighten dialogue or action," "cuts of repeated material mostly made before the opening in Boston," and "cuts to shorten the opera," the openings of three scenes were greatly reduced. By the time *Porgy and Bess* reached New York, only twenty measures of Jazzbo Brown's music remained before "Summertime" (and even these were eliminated a few days later), and the "six prayers" that opened act II, scene 4 were removed (though a far shorter reprise could still be heard at the end of the scene). More than two hundred measures from act III, scene 3, had also been discarded, including much of the trio portion of "Oh, Bess, Oh Where's My Bess."

An examination of one deleted portion, Porgy's "Buzzard Song" from act II, scene 1, might help to shed light on the complex issues of "authenticity" and the relative virtues of "absolute completeness."[29] As in the play *Porgy*, by Dorothy and DuBose Heyward, upon which the opera libretto is based (rather than on the novel *Porgy*), the libretto draft that DuBose sent to George on February 6, 1934 concludes this scene with the appearance of a buzzard.[30] In the play, the fact that the buzzard lights over Porgy's door represents the end of the protagonist's newly acquired happiness and peace of mind with Bess and prompts the final stage direction of the scene, "Porgy sits looking up at the bird with an expression of hopelessness as the curtain falls."[31]

The text of the "Buzzard Song" in the libretto shows Porgy's superstitious response to and fear of the buzzard, but in keeping with his attempt to be more upbeat in his adaptation from play to opera, Heyward presents a triumphant protagonist who reminds the buzzard that a former Porgy, decaying with loneliness, "don't live here no mo'."[32] Because he is no longer lonely, the Porgy in the first draft of Heyward's libretto revels in his victory over superstition and loneliness: "There's two folks livin' in dis shelter / Eatin', sleepin', singin', prayin'. / Ain't no such thing as loneliness, / An' Porgy's young again."[33]

Several pages earlier in the libretto manuscript, George wrote the words "Buzzard Song" shortly after the first appearance of the bird in the scene and Porgy's observation that "once de buzzard fold his wing an' light over yo' house, all yo' happiness done dead."[34] By placing the "Buzzard Song" earlier in the scene, Gershwin paved the way for the following duet between Porgy and Bess, "Bess, You Is My Woman Now," a subsequent addition.

Shortly before *Porgy and Bess* premiered in New York, the "Buzzard Song" was among the deletions agreed to by Gershwin and director

Rouben Mamoulian. There is general agreement among various first and secondhand explanations for this cut. Mamoulian, in his 1938 tribute to Gershwin, wrote that "no matter how well he loved a musical passage or an aria (like the Buzzard Song in *Porgy and Bess* for instance), he would cut it out without hesitation if that improved the performance as a whole."[35] According to Edith Garson's completion of Isaac Goldberg's 1931 Gershwin biography, the composer agreed to this particular cut for practical reasons: "In fact, during the Boston run, it was George who insisted on cutting fifteen minutes from one section, saying to Ira, 'You won't have a Porgy by the time we reach New York. No one can sing that much, eight performances a week.' "[36] David Ewen writes that "Porgy's effective 'Buzzard Song' and other of his passages were removed at George's suggestion."[37] Edward Jablonski explains, "Unlike recent productions of Porgy and Bess, the 1935 production had but one Porgy. So 'Buzzard Song' was among the first cut, in order to provide [Todd] Duncan with a chance to breathe between songs."[38]

There is little doubt that Heyward and the brothers Gershwin (mainly, of course, George) agreed to relocate the buzzard number prior to the composition of the short score that served as the foundation of the published piano-vocal version used in rehearsal. It can also be determined that those most involved in the production, particularly the composer and the director, agreed to cut the "Buzzard Song," perhaps on the eve of the New York premiere. Presumably the cut was made primarily for the practical reason that the opera was forty-five minutes too long and that Porgy already had two big numbers in this scene.

But the buzzard would light again with remarkable tenacity. Even during the initial run of the Broadway *Porgy and Bess,* the discarded "Buzzard Song" would appear among the first recorded excerpts from the opera. It was ironic that the singer on the recording—Lawrence Tibbett—was white. According to Gershwin, Tibbett was the likely candidate for a Metropolitan Opera production rather than the original Porgy, Todd Duncan.[39] Duncan himself sang the "Buzzard Song" along with "I Got Plenty o' Nuttin' " and "Bess, You Is My Woman Now" (with Marguerite Chapman) in the Los Angeles Philharmonic concerts organized by Merle Armitage in February 1937, and he included it along with other excerpts for a recording released in 1942.[40]

The "Buzzard Song" was also one of the few items cut from the Boston tryouts to resurface on the first nearly complete *Porgy* recording (and first published libretto in English) in 1951 produced by Goddard Lieberson and conducted by Lehman Engel, with Lawrence Winters and Camilla Williams singing the title roles.[41] And the song was among those portions reinstated for the Blevins Davis/Robert Breen revival that premiered in Dallas in 1952 and toured Europe later that year.[42] But in 1952 the buzzard did not appear until the final scene of the opera, perhaps to symbolize Porgy's bad luck in losing Bess.[43]

Does the "Buzzard Song" belong in future productions of *Porgy and Bess*? The central practical issue that led to its original omission was not really its length (less than four minutes, including the recitative with the lawyer Archdale), but the strain on Porgy's voice. Does this mean that if several Porgys had been available or if the Broadway equivalent of Lauritz Melchior had surfaced, the composer might have fought for its inclusion? Not necessarily.

The artistic aspects are naturally more problematic than the practical ones. Can we interpret Gershwin's remarks in 1935—"The reason I did not submit this work to the usual sponsors of opera in America was that I hoped to have developed something in American music that would appeal to the many rather than to the cultured few"—to justify the removal of forty-five expendable minutes?[44] What are present-day audiences to make of Gershwin's contemporaries, many directly involved in the first production, who without exception concluded that *Porgy and Bess* was better off with the cuts, including that of the "Buzzard Song"?

Clearly, even if Gershwin strove to approximate the "beauty of *Meistersinger*," he did not want to approximate its length, at least not on Broadway.[45] But opera epicureans used to *Die Meistersinger* and desirous of savoring every possible morsel of a work might eagerly welcome back the deleted forty-five minutes and perhaps endorse portions of the opera that never made it even to Boston, for example, the reconciliation duet between Bess and Serena in act III, scene 1.[46] The Houston Opera producers, who felt no remorse at dividing the work into two long acts rather than the specified three in order to save overtime labor costs, perhaps did not even consider the option of cutting the "Buzzard Song."

Several years before the Cleveland and Houston recordings were issued, Wayne Shirley, an authority on the opera and a persuasive advocate for a score that represents the composer's intentions, wrote that the "Buzzard Song" "is always cut, since Porgy has two other strenuous numbers in the scene, and the work flows better for the cut."[47] And although he does not offer an artistic justification for deleting this particular song, Hamm, who contends, as we have seen, that "most cuts made for apparently practical reasons were of passages already questioned on artistic grounds," would presumably support Fred Graham, who introduces *Kiss Me, Kate* with the line, "Yes, the cut's good, leave it in."[48] In contrast to Shirley and Hamm, Wilfrid Mellers has argued that the "Buzzard Song" constitutes "the turning-point of the opera, for it forces him [Porgy] to face up to reality and suffering. . . . The appearance of the buzzard marks Porgy's realization of the significance of his love."[49]

Some might argue for the retention of the "Buzzard Song" on musical grounds; others might conclude with equal justification that the song creates a dramatic intrusion. Certainly the "Buzzard Song" undermines the effect of a scene that otherwise successfully shows Porgy and Bess as fully accepted members of the Catfish Row community and, of course, illustrates their genuine and optimistic love. Because Porgy's superstitious nature had been de-emphasized in the adaptation of play to opera, its sudden appearance in this scene, despite Porgy's ultimate ability to conquer his fear, creates an ominous tone that the love duet "Bess, You Is My Woman Now" cannot overcome. Porgy's extraordinary fear in act III, scene 2, when he learns that he must look on Crown's face or serve time in jail, is generated by his sense of guilt at having murdered Crown rather than by irrational superstition. (For this reason, its placement in act III of the Davis/Breen libretto makes artistic sense despite the absence of historical justification.) To historians troubled by the dramatic effect of the song, it comes as a relief to learn that the composer had agreed to and perhaps even suggested its deletion.

Since the late 1970s the prevailing view holds that an uncut version of Gershwin's rehearsal vocal score best represents the composer's final intentions for the work. The more complete, the more authentic. For this reason few of the cuts noted by Hamm are in fact observed in current productions (although interestingly the video directed by Trevor Nunn in 1993 omitted the "Buzzard Song"); virtually none are observed in the three recordings of the work.[50] The merits of the cuts can and should be argued on aesthetic as well as historical grounds, and perhaps *Porgy*'s cuts should be disregarded, especially on recordings, which are less beholden to the time contraints of a Broadway production. But any careful consideration must acknowledge that the published score does not represent what Theatre Guild audiences heard during the initial run and may be alien to Gershwin's considered thoughts on the work.

The criticism leveled at Gershwin for making his Broadway opera through-composed and for straddling two worlds with his concoction of sung speech and hit songs has somewhat abated in recent years. More persistently controversial is Gershwin's claim that his "folk opera" expressed the African-American experience. Criticisms of Gershwin's racial presumptions appeared as early as the 1935 Broadway premiere, but in contrast to the gradual tolerance and eventual appreciation of his musical ambitions and the work's length, the hubris of Gershwin's depiction of black culture has not diminished over time despite the proliferation of performances throughout the world.[51] In fact, the growing "classic" stature of *Porgy and Bess* may actually have fueled racial controversies in recent years to a point where the problems brought about by what is perceived as cultural colonization and exploitation seems destined to remain central to the work in the minds of many for some time to come.[52]

In chapter 2 it was noted that the creators and future producers of *Show Boat* made some revisions in response to evolving racial sensibilities. Hammerstein replaced the word "niggers" with "coloured folks" as early as the 1928 London production ("colored" in 1946) as the first words of the show. For his screenplay to the 1936 film Hammerstein substituted "Darkies all work on de Mississippi," and in the 1946 film biography of Kern audiences heard "Here we all work on de Mississippi." Miles Kreuger wrote that in a 1966 Lincoln Center revival, "Nobody works on the Mississippi, because the Negro chorus was omitted altogether from the opening number."[53] In the 1994 Broadway revival directed by Hal Prince, "Brothers all work on the Mississippi."

Accounts of the genesis of McGlinn's recording of the "authentic" *Show Boat* of 1927 report that the contracted African-American chorus refused to sing the offending word "niggers" and therefore was replaced by the Ambrosian Chorus, who had been contracted to sing the white choral parts. To show his solidarity with the black chorus, Willard White, the Joe for this recording, resigned, and only after consultation with Eartha Kitt, a black performer and an articulate and influential opponent of racial indignities, did Bruce Hubbard consent to sing the role of Joe and the word "niggers." Earlier, Etta Moten Barnett, who sang Bess in the popular 1942 revival of *Porgy and Bess,* recalled that the cast "refused to used the word 'nigger,' and it was removed from all of the lines except those spoken by white characters."[54] As mentioned in chapter 2, some productions of *Show Boat* tried to circumvent the issue by minimizing the role of blacks, but this type of circumvention was, of course, impossible to accomplish with *Porgy and Bess,* Thus, from his time to ours Gershwin's opera has been chastized for its composer's presumption to speak for another race.

Thomson in his 1935 review takes Gershwin to task for attempting a folk subject: "Folk-lore subjects recounted by an outsider are only valid as long as the folk in question is unable to speak for itself, which is certainly not true of the American Negro in 1935."[55] A more detailed and closely reasoned critique of what Thomson termed "fake folk-lore" can be found in a review of the opera by Hall Johnson that appeared in the African-

American journal *Opportunity* a few months after the Theatre Guild premiere.[56] As the composer of *The Green Pastures* (1930) and *Run, Little Chillun!* (1933), two undisputed examples of authentic black folklore, Johnson's credentials were impeccable for this task.

Although Johnson, like Downes and Thomson, criticizes Gershwin's craftsmanship, again mainly in the recitatives, most of his remarks focus on Gershwin's misunderstanding of the African-American character and experience.[57] According to Johnson, the first of Gershwin's many inauthentic elements is his failure to capture "Negro simplicity." For Johnson, Gershwin's music "suggests sophisticated intricacies of attitude which could not possibly be native to the minds of the people who make up his story."[58] What makes the work "genuine" are the performances, particularly that of John W. Bubbles, of the vaudeville team Buck and Bubbles, who as Sporting Life played the central nonoperatic character among the leading players. But despite Bubbles's genuineness, Johnson viewed "It Ain't Necessarily So" as "so un-Negroid, in thought and in structure, that even Bubbles cannot save it."[59] On the other hand, perhaps because its derivations were more urban than folk, Johnson praises the authenticity of Sporting Life's "There's a Boat Dat's Leavin' Soon for New York" as a "real Negro gem."[60]

Criticism of *Porgy and Bess* on racial grounds reached a new level of intensity in the 1950s and 1960s, the era of *Brown v. Board of Education* and the civil rights struggles for equality. Many blacks resented the fact that the State Department, in sponsoring a global tour in 1952, was propagating negative stereotypes. On a televised broadcast playwright Lorraine Hansberry, author of *Raisin in the Sun,* criticized Otto Preminger, director of the 1959 film version of the opera, for "portraying Negroes at their worst."[61] A. S. "Doc" Young wrote in the *Los Angeles Sentinel* that *Porgy and Bess* "is completely out of context with modern times . . . it perpetuates old stereotypes that right-thinking people have buried long ago."[62]

Social historian Harold Cruse takes Hansberry to task for focusing on content in her criticism of *Porgy and Bess.*[63] Cruse instead sees the work "as the most perfect symbol of the Negro creative artist's cultural denial, degradation, exclusion, exploitation and acceptance of white paternalism."[64] He deeply resents the fact that blacks themselves did not produce their own authentic folk opera. He also considers it as indisputable that even if blacks had written such a work, it "would never have been supported, glorified and acclaimed, as *Porgy* has, by the white cultural elite of America."[65]

In Gershwin's time knowledgeable black critics responded negatively to the composer's attempt to come "as close to the Negro inflection in speech as possible" in his recitatives.[66] Even the normally circumspect and polite Duke Ellington was reported to have said that *Porgy and Bess* "does not use the Negro musical idiom" and that "it was not the music of Catfish Row or any other kind of Negroes."[67] Others find the idea of whites speaking for blacks and the subject matter itself rather than the final product the principal source of consternation.

Even those who for the most part reject Gershwin's "fake folk-lore" might find something to appreciate in Gershwin's assimilation of black culture inspired by his month at Folly Beach in 1934. Although simplistic by the standards of a master drummer, the polyrhythmic drumming that precedes "I Ain't Got No Shame" in act II, scene 2 comes closer to black African drumming style than most jazz drumming (by drummers of any race) before the 1950s. Similarly, Gershwin's attempt to capture the effect he and Heyward heard while listening outside a Pentecostal church in the opening and closing of act II, scene 4, "Oh, Doctor Jesus," in which six prayers are presented in a six-part texture (unfortunately mostly cut in Boston and New York), is a dazzling translation of the black experience.[68] Certainly these two examples possess a "fake authenticity" analogous to nineteenth-century slave narratives written by whites or Forrest Carter's best-selling bogus biography of the Cherokee Indian, *The Education of Little Tree*.[69] If we use Henry Louis Gates Jr.'s "blindfold test" (in which an expert usually failed to determine the race of various jazz trumpeters without previous knowledge) to judge a work's authenticity, Gershwin's evocation of African-American drumming and prayer meetings might be heard more charitably.[70]

For the sake of musical homogeneity Gershwin in most instances purposefully created his own idiosyncratic pseudo-spirituals rather than copy those he had heard. He also preferred to freely adapt his own Russian-Jewish ethnicity into a personal interpretation of the African-American experience rather than slavishly imitate it. The strong kinship between these musically compatible traditions is evident in Sporting Life's theme, which might be interpreted as a chromatic transformation of the Jewish blessing that precedes and follows the reading of the Torah (Example 4.2b, p. 80).[71]

How do we judge *Porgy and Bess* today, an opera that plays on black stereotypes and has served as a negative symbol of black exploitation? Is it enough to counter that the "civilized" and, moreover, nonsinging whites in the drama "are also more unemotional, drab and dull" and, as Edith Garson says in her completion of Goldberg's biography, "cruel and foolish"?[72] In the 1980s Lawrence Starr attempted to defuse the passions of this debate: "To insist on viewing *Porgy and Bess* as a racial document is to apply criteria which lie wholly outside the tradition to which this work relates, with the consequent risk of blinding oneself to the virtues it possesses."[73] Unfortunately, when considering the escalating tensions between Jews and African Americans (relatively unusual in 1935), it seems less likely in the 1990s that the universal values of Gershwin's opera espoused by Starr will soon transcend artistically as well as politically divisive racial issues.

Establishing and Transforming Musical Character

It was previously observed in *Show Boat* that Kern chose musical themes in part for their symbolic possibilities and reworked these themes in order to reveal dramatic connections and oppositions (see the "River Family" of motives, Example 2.2, p. 30). Kern also transformed two themes, Captain Andy's musical signature and Magnolia's piano music, to convey the continuity that underlies changing dramatic situations. Gershwin's treatment of the first technique is similar to that of Kern, since Gershwin assigns specific themes to important characters (or to a thing like "happy dust") and allows his listeners actively or subliminally the possiblity of attributing dramatic significance to these themes.

But Gershwin went beyond Kern in discovering varied and ingenious new ways to transform his melodies (even his hit tunes) for credible dramatic purposes. In altering Captain Andy's theme and Magnolia's piano theme, Kern altered tempo and character—and presumably asked Robert Russell Bennett to orchestrate these transformations—but he did not change the pitch content of either theme. When Gershwin musically responds to the ever-changing dramatic circumstances of his characters and their relationships, he frequently alters the pitches of the initial melodies by using a technique known as paraphrase. As his characters evolve, Gershwin adds and subtracts pitches and alters rhythms to create new melodies. In most cases these new melodies retain the identity inherent in their fundamental melodic contours. Some of Gershwin's melodic transformations are difficult to perceive and are consequently meaningless to most listeners. Other transformations are questionably related to the central themes. The remarks that follow will focus on the most audible and dramatically meaningful of Gershwin's melodic manipulations, a union of craft and art.

Musicals, operatic and otherwise, thrive when they show two people in love whom audiences can care about. The opera *Porgy and Bess,* like all the adaptations treated in this book, similarly places its greatest dramatic emphasis on the love-story component of its literary source. A related theme

Porgy and Bess, act II, scene 1. Todd Duncan in window at right (1935). Museum of the City of New York.

is the attempt of the principal characters to overcome their physical and emotional handicaps and dependencies, their loneliness and poor self esteem, and to establish themselves as fully-accepted members within a loving community. Act II, scenes 1 and 3 provide a good introduction to how Gershwin created a symbolic musical language to express these great dramatic themes.

At the musical heart of the opera stands (or kneels) Porgy, not only because Gershwin gives him several themes but because these themes relate so closely to the Catfish Row community.[74] Porgy may not feel as though he is a "complete" man (until ironically he gains his manhood and loses his humanity by killing Crown and then gloating over it), but from the outset of the drama he is definitely, unlike Bess, part of the community. It is fitting, then, that his main theme, shown in Example 4.1a, introduced by the orchestra rather than by Porgy himself, emphasizes a pure (or perfect) fifth and a minor (or blue) third, intervals that reasonably (if somewhat inexplicably) represent both the solidity and folk-like nature Porgy shares with Catfish Row as well as his sadness before he met Bess.[75] Soon after his introduction in act I Porgy sings the first of two loneliness themes,

"They pass by singin' " (Example 4.1b), a theme that thematically consists entirely of minor thirds and a theme that will retain its strong rhythmic profile in many future contexts.[76]

Moments later in this same monologue Gershwin has Porgy introduce a second loneliness theme (Example 4.1c), a melody that emphasizes a major second on "night time, day time" and "lonesome road" and a prominent syncopated rhythm ($\flat$ $\flat$.) derived from the last two notes of Porgy's central theme (Example 4.1a) and the rhythm of "singin' " (Example 4.1b).[77] Having introduced these three rhythmically connected Porgy themes in the opening scene, Gershwin will, in act II, scene 1, establish connections between Porgy and his community to reveal how Bess and Catfish Row work together to eliminate Porgy's loneliness.

Porgy's loneliness themes will undergo further audible transformations in the "Buzzard Song." Throughout much of the "Buzzard Song" Gershwin emphasizes the minor thirds that were so prominent in Porgy's central theme (e.g., "Don' you let dat buzzard keep you hangin' 'round my do' "), and he also retains the syncopations of the loneliness theme. But as seen in Example 4.1d, Gershwin intensifies Porgy's loneliness by contracting his major second a half step in the song's principal melodic motive to create a still-harsher minor second. Even if one questions the dramatic effect of the "Buzzard Song" on this scene and the drama as a whole and embraces the decision to remove it, its omnipresent syncopations and dissonant minor seconds certainly provide a fitting musical counterpart to Porgy's sudden apprehension upon seeing a buzzard.

The original form of Porgy's loneliness theme returns in act II, scene 1 to introduce the duet between Porgy and Bess, "Bess, You Is My Woman Now." The dramatic point of this duet, that Bess's love can eliminate Porgy's loneliness, soon becomes apparent when we hear Bess sing the second loneliness theme, "I ain' goin'! / You hear me sayin', / if you ain' goin', / wid you I'm stayin' " (Example 4.1e). Significantly, Porgy does not sing about his loneliness with Bess, and when Bess returns to it later in the song, Porgy sings a different counter line. In their fleeting, almost magical, moment of happiness Bess has thus absorbed Porgy's loneliness while at the same time relieving her own. Act II, scene 1 is thus the only scene in which Porgy and Bess express their love with uninhibited optimism for their future together. Musically, "Bess, You Is My Woman Now," as Starr has noted, marks a special and ephemeral moment of F-sharp major, a distant key heard nowhere else in the opera.[78]

The final transformation of Porgy's loneliness in act II, scene 1 occurs in the pseudo-spiritual "Oh, I Can't Sit Down!" that immediately follows Porgy and Bess's love duet, a spiritual that could, without stretching things

(a)

Porgy enters in goat cart—crowd greets him.

(b)

They pass by sing-in',——

(c)

Night time, day time, he got to trab-ble dat lone-some road,——

(d)

Buz-zard keep on fly-in' o-ver, take a-long yo' shad-ow——

(e)

I ain' go-in'! You hear me say-in', if you ain' go-in', wid you I'm stay-in'.

Example 4.1. Porgy's themes
  (a) Porgy's central theme
  (b) Loneliness theme
  (c) Loneliness theme
  (d) Loneliness theme in "Buzzard Song"
  (e) Loneliness theme in "Bess, You Is My Woman Now"

too much, be interpreted as a transformation of "It Take a Long Pull to Get There" and especially "I Got Plenty o' Nuttin'." In any event all of these melodies display the short-long syncopated loneliness rhythm (in most cases the short note receives an accent) prominently at the ends of many phrases.[79] In the main portion of this final chorus Gershwin not only preserves the G major tonality of Porgy's earlier tune, he creates another melody that manages to sound new while operating completely within Porgy's perfect fifth. More strikingly, Gershwin in "Oh, I Can't Sit Down" maintains the melodic connection with Porgy's central theme (the prominent minor thirds in the opening musical line that correspond to the song title) and the rhythmic connection (the characteristic syncopation on "happy feelin'," "no concealin'," and many other words) with Porgy's loneliness theme.

Through such devices Gershwin conveys the message that the most effective way to overcome loneliness is to acknowledge it musically, then transform its character, also musically. Not only has Bess's love for Porgy at least momentarily conquered Porgy's loneliness, Catfish Row revels in this transformation. Ironically, at the end of this scene Bess does in fact leave Porgy, albeit at his urging, to join the community at their picnic, an act that sets up her eventual fall from grace. Nevertheless, the people of Catfish Row invite Bess to join them on Kittiwah Island, a strong sign of her successful integration into the community.

If Porgy's themes and their transformations in community songs serve to emphasize the unity between Porgy and Catfish Row, Sporting Life's central theme—both at his entrance in act II, scene 1 and in the main melody of "It Ain't Necessarily So" in act II, scene 2—demonstrates his separation and estrangement from this same community (Example 4.2). Just as Captain Andy's shrewish wife Parthy possesses a melody that cannot live in harmony with the other themes that dwell within the secure perfect fourths of the Mississippi River (Example 2.3, p. 31), Sporting Life's attempt to be a part of Catfish Row is demonstrably false, musically as well as dramatically.

Like Porgy's theme, the melody that Gershwin assigned to Sporting Life is encompassed within a perfect fifth and concludes with a prominent minor (or blue) third. What betrays Sporting Life as an unwelcome outsider, however, is the prominence of the diminished fifth (the same sound as Parthy's dissonant augmented fourth, or tritone), an interval that has been associated with the devil since the Middle Ages when it was known as the *diabolus in musica*. The chromatic machinations of Sporting Life's theme appropriately enough suggest the movements of a snake-in-the-grass, analogous to the serpent who manages to tempt Eve out of the Garden of Eden.

Example 4.2. Sporting Life's themes
   (a) Sporting Life
   (b) Jewish prayer ("Boruch attah adonoi")
   (c) Happy Dust theme

The agent of Sporting Life's evil, his "happy dust" (heroin), receives a suitably chromatic, serpentine theme (Example 4.2c).[80] Even if one takes the optimistic view that Porgy will eventually find Bess after the final curtain, it must be acknowledged that both Bess and Porgy have been forced to leave Eden and search elsewhere for the Promised Land.

The third principal male character, Crown, exhibits a highly charged orchestral theme that contrasts markedly with Porgy's theme (Example 4.3).

Example 4.3. Crown's theme

Crown's strength and restless vitality, like that of a caged animal, is evident in the relentless syncopation of his theme. Musically, Crown's theme is also confined, within the narrow limits of a minor third. Further, in keeping with his dominating presence, whenever Crown appears all other themes are subordinate. His music even dominates the final struggle with Porgy in act III, scene 1, before Porgy states his musical supremacy and manages to overcome and kill his nemesis. In act II, scene 1, however, Crown, who has been absent a month from Catfish Row, does not exert any dramatic influence on the actions or thoughts of Porgy and Bess, and his musical theme is appropriately absent from this peaceful scene.

What about Bess? Does she not merit a theme of her own? Commentators on the opera have without exception neglected to assign her one.[81] Crown's music dominates his fight to the death with Porgy, but Bess's musical identity is less assertive and strongly influenced by the man she is with at the time (Porgy, Crown, or Sporting Life). Although Bess certainly holds her own musically, the two songs that she sings to her men, "What You Want Wid Bess?" (to Crown) and "I Loves You Porgy" (to Porgy) (Example 4.4), bear striking melodic or rhythmic resemblances to Porgy's themes, the former a paraphrase of Porgy's central theme (Example 4.1a) and the latter a new melody that uses the rhythms of "They pass by singin'" (Example 4.1b). When she sings "Summertime" to Clara's orphaned baby in act III, scene 1, Bess demonstrates her hard-won acceptance into the Catfish Row community by singing one of their songs.

Example 4.4. "I Loves You Porgy"

It is not surprising, then, that Bess's weaknesses and chameleon-like nature as a character have caused writers to overlook that Gershwin did in fact associate a specific theme with his heroine. We know this from Heyward's original libretto typescript, which he sent to Gershwin. On page 2-17 Gershwin indicated in a handwritten notation that a "Bess theme" should accompany the words sung by Bess, "Porgy, I hates to go an' leave you all alone."[82] At this point in the genesis of the work the idea of a love

duet between the principals, the future "Bess, You Is My Woman Now"—
which does not have a counterpart in the play *Porgy*—had not yet been
hatched.

Earlier it was noted that the eventual insertion of "Bess, You Is My
Woman Now" was the most substantial alteration to Heyward's typescript
for this scene. As act II, scene 1 takes shape in Gershwin's handwritten
notes, it is possible to observe the composer's realization that the principal
tune of this famous duet (even if Porgy sings it) belongs to Bess (Example
4.5).[83] And of course it is reasonable (and egalitarian) that Bess, who is
capable at this point in the drama of dispelling Porgy's loneliness, deserves
her own theme, especially since she is deprived of a solo aria in act III,
scene 3. Surely it is significant that her opening intervals consists mainly
of consonant major thirds and sixths and that her principal minor third is
gently completed by an intervening step, just as Bess fills in the gap of
Porgy's lonely existence. Interestingly, her theme also figures prominently
in the orchestra in the opera's final scene, act III, scene 3, when Porgy
inquires for Bess upon his return from jail and she is not there to sing her
theme. In the last moments of the opera Bess's theme—again presented in
the orchestra in her absence—connects with Porgy's own central theme for
the first time to seal their fate.[84]

Example 4.5. Bess's theme ("Bess, You Is My Woman Now")

Act II, scene 1, provides abundant evidence of Gershwin's skill in making
dramatic connections and distinctions through his use of musical signatures or leitmotivs. Once he has shown, for example, that Bess's theme and
the Catfish Row songs can at least temporarily transform Porgy's loneliness
into hope, Gershwin's motivic transformations reveal a great deal about
the meaning and significance of future dramatic events. One such scene,
act II, scene 3, which takes place one week after Bess left Porgy to join the
Catfish Row picnic on Kittiwah Island, offers a particularly vivid demon-

stration of Gershwin's ability to establish dramatic meaning through motivic transformation and paraphrase.

For the week that followed Bess's meeting with Crown on the island in the previous scene (act II, scene 2), Bess was "out of her head" back in Catfish Row. She remains in precarious condition at the opening of scene 3. Before we see Bess, however, we hear Jake's melody and a reprise of "It Take a Long Pull to Get There." In a passage cut from the New York production Bess sings "Eighteen mile to Kittiwah, eighteen mile to trabble," a musical line that might be interpreted as another of the many transformations of Porgy's central theme. Like Porgy's theme (Example 4.1a) it is encompassed within a perfect fifth and contains a prominent descending minor third (at the end of its second measure). It also reuses the syncopated rhythm of Porgy's loneliness (on "trabble") and combines this rhythm with the half-step interval that dominated the "Buzzard Song" (Examples 4.1c and 4.1d).

Bess's recitative also shows the influence of Sporting Life with its glaring and ominous augmented fourth (A-D♯) (the same sound as the diminished fifth (G-D♭) in Example 4.2). When she returns to this phrase moments later with the words, "Oh, there's a rattle snake in dem bushes," one can imagine the devilish and sepentine Sporting Life lurking in the bushes as well. After Bess sings this brief passage she collapses and Porgy sings his first words of the scene, "I think dat may-be she goin' to sleep now," an easily perceptible transformation of his central theme untarnished by any intrusion of Sporting Life. The devil is taking a nap and Bess will recover.

Serena prays on Bess's behalf and in answer to these prayers Catfish Row comes back to life with Jake's theme and the music of street vendors hawking their wares.[85] We know that Bess has recovered when we hear the orchestra play the opening of her theme (unsupported by harmony), and her conversation with Porgy is underscored by the continuation of "Bess, You Is My Woman Now." In their conversation Porgy tells Bess that he knows she has "been with Crown" on Kittiwah Island, because "Gawd give cripple to understan' many thing he ain' give strong men." Bess, too, understands many things about herself, including the fact that when Crown comes for her, she will be incapable of resisting him. When, near the end of "I Loves You Porgy," she sings, "If you kin keep me I wants to stay here wid you forever. — / I got my man" (Example 4.4), she uses the rhythm of "They pass by singin' " (Example 4.1b) to plead with Porgy to keep her safe from a man who possesses a harmful power over her.

Although Bess survives her illness and is able to express her love for Porgy once again, the moment of hope that concluded "Bess, You Is My Woman Now" has vanished forever (along with the key of F♯ major reserved for their brief moment of bliss). With her realization that the irresistible Crown, who was conspicuously absent in the earlier scene, now represents a menace to her future happiness with Porgy and that she is now unworthy of the man she loves, Bess has been rendered incapable of defusing Porgy's loneliness. Gershwin conveys this dramatic point simply and effectively when he gives Bess a new melody that is rhythmically identical to Porgy's loneliness theme. Bess has now become so overwhelmed by Porgy's loneliness that its rhythm has become a consuming obsession. She cannot sing anything else, despite Porgy's assurances of a better life and a sturdy statement of Porgy's central theme to conclude their duet.[86]

Later, in act III, scene 2, Sporting Life mocks the hero (who is about to lose the love of his life) by singing the short-long rhythm of Porgy's loneliness themes (Examples 4.1b and c) no less than four times in the first six measures of his "There's a Boat Dat's Leavin' Soon for New York." But it is Bess's fatalistic sense of defeat in act II, scene 3 rather than Sporting Life's powers of mockery and seduction that enables us to understand why she is so easily persuaded she belongs in New York rather than in Catfish Row.

We will meet Ira Gershwin again five years after *Porgy and Bess* as Kurt Weill's lyricist for *Lady in the Dark* (see chapter 7). For the first two of these years, George was only able to compose a pair of film scores, *Shall We Dance* (1936) and *A Damsel in Distress* (1937), and start a third, *The Goldwyn Follies*, which was completed by Vernon Duke after Gershwin's sudden death of a brain tumor in July 1937.

Assessments on the relative merits of Gershwin's twenty musicals and one opera continue to vary, even among music historians. For example, while H. Wiley Hitchcock concludes that *Porgy and Bess* was "a more pretentious but hardly more artistically successful contribution" than Gershwin's musical comedies and political satires, Hamm writes unreservedly that Gerswhin's opera "is the greatest nationalistic opera of the century, not only of America but of the world."[87] From Gershwin's time to ours the comedies and satires have seldom been revived in anything approaching their original state, even though nearly all contain one or more songs of lasting popularity and extraordinary musical, lyrical, and dramatic merit. In contrast, Gershwin's sole surviving opera, a work that began its career on Broadway, has, despite its pretensions and attendant artistic and political controversies, long since demonstrated a stageworthiness matched only by the memorability of its tunes.

CHAPTER FIVE

ON YOUR TOES AND PAL JOEY

Dance Gets into the Act and "Sweet Water from a Foul Well"

The historic collaboration of Richard Rodgers (1902–1979) and Lorenz Hart (1895–1943) began inauspiciously, shortly after their first meeting in 1919, when one of their first songs, "Any Old Place with You," was interpolated into a Broadway show. Hart was twenty-four and Rodgers only seventeen. The next year the new partners produced the first of three varsity shows at Columbia University and placed seven interpolated songs in a modestly successful Sigmund Romberg musical, *The Poor Little Ritz Girl*. After five years of failures and frustrations (Rodgers was on the verge of quitting show business to become a babies'-underwear wholesaler), the duo enjoyed two big hits in 1925, *The Garrick Gaieties*, a revue that included among its seven Rodgers and Hart songs the still-popular "Manhattan," and *Dearest Enemy*, a romantic musical set during the Revolutionary War.

These two shows launched a succession of popularly received musicals, each containing at least one future perennial song favorite: *Peggy-Ann* in 1926 ("Where's That Rainbow?"), *A Connecticut Yankee* in 1927 ("My Heart Stood Still" and "Thou Swell"), *Present Arms* in 1928 ("You Took Advantage of Me"), and *Evergreen* in 1930 ("Dancing on the Ceiling"). In 1930 the pair began a five-year sojourn in Hollywood where they produced the much discussed but rarely seen *Love Me Tonight* (1932), directed by Rouben Mamoulian, the future stage director of *Porgy and Bess*, *Oklahoma!*, and *Carousel*. A circus musical spectacular, *Jumbo*, marked their return to Broadway in 1935 and the beginning of their greatest successes: *On Your Toes* (1936), *I'd Rather Be Right* and *Babes in Arms* (1937), *I Married an Angel* and *The Boys from Syracuse* (1938), *Pal Joey* (1940), *By Jupiter* (1942), and a revised *A Connecticut Yankee* (1943).

Before the belated triumphs of 1925, Rodgers, who like Hart had dropped out of Columbia University without earning a degree, decided at the age of twenty that he needed to acquire a more rigorous musical education. As an adolescent Rodgers had received informal instruction both from his mother, an amateur pianist, and from his father, an enthusiastic amateur singer. For two years beginning in 1922 he studied harmony with the noted theorist and author Percy Goetschius at the Institute of Musical Art (which became the Juilliard School of Music in 1926).

Complementing this musical training was a legendary facility in the creation of melody. Rodgers's early biographer David Ewen reports that after Hammerstein had labored many hours and sometimes weeks, Rodgers needed only about twenty minutes to compose "June Is Bustin' Out All Over" and another twenty minutes for "Happy Talk"; the complex "Soliloquy" from *Carousel* allegedly occupied "about three hours."[1] Although in his autobiography, *Musical Stages,* Rodgers emphasizes the months of precompositional discussions with Hammerstein rather than his own speed, he corroborates the story that "Bali Ha'i" "couldn't have taken more than five minutes."[2] It therefore comes as something of a shock and perhaps a relief that the opening of the chorus to "I Could Write a Book" in *Pal Joey* took Rodgers the three tries illustrated in Example 5.1 before he found a version that satisfied him.

Example 5.1. "I Could Write a Book," three sketches for the opening four measures

Throughout his long career Rodgers placed innovation and integration among his loftiest goals for a musical. In *Musical Stages* he writes with pride that *Dearest Enemy* (1925), his first book musical with Hart, gave his team the welcome "chance to demonstrate what we could do with a score that had at least some relevance to the mood, characters and situations found in a story."[3] Rodgers took similar pride the following year in *Peggy-Ann*'s distinction as the first musical comedy to express Freud's theories on the stage "by dealing with subconscious fears and fantasies."[4]

Rodgers prefaces his remarks concerning the ill-fated musical about castration, *Chee-Chee*, a musical that received an all-time Rodgers and Hart low of thirty-one performances in 1928, with the suggestion that long before *Pal Joey* (1940) and *Oklahoma!* (1943), Rodgers with Hart "had long been firm believers in the close unity of song and story."[5] *Chee-Chee* provided their first opportunity "to put our theories into practice," as Rodgers explains:

> To avoid the eternal problem of the story coming to a halt as the songs take over, we decided to use a number of short pieces of from four to sixteen bars each, with no more than six songs of traditional form and length in the entire scene. In this way the music would be an essential part of the structure of the story rather than an appendage to the action. The concept was so unusual, in fact, that we even called attention to it with the following notice in the program: NOTE: The musical numbers, some of them very short, are so interwoven with the story that it would be confusing for the audience to peruse a complete list.[6]

On Your Toes

By the time Rodgers and Hart returned from Hollywood in 1935, their desire to create innovative musicals reached a new level. One year later they wrote *On Your Toes*. The genesis of the show can be traced to the Hollywood years, however, when Rodgers and Hart conceived the idea of a movie musical about a vaudeville hoofer (to be played by Fred Astaire) who becomes involved with a Russian ballet company.[7] Astaire, then busy with his series of films with Ginger Rogers, declined the role and Hollywood rejected their scenario. Soon, however, Broadway bought the idea as a vehicle for a new dancing sensation, Ray Bolger, the scarecrow in Hollywood's *The Wizard of Oz* in 1939, and the star of Rodgers and Hart's final Broadway show, *By Jupiter*, in 1942 and Frank Loesser's first Broadway triumph, *Where's Charley?*, in 1948. Boston tryouts took place between

On Your Toes. Ray Bolger and Tamara Geva (1936). Photograph: White Studio. Museum of the City of New York.

March 21 and April 8, 1936, and *On Your Toes* opened at the Imperial Theatre three days later. When it concluded its run at the Majestic Theatre the following January 23, the hit show had been performed 315 times.

The history of *On Your Toes* after its initial critically and popularly acclaimed run differs markedly from the history of its more popular predecessor, Porter's *Anything Goes* (discussed in chapter 3). The first major revival of *Anything Goes* in 1962 offered a new book and many interpolated songs, and made a respectable Off-Broadway run of 239 performances; the first revival of *On Your Toes* in 1954, with one interpolation and several other modest alterations, folded after only sixty-four showings. More in-

criminatingly, the work itself, not the production, was considered the principal reason for its failure.

In 1936 Brooks Atkinson had written that "if the word 'sophisticated' is
not too unpalatable, let it serve as a description of the mocking book which
Richard Rodgers, Lorenz Hart and George Abbott have scribbled."[8] By
1954 the integrated musicals of Rodgers and Hammerstein and even Rodgers and Hart's recently revived *Pal Joey*—which Atkinson had reviewed
disparagingly in 1940 before extolling its virtues in 1952—had created new
criteria that musicals like *On Your Toes* did not match. Thus eighteen years
after his initially positive assessment Atkinson attacked as "labored, me-
chanical and verbose" the book he formerly had deemed sophisticated. For
Atkinson and his public "the mood of the day," which had recently caught
up to *Pal Joey*, had "passed beyond" *On Your Toes*. The "long and ener-
vating" road to the still-worthy "Slaughter on Tenth Avenue" ballet at the
end of the second act simply was not worth the wait.[9]

In the 1936 *On Your Toes* Rodgers and Hart attempted an integration of
music and drama that went beyond their successful innovations in *Peggy-
Ann* and their unsuccessful ones in *Chee-Chee*. In *Musical Stages* Rodgers
discusses his ambitious new artistic intentions in the following terms:

> One of the great innovations of *On Your Toes,* the angle that had
> initially made us think of it as a vehicle for Fred Astaire, was that
> for the first time ballet was being incorporated into a musical-
> comedy book. To be sure, Albertina Rasch had made a specialty
> of creating Broadway ballets [for example, *The Band Wagon* of
> 1931], but these were usually in revues and were not part of a
> story line. We made our main ballet ["Slaughter on Tenth Ave-
> nue"] an integral part of the action; without it, there was no con-
> clusion to our story.[10]

Despite such claims, the degree to which coauthors Rodgers and Hart
and Abbott succeeded in their attempt to integrate dance, especially
"Slaughter on Tenth Avenue," has been questioned by Ethan Mordden:

> Much has been made of "Slaughter on Tenth Avenue"'s impor-
> tance as a book-integrated ballet, but it was, in fact, a ballet-
> within-a-play ... *not* a part of the story told in choreographic
> terms. Only towards the ballet's end did plot collide with set piece
> when the hoofer learned that two gangsters were planning to gun
> him down from a box in the theatre at the end of the number.
> Exhausted, terrified, he must keep dancing to save his life until

help comes, and thus a ballet sequence in *On Your Toes* turned into the *On Your Toes* plot.[11]

Mordden's challenge does not obscure the fact that *On Your Toes* treats a vexing artistic issue: the conflict and reconciliation between classical and popular art. Much of the plot and the comedy in *On Your Toes* evolves from the tensions between the cultivated and the vernacular, between high-brow and lowbrow art. Even the barest outlines of the scenario reveal this.

When in act I, scene 3 we meet Phil Dolan III ("Junior") as an adult, he is employed as a music professor at a W.P.A. (Work Projects Administration) Extension University, having renounced his career as a famous vaudeville hoofer sixteen years earlier at the insistence of his parents (scenes 1 and 2). His student and eventual romantic partner, Frankie Frayne, writes "cheap" (1936) or "derivative" (1983) popular songs, including "It's Got to Be Love," "On Your Toes," and "Glad to Be Un-happy"; another student, Sidney Cohn, who supposedly possesses greater talent (to match his pretensions and ambition), has composed "Slaughter on Tenth Avenue," which will be performed by the Russian Ballet in act II.

The Cat and the Fiddle, a 1931 hit with lyrics by Otto Harbach and music by Kern, had explored the tensions and eventual accommodation of clas-sical and popular music in a European setting in which a "serious" Ro-manian male composer and a jazzy American female composer (at the beginning of the show she is already well known as the composer of "She Didn't Say Yes") eventually produce a harmonious hybrid. *On Your Toes* contrasted the cultivated and vernacular traditions through dance, two full-length ballets, both choreographed by George Balanchine (1904–1983), a star in Diaghilev's ballet company the previous decade: a classical ballet to conclude act I ("La Princesse Zenobia") and a jazz ballet ("Slaughter on Tenth Avenue") as a climax for act II. In the title song tap dancing and classical ballet alternate and compete for audience approbation in the same number. Further, the Russian prima ballerina (Vera Baranova) and her partner (Konstantine Morrosine) have important dramatic (albeit nonsing-ing) parts as well as their star dance turns. By contrast, in the dream ballet that concludes act I of *Oklahoma!*—the musical which almost invariably receives the credit for integrating dance into the book—the dancing roles of Laurey and Curley are played by separate and mute dancers.

That *On Your Toes* is a musical about Art is frequently evident in the dialogue, especially its original 1936 manifestation. For example, in her efforts to convince the Russian ballet director, Sergei Alexandrovitch, that Sidney Cohn's ballet is worthy of his company, manager and principal benefactress Peggy Porterfield explains the case for branching out: "Your public is tired of *Scherezade, La Spectre de la Rose*—they've seen all those Russian turkeys at the Capital for 40 cents—this is something different— it's a jazz ballet—they can't understand the music without the story and nobody can understand the story—they'll say it's art."[12] Vera considers herself "a great artist" because she has convinced Junior that her "dancing [has] a virginal charm."[13] And when Morrosine tells a gangster that he "must wait till he [Junior] stops dancing" before shooting him, Art takes precedence over jealousy and revenge.[14]

More specifically, the libretto also explores conflicting attitudes on the relative merits of classical and jazz dance. Frankie questions Junior's priorities in giving up his potential as "a headliner in vaudeville" to be a supernumerary in the Russian ballet.[15] In the 1936 libretto Morrosine's infidelities and obnoxious behavior toward his partner and paramour Vera are acceptable, but he is denied the lead role in the jazz ballet for artistic reasons: "he does not understand American Jazz Rhythm" and "does not know how to dance on the off beat."[16]

On Your Toes *in 1936 and 1983*

In 1983, nearly thirty years after it had previously stumbled in its first Broadway revival, *On Your Toes* was again revived, this time with a new book from nonagenarian Abbott, the principal contributor to the original book. Echoing Atkinson's condemnation of the earlier production, Frank Rich of the *New York Times* wrote that the 1954 failure "was no fluke" and that "its few assets as entertainment are scattered like sweet and frail rose petals on a stagnant pond."[17] With the exception of Rich the new production received mostly favorable reviews and ran 505 performances, after the 1952 revival of *Pal Joey* (542 performances) the second longest-running Rodgers and Hart production and, like *Pal Joey, Porgy and Bess, Guys and Dolls*, and *Candide*, one of the few musical revivals to surpass its initial run.

What made the 1983 *On Your Toes* revival especially newsworthy was the approach of the revivalists. In contrast to the drastic book revisions and interpolated songs of the 1962 and 1987 revivals of *Anything Goes*, the 1983 *On Your Toes* in most respects closely followed its 1936 model. And unlike the 1954 revival, which had contained the interpolated "You Took Advantage of Me" (originally heard in *Present Arms* of 1928) in act II, scene 3 and dropped the first number, "Two a Day for Keith," soon after opening night, no interpolations or deletions in 1983 disturbed the "authenticity" of the original. That the 1983 production attempted to offer a faithful reenactment of the 1936 show is evident also in the reinstatement of the original dance and vocal arrangements, for the most part uncut and unedited, and the resuscitation of Hans Spialek's 1936 orchestrations. Although some of the original choreography was lost, "Donald Saddler, who restaged the non-ballet numbers, took care to use only movements that belong to the dance of the time."[18]

The considerable success of the 1983 revival prompted the publication of the first complete vocal score two years later with the following introductory remarks from Theodore S. Chapin, Managing Director of the Rodgers & Hammerstein Organization:

> This score corresponds to the 1983 production of ON YOUR TOES which used the orchestrations and arrangements created for the original production in 1936. A few slight changes were necessary and were made by Hans Spialek, the man who orchestrated the show forty-seven years earlier. Therefore, what you have in your hands is a record of a 1936 Rodgers and Hart score as it sounded when first presented to the public, as well as a documentation of a successful revival. That a score of this nature could be presented as its creators intended, and that those intentions could seem as vital today as they were in 1936, is a testament not only to the timelessness of Rodgers and Hart, but to the dedication and affection lavished on the 1983 production.[19]

Chapin neglects to mention that the vocal score issued in 1985 by Chappell does not entirely preserve the original order of these authentic 1936 orchestrations and arrangements. The brackets and other emendations in Appendix G reveal, for example, that "The Heart Is Quicker Than the Eye" (sung in 1936 by Peggy and Junior in act I, scene 6) has been transferred to the first scene of the second act to replace "Quiet Night" so that Ms. Porterfield would have something to sing in both acts. "Quiet Night" in 1936 opens act II, sung by a character identified only as Crooner; in 1983 "Quiet Night" is sung one scene later by a named nonentity (Hank J. Smith) and a female trio and reprised in scene 4 by the Russian ballet impresario Sergei Alexandrovitch and an off-stage chorus.

Gone also is the act II reprise by Sergei and Peggy of Junior's and Frankie's "There's a Small Hotel." Even if one refrained from asking how Sergei and Peggy came to know this song, its second act appearance in 1936 seemed somewhat gratuitous. In 1983 Sergei and Peggy sing a reprise of "Quiet Night" instead. Both productions allow everyone to learn "There's a Small Hotel" well enough to sing it at the end of the show.

The 1983 version also changed the locale of a few scenes. For example, the schoolroom scene in act I, scene 5, originally took place in Central Park at night, a setting for "There's a Small Hotel" that even the staunchest advocates of authenticity might consider laughable in 1983. But these changes do not contradict Chapin's assertion that for the most part Abbott & Co. as well as Chappell & Co. remained faithful to their musical source to a degree that was remarkable for a 1980s revival of a 1930s musical.

Thirty years earlier, as a result of his dissatisfaction with director Dwight Wiman, Abbott left for Palm Beach before rehearsals had begun in February, returning after Rodgers reminded him that as co-(*de facto* principal) author Abbott had an "obligation to come and protect it."[20] In his autobiography Abbott explains his reaction and solution:

> Arriving in Boston, where *On Your Toes* was playing its final week, I found things in better shape than I had expected. Ray Bolger was sensational in the lead, and "Slaughter on Tenth Avenue" remains in my memory as one of the best numbers I've ever seen in the theatre, both musically and choreographically. The book, however, was a mess; the story line had been destroyed by experimenting, and the actors were out of hand. I behaved ruthlessly to the cast to force them to play parts instead of fighting for material, and I straightened the book out by the simple device of putting it back the way I had written it in the first place.[21]

When he returned to the script in 1983, Abbott (now ninety-five) had had time to rethink and reinterpret his responses and actions of 1936. He now recalled the situation somewhat differently than in both his and Rodgers's published autobiographies: "I respected Rodgers and Hart so much in that field . . . I didn't do as much as I should have done. . . . I threw out three sets. . . . In the old days, if they wanted to sing a song, they set it in Central park or the Palladium. What for? To sing a song like 'Quiet Night'? I made 'Quiet Night' part of the plot."[22]

In order to further integrate plot and music as well as to establish greater credibility (and, of course, accessibility) for a 1980s audience, Abbott altered his original libretto. In 1936 Sergei and Vera had been several times married; in 1983 Sergei is given some romantic potential with Peggy (as revealed in their reprise of "Quiet Night," now "part of the plot") and Vera and Konstantine are lovers both on and off the stage. Also in 1983 the original meeting between Junior and Peggy is made more understandable; Frankie now knows a friend of Peggy's uncle who can introduce them.

The main changes between the 1936 and 1983 books, however, deal less

with plot than with language. The earlier version is more sexually suggestive and, still more surprisingly, perhaps even funnier. Here, for example,
is what 1936 audiences heard in the dialogue that precedes Vera's meeting
with Junior in act I, scene 4:

PEGGY: You're to be a strip tease girl in a burlesque show.
VERA: Well, if he's got ideas like that, why should I bother to dress?
PEGGY: Darling, he thinks you are an actress. He doesn't know we
are casting to type.

In 1983 Vera is cast as a primmer prima ballerina who has the *potential* to
play a striptease character when given time to consider such an outrageous
thought. Abbott is clearly no longer casting to type:

PEGGY: You're going to love the part—it's a striptease girl in a burlesque show. It will shock the dance world. It will show us as the
progressive ballet company I want us to be.
VERA: What about Sergei Alexandrovitch? He will say no.
PEGGY: First you have to like it. This young man who is coming will
play the music and tell you all about it.
VERA (*Begins to play the part*): Sure, a striptease girl—why not?

As a sexually liberated goddess of the ballet world, the original Vera is
allowed to conclude the scene in her apartment with a risqué punchline
that indicates her desire to see more of Junior. After the foreplay of dancing
to the "Zenobia" ballet with Junior, they climb on her bed and she takes
his glasses off. When Junior tells Vera his real name and his nickname,
Vera replies with a line that could have been stolen from a Mae West film:
"But I'll call you Phillip. I can't call you Junior. For very soon you will be
a great big boy."[23]

The original book of *On Your Toes* had fewer Groucho Marx–Margaret
Dumont–type exchanges than the 1934 *Anything Goes*, but those that remained were carefully expurgated. Thus in Abbott's 1983 revised book (act
1, scene 6) Sergei learns of the glitch that will pave the way for Junior to
escape from his role as a supernumerary to become a star of the "Zenobia"
ballet: the dancer Leftsky has been detained in jail. This change obscures
the politically topical nature of the 1936 version which finds Lefsky (less
obviously named than his 1983 counterpart) in a hospital.

SERGEI: He got in fight with union delegates—All afternoon we are
waiting and waiting for him—

PEGGY: Waiting for Lefsky![24]

Theater audiences in 1936 would not have had any trouble relating this
reference to Clifford Odets's then widely known union play produced the
previous year, *Waiting for Lefty,* in which members of a taxi drivers' union
are waiting in vain for their leader, who has been killed.

The Classroom Scene

A comparison between the 1936 and 1983 versions of the first classroom
scene, act I, scene 3, further demonstrates evolving social attitudes. In 1936
Junior not only derogates as "cheap" the musical ditty Frankie has composed, he displays a favoritism towards his "serious" jazz (and, not incidentally, male) student composer Sidney Cohn. In fact, he is so engrossed
in his protégé that he is oblivious to Frankie's feelings. Although Frankie
is still the one who will return to apologize for leaving so abruptly, by
1983 Junior has learned something from the feminist movement of the
intervening years. At least he realizes that he has hurt her feelings.

Gone from both the lyrics and the vocal score of "The Three B's" in
1983 are Hart's virtuosic and delectably absurd rhymes in 1936 that called
attention to their brilliance: "Who are the three 'B's' of music? / Name the
holy trinity / Whose true divinity / Goes stretching to infinity / No asi-
ninity / In this vicinity / Who are the three "B's" of music?"[25]

In 1983 Junior offers the following interpretation of romantic lieder:
"and thus we note the painless transition into the next phase. The early
19th century brought forth a renaissance of what we could term singing
composers. The great music of that period was idealized folk song. Chopin,
Schumann, Mendelssohn, and, last but not least, Franz Schubert."[26]

The following dialogue from 1936 (abandoned in 1983) introduces "The
Three B's" from quite a different perspective:

JUNIOR: You will notice I am careful of the pronunciation, Schu-*bert*,
not Shubert [a reference to the organization which, then as now,
owned a considerable number of Broadway theaters]. (*Walks to
piano*) Let us take this lovely melody. (*He plays the* Ständchen *and
sings*) "Dein ist mein Herz" which means "Yours is my heart." We
are all familiar with that melody but I wonder is there anyone
who can tell me what life force may have inspired Franz Schubert?
(*Hands are raised by some of the class*) Yes, Miss Wasservogel?

MISS WASSERVOGEL: A beautiful girl.

JUNIOR: Miss Frayne?

FRANKIE: A handsome young man.

SEVERAL STUDENTS: A girl—a girl.

OTHERS: A boy.

JUNIOR: No—a pork chop, a glass of beer and liverwurst; Schubert
should be very close to our hearts here for he was born poor with
no W.P.A.[27]

Abbott's 1936 dialogue lets audiences know unequivocally that Frankie—a contemporary Schubert—is the one inspired by "a handsome young man."[28] Also in 1936, with a remark that would mean more to Depression audiences, Junior disregards love as a motive and attributes Schubert's inspiration to a good meal. "The Three B's" in the 1936 version (renamed "Questions and Answers" in 1983) also demonstrates the essence of the conflict between classical music and jazz so central to *On Your Toes*. Classical music, with its "charms of Orpheus," throws lovers of popular music "right into the arms of Morpheus." Although the scholarly establishment would not lower itself in 1936 (or even a 1983 version of 1936) to explain the artistic merits of jazz in a university classroom, classical music is characterized as boring for all its artistic pretensions while jazz, a "cheap" (or "derivative") pseudo-art, provides much greater entertainment.

Throughout "The Three B's" the jazz-loving W.P.A. Extension University class unabashedly reveals its ignorance of and derision for art music. To the strains of the Symphony in D Minor and *Les Préludes* they mispronounce César Franck's name as Seezer Frank and convert Liszt's popular classic into a drinking song (Example 5.2).[29] Next they add ignorance to sacrilege when they confuse Shostakovich's recently banned opera, *Lady Macbeth of Mtsensk*, with celebrity stripper Gypsy Rose Lee's burlesque house Minskys, and reach a "new low" (to rhyme with "Von Bülow") when they assert that Puccini wrote the popular song classic "Poor Butterfly" instead of *Madame Butterfly*. In exclaiming in the chorus of "Bach, Beethoven, and Brahms" that "two of them wrote symphonies and one wrote psalms," they add the sin of a weak rhyme "Brahms/psalms" to a tenuous historical claim (Bach wrote chorales, after all, not psalms). But the students show that they are not complete dunces when they place "the man who wrote *Sari*"—the now-obscure Emmerich Kálmán (1882–1953)—on a par with Bernardino Molinari (1880–1952).[30] To paraphrase a line from *Pal Joey*'s "Zip," "Who the hell is Molinari?"

The dramatic context of the song "It's Got to Be Love" in act I, scene 3

Example 5.2. "Questions and Answers (The Three B's)"
(a) with Franck Symphony in D Minor and Liszt *Les
Préludes* borrowings

(b)

(b) Liszt's *Les Préludes*

is a pretext for Frankie to sing the song she wrote (with Junior in mind).
Here is the exchange that leads to it in 1936:

> JUNIOR: Well, I seem to remember that primarily you wanted to talk
> about the song of yours.
> FRANKIE (*cross to desk*): Oh, no, not really. It's so unimportant. Just
> look at the title, "It's Got to Be Love"—that's unimportant to start
> with, isn't it?
> JUNIOR: I wish I knew.
> FRANKIE: What?
> JUNIOR: I mean, well, perhaps if you play it for me a few times, I'll
> change my mind.
> FRANKIE: You really want me to?
> JUNIOR: Of course I do, Miss Frayne.
> FRANKIE (*crossing to piano*): Alright—by the way, the name's Frances,
> but you may call me Frankie.
> JUNIOR: Frankie? I like that name—Frankie.
> FRANKIE: Professor Dolan, may I call you Junior?[31]

Following a five-measure introduction and a tuneful verse of twenty-three measures, which provides a smooth musical transition between spoken dialogue and a song hit (Frankie has indeed composed a hit worthy of Rodgers), Frankie and Junior sing two thirty-two-bar choruses. The melody of the first chorus (A-B-A-B' form) is shown in Example 5.3.

> A a [It's] got to be love! [upbeats in brackets]
> It couldn't be tonsilitis;
> It feels like neuritis,
> But nevertheless it's love.
> (8 measures, mm. 1–8)
> B b [Don't] tell me the pickles and pie à la mode
> (2 measures, mm. 9–10)

Ex. 5.3: *It's Got to Be Love* (chorus)

Example 5.3. "It's Got to Be Love" (chorus)

    a'   [They] served me
           Unnerved me,
           And made my heart a broken down pump!
           (6 measures, mm. 11–16)

A   a   [It's] got to be love,
           It isn't the morning after,
           That makes every rafter
           Go spinning around above.
           (8 measures, mm. 17–24)

B'   b'   [I'm sure] that it's fatal, or why do I get
         That sinking feeling?
         (4 measures, mm. 25–28)
     a"   [I] think that I'm dead.
         But nevertheless it's only love!
         (4 measures, mm. 29–32)

The first eight measures start off conventionally enough and present what anyone familiar with the standard popular song form would interpret as an A section. Instead of the more conventional repeat of A, however, the words "Don't tell me the pickles and pie à la mode" during the next two measures inaugurate a new section, B. More surprisingly (other popular songs are in A-B-A-B form instead of A-A-B-A), two measures later, within this B section (beginning with "served me"), Rodgers interrupts the new melody and returns to a version of A, albeit much transformed through condensation. Probably relatively few listeners would recognize that *a'* (mm. 11–16) in this B section is fundamentally the same as *a* (mm. 1–8) of the A section, albeit stripped of all but the bare essential notes of the earlier phrase.

Rodgers offers another surprise when he returns to B' and its first part, *b'*, is now doubled in length from two measures to four (mm. 25–28). The added measures (mm. 27–28), for which Hart wrote the words "sinking feeling," stand out from the rest of the song as the only occasion (other than the ends of phrases) where a note is held longer than a single beat. Hart understood that the descending melodic line of these measures, D-C♯-B-B♭, aptly fits the sentiment of the lyric here, just as in the previous line he set the melody that turns around the note E to capture the feeling of "spinning around above" (m. 23). When he arrives at the phrase that inspired Hart's "sinking feeling," Rodgers also presents a harmonic rhythm dramatically altered from everything that came before in the song. Instead of allowing several melody notes for each chord, he now allots one note per chord.[32]

"It's Got to Be Love" contains a characteristic Hartian sentiment about love as an unwelcome malady and its negative effect on the body and spirit. Two years later in *The Boys from Syracuse*, Rodgers and Hart composed a sequel, "This Can't Be Love." Why not? Because Luciana and Antipholus of Syracuse "feel so well—no sobs, no sorrows, no sighs . . . no dizzy spell." In the earlier lament from *On Your Toes* Rodgers and Hart present a love song composed by a woman so smitten that her lover's hair, even if it "couldn't possibly be duller," would be perceived as pure gold. Since at this stage in the show Frankie cannot admit that Junior is the reason her heart has become "a broken down pump," the jazzy tune, like the lyrics (with the exception of "that sinking feeling"), creates a surface lightness that masks the underlying truth: Frankie is literally as well as figuratively lovesick. Perhaps even more ingeniously than in Vera Simpson's open admission of her obsession with Joey in "Bewitched," discussed later in this chapter (Example 5.6), "It's Got to Be Love" displays a descending two-note figure in nearly every measure that subtly betrays Frankie's obsession with her teacher Junior.

In his notes to the 1983 revival recording conductor John Mauceri writes tantalizingly of musical organicism in *On Your Toes:*

> The score is full of musical "cross-references" like the theme of
> the pas de deux in "Princesse Zenobia" having the same rhythmic
> structure as "There's a Small Hotel" [Example 5.4]. The great
> composers of the American musical theater were not merely tune-
> smiths, but composers of songs, ensembles and occasionally larger
> structures, like Schumann, Mendelssohn and Schubert a century
> before them."[33]

Mauceri's message is that great works of theatrical art like *On Your Toes* possess unity and structural integrity not usually associated with musical comedy—and, by implication, that large works are more worthy of praise than "mere" tunes. And certainly "There's a Small Hotel" and "Princesse Zenobia" have much in common melodically as well as rhythmically. Since this song has previously served as the love duet between Junior and Frankie, it is dramatically convincing when Rodgers uses a transformed version of this song for a *pas de deux* (the balletic equivalent of a love song) that depicts the love between the Beggar (Morrosine) and the Princesse (Vera).

Additional examples of organicism include the rhythmic and sometimes melodic connections between the release or B section of "There's a Small Hotel" (which, unlike "It's Got to Be Love," displays the more usual A-A-B-A thirty-two-bar form) and the first phrase of "The Heart is Quicker Than the Eye" (also A-A-B-A) shown in Example 5.5. Mauceri might have noted that Rodgers reuses the dotted rhythmic accompaniment of "Small Hotel" to accompany the main theme of "Slaughter" for the jazzy duet between Junior (who knows the tune pretty well by now) and the stripper Vera. He might also have mentioned that the accompaniment of the second half of the verse, beginning with the words "see . . . looks gold to me" of

(a)

(b)

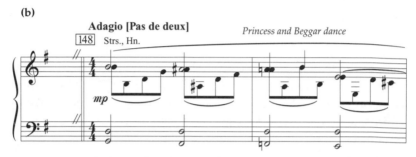

Example 5.4. "There's a Small Hotel" and "La Princesse Zenobia" Ballet
(a) "There's a Small Hotel," original song
(b) transformation in "La Princesse Zenobia" ballet

"It's Got to Be Love" also anticipates the rhythmic accompaniment throughout "There's a Small Hotel" and the *pas de deux* between Junior and Vera in "Slaughter." Nevertheless, in contrast to the vast network of connections previously observed in *Show Boat* and *Porgy and Bess*, examples of organicism in *On Your Toes* are comparatively rare. More important, Rodgers, although he does employ the musical device of foreshadowing for dramatic purposes, especially of his second ballet, "Slaughter on Tenth Avenue," for the most part does not exploit the dramatic potential of his musical connections as he would later with Hammerstein.[34]

Musical comedies before *Oklahoma!* and *Carousel* are almost invariably criticized for their awkward transitions from dialogue into music. The segue into "There's a Small Hotel" (act I, scene 6), a big hit song in the original production, provides a representative example by its absence of any references in the dialogue that lead plausibly, much less naturally or inevitably, to the song. In his 1983 revision Abbott tries to remedy this:

(a)

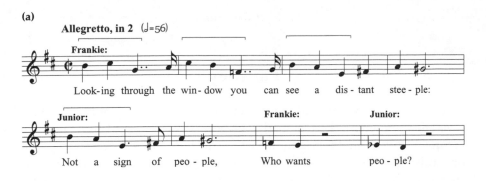

(b)

Example 5.5. "There's a Small Hotel and "The Heart Is
Quicker Than the Eye"
(a) "There's a Small Hotel" (release or B section)
(b) "The Heart is Quicker Than the Eye" (opening of
chorus)

FRANKIE: Oh, Junior, I wish we were far away from all this.
JUNIOR: Yes, so do I. With no complications in our lives.
FRANKIE: Yes.
JUNIOR (*Goes to her*): Oh yes . . . very far away . . . Paris maybe.[35]

If the revised dialogue constitutes an improvement over the Central
Park setting of the 1936 original, where "There's a Small Hotel" almost
literally comes out of nowhere, it does not fully solve the problem of how
a librettist or an imaginative director can successfully introduce a song like
"There's a Small Hotel." "It's Got to Be Love" may subtly reflect Frankie's
disguised obsession with veiled descending melodic sequences, but not
even with all the wisdom of his advancing years could a genius such as
Abbott make these songs grow seamlessly out of the dramatic action. But
perhaps the point is that, with songs such as these, who needs integrated
dramatic solutions?

Pal Joey

Several days before *Pal Joey*'s 1952 revival, Rodgers wrote in the *New York Times* that "Nobody like Joey had ever been on the musical comedy stage before."[36] In his autobiography Rodgers concluded that of the twenty-five musicals he wrote with Hart, *Pal Joey* remained his favorite, a opinion also shared by his lyricist.[37] Porter's *Anything Goes* may be more frequently revived. Several Rodgers and Hart shows, including *A Connecticut Yankee* in its revised 1943 version and *The Boys from Syracuse* from 1938 can boast as many hits. The scintillating *On Your Toes* can claim two full-length ballets and an organic unity unusual in musical comedies. Despite all this, only *Pal Joey* has proven that it can be successfully revived without substantial changes in its book or reordering of its songs.

The genesis of the musical *Pal Joey*, based on John O'Hara's collection of stories in epistolary form, can be traced to 1938 when a single O'Hara short story, "Pal Joey," was published in the *New Yorker*. By early 1940, shortly after Rodgers had received O'Hara's letter suggesting a collaboration on a musical based on his collection, an additional eleven Joey stories (out of a total of thirteen) had appeared.[38] A normal five-week rehearsal schedule began on November 11 and tryouts took place in Philadelphia between December 16 and 22. Directed by Abbott and starring Gene Kelly as Joey and Vivienne Segal as Vera Simpson, the musical made its Broadway premiere at the Ethel Barrymore Theatre on Christmas Day and closed 374 performances later at the St. James Theatre on November 29, 1941.[39]

In his now-infamous review *New York Times* theater critic Brooks Atkinson found *Pal Joey* "entertaining" but "odious." Referring to the disturbing subject matter, including adultery, sexual exploitation, blackmail, the somewhat unwholesome moral character of the principals, and a realistic and unflattering depiction of the seamy side of Chicago night life, Atkinson concluded his review with the question, "Although it is expertly done, can you draw sweet water from a foul well?"[40] Other critics greeted *Pal Joey* as a major "advance" in the form. Burns Mantle, for example, compared it favorably with the legitimate plays of the season and expressed his delight "that there are signs of new life in the musicals."[41] And in *Musical Stages* Rodgers proudly quotes Wolcott Gibbs's *New Yorker* review as an antidote to Atkinson: "I am not optimistic by nature but it seems to me just possible that the idea of equipping a song-and-dance production with a few living, three-dimensional figures, talking and behaving like human beings, may no longer strike the boys in the business as merely fantastic."[42]

Pal Joey. Gene Kelly in right foreground (1940). Photograph: Vandamm. Museum of the City of New York.

Some reviewers noted weaknesses in the second act, but most praised O'Hara for producing a fine book. John Mason Brown described the work as "novel and imaginative."[43] Sidney B. Whipple lauded the "rich characterizations" and concluded that it was "the first musical comedy book in a long time that has been worth the bother."[44] Its successful original run was surpassed by Rodgers and Hart only in their final and now largely forgotten *By Jupiter* (1942), which received 427 performances.

Pal Joey appeared several years before the era of cast recordings, but in September 1950, ten years after its Broadway stage debut, a successful recording was issued with Vivienne Segal, the original Vera Simpson, and Harold Lang as a new Joey. The recording generated considerable interest in the work and soon led to a revival on January 3, 1952, a sequence of events that foreshadowed the trajecteries of several Andrew Lloyd Webber musicals of the 1970s and 1980s that were introduced as record albums and later evolved into stage productions. The 1952 *Pal Joey* became the second major revival (after Cheryl Crawford's 1942 revival of *Porgy and Bess*) to surpass its original run and, at 542 performances remains the longest-running production of any Rodgers and Hart musical, original or revival. Even Atkinson, while not exactly admitting that he had erred in his 1940 assessment, lavishly praised the work as well as the production in 1952, including "the terseness of the writing, the liveliness and versatility of the score, and the easy perfection of the lyrics."[45]

After two successful revivals at the New York City Center in 1961 and 1963 (both with Bob Fosse in the title role), the artistic and commercial failure of a 1976 revival at New York City's Circle in the Square—abandoned by New York City Ballet star Edward Villella shortly before opening night—would not cause *Pal Joey* to lose its place as a classic American musical, a place firmly established by the 1952 revival. As another sign of its artistic stature *Pal Joey* became the earliest musical to gain admittance in Lehman Engel's select list of fifteen canonic musicals.[46] For Engel, *Pal Joey* inaugurated a Golden Age of the American musical.[47]

Pal Joey *in 1940 and 1952*

Compared to the liberties taken with the 1962 *Anything Goes* and the 1954 *On Your Toes*, the 1952 *Pal Joey* revival followed its original book and song content and order tenaciously. Nevertheless, some of what audiences heard and saw in 1952 departs from the original Broadway production. For example, in the 1952 revival, "Do It the Hard Way," is placed outside of its original dramatic context (act II, scene 4), when it is sung by Joey to Vera in their apartment; in 1940 this song is presented as a duet between Gladys and Ludlow Lowell in Chez Joey one scene earlier.[48]

The 1952 lyrics also depart in several notable ways from O'Hara's 1940 typescript.[49] In 1940 Hart concluded the chorus of "That Terrific Rainbow" (act I, scene 3) with the following quatrain: "Though we're in those GRAY clouds / Some day you'll see / That terrific RAINBOW / Over you and me" (preserved on the prerevival recording); for the 1952 revival someone (presumably not Hart) replaced two lines of this lyric with one that is grammatically incorrect, perhaps to emphasize the amateurish nature of the song. Thus "Some day you'll spy" now rhymes with "Over you and I" (Hart rhymed "someday you'll see" with "over you and me"). This alteration was adopted in the 1962 vocal score published by Chappell & Co.

The topical "Zip"—a song in which newspaper reporter Melba Snyder (played in the revival by Elaine Strich) acts out her interview with Gypsy Rose Lee, "the star who worked for Minski"—also underwent several lyrical changes in 1952. In the revival Melba opened the song with Hart's earlier version of the first lines when she recalls her interviews with "Pablo Picasso and a countess named di Frasso." It is possible that Picasso and di Frasso were more recognizable to an early 1950s audience than the revised 1940 lyric that paired Leslie Howard and Noël Coward. In the final chorus the then-better-known Arturo Toscanini replaced Leopold Stokowski as the leader of the "the greatest of bands," and one stripper (Lili St. Cyr) replaced another (Rosita Royce). Even present-day trivia buffs could not be expected to know who either stripper is (although it might be said that Lili St. Cyr has achieved immortality by being mentioned in "Zip"). The 1952 version of "Den of Iniquity" (act II, scene 2) replaced Tchaikovski's *1812 Overture* with Ravel's *Boléro* and added a final lyrical exchange between Joey and Vera after their dance.[50]

In his autobiography Abbott somewhat exaggeratingly refers to a preliminary script by librettist O'Hara as "a disorganized set of scenes without a good story line [that] required work before we would be ready for rehearsal."[51] In fact, although it contains no lyrics among its indications for songs and displays several notable deletions and departures from his Broadway typescript in 1940 (including an ending in which Linda and Joey are reconciled), in most respects O'Hara's preliminary typescript follows the story line of the 1940 version closely.[52]

Some songs that became part of the Broadway draft, "That Terrific Rainbow," "Happy Hunting Horn," and even "Bewitched," were not given any space at all in O'Hara's preliminary script. Further, the early typescript offers no indication for a ballet, an idea that Abbott credits scene and lighting designer Jo Mielziner for suggesting during rehearsals.[53] The dialogue that precedes "The Flower Garden of My Heart" in the published libretto is also missing from the earlier draft, but in this case O'Hara's description of this production number (original draft, beginning of Act II) leaves no room for doubt that he was responsible for the idea of the ballet:

> The song is Richman corn [Harry Richman, who introduced "Putting on the Ritz" in *Face the Music,* 1932], the flower number kind of thing—every girl reminds me of a flower; here is a hydrangea, here is a crocus, etc. a YOUNG MAN stays in the spotlight, holding out a hand for Hydrangea, who is in silly nudish costume. He never quite lets her get all the way in the light, but hands her away with one hand as he reaches for Crocus with the other. He looks at the fannies etc. in a way to make them ridiculous, and is mugging terribly, even in rehearsal.

Song and Story

O'Hara's typescript of the 1940 Broadway libretto (I-6-36) contains handwritten changes for "Bewitched," the biggest song hit from *Pal Joey.* Here are the typed lyrics as they once appeared in the B and final A sections of the third A-A-B-A chorus.

B   We can fight—we start shrieking
     Always end in a row,
     Horizontally speaking is not the whole thing now,
A   I'm dumb again
     And numb again
     Like Fanny Brice singing "Mon Homme" again.
     Bewitched, bothered and bewildered am I.

The draft poses a cultural literacy problem for those who might not know, even in 1940, that Fanny Brice sang "My Man" in *Ziegfeld 9 O'Clock Frolic* (1920) and *Ziegfeld Follies* (1921), or that this song was originally the French song "Mon Homme" by Maurice Yvain and Channing Pollock.[54]

Fortunately this lyric was abandoned. The first three lines were crossed out and replaced with the following handwritten script for the B section:

When your dream boat is leaking
And your pal ain't your pal
Geometrically speaking just keep it vertical

The final version published in 1940 is not indicated in the O'Hara typescript:

B   Though at first we said, "No sir,"
     Now we're two little dears.
     You might say we are closer
     Than Roebuck is to Sears.
A   I'm dumb again
     And numb again,
     A rich, ready, ripe little plum again—
     Bewitched, bothered and bewildered am I.

All of these versions are variations on a theme that Hart explored in numerous songs, including "It's Got to Be Love" discussed earlier: love as a sickness. Vera, the restless wife of the wealthy Prentiss Simpson, is generally in control of her emotions and entertains no delusions about the cause of her sleepless nights. In the verse that precedes the chorus she even refers to Joey as a "fool" and a "half-pint imitation," but even this realization does not prevent her from catching the dreaded disease.

In his autobiography Rodgers recalls what he learned from his training in Goetschius's class of five students: "Whenever Goetschius talked about ending a phrase with a straight-out tonic chord (the first, third and fifth step of any scale), he would call it a 'pig,' his term for anything that was too easy or obvious. Once I heard the scorn in Goetschius' voice I knew that I'd avoid that 'pig' as if my life depended on it."[55] In "Bewitched" (Example 5.6) Rodgers avoids the infelicitously named "pig" at the end of the second eight-measure A section. He does this by moving to an A in measures 15 and 16 on the word "I" rather than the expected first note of the scale, F (also on the word "I"), that he set up at the end of the first A section in measures 7 and 8.

Rodgers also finds an effective musical means to capture Hart's virtuosic depiction of Vera's obsession. Hart conveys the society matron's *idée fixe* by giving her thrice-repeated lyrics to conclude the first three lines of each A section, as in "I'm wild *again!* / Beguiled *again!* / A whimpering, simpering child *again*," before delivering the "hook" of the song's title, "bewitched, bothered and bewildered," to conclude each A section. It is tempting to conclude that Rodgers's musical characterization of Vera's emotional state corresponds with uncanny accuracy to the lyrics. But since the lyrics apparently followed the music—in contrast to Rodgers's subsequent *modus operandi* with Hammerstein—it is more accurate to admire Hart's special sensitivity to Rodger's music, which presents an equally repetitive musical line, the note B ascending up a half-step to C. By inverting the musical line (turning it upside down) in the B section (mm. 17–24), Rodgers manages to maintain Vera's obsession while providing welcome musical contrast to the repetitive A sections.

Vera's ability to rhyme internally reflects her complexity and sophistication—or, as Sondheim would say, her education.[56] Rodgers matches this richness musically when he offers several subtle harmonic touches in "Bewitched." He first treats the melodically conventional F (on "I") in measures 7 and 8 as the third of a D minor triad (D-F-A) rather than the root of an F major triad (F-A-C) as expected. At measure 15 he then balances the surprise melodic note A (also on "I," the note that avoided the "pig") with the expected F major triad (in this new context a surprise) before reharmonizing the A as the dominant of D minor first heard in measures 7 and 8.

In other songs Hart's lyrics convey literal lyrical parallels to Rodgers's music. Examples of textual realism include Joey's monotonous recitation of the alphabet and numbers to match the repeated notes in the verse of "I Could Write a Book," the word "blue" in the phrase "but I'm blue for you" to match Rodgers's "blue note" (a blue seventh) in the first period of "That Terrific Rainbow," and the hunting imagery that corresponds to

Example 5.6. "Bewitched" (chorus)

the horn-like fifths in "Happy Hunting Horn." Other pictorial examples include the gun shot at the end of this last song to suggest fallen prey, the graphic chord each time Melba Snyder sings the word "Zip!", and the dissonant chord cluster after she mentions "the great Stravinsky."

Perhaps in an effort to musically integrate his *Pal Joey* songs Rodgers maintains his obsession with the prominent half-steps that characterized "Bewitched." No less than three other songs in *Pal Joey* prominently em-

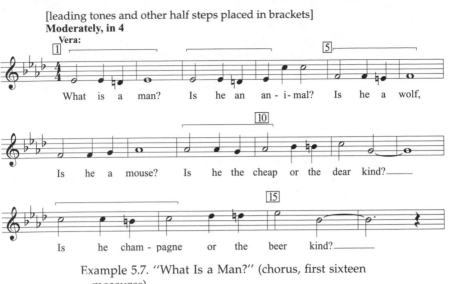

[leading tones and other half steps placed in brackets]

Example 5.7. "What Is a Man?" (chorus, first sixteen measures)

ploy various melodic permutations of the half-step interval. Can we attribute any dramatic meaning to this? By emphasizing this interval in both of Vera's solo songs, "What Is a Man?" and "Bewitched" (Examples 5.7 and 5.6), Rodgers helps establish the musical identity of a woman who has allowed herself the luxury of an obsession. When Vera is with her paramour and sings with him, she has no need to obsess about him. Consequently, the half-step is absent in her duet with Joey, "Den of Iniquity." Why Joey should sing half-steps so often in "Plant You Now, Dig You Later" is less explicable.[57] What remains consistent is that the songs prominently displaying the half-step are the "off-stage" songs, not the songs sung in rehearsal or as part of the entertainment in Mike Spears's nightclub or Chez Joey.

The seemingly irresistible musical and psychological pull that characterizes the move from the seventh degree of a major scale (aptly labelled the leading tone) to the tonic one half-step higher (e.g., B-C in the key of C) was also used to produce meaningful dramatic effects in other shows. In *South Pacific* (1949) Rodgers (with Hammerstein) greases rather than avoids the "pig" (an F) for the sake of verisimilitude in "I'm Gonna Wash That Man Right Outa My Hair." In this well-known song Rodgers conveys Nellie Forbush's delusion by introducing the oft-repeated title line with an equally repetitive ascending scalar phrase (C-D-E-F) that relentlessly and obsessively returns to the central key and thereby exposes her failure to accomplish her task. Later in the show when she admits to herself and her fellow nurses that she is, in fact, "in love with a wonderful guy," Nellie sings an exaggerated eighteen repetitions of the half-step interval (again from the leading tone up to the tonic) on the repeated words "love, I'm in" (B-C-C, B-C-C, etc.). In "Bali Ha'i," also from *South Pacific,* Rodgers convincingly conveys the mysterious quality and seductive call of the exotic island by its emphasis on repeated half-steps (e.g., "Ha'i may call you" becomes F♯-F♯-F♯-G).

Not to be overlooked is Rodgers and Hart's ability in *Pal Joey* to write first-rate songs appropriate for their second-rate surroundings, a delicate balancing act that will also be used by Frank Loesser in the Hot Box numbers of *Guys and Dolls.* In "That Terrific Rainbow," for example, Hart presents a staggering array of trite and clichéd images to create his rainbow:

> I'm a RED-hot mama,
> But I'm BLUE for you.
> I get PURPLE with anger
> At the things you do.
> And I'm GREEN with envy
> When you meet a dame.
> But you burn my heart up
> With an ORANGE flame.
>
> I'm a RED-hot mama
> But you're WHITE and cold.
> Don't you know your mama
> Has a heart of GOLD?
> Though we're in those GRAY clouds,
> Some day you'll see
> That terrific rainbow
> Over you and me.

When Mike Spears's club is converted to Chez Joey in act II, the lyrics of the more elaborate and pretentious new opening production number, "The Flower Garden of My Heart," read like a parody of the hackneyed and formulaic Mother Goose rhyme "Roses are Red": "In the flower garden of my heart / I've got violets blue as your eyes. / I've got dainty narcissus / As sweet as my missus / And lilies as pure as the skies." In the same chorus Hart gives Gladys the couplets, "Just to keep our love holy / I've got gladioli," and in ensuing choruses "Oh, the west wind will whisk us / The scent of hibiscus," and "You will look like sweet william / And smell like a trillium." Was Rodgers perhaps too successful in achieving conventionality and mediocrity in this song, since it was one of only two numbers—the other is "A Great Big Town"—excluded from the prerevival cast album?

After *Pal Joey* and his final collaboration with Rodgers, *By Jupiter*, Hart possessed neither the interest nor the will to tackle a setting of Lynn Riggs's play, *Green Grow the Lilacs* (1931). Rodgers therefore left his "partner, a best friend, and a source of permanent irritation," and turned to Hammerstein to create *Oklahoma!* in 1942 and early 1943. In the increasingly small intervals between drinking binges Hart managed to create a few new songs for the successful 1943 revival of the 1927 hit *A Connecticut Yankee* (including the bitingly funny "To Keep My Love Alive"), but within a few months of *Oklahoma!*'s historic debut he was dead.

The new team of Rodgers and Hammerstein and the integrated ideal would dominate the American musical until Hammerstein's death in 1960. But something irreplaceable was also lost when the Rodgers and Hammerstein era replaced Rodgers and Hart. The new partners would continue to compose excellent songs that, although integrated, can be sung successfully outside of their carefully considered contexts. Only rarely, however, would Rodgers recreate the rhythmic energy and jazzy melodic vernacular that distinguished so many of his songs with Hart, songs such as "You Mustn't Kick It Around," "Happy Hunting Horn," "Plant You Now, Dig You Later," and "Do It the Hard Way" in *Pal Joey* and "It's Got to Be Love" "Slaughter on 10th Avenue," and the title song in *On Your Toes.*

Alec Wilder addresses this point in *American Popular Song: The Great Innovators 1900–1950*, an idiosyncratic survey that until recently was the only book seriously to discuss the musical qualities of popular songs.[58] Although Wilder treats the songs show-by-show, he scrupulously avoids discussing their dramatic context or even their texts, and consequently evaluates them solely on their autonomous musical merits. For this reason he remains impervious to the psychological insights in "Bewitched" and instead berates Rodgers's repetitive "device" that was "brought to a sort of negative fruition in that it finally obtrudes as a contrivance."[59] Nevertheless Wilder devoted fifty-three pages to Rodgers and Hart and only six to Rodgers and Hammerstein, and he tells us why:

> Though he wrote great songs with Oscar Hammerstein II, it is my belief that his greatest melodic invention and pellucid freshness occurred during his years of collaboration with Lorenz Hart. The inventiveness has never ceased. Yet something bordering on musical complacency evidenced itself in his later career. I have al-

ways felt that there was an almost feverish demand in Hart's writing which reflected itself in Rodger's melodies as opposed to the almost too comfortable armchair philosophy in Hammerstein's lyrics.[60]

Musical comedies in general, like their nonmusical stage counterparts, stand unfairly as poor relations to tragedies (or musicals that aspire to nineteenth-century tragic operas filled with thematic transformations and conspicuous organicism). *Pal Joey* is a brilliant musical comedy that has not lost its relevance or its punch since its arrival in 1940. Despite its many virtues, however, this first musical in "long pants," as Rodgers described it in 1952, and the first major musical to feature an anti-hero, lacks the great themes of *Show Boat* and *Porgy and Bess* and their correspondingly ambitious and complex dramatic transformations of musical motives. The transformation of "Bewitched" in Joey's ballet from a ballad in duple meter to a fast waltz in triple meter, for example, does not convey the dramatic meaning inherent in Kern's transformations of Magnolia's piano theme, nor does it come close to attaining Gershwin's dramatic application of his melodic and rhythmic transformations and paraphrases.

In contrast to Porter's *Anything Goes* and Rodgers and Hart's *On Your Toes*, however, *Pal Joey* possesses a book that can be and is frequently revived in nearly its original state (albeit relatively rarely on Broadway), and its songs, nearly all gems, grow naturally from the dramatic action and tell us something important about the characters who sing them. For discerning critics such as Lehman Engel as well as for modern audiences, the bewitching *Pal Joey* survives on its own terms as perhaps the first enduring Broadway classic of its genre and of its time.

CHAPTER SIX

THE CRADLE WILL ROCK

A Labor Musical for Art's Sake

Marc Blitzstein (1905–1964) remains an obscure figure. With few exceptions his music either was never published or is currently out of print. As late as the early 1980s, one decade before her company, under new leadership, revived the work, Beverly Sills of the New York City Opera was rejecting *Regina,* Blitzstein's 1949 adaptation of Lillian Hellman's *Little Foxes,* as "too old-fashioned" for present-day tastes.[1] Bertolt Brecht scholar Martin Esslin had already dismissed Blitzstein's "sugar-coated" English translation of Brecht and Weill's *The Threepenny Opera*—the version which during the years 1954–1960 became the longest Off-Broadway musical in history and Blitzstein's best-known achievement—as unworthy of Brecht's vision.[2]

Although he is seldom treated as a major figure, the authors of most comprehensive histories of American music, as well as more idiosyncratic surveys, offer Blitzstein some space and a generally good press.[3] Aaron Copland gives Blitzstein equal billing with Virgil Thomson in a chapter in *Our New Music.*[4] Wilfrid Mellers presents Blitzstein along with Ives and Copland as one of three distinguished and representative American composers in *Music and Society* (1950).[5] In *Music in a New Found Land,* published the year of Blitzstein's death and dedicated to his memory, Mellers focuses on *Regina* in a laudatory chapter which pairs it with Bernstein's *West Side Story.*[6] Blitzstein's Broadway opera *Regina* (1949), successfully revived and recorded in 1992 by the New York City Opera, now stands poised for the

Marc Blitzstein. © Al Hirschfeld. Drawing reproduced by special arrangement with Hirschfeld's exclusive representative, The Margo Feiden Galleries Ltd. New York.

possibility of future enshrinement. Several years earlier the composer of *The Cradle Will Rock* was the subject of the longest biography to date of an American composer.[7]

Historians and Broadway enthusiasts relatively unfamiliar with either Blitzstein or *The Cradle Will Rock* may nevertheless know something of the circumstances behind this work's extraordinary premiere on June 16, 1937 (directed by Orson Welles). As reported on the front page of the *New York Times* the next day—and almost invariably whenever the work is mentioned for the next sixty years—the show, banned from a padlocked Maxine Elliot theater, its government sponsorship revoked, moved its forces and its assembled audience twenty blocks uptown to the Venice Theater. Once there, in conformance to the letter (if not the spirit) of the prohibitions placed upon its performance, cast members sang their parts from the audience while Blitzstein took the stage with his piano.[8]

After nineteen performances at the Venice, *Cradle* moved to the Mercury Theater for several months of Sunday evening performances. On January 3, 1938 the controversial show opened on Broadway at the Windsor for a short run of 108 performances (sixteen performances fewer than *Porgy and Bess* and in a smaller theater).[9] The play was published a few months later by Random House, and the following year *Cradle* was anthologized in a volume that included Clifford Odets's *Waiting for Lefty*, a play to which *Cradle* is frequently associated and compared.[10] A recording of the original production issued in 1938 became the first Broadway cast album, a historical distinction almost invariably and incorrectly attributed to *Oklahoma!*[11]

Reviews were generally positive. Although he wrote that the "weak ending" was "hokum" and a "fairy-tale," Thomson also concluded that after six months of the 1937 production "*The Cradle* was still a good show and its musical quality hasn't worn thin" and that the work was "the most appealing operatic socialism since *Louise*" [Gustave Charpentier's realistic opera that premiered in 1900].[12] Brooks Atkinson considered the musical "a stirring success" and "the most versatile artistic triumph of the politically insurgent theatre."[13] Edith J. R. Isaac wrote that the work "introduces a persuasive new theatre form."[14] Somewhat less sympathetically, the notorious George Jean Nathan concluded his acerbic review with the often-quoted barb that *Cradle* was "little more than the kind of thing Cole Porter might have written if, God forbid, he had gone to Columbia instead of Yale."[15]

In common with most of the musicals discussed in this survey *Cradle* has been revived with relative frequency, including a production in 1947 under the direction of Leonard Bernstein, who had presented the work at

Harvard in 1939 while an undergraduate (playing the piano part from memory), a New York City Opera production in 1960 (the most successful work of their season), and an Off-Broadway production in 1964 that led to the first complete recorded performance of the work. In 1983 an Off-Broadway production and London run starring *Evita* superstar Patti Lupone (doubling as Moll and Sister Mister) and directed by John Houseman, who produced the premiere, generated a second complete recording and a television broadcast.[16] Of all these performances only the 1960 production resuscitated the orchestral score that Blitzstein had completed in May 1937 and Lehman Engel conducted at the dress rehearsal before the eventful opening night. The performances with Blitzstein alone on his piano launched a tradition that has long since become entrenched and seemingly irrevocable.[17]

Singing a Song of Social Significance

Authentic avant-garde works achieve their status in part by their continued ability to shock audiences out of their complacency and to bite the hand that feeds. For this reason the purposeful retraction of government funding when the political wind began to blow in a different direction in 1937—even if the government was not initially targeting *Cradle*—arguably gives *Cradle* more credibility than those works that were ideologically safe, including Blitzstein's earlier modernistic works. *Cradle* also joins other works of the 1930s, most notably the Gershwins' *Of Thee I Sing* (1931) and *Let 'Em Eat Cake* (1933) and composer-lyricist Harold Rome's *Pins and Needles* (1937), in its representation of politically satirical or antiestablishment themes.

Contributing to the continued problematic taxonomic status of *The Cradle Will Rock* is its musical incongruity with both the avant-garde and the conventional popular theater of the 1930s. Particularly jarring is *Cradle*'s conflicting allegiances to vernacular song forms and styles and modernistic characteristics and emblems, the latter including harsh dissonances and chords that thwart expectations. How many musicals would encourage the musically shrill hysteria of Mrs. Mister in the Mission Scene (scene 3) when she asks Reverend Salvation in 1917 to pray for war in order to support her husband's military machine? What other musicals would permit the dissonance of the recurring gavel music that proclaims order in the Night Court before a new flashback? On the other hand, although the work is for the most part through-sung and contains proportionally far less talk than most *Singspiels*, including Mozart's *The Magic Flute*, *Cradle*'s treatment of popular vernacular and its nonreliance on opera singers contributes further to the difficulty of placing the work with one genre or another.

In contrast to Gershwin, who began as a popular songwriter before transforming his popular music into art music, Blitzstein, like Copland and Weill, began his musical career as a modernist who then converted to populism. As a student of both Stravinsky-advocate Nadia Boulanger in Paris and Schoenberg in Berlin, Blitzstein became intimately acquainted early in his career with the two primary tributaries to the modernist mainstream and reflected their values in early works such as his Piano Sonata (1927) and Piano Concerto (1931). Blitzstein's modernist phase prior to 1933 also embraces the "art for art's sake" ideology that he would soon come to loathe and indict in his first major populist work, *The Cradle Will Rock.*

One month after he had completed *Cradle* Blitzstein, a prolific essayist, published an article in the left-wing magazine *New Masses* on July 14 (Bastille Day) in 1936 in which he viewed modernism as an inevitable reaction against the excesses required of "a capitalist society turning imperialist."[18] Although Blitzstein thought that Schoenberg and Stravinsky wrote "the truth about the dreams of humanity in a world of war and violence," he concluded this essay by asserting that these premier modernists were limited by their inability to confront the social issues of their time: "It is too much to say that the new men sought deliberately and fundamentally to battle the whole conception. They were still the 'art-for-art's-sake' boys, they didn't see much beyond their artistic vision."[19]

One week later, in *New Masses*, Blitzstein praised the *Gebrauchsmusik* movement (variously translated as "utility music" or "music for use") for its sense of direction and its topicality. At the same time he faulted it because its exponents—principally Paul Hindemith, who at that time was only slightly less highly regarded than Schoenberg and Stravinsky—"had little political or social education."[20] The value of *Gebrauchsmusik* for Blitzstein was its spawning of men such as Brecht who possessed the necessary education and who "saw the need for education through poetry, through music."[21]

Earlier in 1936, in an article published in *Modern Music*, Blitzstein concluded that Hanns Eisler and Weill, two of Brecht's musical collaborators, "write the same kind of music, although their purposes are completely at variance. . . . Weill is flaccid (he wants to 'entertain'); Eisler has spine and nerves (he wants to 'educate')."[22] By the time he composed *Cradle* Blitzstein revealed in print that he shared Eisler's ideology and had become a card-carrying member of the musical-theater proletariat led by Brecht. He ends his *New Masses* manifesto with a call to political action. Blitzstein himself had taken such action the previous month when he had completed his

Cradle after five weeks of composing at "white heat." "The composer is now willing, eager, to trade in his sanctified post as Vestal Virgin before the altar of Immutable and Undefilable Art, for the post of an honest workman among workmen, who has a job to do, a job which wonderfully gives other people joy. His music is aimed at the masses; he knows what he wants to say to them."[23]

Contributing to the changes in Blitzstein's thinking was his meeting several months earlier (probably in December 1935) with Brecht, at which the playwright and poet shared his response to Blitzstein's song "Nickel Under the Foot." The scene was reported by Minna Lederman, the editor of *Modern Music*:

> Marc said to Brecht, "I want you to hear something I've written," and, sitting at his piano, played and sang "The Nickel under the Foot." This immediately excited Brecht. He rose, and I can still hear his high, shrill voice, almost a falsetto, exclaiming, "Why don't you write a piece about all kinds of prostitution—the press, the church, the courts, the arts, the whole system?"[24]

Cradle's dramatic structure follows Brecht's suggestion to the letter, and most of the work's ten scenes in "Steeltown, U.S.A. on the night of a union drive" focus on the metaphoric prostitution of various prototypes.[25] The only uncorruptible figures are Moll, who literally prostitutes herself but does not metaphorically sell out to Mr. Mister and at least has something genuine to sell, and Larry Foreman, who refuses to be corrupted by Mr. Mister and eventually leads the unions to thwart the union buster's corrupt use of power.

Undoubtedly, the ideological nature of *The Cradle Will Rock* has obscured its artistic significance. That the work deserves its frequently designated status as an agit-prop musical is evident by the degree to which it was imitated by life. Only a few months after its opening America seemed to heed its call to action with the formation of a strong national steel union, Little Steel. If *Cradle*'s prounionist and anticapitalist stance now seems dated, its central Brechtian theme, the indictment of a passive middle-class that sells out to the highest bidder, continues to haunt and disturb. As Blitzstein himself wrote: " 'The Cradle Will Rock' is about unions but only incidentally about unions. What I really wanted to talk about was the middleclass. Unions, unionism as a subject, are used as a symbol of something in the way of a solution for the plight of that middleclass."[26]

With the exception of "Nickel Under the Foot," which observes Brecht's call for an epic theater and "the strict separation of the music from all the other elements of entertainment offered," Blitzstein, in contrast to Brecht and Weill, created a work in which music and words were inseparable from the axis of the work.[27] Despite this aesthetic descrepancy, the integrated songs of *The Cradle Will Rock* remain faithful to Brecht's larger social artistic vision. Consequently, the *Cradle* songs, like those of Brecht and Weill, both embrace the didactic element espoused by Brecht's epic theater and reject the "hedonistic approach" and "senselessness" common to operas (and of course musicals as well) before *The Rise and Fall of the City of Mahagonny* of 1930.[28]

Two Scenes: Lawn of Mr. Mister and Hotel Lobby

Scene Four, which contains four songs ("Croon-Spoon," "The Freedom of the Press," "Let's Do Something" and "Honolulu") opens on the lawn of Mr. Mister's home, where his children, Junior and Sister Mister, are lounging on hammocks.[29] The stage directions describe Junior as "sluggish, collegiate and vacant; Sister is smartly gotten up and peevish." Unlike most of the characters in Blitzstein's morality tale, Junior and Sister Mister have nothing to sell and therefore cannot be indicted for selling out. But they do possess vacuous middle-class values that Blitzstein targets for ridicule in their duet which opens the scene, "Croon–Spoon" Examples 6.1 and 6.2), a spoof of the type of trivial and ephemeral popular song on recordings, dance halls, and nondidactic Broadway shows.

Blitzstein's opinion of the idle rich, who spend their time singing songs that do not convey a message of social significance, is apparent from the opening lyrics 'to "Croon–Spoon" when Junior sings, "Croon, Croon till it hurts, baby, / Croon, My heart asserts, baby, / Croonin' in spurts, baby, / Is just the nerts for a tune!"[30] True, Blitzstein permits Junior to begin on a note that belongs to a chord in the key of the song, an F♯ (the third of the tonic D major triad). But this F♯ is the last note in a tonic chord that Junior manages to assert in his opening seven-measure phrase (one measure less than the nearly ubiquitous eight of Tin Pan Alley and Broadway songs). The "conventional" theater song (e.g., "Anything Goes") would present four eight-measure phrases to create an A-A-B-A or thirty-two-bar song form. Blitzstein's altered phrase lengths (A[7]-A[7]-B[6+6+2]-A[7+4] measures) within the A-A-B-A structure manages to acknowledge convention at the same time he defies and ridicules it.

In contrast to Junior Mister, who concludes his first A section a half-step too low for the accompanying harmony (E♯ against a D major chord),

Ex. 6.1: *Croon Spoon* (beginning)

Example 6.1. "Croon-Spoon" (beginning)

Sister Mister, in her complementary seven-measure phrase (the second A of the askew A-A-B-A), manages to conclude correctly on a tonic D in the melody. Blitzstein, however, subverts the harmonic implication of Sister's more self-assured D (again on the word "spoon") with harmony that will rapidly depart from the home tonic. The B section, which begins in F♯ minor (Example 6.2) and consists of two nearly melodically identical six-bar phrases followed by Sister Mister's two-bar patter that leads back to the final A section, is remarkable for the C♮ in measure 17 (on "-la-" of

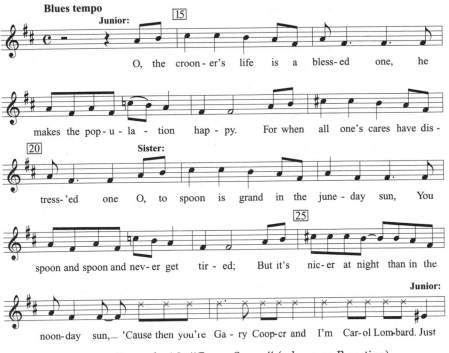

Example 6.2. "Croon-Spoon" (release or B section)

"pop-u-la-tion") and measure 23 (on "nev-" of "nev-er"), a lowered or blue fifth that is relatively rare in Broadway songs (and even somewhat unusual in jazz before the 1940s).

The punchline of the final A derives from the inability of either Junior or Sister Mister to successfully resolve the harmony. After six measures Junior should be ready to conclude the song one measure later to preserve the odd but symmetrical seven-bar units of the first two A sections. Instead, Sister Mister, after a fermata (a hold of indefinite length), repeats her brother's last three measures and Junior, after another fermata, repeats the third measure one more time before the siblings screech out the original tonic to conclude the thirty-nine-measure tune.

Following Brecht and his own evolution as a reformed modernist with a social agenda, Blitzstein is of course telling us to avoid singing what he considers to be vapid songs about Croon, spoon, and June, even as Junior tells us in the bridge of this song that "Oh, the crooner's life is a blessed one, / He makes the population happy." Junior concludes his song with his own didactic message directed toward the poor who are "not immune" to the wonders of croon spoon. "If they're [the poor] without a suit, / They shouldn't give a hoot, / When they can substitute—CROON!" In

Pins and Needles, the inspired and phenomenally popular revue presented by the International Garment Workers Union the same year as *Cradle*, Rome asks his audience to "Sing a Song of Social Significance." "Croon–Spoon," a song far removed from social significance, serves as a forum in which Blitzstein can lambaste songs that do not respond to his call for social action and provides the composer-lyricist with an irresistible opportunity to ridicule performers who sing socially useless songs.[31]

During the Windsor run of *Cradle*, Blitzstein concluded an article, "On Writing for the Theatre," with some remarks on the relationship between theory and practice in this work.

> When I started to write the *Cradle* I had a whole and beautiful theory lined up about it. Music was to be used for those sections which were predominantly lyric, satirical, and dramatic. My theories got kicked headlong as soon as I started to write; it became clear to me that the theatre is so elusive an animal that each situation demands its own solution, and so, in a particularly dramatic spot, I found the music simply had to stop. I also found that certain pieces of ordinary plot-exposition could be handled very well by music (*The Freedom of the Press* is a plot-song).

"The Freedom of the Press" begins immediately ("*attacca subito*") after Mr. Mister excuses Junior and Sister Mister, an exit underscored by the vamp that began "Croon-Spoon." Blitzstein called this duet between Mr. Mister and Editor Daily a plot-song because the song narrates (or plots) the entire process by which Daily reinterprets the meaning behind its title: the freedom of the press can be a freedom to distort as well as to impart the truth. The plot is as follows: Daily reveals that he is willing to sell out to the highest bidder (first stanza, A); Daily expresses his willingness to change a story, i.e., "if something's wrong with it [the story] why then we'll print to fit" (second stanza, B); and Daily learns that Mr. Mister had purchased the paper that morning (third stanza, Mr. Mister's final A).

Following a vigorous six-measure introduction the form of the song is strophic in three identical musical stanzas. Blitzstein subdivides each stanza into an *a-b-a-b-c-d* form, in which the melody of the rapid ($\downarrow$-160) *a* sections (eight measures each) sung by Mr. Mister are tonally centered in F (concluding in C minor) and the equally fast *b* sections (also eight measures) are answered by Editor Daily in a passage that begins abruptly one step higher in D major ("All my gift . . .") and modulates to A major

Example 6.3. "The Freedom of the Press"
(a) A section

(on "very kind") before Mr. Mister returns to the *a* section and F with equal abruptness (Example 6.3).[32]

When Editor Daily returns to his *b* section ("Just you call . . ."), Blitzstein has him sing a whole step higher than his original D major (in E major) for greater intensity. In the brief *c* section Mr. Mister departs from the relentlessness and speed of his (and Editor Daily's) earlier material and for

(b)

Editor Daily:

|15|

All   my   gift   at   prose - 'll   Be   at   your dis - pos - al
Yes,   we've   heard   of   him,   In   fact   good   word   of   him,   He
Just   a   min - ute,   I'm   not   be   -   ing   in - dis - creet!   I

|20|

Mis   -   ter   Mis - ter, you've been   ver   -   y   kind.
seems   quite   pop - u - lar with   work - ing   men.
must   con   -   sult   the   own - er   of   my   sheet.

Example 6.3. "The Freedom of the Press"
(b) B section

four measures sings, *"lento e dolce"* (slow and sweetly), the menacing
words "Yes, but some news can be made to order" to match the menacing
underlying harmony. In the *d* section (twenty measures) the music resumes
the original tempo and Mr. Mister and Editor Daily sing the main refrain.
"O, the press, the press, the freedom of the press . . . for whichever side
will pay the best!"[33]

After "The Freedom of the Press," the music stops for the first time in
the scene and in spoken dialogue Editor Daily quickly agrees with his new
boss that Junior "doesn't go so well with union trouble" and would be a
good candidate for a correspondent's job "out of town, say on the paper."
Junior and Sister enter to a brief and frenetic dance and jazzy tune, "Let's
Do Something." Editor Daily, now firmly ensconced as a stooge of his new
boss, proposes the "something" that will both satisfy Mr. Mister and appear palatable to Junior: "Have you thought of Honolulu?"

In his survey of American music H. Wiley Hitchcock writes that the first
twelve measures of "Honolulu" illustrate "Blitzstein's subtle transforma-

tion of popular song style," in which "the clichés of the vocal line are cancelled out by the freshness of the accompaniment."[34] Hitchcock singles out the "irregular texture underlying" the "hint of Hawaiian guitars" in the first eight measures (a four-measure phrase and its literal repetition), the "offbeat accentuation of the bass under the raucous refrain," which produces a phrase structure of 3+4+1+3+4+1, and an "acrid" harmony (in technical terms, an inverted dominant ninth) on the word "isle." If the first four measures are labelled A and measures 9–12 B (Example 6.4) the overall form of the song looks like this:

A A B A'   A' A' A B   A A A' A'   B A' A' A'   A' B A A'
4 4 4 4   4   4   2 4   4 4 6   4   4 4   4   4   6 4 6 3

The irregularity of the form and the unpredictibility of the less frequent B entrances goes a long way to save "Honololu" from the banality it is trying to satirize, just as the unconventional phrase lengths and unorthodox relationship between melody and harmony earlier spared "Croon-Spoon" from a similar fate.

If "Croon–Spoon" and "Honolulu" ridicule the vapidity of ephemeral popular music and some of the people who sing them, the songs in the Hotel Lobby Scene (scene 6) convey a more direct didactic social message about the role of artists and their appropriate artistic purposes. Blitzstein saves his sharpest rebuke for the artists themselves, the painter Dauber and the violinist Yasha who meet by accident in a hotel lobby in scene 6.[35] Like the other members of Mr. Mister's anti-union Liberty Committee, Dauber and Yasha have sold themselves to the highest bidder, in this case to the wealthy Mrs. Mister. The painter and the musician, like the poet Rupert Scansion to follow, have come to the hotel to curry favor with their patroness in exchange for a free meal and perhaps a temporary roof over their heads.

Blitzstein presents Dauber and Yasha as caricatures of artists who, in their espousal of art-for-art's-sake, have rejected nobler socially conscious artistic visions. The audience learns immediately that they are second-rate artists who fail whenever they are forced to rely on their talent alone. Then, in the course of their initial exchange (a combination of song and underscored dialogue), Dauber and Yasha learn that both of them have appointments with Mrs. Mister. In the ensuing tango (shades of Brecht and Weill), appropriately named "The Rich," they expose the foibles and inadequacies of the "moneyed people" in such lines as "There's something so damned low about the rich!" and "They've no impulse, no fine feeling, no great itch!" The answer to the question "What have they got?" is money; the

Example 6.4. "Honolulu"
  (a) A phrase
  (b) B phrase

(Quasi Egmont Overture)

Mrs. Mister:

Yasha, those are perfect.
Imagine, he went and had the
horns on my Pierce Arrow tuned to
that motive in Beethoven's *Egmont* Overture. . .
YOU KNOW!

ta   ta   ta   ta   ta   ta   ta   ta   Yoo Hoo!

Example 6.5. Scene Six, Hotel Lobby
Entrance of Mrs. Mister and Beethoven *Egmont* Overture

answer to the question "What can they do?" is support you. Clearly
Dauber and Yasha hate the rich as much as Blitzstein does.

At this point the object of their scorn, Mrs. Mister, enters to the accompaniment of the horn motive from Beethoven's *Egmont* Overture based on
Goethe's play of the same name: "you know: ta, ta, ta-ta-ta, ta-ta-ta, yoo
hoo!" (Example 6.5). In Blitzstein's satire of *Gebrauchsmusik*, Goethe's tale
of a great man who loses his life in his efforts to overcome the tyrannical
bonds of political oppression is demeaned: Beethoven's heroic horn call
now serves as the horn call on Mrs. Mister's Pierce Arrow automobile.
This horn also includes the violin answer that was interpreted by nineteenth-century Beethoven biographer Alexander Wheelock Thayer as depicting the moment when Egmont was beheaded.[36] Clearly, the Pierce
Arrow usurpation of Beethoven's horn motif consitues a sacrilegious use
of an art object.

That Mrs. Mister expects Dauber and Yasha to pay a price and kiss the
hand that feeds these untalented artists becomes clear near the end of the
scene, when she asks them to join her husband's Liberty Committee,
formed to break the unions led by Larry Foreman, a heroic figure analogous to Egmont. This is the same committee of middle-class prostitutes of
various professions who were mistakenly rounded up in scene 1 and taken
to night court in scene 2 before the flashbacks began in scene 3. Dauber
and Yasha are only too eager to oblige, and when Mrs. Mister asks them,
"But don't you want to know what it's all about?" they reply that they
are *artists* who "love art for art's sake."

It's smart, for Art's sake,
To part, for Art's sake,
With your heart, for Art's sake,

Example 6.6. Scene Six, Hotel Lobby
(a) "Art for Art's Sake"
(b) "The Rich"

And your mind, for Art's sake—
Be blind, for Art's sake,
And deaf, for Art's sake,
And dumb, for Art's sake,
Until, for Art's sake,
They kill, for Art's sake
All the Art for Art's sake![37]

As shown in Example 6.6a Blitzstein's choice to state each of these lines with a nearly monotonal melody reinforces the pervasiveness of Dauber's and Yasha's political vacuity. The fact that Blitzstein reharmonizes the B on the downbeat of each measure with increasingly dissonant chords bears some similarity to the notorious nineteenth-century "Art" song by Peter

Cornelius, "Ein Ton," in which a single pitch is harmonized to an almost absurd degree by evolving chromaticism. Through his relentless dissonant harmonization of the Johnny-one-notes Blitzstein creates a musical equivalent to support his single-mindedly vitriolic text.

Because Blitzstein himself is a genuine artist, in contrast to Dauber and Yasha, he cannot resist using Beethoven for his own artistic purposes as well. He does this by making two simple rhythmic alterations that effectively disguise the *Egmont* horn motive. The first allusion to *Egmont* occurs in the second chorus of their initial vaudeville routine when Dauber sings "Your lady friend does resemble a lot / Some one, and that's very queer." By adding one beat to the first note of the horn motive Blitzstein accommodates the difference between the triple meter of Beethoven's original motive and the duple meter of the vaudeville routine, a subtle but recognizable rhythmic transformation (Example 6.6b). In the second allusion, the art-for-art's-sake passage previously discussed in Example 6.6a, Blitzstein keeps the rhythmic integrity of Beethoven's motive but distorts it almost (but not entirely) beyond recognition in a duple context with contrary accentual patterns.

It is possible, albeit unlikely, that Blitzstein's rhythmic distortions, which parallel his bizarre atonal harmonizations of the B♮ ("Art for Art's sake," "smart for Art's sake," etc.) can be interpreted as a critique of Beethoven's noble purposes in *Egmont* as well as an indictment of Yasha and Dauber's art. In any event, Blitzstein's incorporation of Beethoven into his Hotel Lobby Scene goes beyond the conventions and expectations of a musical. It also shows that a revered European master can serve Blitzstein's artistic as well as satiric purposes.

In contrast to *Show Boat* and *Porgy and Bess,* Blitzstein's *Cradle* does not offer a grand scheme of musical symbols and musical transformations that reflect large-scale dramatic vision and character development. Unlike their counterparts in the other musicals discussed in this survey, the characters in *Cradle* for the most part sing their songs and then either assume a secondary role, merge into a crowd, or vanish entirely from the stage. The work is episodic within a structured frame; the characters, vividly outlined, are not filled in.[38]

It is significant that Moll, the pure prostitute, and Larry Foreman, who represents the juggernaut of the oppressed, are the only characters permitted to recycle musical material. In fact, both of the Moll's songs are reprised. The melody of "I'm Checkin' Home Now," the first music heard in the show, returns as underscoring for Moll's spoken introduction to her song "Nickel Under the Foot" in scene 7.[39] Before her big scene Moll had sung most of "Nickel" (using other words) in her conversation with Harry

Druggist in scene 2. "Nickel" returns a last time in scene 10 against a din of conversation before Larry Foreman and the chorus of union workers conclude the work with a reprise of the title song.

Although *Cradle* has been called "the most enduring social-political piece of the period" and has generally received high marks as the musical equivalent of *Waiting for Lefty*, its didacticism has unfortunately overwhelmed its rich intrinsic musical and dramatic qualities.[40] If other musicals of the time rival *The Cradle Will Rock* as a work of social satire, few musicals of its time (for example, those by Brecht and Weill the previous decade or E. Y. Harburg and Harold Arlen in the next) and few works since, combine Blitzstein's call for social action with a vernacular of such musical sophistication and, yes, artistry.[41] In contrast to many avant-garde works eventually absorbed into the mainstream, *The Cradle Will Rock*, despite its intent to reach a wider public, has managed to sustain its anomalistic status remarkably well. After nearly sixty years it continues to resist artistic classification within a genre. It also continues to offend its intended audience of middle-class capitalists through its messages, its devastating caricatures of clergy, doctors, and even university professors, and its occasionally difficult and unconventional score. With due respect to Blitzstein's sincere didacticism, Blitzstein's *Cradle*—cult musical, historical footnote, and agent of social change—might, even as it agitates and propagandizes, someday achieve the recognition it deserves as a work of musical theater art (for art's sake).[42]

CHAPTER SEVEN

LADY IN THE DARK AND ONE TOUCH OF VENUS

The Broadway Stranger and His American Dreams

Within a year after Kurt Weill (1900–1950) immigrated to America his *Johnny Johnson* (1936) had appeared on Broadway. By the time he ended his brief but productive American career with *Lost in the Stars* (1949), the German refugee had managed to produce no less than eight shows in his adopted homeland, including two certifiable hits, *Lady in the Dark* (467 performances) and *One Touch of Venus* (567 performances). At the risk of minimizing such a notable achievement, it must be said that Weill's hits did not run significantly longer than the disappointing 315 performances suffered by Rodgers and Hammerstein's *Allegro* (1947), which closed only a few months after *Oklahoma!*'s five-year run.

Furthermore, while all three of Rodgers and Hammerstein's 1940s hits, *Oklahoma!*, *Carousel*, and *South Pacific*, have gone on to form part of the nucleus of the Broadway repertory, Weill's two contemporaneous hits have nearly vanished. With the escalating success of *Street Scene* (1947) and *Lost in the Stars* and the championing of his previously neglected European music from both sides of the Atlantic, however, Weill's critical and popular star continues to rise. At the same time, with the notable exception of the perennially popular *Threepenny Opera* (Off-Broadway 1954–1960), the once-popular Broadway Weill remains largely overlooked in print (including Broadway surveys) as well as in performance.[1]

Weill, like Bernstein to follow, entered the world of Broadway after rigorous classical training. In contrast to Bernstein, Weill made his mark

133

as an avant-garde composer *before* succumbing to the siren song of a more popular musical theater. The trajectory of Gershwin's career perhaps better exemplifies the more usual evolutionary pattern of the Tin Pan Alley composer who harbored more lofty theatrical ambitions. Unlike most of his Broadway colleagues (including Gershwin), Weill, years before his arrival in America, had established himself as a reputable classical composer from Germany in what Stravinsky called the "main stem" of the classical tradition. At fifteen he began studying theory and composition as well as piano, at sixteen he was creating "serious" compositions, and by seventeen he was acquiring skills in instrumentation, orchestration (unlike most Broadway composers Weill would score his own shows), and scorereading. In 1918 he enrolled at Berlin's Hochschule für Musik to study composition with Engelbert Humperdinck, the composer of *Hänsel und Gretel*. Conducting and counterpoint studies with equally distinguished teachers would continue.

At twenty Weill was accepted as one of Ferruccio Busoni's six composition students at the Prussian Academy of Arts in Berlin. After composing an impressive series of instrumental as well as stage works, Weill made his pivotal decision to devote his career to the latter in 1926. The next year he began his most famous collaboration with Bertolt Brecht, a collaboration that over the next six years yielded the works by which Weill remains best remembered and most appreciated: *Die Dreigroschenoper (The Threepenny Opera)* (1928), *Happy End* (1929), and *Aufstieg und Fall der Stadt Mahagonny (The Rise and Fall of the City of Mahagonny)* (1930).

Those who see the collaborations with Brecht as the summit of Weill's creative life have concluded that when Weill immigrated to America after a two-year Parisian interregnum, he traded in his artistic soul for fourteen years of hits—and still more misses—in the cultural wasteland of Broadway. Even writers sympathetic to his American musicals recount the compromises that Weill was forced to make to reach the lowest common Broadway denominators.[2] Just as politicians frequently do not survive a change of party allegiance or a conspicuous change of mind on a sensitive issue, composers who abandon the trappings of "high culture" for the commercial marketplace can be expected to pay a price for their pact with Mammon. Schoenberg's idea that great works are inherently inaccessible to general audiences and that audiences who like great works cannot possibly understand them, is dying a slow and lingering death.

In a reflective entry in *The New Grove Dictionary of Music and Musicians* Weill authority David Drew helps to place the transplanted German's "divided" career in perspective when he points out that even with his sharperedged collaborations with Brecht, Weill had also aimed to please a particular audience in a particular time and place.³ According to Drew, Weill discovered with *Die Dreigroschenoper* "that a 'serious' modern composer could still reach the broad masses without sacrifice of originality or contemporaneity." Similarly, when discussing the Broadway works, Drew helps to clarify the altered aesthetic transformation between the "cultural implications" of a work like *Mahagonny* and the Broadway period:

> The creation of 'works of art' was not Weill's primary concern. . . . Weill now attempted to subordinate all aesthetic criteria to purely pragmatic and populist ones. Musical ideas, and dramatic ones too, were not to be judged in terms of originality or intrinsic interest . . . but in terms of their power to evoke, immediately and unambiguously, the required emotional response from a given audience.

Drew goes on to remark that Weill continued to take risks on Broadway in dramatic form or subject matter. Even in the conventional *One Touch of Venus* Weill took a risk by allowing dance to tell a story and by teaming up with Broadway newcomers, librettist S. J. Perelman (1904–1979) and lyricist Ogden Nash (1902–1971). But Drew seems to share the view held by even those sympathetic to Weill's American adventure when he writes that Broadway "exacted from him a degree of self-sacrifice greater than any that would have been demanded by a totalitarian ministry of culture." In Europe Weill was a leading modernist and a composer "accustomed to measure his talents and achievements against those of the most eminent of his German contemporaries, Paul Hindemith." In America, "the composer whom he now saw as his chief rival was Richard Rodgers." Nevertheless, Weill's "aural imagination" and "highly cultivated sense of musical character and theatrical form" enabled him to secure "a special place in the history of American popular music."

Drew and other Weill biographers assume that Weill sacrificed his potential for growth and artistic achievement (albeit willingly) in order to serve "a larger interest than his own, namely that of the American musical theatre." In any event, the absence of subsidized American theater and the scarce opportunities for new works to be performed in what he viewed as artistically stagnant American operatic institutions allowed Weill no place to turn but to the somewhat restricted world of Broadway.

In its English translation by Blitzstein *Die Dreigroschenoper* has demonstrated its durability in the American musical theater repertory as *The Threepenny Opera*. Of the works originally composed for American audiences perhaps only *Street Scene* (1947), a modest success in its own time with 148 performances, and the comparably successful *Knickerbocker Holiday* (1938) and *Lost in the Stars* (1949) (168 and 273 performances, respectively) have in recent years gained increasing popular and critical acclaim. In particular, *Street Scene* seems destined to achieve a reasonably secure place in the operatic repertory. Meanwhile, neither of Weill's wartime hits, *Lady in the Dark* and *One Touch of Venus*, has returned to the Broadway stage. It is indeed a peculiar legacy that Weill's popularly designed American works remain unrevived and perhaps unrevivable.[4]

Lady in the Dark can be found in nearly every list of notable musicals. While it failed to make Lehman Engel's short list, this pioneering critic confidently but incorrectly predicted that it "will come back again and again."[5] *One Touch of Venus* was greeted as "an unhackneyed and imaginative musical that spurns the easy formulas of Broadway" and "the best score by Mr. Weill that we recall."[6] Even Weill, in a letter to Ira Gershwin, expressed the opinion that he had for the most part succeeded in producing an audience-worthy show: "I was rather pleased to find, looking at it cold-bloodedly, that inspite [*sic*] of all the faults and mistakes it is a very good and interesting show and that it holds the audience all through once they sit through the first 15 minutes which are pretty awful."[7] Despite such public and private endorsements, *Venus,* like its wartime predecessor, has so far failed to establish itself in the Broadway (or any other) repertory. The issues raised by *Venus*'s demise deserve more attention than they have so far received.

In his final years Weill himself seemed to repudiate his Broadway hits when he interpreted his creative evolution in America to show its culmination in *Street Scene.* In his notes to its recording the composer confesses that he "learned a great deal about Broadway and its audience" as a result of his first effort, *Johnny Johnson,* "a continuation of the [European] formula."[8] According to Weill's revisionism, *Lady in the Dark* and *One Touch of Venus,* the former especially "with its three little one-act operas," were merely way stations on the road to the development of "something like an American opera."[9] Just as Gershwin opted for a Broadway home for *Porgy and Bess* and Rodgers was content to present his brand of opera (*Carousel*) on the Great White Way, Weill concluded that his Broadway operas "could only take place on Broadway, because Broadway represents the living theatre in this country."[10] Weill continues: "[It] should, like the products of other opera-civilizations, appeal to large parts of the audience. It should have all the necessary ingredients of a 'good show'."[11]

Additional evidence that Weill appreciated audience-pleasing shows can be found in his remarks to Ira Gershwin regarding *Oklahoma!* Weill had seen the tryouts in New Haven and was surprised that "they still haven't got a second act" (although he quickly added that "they don't seem to need one").[12] After praising Rouben Mamoulian's work, the production as a whole, the direction and the songs ("just perfect for this kind of show"), and Hammerstein's singable lyrics, Weill made this final assessment: "On the whole, the show is definitely designed for a very low audience . . . and that, in my opinion explains the terrific success."[13]

Two Compromising Ladies

According to theater lore, Moss Hart (1904–1961) wrote *I Am Listening* when his psychiatrist advised him to cease his successful but inhibiting collaboration with George S. Kaufman and write a play of his own. As Hart tells it: "My psychoanalyst made me resolve that the next idea I had, whether it was good or lousy, I'd carry through."[14] In fact, three years before the creative crisis that led to *Lady in the Dark*, Kaufman and Hart had drafted the first act of a musical based on psychoanalysis starring Marlene Dietrich before settling on *I'd Rather Be Right* with Rodgers and Hart and George M. Cohan as Franklin Roosevelt. *I Am Listening* also shares much in common with the Fred Astaire–Ginger Rogers film musical *Carefree* (1938), in which Rogers plays a woman similar to Liza Elliott who "can't make up her mind" about marriage, a problem solved in the film by psychiatrist Astaire when he falls in love with her.[15]

One Touch of Venus is based on Thomas Anstey Guthrie's novella *The Tinted Venus* (1885).[16] Sources disagree as to how Weill learned about this relatively obscure work of fiction by the man who published under the pseudonym F. Anstey, but most credit him as the person who persuaded Cheryl Crawford to produce the show.[17] Crawford then asked Sam and Bella Spewack, who had earlier worked on an abandoned Weill project, *The Opera from Mannheim* (1937), to write a libretto; light-verse poet Nash, a Broadway novice, would provide the lyrics. In August the Spewacks drafted the first act of *One Man's Venus*. After at least five lyrics and as many as eight songs, the Spewack libretto, now Bella's alone, was dismissed as beyond repair, and a new book was commissioned from Perelman, best known as the author of the Marx Brothers screenplays *Monkey Business* (1931) and *Horsefeathers* (1932), but untested in a book musical.[18]

Crawford articulates the causes for her dissatisfaction with Bella Spewack's libretto: "The idea that had enticed me was the irreconcilable differences between the world of mundane, conventional human beings and the free untrammeled world of the gods. But this theme had not been developed."[19] In Perelman's rewrite Anstey's Victorian England was trans-

Moss Hart. © Al Hirschfeld. Drawing reproduced by special arrangement with Hirschfeld's exclusive representative, The Margo Feiden Galleries Ltd. New York.

formed into contemporary Manhattan. Foremost among other significant alterations was the character of Venus herself, more threatening and forbidding than sensual in Anstey's novella, and a goddess who would return to her stone form for hours at a time. Rather than succumbing to her demands (as opposed to charms) the unfortunate barber (Leander Tweddle) remains steadfast in his love for his eventually understanding fiancée (Matilda Collum). By appealing to Venus's vanity, Leander in the end manages to trick her into relinquishing the ring that gave her life.[20]

Throughout his career Weill rarely failed to surround himself with strong artistic figures. In Germany he collaborated with Brecht and Georg Kaiser. For the American musical stage he worked with a series of distinguished partners as the following list attests: Paul Green (*Johnny Johnson*); Maxwell Anderson (*Knickerbocker Holiday* and *Lost in the Stars*); Elmer Rice and Langston Hughes (*Street Scene*); and Alan Jay Lerner (*Love Life*). Similarly, the productions of *Lady in the Dark* and *One Touch of Venus* evolved under dynamic leadership, and his principal collaborators, Hart and Gershwin (*Lady*), Nash and Perelman (*Venus*), all possessed strong artistic personalities and identities. The *One Touch of Venus* team could boast an especially impressive talent roster. The previous year alone Crawford produced the immensely popular revival of *Porgy and Bess*, Elia Kazan directed his first memorable production, Thornton Wilder's *The Skin of Our Teeth*, and Agnes de Mille had choreographed Copland's ballet classic *Rodeo*. Only six months before *Venus* came to life in 1943 de Mille had gained enormous Broadway distinction as the choreographer of *Oklahoma!*[21]

Even in this venerable company the composer could still play a major role in the creative process of a musical, although he would not occupy the center stage enjoyed by Mozart and Da Ponte, Verdi and Boito, and Wagner. Theater critics appreciated the imagination of the *Lady in the Dark* and *One Touch of Venus* teams, but music critics who focused on Weill felt betrayed by his collaboration with the enemy, men and women of the theater who helped Weill to sell out. Critics Virgil Thomson and Samuel Barlow respectively accused Weill of banality and phoniness and wrote that the transplanted European had lost his sophistication and his satirical punch in his efforts to please the lower-class inhabitants of Broadway.[22]

Considering the experience and prestige of his collaborators, especially Hart and Gershwin, it should come as no surprise that Weill would be asked to defer to the judgment of these collaborators during the writing of *Lady in the Dark*.[23] As a result one complete dream in *Lady* (first described as the "Day Dream" and later as the "Hollywood Dream") was rejected before its completion, allegedly to help trim escalating costs. To add pizzazz (and perhaps to avoid racial stereotypes), the "Minstrel Dream" metamorphosed into the "Circus Dream." "The Saga of Jenny" was a response to Hart's and producer Sam H. Harris's assessment that Gertrude Lawrence's final number was not funny enough, and the patter number which preceded it, "Tschaikowsky," was added as a vehicle to feature the talented new star Danny Kaye.

Crawford credits de Mille with many of the small cuts in the *One Touch of Venus* ballets, summarizes the problem of the original ending, and explains how Weill's collaborators achieved a satisfactory solution:

The bacchanal of the nymphs, satyrs, nyads and dryads who carry Venus off was very effective, but it left the audience hanging. It seemed very unsatisfactory for Venus to disappear into the clouds, leaving the poor barber all alone: the ending needed ooomph, something upbeat. It was Agnes who thought of having Venus come back as an "ordinary" human girl, dressed in a cute little dress and hat—a sort of reincarnation.[24]

This new ending necessitated the shortening of Weill's Bacchanale ballet, which de Mille (as remembered by Crawford) considered "the best thing he'd done since *Threepenny Opera*" and Weill himself treasured as "the finest piece of orchestral music he had ever written."[25] But since Weill "wanted a success" and was "predominantly a theatre man," he acquiesced to de Mille's suggestion.

It is likely that the musical starting point for both *Lady* and *Venus* were songs that Weill had written for earlier contexts. Both of these songs, *Lady's* "My Ship" and *Venus's* "Westwind," would become pivotal to the musical story. Since "My Ship" was originally the only song Hart had in mind when he drafted his play *I Am Listening*, it is not surprising that this was the first song Weill wrote for the show.[26]

In the midst of his sketches for *Lady*, including a draft for "My Ship," Weill sketched a tune that with some modifications would eventually become "Westwind" (Example 7.2a p. 152). In the early stages Weill used its melody solely for the "Venus Entrance" music (and he would continue to label this tune as such throughout his orchestral score). Long after the entire show had taken shape, the music of the future "Westwind" was still reserved for Venus.[27] At a relatively late stage Weill decided to show Savory's total captivation with Venus musically by adopting her tune as his own. After their first meeting his identity is now fully submerged in the woman he idealizes.[28]

The extant manuscript sources and material of *Lady in the Dark* provide an unusually rich glimpse into the compositional process of a musical: Hart's complete original play *I Am Listening*, two revised scenes for this play, and two typescript outlines for two dreams not included in this play; Gershwin's lyrics drafts, including those for the discarded "Zodiac" song; and two hundred pages of Weill's sketches and drafts. Also extant are twenty letters between Weill and Gershwin exchanged between September 1940 and February 1944 ("with random annotations" by Gershwin in 1967) that occasionally reveal important information and attitudes about the compositional process.[29]

Gershwin had travelled from Los Angeles to New York in early May 1940 to work with Hart and Weill, and the letters from Weill began one or two weeks after Gershwin's return in August. The two Weill letters in September are especially valuable because they precede the opening night (the following January 23). On September 2 Weill sets the context for his following suggestions with a budget report: the show was $25,000 above its projected $100,000. Hart and Hassard Short "read the play to the boys in the office," who were "crazy about the show" but thought "that the bar scene and the Hollywood dream had nothing to do with the play."[30] Hart asked Weill to cut the Hollywood Dream, and the composer agreed to do this if Hart agreed to delete the bar scene as well.

Did this compromise breach Weill's artistic sensibilities? Apparently Weill did not think so. He explains his positive reaction to the excision of the Hollywood Dream:

> I began to see certain advantages. It is obvious that this change would be very good for the play itself because it would mean that we go from the flashback scene directly into the last scene of the play. The decision which Liza makes in the last scene would be an immediate result of the successful analysis. The balance between music and book would be very good in the second act because we would make the flashback scene a completely musical scene.[31]

Although Weill regretted losing "an entire musical scene and some very good material," he saw artistic benefits as well as financial ones, and agreed to these changes.

After more discussion on the relationship between the Hollywood Dream and the Hollywood sequence, both eventually discarded, Weill turned to the "Circus Dream." Here Weill was less acquiescent to Short's suggestions. Although he understood that "Gertie" (Gertrude Lawrence) might remain dissatisfied until he provided "a really funny song" for her, Weill was not yet ready to abandon his "Zodiac" song and defended its place in the show to Gershwin. Although Weill acknowledged that the "Zodiac" song "is not the kind of broad entertainment which Hassard has in mind," he concluded that "it is a very original, high class song of the kind which you and I should have in a show and for which we will get a lot of credit." Because Weill also recognized "the necessity to give Gertie

Lady in the Dark. "Circus Dream." Gertrude Lawrence sitting on the left, Danny Kaye on the horse at right (1941). Photograph: Vandamm. Museum of the City of New York. Gift of the Burns Mantle Estate.

a good, solid, entertaining, humorous song in the Circus dream," he offered to make the "Zodiac" song "musically lighter, more on the line of a patter, and to think about another song for Gertie."

On September 14 Weill again commented on the evolving Circus Dream:

> So Moss and Hassard suggested that we give the Zodiak song back to Randy and I thought this might be good news for you because that's what we always wanted. Here is Moss's idea: the Zodiak song would become Randy's defense speech, just the way you had originally conceived it, but we should try to work Gertie into it. . . . When they have won over everybody to their cause, Liza should go into a triumphant song. . . . That would give Liza her show-stopping (??) song near the end of the dream and at a moment where she is triumphant and which allows her to be as gay or sarcastic as you want."[32]

From Ira Gershwin's 1967 annotations that accompany his manuscripts as well his published comments in *Lyrics on Several Occasions,* we learn that the "Circus Dream" was originally planned as a "Minstrel Dream" and "an environment of burnt cork and sanded floor" was transformed "to putty nose and tanbark."[33] Gershwin divides the "Zodiac" into two parts,

"No Matter Under What Star You're Born" and "Song of the Zodiac," "both of which were discarded to make way for "The Saga of Jenny.""[34] He also notes that he and Weill "hadn't as yet introduced "Tschaikovsky.""[35]

Weill's musical manuscripts add credence to the letters and Gershwin's annotations and reveal that when most of the Circus Dream nearly reached its final form, "The Saga of Jenny" was just taking shape. It is ironic that Gertrude Lawrence's final number and Danny Kaye's patter show stopper that directly preceded it were the only musical portions originally written for this dream. All the other musical material—with the exception of some recitative—was borrowed from earlier shows. Even the lyrics to "Tschaikovsky" were borrowed unchanged from a 1924 poem published in "the then pre-pictorial, humorous weekly *Life*" that Ira published under the pseudonym Arthur Francis.[36]

Weill's 1935 London box office debacle, *A Kindom for a Cow*, served as an important musical link between the German Weill and the American Weill. In his *Handbook* Drew lists thirteen major instances of Weill's recycling ideas from this most recent European venture into every American stage work from *Johnny Johnson* and *Knickerbocker Holiday* (two borrowings each) to *The Firebrand of Florence*.[37] The two *Kingdom for a Cow* borrowings in *Lady in the Dark* both occur in the Circus Dream: the opening circus march, "The Greatest Show on Earth," and "The Best Years of His Life." The single borrowing in *One Touch of Venus* occurs more obliquely in "Very, Very, Very."

Of the *Kingdom for a Cow* borrowings in *Lady* and *Venus* "The Best Years of His Life" comes closest to quotation. In fact, Kendall Nesbitt's melody in *Lady* is identical to the choral melody in the first act finale of *Kingdom*, and the rhythmic alterations are insubstantial. Weill takes significant transformational liberties, however, in adapting "Very, Very, Very" from *Kingdom* to *Venus* (where it is sung by Savory's assistant Molly). On this occasion Weill uses two recognizable but highly disguised melodic fragments of "Madame Odette's Waltz" from the second act finale of *Kingdom*.

Weill's remaining borrowing falls between these extremes. "The Greatest Show on Earth," the rousing march which opens the Circus Dream, borrows significantly from the melody, rhythm, and dissonant harmonic underpinning of the refrain of *Kingdom*'s "Auftrittslied des General." When drafting his melody in its new context and new meter, Weill began by retaining the rhythmic *gestus* (to be discussed shortly) and symmetrical phrasing of its predecessor, altering only the pitch. By the time

Weill completed his transformation, he had added a new syncopation at the ends of phrases and reinforced the sense of disarray by concluding his phrase one measure earlier than expected. In real (and especially military) life, marches contain symmetrical four-measure phrases; in Liza's confused dream message a seven-measure phrase makes more sense.

Partisans of Brecht may be disconcerted to hear the choral refrain "In der Jugend gold'nem Schimmer" from *Happy End* (1929) set to Nash's words in the opening verses of "The Trouble With Women." At the time Weill recast Brecht, he had abandoned the possibility of a staged revival of this show, although he had tried in 1932 to interest his publisher in "a kind of *Songspiel* with short spoken scenes."[38] Perhaps his sense that all was lost with *Happy End* prompted Weill to recycle no less than three numbers from this German show in his Parisian collaboration with Jacques Déval, *Marie Galante* (1934). One of these reincarnations is once again "In der Jugend gold'nem Schimmer," this time altered from triple to duple meter in the refrain of "Les filles de Bordeaux." Despite some modest melodic changes at the opening and closing and the metrical change from the German and American waltzes to the French fox trot, the two—or three—Weills are here much closer to one.[39]

The process by which *A Kingdom for a Cow, Happy End,* and *Marie Galante* would reemerge in *Lady in the Dark* and *One Touch of Venus* suggests a deeper than generally acknowledged connection between the aesthetic and working methods of the European and the American Weills. The connecting link is embodied in the concept of *gestus*, a term that eludes precise identification. According to Kim Kowalke, "the crucial aspect of *gestus* was the translation of dramatic emotion and individual characterization into a typical, reproducible physical realization."[40] In any event, the principle of a gestic music based on rhythm is demonstrable in the aesthetic framework and the compositional process of Weill's music in America as well as in Europe.

In his 1929 essay on this subject, "Concerning the Gestic Character of Music," Weill, after explaining that "the *gestus* is expressed in a rhythmic fixing of the text," makes a case for the primacy of rhythm.[41] Once a composer has located the "proper" *gestus*, "even the melody is stamped by the *gestus* of the action that is to be represented." Weill acknowledges the possibility of more than one rhythmic interpretation of a text (and, one might add, the possibility of more than one text for a given *gestus*). He also argues that "the rhythmic restriction imposed by the text is no more severe a fetter for the operatic composer than, for example, the formal schemes of the fugue, sonata, or rondo were for the classic master" and that "within the framework of such rhythmically predetermined music, all methods of melodic elaboration and of harmonic and rhythmic differentiation are possible, if only the musical spans of accent conform to the gestic proceeding."

Weill concludes his discussion of gestic music by citing an example from Brecht's version of the "Alabama-Song," in which "a basic *gestus* has been defined in the most primitive form."[42] While Brecht assigns pitches to his *gestus*—which may explain why he tried to assume the credit for composing Weill's music—Weill considers Brecht's attempt "nothing more than an inventory of the speech-rhythm and cannot be used as music."[43] Weill explains that he retains "the same basic *gestus*" but that he "composed" this *gestus* "with the much freer means of the musician." Weill's tune "extends much farther afield melodically, and even has a totally different rhythmic foundation as a result of the pattern of the accompaniment—but the gestic character has been preserved, although it occurs in a completely different outward form." Several compositional drafts and self-borrowings reveal that in America as well as in Germany, Weill, like Loesser to follow, continued to establish a rhythmic *gestus* before he worked out his songs melodically.

Kowalke suggests that eighteenth-century Baroque *opera seria* served as the aesthetic model for Brecht and Weill's music drama of alienation widely known as epic opera.[44] Kowalke goes on to describe more specific stylistic similarities, including the relationship between the Baroque doctrine of affections[45] and Weill's interchangeable song types based on a related gestus. An especially applicable example can be found in the genesis of "My Ship" from *Lady in the Dark*. Both the opening of the second sketch draft and the final version feature a rising diminished seventh, F♯-A-C-E♭ (a resemblance noted by bruce d. mcclung).[46] It is also clear that Weill had established a *gestus*, if not the melodic working out, by the time he drafted this second draft of five eventual versions.

Just as "Surabaya Johnny" (*Happy End*) constitutes a trope of the "Moritat" ("The Ballad of Mack the Knife") from *Die Dreigroschenoper*, the borrowed songs in *Lady* and *Venus* may be considered tropes from Weill's European output. Weill's practice of salvaging material from failed shows closely parallels the practice of other Broadway as well as European operatic composers as far back as Handel in the Baroque era.[47] What makes such salvaging possible for Weill is a shared *gestus* that might, like the Baroque affections, serve several dramatic situations with equal conviction. Weill would continue to develop this particular brand of transformation within his American works. *Lady* and *Venus* exhibit an especially notable

Example 7.1. "The Saga of Jenny" and "Dr. Crippen"
    (a) "The Saga of Jenny" (*Lady in the Dark*)
    (b) "Dr. Crippen" (*One Touch of Venus*)

example as shown in Example 7.1. Even the theater reviewer, Lewis Nichols, remarked after a single hearing in his opening night review of *Venus* that at the conclusion of act I Savory "sings the sad story of 'Dr. Crippen' in a mood and a tune not unlike that of Mr. Weill's celebrated 'Saga of Jenny'."[48]

Lady in the Dark *and* One Touch of Venus *As Integrated Musicals*

Despite his careful selection of librettists and lyricists and his devotion to theatrical integrity, Weill's Broadway offerings for the most part share the posthumous fate of such popular contemporaries as Kern, Porter, and Rodgers and Hart who are similarly remembered more for their hit songs in most of their shows.[49] Even in the case of *The Threepenny Opera*, an extraordinarily popular musical in its Off-Broadway reincarnation, "The Ballad of Mack the Knife," remains by far its most remembered feature.

It is additionally ironic that the ideal of Weill's most successful musical deliberately disregards the principle of the integrated model popularized by Rodgers and Hammerstein, a principle that would hold center stage (with some exceptions) at least until the late 1960s. In Europe the apparent interchangeability of arias (providing the proper affects were preserved) in *opera seria* gave way to the increasingly integrated, albeit occasionally heterogeneous, operas of Mozart, Verdi, Wagner, Strauss, and Berg. Many Broadway shows before Rodgers and Hammerstein (and some thereafter), like their Baroque opera counterparts, emphasized individual great songs, stars, and stagecraft, more than broader dramatic themes and treated their books and music as autonomous rather than integrated elements.

After *Oklahoma!* and *Carousel* the aesthetic goals of Broadway shifted. Two years after the disastrous *Firebrand of Florence* in 1945 (43 performances), Weill too composed an integrated dramatic work, *Street Scene* (148 performances), that would eventually achieve a commercial success roughly commensurate with its critical acclaim. The dream that Weill shared on his notes to the cast album of this Broadway opera, a "dream of a special brand of musical theatre which would completely integrate drama and music, spoken word, song and movement" was also the dream of his chief Broadway rival in the 1940s, Rodgers, who was composing *Oklahoma!, Carousel, Allegro,* and *South Pacific* during these years.[50]

In his notes to *Street Scene* Weill acknowledges that he and his earlier collaborator Brecht "deliberately stopped the action during the songs which were written to illustrate the 'philosophy,' the inner meaning of the play."[51] It was not until *Street Scene,* however, that Weill achieved "a real blending of drama and music, in which the singing continues naturally where the speaking stops and the spoken work as well as the dramatic action are embedded in overall musical structure."[52] Three years before he completed his long and productive theater career Weill appeared to repudiate the aesthetic he had worked out with Brecht and achieved his integrated American opera.

Thus Weill, by now a wayward branch from the German stem, did not begin his serious attempt to integrate drama and music until after he ceased collaborating with Brecht. On the other hand the American Rodgers, as early as Brecht and Weill's *Threepenny Opera,* was already somewhat paradoxically striving to compose integrated musicals in a marketplace somewhat indifferent to this aesthetic.[53] Weill's contemporary and posthumous success with *Threepenny Opera,* both its German production in the late 1920s and its Broadway adaptation by Blitzstein in the middle and late 1950s, rests in part in the alienation between and separation of music and story. Even those who remain impervious to the quality and charm of Weill's many other works acknowledge the artistic merits of *Threepenny Opera* and usually grant it masterpiece status.

Shortly before the debut of *Lady in the Dark* Weill informed William King in the *New York Sun* that, in contrast to Schoenberg who "has said he is writing for a time fifty years after his death," Weill wrote "for today" and did not "give a damn about writing for posterity."[54] Between the extremes of his two posthumous success stories, *Threepenny Opera* and, to a lesser degree, *Street Scene*, lie Weill's two greatest and—if posterity be damned—most meaningful hits. Both *Lady* and *Venus* exhibit integrative as well as nonintegrative traits. On one level *Lady in the Dark* might be considered the least integrated of any book show by any Broadway composer, since the play portions and the musical portions are unprecedentedly segregated. In this respect *Lady* shares much in common with film adaptations of musicals which remove the "nonrealistic" portions of their Broadway source.[55]

With the exception of "My Ship" virtually all the music of the show appears in three separate dream sequences that comprise half of the show—the Glamour Dream and the Wedding Dream in act I and the Circus Dream in act II—and nowhere else. In each of these dreams virtually everything is sung or underscored by continuous music, while the other half is composed entirely of spoken dialogue. Hart's original intent, evident in his draft of the play *I Am Listening*, was to have a play with a small amount of musical interjections rather than "three little one-act operas."

Once Hart had decided to create a play that could accommodate Weill's music, he fully embraced the integrated ideal (for the dreams) that within a few years would dominate Broadway. In his prefatory remarks to the published vocal score, Hart expressed the desire for himself and his collaborators not only to avoid "the tight little formula of the musical comedy stage," but to create a show "in which the music carried forward the essential story." "For the first time . . . the music and lyrics of a musical 'show' are part and parcel of the basic structure of the play."[56]

With due respect to Hart, the music in *Lady in the Dark* might more accurately be described as a conscious interruption of a play. But since an important component of the story is the disparity between Liza Elliott's drab quotidian existence and the colorful pizzazz of her dream world, it makes sense for her to only speak in her waking life and reserve music for her dreams. The dream pretext also allows Weill to present the interruptions within the discontinuity of a dream, since, after all, audiences should not expect dreams to be totally logical. Dreams, as Weill wrote in his thoughts on dreams that he typed out in preparation for *Lady in the Dark*, "are, at the moment of the dreaming, very realistic and don't have at all the mysterious, shadowy quality of the usual dream sequences in plays or novels."

Liza's dreams differ no more from her daily life than escapist musicals of the late 1930s differed from the daily lives of their audiences.[57] The musical and dramatic non sequitur that launches "Tschaikowsky" may be equally abrupt as the opening gambits in 1930s musical comedies, for example, "There's a Small Hotel" in *On Your Toes*. After Liza, accompanied by a chorus, concludes her musical defense—"Tra-la—I never gave my word"—in the breach of promise suit for failing to marry Nesbitt (clearly reminiscent of Gilbert and Sullivan's *Trial by Jury*), the music comes to a halt with a soft cymbal. The Ringmaster (*Allure* photographer Randy Paxton in real life) then breaks the silence with "Charming, charming, who wrote that music?", the Jury answers, "Tschaikowsky!", and the Ringmaster says, "Tschaikowsky? I love Russian composers!" Part of the joke, of course, is that Tchaikovsky did not compose "The Best Years of His Life" (Weill himself had composed this song several years earlier in *Kingdom for a Cow*). Moreover, in the slightly askew chronology of dreamland, the exchange between the Ringmaster and the Jury actually anticipates a real, albeit small, dose of Tchaikovsky's "Pathétique" Symphony (third movement).

While a major theme of *Lady in the Dark* is the disparity between Liza Elliott's real and dream worlds (although she retains her name in her dreams), her coworkers often appear in her dreams as metaphors for their roles in Liza's waking life. The metaphors also become increasingly obvious as Liza comes to understand the meaning of her dreams. Of the four men in her life, the "mildly effeminate" Paxton (Danny Kaye) plays a neutral role in Liza's romantic life and serves the dreaming Liza with equal neutrality (a chauffeur in the Glamour Dream and the ringmaster in the Circus Dream). Nesbitt (Bert Lytell), who "waits" for Liza in real life, plays the role of a head waiter in a night club in the Glamour Dream and the real-life role of Liza's expectant groom in the Wedding Dream before appearing as the first witness for the prosecution in the Circus Dream. The glamorous movie star Randy Curtis (Victor Mature), who appreciates and defends Liza's lack of glamour, naturally appears as Liza's defense attorney in the Circus Dream.

Similarly, Hart captures the complexity of Liza's relationship with her obnoxious advertising manager, Charley Johnson (MacDonald Carey). In the Glamour Dream Johnson plays the marine who paints Liza's portrait for the two-cent stamp, not as Liza sees herself in the dream, but as others see her in real life. Already in the first dream he has established himself as firmly grounded in reality and the person who truly sees Liza for what she is (significantly, Johnson's realism is bound to speech and he never sings in the dreams, although he will eventually sing "My Ship" for Liza). In the Wedding Dream Johnson appears twice, first as the salesman who offers a dagger instead of a ring and then as the minister who, merely by asking the standard question, "If there be any who know why these two [Liza and Nesbitt] should not be joined in holy wedlock let him speak now or forever hold his peace," prompts a truthful response from his congregation that exposes the wedding as a sham: "This woman knows she does not love this man."

In the Circus Dream Johnson acts as the prosecuting attorney and as a surrogate for Dr. Brooks, when he repeats the psychiatrist's diagnosis nearly word for word, adding a new accusatory tone at the end of the dream: "You're afraid. You're hiding something. You're afraid of that music aren't you? Just as you're afraid to compete as a woman—afraid to marry Kendall Nesbitt—afraid to be the woman you want to be—afraid—afraid—afraid!" "That music" is of course the song "My Ship," or rather the opening portion of this song that either leads to dreams (Glamour and Wedding Dreams) or makes a dream come to a stop (the Circus Dream).

In her final session with Dr. Brooks Liza manages to recall the entire song as she formerly sang it to a boy named Ben. Ben, the Handsomest Boy at Mapleton High, many years earlier had abandoned the teenage Liza, the Most Popular Girl, to return to the Most Beautiful Girl. While she waits for Ben to return, another boy asks to take Liza to dinner (Liza prefers to wait). The boy's name is Charles, yet another clue that someday a prince named Charley will come. In the final scene Charley Johnson offers more substantive evidence that he is indeed Mr. Right for Liza Elliott: he knows "My Ship" and will sing it with her as their ship sails off into the golden sunset.

The central musical unifying musical element of *Lady in the Dark* is certainly "My Ship," the opening portion of which appears in various harmonizations in each dream before Liza manages to sing it completely in the otherwise musically silent Childhood Dream.[58] The musical material of the three main dreams are internally "unified" around a characteristic rhythm (a rhumba for the Glamour Dream, a bolero for the Wedding Dream, and a march for the Circus Dream). The Glamour dream contains the greatest use of internal thematic transformation. Beyond the reuse and development of "My Ship," however, organic unity is not especially prominent from one dream to the next.

In *One Touch of Venus* the use of song to musically interrupt rather than continue the action may be a characteristic shared with the nonintegrated musicals of Porter before *Kiss Me, Kate*. It also suggests a return structurally, if not ideologically, to Weill's epic creations with Brecht (*Threepenny Opera, Happy End,* and *Mahagonny*). Venus's final song, "That's Him," is representative of Weill's earlier ideal by distancing the singer from the object and providing a commentary on love rather than an experience of it. Venus even speaks of her love object in the third person.

Dramatic unity in *One Touch of Venus,* outwardly more conventional than the intricate continuous dream scenes in *Lady in the Dark,* nevertheless corresponds closely to the contemporary *Oklahoma!* model based on such devices as thematic transformation in narrative ballets and the use of strong rhythmic profiles to reflect character.[59] These two techniques converge in Weill's recasting of Venus's (Mary Martin's) jazzy and uninhibited opening song, "I'm a Stranger Here Myself" moments later in the ballet "Forty Minutes for Lunch," described in the libretto as "a series of formalized dance patterns parodying the tension of metropolitan life."[60]

Like the composers of *Anything Goes, Carousel, Guys and Dolls,* and *West Side Story* Weill uses quarter-note triplets when he wants to show his characters moving emotionally beyond their metrical boundaries.[61] Weill uses the quarter-note triplet most prominently in Whitelaw Savory's love song "Westwind" (Example 7.2a), previously noted as based, appropriately enough as it turns out, on Venus's Entrance Music. Even Rodney Hatch, when serenading his fiancée Gloria Kramer in his characteristically rhythmically square fashion, manages a few quarter-note triplets in the release of his "How Much I Love You" when he sings "I love you" and "I yearn for you." But by the time he sings of his "Wooden Wedding" near the end of the show, quarter-note triplets have vanished, and Venus will soon follow.

Venus herself, who tells Savory at their first meeting that "love isn't the dying moan of a distant violin—it's the triumphant twang of a bedspring," generally prefers swing rhythms, but quarter-note triplets remain a prominent part of her musical character (as well as of the Venus Theme).[62] She sings them prominently in the swinging and highly syncopated "I'm a Stranger Here Myself," and even opens the verse of the waltz "Foolish Heart" with a quarter-note triplet group. By the time Venus sings "Speak Low" with Rodney, every phrase of both the main portion and the release includes quarter-note triplets (Example 7.2b), and her characteristic swinging rhythms are submerged in the accompaniment.

In the spoken dialogue that prepares for her final song Venus confesses that while the ring brought the statue to life, it was not responsible for making her love him. Nevertheless, Venus wastes no time in asking Rodney to part his hair on the other side. The song itself, "That's Him," lyrically and musically captures Venus's ambiguity towards Rodney. On one hand Venus literally compares her potential mate to Gershwin's *Rhapsody in Blue,* she could "pick him out" from the millions of men in the world,

Example 7.2. Quarter-note triplets in *One Touch of Venus*
(a) "Westwind"
(b) "Speak Low"

and she concludes her A sections by singing "wonderful world, wonderful you." On the other hand, despite his endearing qualitites, Rodney remains an unlikely romantic partner, especially for a Venus. He is "simple," "not arty," "satisfactory," and appreciated primarily for his functionality, "like a plumber when you need a plumber" and "comforting as woolens in the winter."

In order to musically express less exalted feelings for her conventional barber, Venus must be deprived of the musical identity she has established for herself in her other songs. Weill conveys this underlying conflict when he does not allow the accompaniment, significantly filled with Venus's characteristic swinging rhythms, to share the implied harmony of Venus's melody. Additionally, although Venus's melodic line contains several telling vocal leaps, it mainly consists of stepwise motion, again in contrast to her previously established melodically disjunct character portrayed in "I'm a Stranger Here Myself" and "Speak Low." Only at the end of the A' sections—the song forms an unusual arch, A-A'-B-A-A' rather than A-A-B-A—do melody and harmony resolve to the C major that Weill has Venus avoid so assiduously for thirty-three measures. Although throughout this B section Venus returns to her jazzy swing rhythms, she will abandon her unrealistic dream of an unambiguous C major existence with Rodney after

One Touch of Venus, act I, scene 4. Mary Martin in the center behind the dressing screen (1943). Photograph: Vandamm. Museum of the City of New York.

three measures. Venus may be in love with a wonderful guy, but a marriage with Rodney would be like Pegasus pulling a milk truck.[63]

At the end of the song, the delusion can no longer be sustained. When Rodney finishes singing his description of their "Wooden Wedding" with its "trip to Gimbel's basement, / Or a double feature [pronounced fee'-tcha] with Don Ameche," Venus must say, "Rodney, I hope I'll be the right kind of wife for you."[64] Venus's nightmarish vision of herself as a conventional "housewife" in the concluding ballet, "Venus in Ozone Heights," finally convinces her to rejoin the gods.

The Possibility of Revival

In contrast to the other musicals discussed in this survey, *Lady in the Dark* and *One Touch of Venus* have yet to receive a staged Broadway revival. They have also remained remarkably impervious to revivals elsewhere. Are these musicals being shortchanged and underappreciated or are they unrevivable? Do they need revised books or more Weill hit songs to succeed like Porter and Rodgers and Hart revivals?

The first of several alleged problems with *Lady in the Dark* is its dependence on a star. After exhibiting an indecisiveness equal to Liza Elliott, the versatile Gertrude Lawrence consulted with her friend and oracle Noël Coward as well as her astrological charts and accepted the demanding title role. When Lawrence left for the summer the show closed, and, unlike most shows, including Mary Martin's *Venus,* Lawrence's *Lady* never went on the road. A second problem is expense. Three revolving sets and the attendant costs of the three dream ballets do not travel cheaply.

But certainly these red herrings mask deeper problems. When Hart wrote the libretto to *Lady,* for example, pyschiatry was still a relatively novel subject for a musical, and the endless series of obligatory dream ballets in musicals were mostly in the future. Nevertheless, even by the standards of the early 1940s, Hart's treatment of psychiatry is simplistic and predictible.

More problematic than the dated treatment of psychiatry are the increasingly volatile subjects of sexism and sexual harassment. To be sure, the sexism in *Lady in the Dark* is rather unpalatable, especially as displayed in the character of Liza's eventual Mr. Right, the fanny-pinching, male-chauvinist Charley Johnson, who tries to give Maggie "a wet kiss" against her will. When Johnson accuses Liza of having "magazines instead of babies and a father instead of a husband," he may be telling it like it was, but his remarks were not destined to please modern Broadway audiences.[65] Instead of getting the girl Johnson today might be obtaining the services of an attorney who specializes in sexual harassment suits; he certainly does not deserve a woman like Liza. The nonsinging Kendall Nesbitt hardly seems a better alternative: "Somehow—I don't know why—it's different for a man, but a woman can have no sense of fulfillment—no real peace and serenity as a woman, living out her life this way."[66] In the 1990s a story about a bright, successful, and powerful woman whose achievement comes at the expense of her feminine identity does not bode well for a box office bonanza, even with Madonna in the title role.

Sexual stereotyping is not reserved for the heterosexual members of the *Lady in the Dark* cast. Russell Paxton, the "mildly-effeminate-in-a-rather-charming-fashion" photographer for Liza's fashion magazine, *Allure,* is introduced as "hysterical, as usual." He also freely acknowledges his physical admiration for male beauty when he describes Randy Curtis: "He's got a face that would melt in your mouth. . . . He's heaven."[67] Although some mystery will remain as to which of Liza's suitors (Curtis, Nesbitt, or Johnson) will eventually win out, Paxton is removed at the outset as a romantic possibility.[68]

The reasons for the demise of *One Touch of Venus* are less explicable. The premise of a cultural alien examining America from another perspective has proven remarkably durable in numerous films over the past two decades, and includes aliens from another country (*Moscow on the Hudson*) and extraterrestrial aliens (*E.T.*) in its wide orbit. A genuine and liberated sex goddess adrift amidst overly romantic types like Whitelaw Savory and prosaic practical types like Rodney Hatch provide for a potentially engaging story, a story wittily realized by Perelman, Nash, and Weill.

While Weill is criticized for abandoning his social conscience in his Broadway musicals, *Venus* manages to effectively satirize a host of American values. We know from the first song that Savory is more than a little eccentric because, in contrast with nearly anyone who loves popular musicals, he firmly believes that (with the notable exception of the classical Anatolian Venus), "New Art Is True Art": "Old art is cold art, / The new art is bold art; / The best of ancient Greece, / It was centuries behind Matisse, / Who has carried us beyond Renoir, / Till our bosoms are tri-an-gu-lar."

The largest target of the Perelman-Nash satire is the contrasting moral values of the very, very rich and the common folk. The loose morals of the wealthy are comically portrayed in the song "Very, Very, Very," when Molly explains that "It's a minor peccadillo / To patronize the wrong pillow, / When you're very, very, very rich." It was previously noted that Venus dismisses Savory's idealistic and bourgeois love by favoring the twang of a bedspring over the moan of a violin. In contrast, Venus's earthbound inamorata, Hatch, expresses his love for his fiancée Gloria through a series of negative prosaic images, e.g., "I love you more than a wasp can sting, / And more than a hangnail hurts." Although Venus helps Hatch to rid himself of his shrewish intended—"*sic transit* Gloria Kramer"—the simple barber retains his desire to live in Ozone Heights, where "every bungalow's just the same" and each has "a radio that looks like a fireplace—and a fireplace that looks like a radio."[69]

If *Street Scene* is the American Weill stage work that posterity has voted retrospectively most likely to succeed, *One Touch of Venus*, the most Broadway-like of any Weill show, may turn out to be the most revivable—the sleeper musical of the 1940s. In short, *Venus* is a first-rate traditional Broadway show, packed with an unprecedented number of song hits and other fine songs by Weill, lyrics that reveal the idiosyncratic Nash at his cleverest, and engaging dialogue by Perelman.

After *Venus*, Nash would abandon Broadway and go back to the more intimate world of comic verse. Perelman's next (and last) musical, three years after *Venus*, closed out of town; he would take time off from his prolific output of comic literary fiction on one more occasion to write the script for Porter's last effort, the television musical *Aladdin* (1958). Hart ended his distinguished Broadway career with a successful play, *Light Up the Sky,* and as the director of *My Fair Lady* and *Camelot.* He also wrote distinguished musical screenplays for *Hans Christian Andersen* (lyrics and music by Loesser) and *A Star is Born* (lyrics by Ira Gershwin and music by Harold Arlen). One year after his failed collaboration with Weill, *The Firebrand of Florence,* Gershwin completed his Broadway career with the poorly received *Park Avenue* (music by Arthur Schwartz). He concluded his career by writing lyrics to several successful films, most notably *A Star is Born,* then spent three decades in creative retirement as the guardian of his brother's legacy. After *Venus* and *Florence* Weill would compose the music to *Street Scene, Love Life,* and *Lost in the Stars*, dying before he could realize his next American dream with Maxwell Anderson (his lyricist-librettist on *Knickerbocker Holiday* and *Lost in the Stars*), a musical based on Mark Twain's *Huckleberry Finn.*

·ACT II·

THE BROADWAY
MUSICAL AFTER
OKLAHOMA!

CHAPTER EIGHT

CAROUSEL

The Invasion of the Integrated Musical

Working under the premise that success begets success, Rodgers and Hammerstein followed the phenomenal triumph of *Oklahoma!* (1943) by assembling much of the same production team for their second hit, *Carousel* (1945). Like their historic opening salvo, *Carousel* was produced by the Theatre Guild and supervised by Theresa Helburn and Lawrence Langer, the pair who had given Rodgers and Hart their big break in 1925, *The Garrick Gaieties*. For their director the Theatre Guild selected Rouben Mamoulian, who had directed *Oklahoma!* as well as Rodgers and Hart's classic film *Love Me Tonight* in 1932, the play *Porgy* in 1927, and the opera *Porgy and Bess* in 1935 (both of the latter were also Theatre Guild productions). Agnes de Mille was again asked to choreograph, and Miles White designed the costumes.

Ferenc Molnár's play *Liliom,* which premiered in Hungary in 1909, had been successfully presented by the Guild in 1921 with the legendary Eva Le Gallienne and Joseph Schildkraut, and more recently in 1940 in a production that starred Ingrid Bergman and Burgess Meredith. After some initial resistance, Molnár, who had allegedly turned down an offer by Puccini (and Weill and perhaps Gershwin as well) to make an opera out of his play, reportedly agreed in 1944 to allow the Theatre Guild to adapt his play: "After fifteen months, all the legal technicalities involved in the production of the musical version of *Liliom* were settled last week."[1] The *New*

Rodgers and Hammerstein. © Al Hirschfeld. Drawing reproduced by special arrangement with Hirschfeld's exclusive representative, The Margo Feiden Galleries Ltd. New York.

York Post went on to say that "the smallest percentage: eight tenths of one percent go to Ferenc Molnár, who merely wrote the play."

The idea for setting Molnár's play came from the Theatre Guild, who naturally wanted to reproduce a second *Oklahoma!* Writing in the *New York Times* four days before the birth of the new sibling, Hammerstein recalled Helburn and Langner propositioning the creators of their previous blockbuster in Sardi's "toward the end of January, 1944." The main obstacle for Hammerstein was the Hungarian setting. When, the following week, the persistent Helburn offered a more promising alternative locale in Louisiana, the required dialect also proved to be "a disconcerting difficulty" for the librettist. Sources agree that the workable idea to "transplant the play to the New England coast" came from Rodgers and that the starting point for the show was Billy Bigelow's "Soliloquy." In *Musical Stages* Rodgers wrote that once the team had conceived "the notion for a soliloquy in which, at the end of the first act, the leading character would reveal his varied emotions about impending fatherhood," the central problem of how to sing *Liliom* was resolved.[2]

Although their contract allowed Rodgers and Hammerstein considerable latitude in their adaptation, they were nonetheless relieved to learn during an early rehearsal run-through that the playwright had given his blessing to their changes, including a greatly altered ending.[3] In the play a defiant Liliom does not regret his actions and is doomed to purgatory for fifteen years. He is then required to return to earth for a day to atone for his sins. While on earth, disguised as a beggar, Liliom slaps his daughter when she refuses the star he stole from heaven; she sends him away, and the play ends on this pessimistic note. In the musical a much more sympathetic Liliom, renamed Billy Bigelow, comes to earth by choice, appears as himself, and can choose either to be seen or to remain invisible. As in the play he has stolen a star and slaps his daughter Louise, but now the slap feels like a kiss (in the play it felt like a caress). In stark contrast to the play, the musical's final scene shows Billy, in his remaining moments on earth, helping his "little girl" at her graduation to overcome her loneliness and misery. To the inspirational strains of "You'll Never Walk Alone," with its somewhat dubious advice if taken literally ("when you walk through a storm keep your chin up high"), Louise finds the courage to live, Julie realizes that her marriage—in Molnár's less family-oriented play she remained Billy's mistress—was worth the pain. Billy redeems his soul, and even the most jaded of contemporary audiences find themselves shedding real tears.

Auditions began in February 1945 and tryouts took place the following months in New Haven (March 22–25) and Boston (March 27–April 15). Elliot Norton describes the principal dramatic alteration made during the Boston tryouts:

> The original heaven of *Carousel* was a New England parlor, bare and plain. In it sat a stern Yankee, listed on the program as He. At a harmonium, playing softly, sat his quiet consort, identified as She. Later some observers [including Rodgers] referred to this celestial couple as Mr. and Mrs. God. . . .
>
> Richard Rodgers, walking back to the hotel with his collaborator afterwards, put it to Oscar Hammerstein bluntly:
>
> "We've got to get God out of that parlor!"
>
> Mild Oscar Hammerstein agreed.
>
> "I know you're right, he said. "But where shall I put Him?"
>
> "I don't care where you put Him," said Richard Rodgers. "Put Him up on a ladder, for all I care, only get Him out of that parlor!"
>
> So Oscar Hammerstein put Him up on a ladder. He discarded

the sitting room too, and put his deity into a brand new sequence. On a ladder in the backyard of heaven, He became the Star-Keeper, polishing stars which hung on lines strung across the floor of infinity, while a sullen Billy Bigelow looked and listened to his quiet admonitions.[4]

Carousel's premiere took place at the Majestic Theatre on April 19, and it closed a little more than two years later on May 24, 1947 after a run of 890 performances. Following a successful national tour *Carousel* began another impressive run of 566 performances at London's Drury Lane on June 7, 1950 (closing on October 13, 1951). Major New York revivals took place at the New York City Center Light Opera in 1954, 1957, and 1967, at the Music Theater of Lincoln Center in 1965, and in 1994 with an acclaimed New York staging based on the Royal National Theater of Great Britain production.

Almost without exception *Carousel* opened to rave reviews. Nevertheless, most critics could not resist the temptation to compare the new work to *Oklahoma!*, then beginning its third year on Broadway. The anonymous reviewer in the *New York World-Telegram* who found "the distinct flavor of 'Oklahoma!'" in "A Real Nice Clambake" was more accurate than he knew, since this song had been discarded from the earlier show, where it had been titled "A Real Nice Hayride."[5] Ward Morehouse's review in the *New York Sun* is representative in its conclusion that the laudatory *Carousel* could not quite match the earlier masterpiece: " 'Carousel,' a touching and affecting musical play, is something rare in the theater. It's a hit, and of that there can be no doubt. If it is not the musical piece to challenge 'Oklahoma' for all-time honors it is certainly one that deserves its place in the 44th Street block. The team of Rodgers and Hammerstein will go on forever."[6]

A handful of reviewers regarded the new musical more favorably than its predecessor. According to John Chapman, " 'Carousel' is one of the finest musical plays I have seen and I shall remember it always. It has everything the professional theatre can give it—and something besides: heart, integrity, an inner glow."[7] Although reviewers then and now found the second-act ballet too long, Robert Garland wrote that "when somebody writes a better musical play than 'Carousel,' written by Richard Rodgers and Oscar Hammerstein, Richard Rodgers and Oscar Hammerstein will have to write it."[8]

By the time it returned to New York in 1954 the climate of critical opinion had shifted further, and Brooks Atkinson could now write that *Carousel* "is the most glorious of the Rodgers and Hammerstein works." Atkinson continued: "Three of the Rodgers and Hammerstein shows have had longer runs than 'Carousel.' It is the stepchild among 'Oklahoma!' 'South Pacific,' and 'The King and I.' But when the highest judge of all hands down the ultimate verdict, it is this column's opinion that 'Carousel' will turn out to be the finest of their creations. If it were not so enjoyable, it would probably turn out to be opera.[9]

Carousel would also remain the pride and joy of its creators. For Rodgers, especially, the second musical with Hammerstein stood as his personal favorite among all his forty musicals. Without any false sense of modesty he conveyed his reasons: "Oscar never wrote more meaningful or more moving lyrics, and to me, my score is more satisfying than any I've ever written. But it's not just the songs; it's the whole play. Beautifully written, tender without being mawkish, it affects me deeply every time I see it performed."[10]

The above critical reception and the judgment of its authors partially explains why *Carousel* and not *Oklahoma!* was selected for examination in the present survey. But given the importance attributed to *Oklahoma!* as the "Eroica" Symphony of the American musical, the question "Why not *Oklahoma!*?" nevertheless lingers and needs to be addressed. The simple answer is that *Oklahoma!*'s incalculable historical importance as the musical that changed all musicals is equalled and arguably surpassed dramatically and musically by *Carousel.* Not content to merely duplicate their earlier success, Rodgers and Hammerstein in their second musical attempted to convey a still richer dramatic situation with characters who were perhaps more complexly realized, through music, than the inhabitants of the Oklahoma Territory.

Further, the artistic ambitions in *Carousel* are matched by a deeper relationship between music and drama. The integrated songs in *Oklahoma!* grow naturally from the action and reflect each character's idiosyncratic nature. But, like *Show Boat* and *Porgy and Bess* before it and *West Side Story* after, the music of *Carousel* develops action and explores nuances of characterization that frequently transcend what the characters themselves understand.[11] The analysis that follows will suggest how Rodgers and Hammerstein's imitation may have surpassed (artistically if not in popularity) not only its model but many other musicals that have had their two or more hours' traffic on the Broadway stage.

The "Bench Scene"

In several respects Julie Jordan, who moves us by her ability to see the good qualities in her abusive husband, Billy Bigelow, and by her uncompromising loyalty to his memory, bears a stronger kinship to Hammerstein's *Show Boat* heroine Magnolia Ravenal than to *Oklahoma*'s Laurey. Even the message of its central song, "What's the Use of Wondrin'," like that of *Carousel* as a whole, echoes Hammerstein's theme in *Show Boat* as embodied in the song "Can't Help Lovin' Dat Man": once fate brings two lovers together "all the rest is talk." Julie shares with Magnolia rather than her Oklahoma cousin a common destiny—to love a man who will eventually generate much unhappiness. Like Magnolia, Julie will also meet the man she will love early in her show.[12]

Also like Magnolia and Ravenal, Julie and Billy—as well as Laurey and Curley in the analogous "People Will Say We're in Love"—describe a hypothetical rather than an acknowledged love, at least at the outset of their duets. The romantic leads in *Show Boat*, however, declare their love in the waltz "You Are Love" at the emotional climax of act I and offer additional explanations for their feelings early in act II when they sing "Why Do I Love You?" (at least before Hal Prince gave this song to Parthy in the 1994 Broadway revival). In contrast, Julie and Billy, more tragically, are unable to express their love directly, not only in their first duet, "If I Loved You," but at any point in the drama while Billy is alive.

In an extremely poignant moment that immediately follows Billy's suicide in act II, scene 2, Julie finally manages to share her feelings with her deceased husband: "One thing I never told you—skeered you'd laugh at me. I'll tell you now—(*Even now she has to make an effort to overcome her shyness in saying it*) I love you. I love you. (*In a whisper*) I love—you. (*Smiles*) I was always ashamed to say it out loud. But now I said it. Didn't I?"[13]

Outside Julie's cottage three scenes later, Billy, whose presence is felt rather than seen or heard, finally sings his love in the following reprise (release and final A section) of "If I Loved You." According to Rodgers, this inspired new idea was, after the removal of Mr. and Mrs. God, the only other major change made during the tryouts. "Longing to tell you, / But afraid and shy, / I let my golden chances pass me by. / Now I've lost you; / Soon I will go in the mist of day, / And you never will know / How I loved you. / How I loved you."[14]

Just as Kern conveys Magnolia's penetration into Ravenal's being by merging her music with his, Rodgers finds subtle musical ways to let audiences know that Julie's love for Billy is similarly more than hypothetical. During the opening exchange between Carrie and Julie, for example, Julie's friend makes it clear that she knows why Julie is behaving so "queerly." First, Carrie describes Julie's recent habit of rising early and sitting silently by the window. Julie lamely denies this circumstantial evidence of love

Example 8.1. The "Mill Theme"

sickness ("I like to watch the river meet the sea"), but Carrie's next and more telling observation of Julie's behavior on the job, the "Mill Theme" (Example 8.1) is incontrovertible: "When we work in the mill, weavin' at the loom, / Y' gaze absent-minded at the roof, / And half the time yer shuttle gets twisted in the threads / Till y'can't tell the warp from the woof!"[15]

Although Julie denies even this evidence with a "'Tain't so!'", her strangeness, even more than Frankie's in *On Your Toes*, cannot be attributed to tonsillitis or to the combination of pickles and pie à la mode: it's got to be love. The sensitive Carrie, now that Julie has a "feller," can inform Julie of her own romantic good fortune in being courted by the young entrepreneur Enoch Snow. This time Julie does not attempt to deny Carrie's presumption. When Julie explains to Billy minutes later how she would behave, hypothetically, "if she loved him," Rodgers and Hammerstein have her describe, again to the "Mill Theme," the behavior that Carrie has in fact already observed. Julie's denial of love may satisfy Billy, but it fails to convince either Carrie or a knowing audience who has more than sufficient textual and musical evidence to catch Julie in her self-deception.

The spark that will eventually set fire to Julie and Billy has already been lit in the pantomimed prelude to act I.[16] During this prelude we see that

Carousel, prelude to act I. Jan Clayton and John Raitt on the carousel (1945). Museum of the City of New York. Gift of Harold Friedlander.

Billy "takes his mind off his work" when he watches Julie and that she gains his attention in part by being the only person who does not "sway unconsciously with the rhythm of his words." The description of the prelude's action points out (parenthetically) that "Billy's attitude to Julie throughout this scene is one of only casual and laconic interest." Although he makes a point of finding the last place on the carousel for Julie, he then "dismisses her from his mind." When he later waves "patronizingly," the omniscient description notes that "it means nothing to him," but that "it means so much to her that she nearly falls!"[17]

"If I Loved You," the climactic moment in the following Bench Scene (act I, scene 1) reinforces these discrepancies in emotional intensity and awareness between the principals. Julie sings as a young woman already in love; Billy, although he admits to having noticed Julie at the carousel "three times before today" (she has actually been there far more often) sings, if not about a hypothetical love, about a love that he does not yet comprehend. Thus Billy can truthfully assert that if he loved Julie he would be "scrawny and pale," and "lovesick like any other guy." So far none of these symptoms has appeared. In fact, Billy does not realize until act II, scene 5, what Mrs. Mullin, the jealous carousel proprietress, has understood only too well as early as the prelude. Already in the pantomimed introduction Mrs. Mullin has demonstrated that she is enamored of Billy.

Also in the prelude Mrs. Mullin has observed his unique attraction to Julie. We learn later that Mrs. Mullin correctly perceived that this peculiar young woman posed a serious threat both to her business (the other young women would patronize the carousel less ardently if Billy were romantically attached) and to any more personal relationship that might develop with her favorite barker.

Although Rodgers and Hammerstein have the two lovestruck mill workers, Carrie and Julie, sing the same tune, "You're a Queer One, Julie Jordan," Rodgers musically differentiates the sharp character distinctions drawn by Hammerstein. He does this by contrasting Carrie's even eighth-note rhythms ("You are quieter and deeper than a well") with Julie's dotted eighths and sixteenths ("There nothin' that I keer t'choose t' tell") (Example 8.2a); revealingly, Billy will whistle Julie's dotted rhythms rather than Carrie's even ones (Example 8.2b). A clue to Rodgers's intention might be found in his autobiography, *Musical Stages*, where he discusses how "It Might As Well Be Spring" from the Rodgers and Hammerstein film musical *State Fair* (Example 8.2c), serves as "a good example of the way a tune can amplify the meaning of its lyric."[18] Rodgers continues: "The first lines are: 'I'm as restless as a willow in a wind storm, / I'm as jumpy as a puppet on a string.' Taking its cue directly from these words, the music itself is appropriately restless and jumpy."[19]

Clearly, Julie's dotted rhythms when she sings "There's nothin' that I keer t' choose t' tell," almost identical in pitch to Carrie's "You are quieter and deeper than a well," successfully contrasts Julie's restlessness with Carrie's stability. When Julie tells Carrie that she likes "to watch the river meet the sea" (Example 8.2d), Rodgers presents a dotted melodic line filled with wide leaps that are unmistakably "jumpy as a puppet on a string." Once Rodgers has established Julie's sharp rhythmic profile in her opening exchange with Carrie, he shows Julie's influence over her friend when Carrie adopts dotted rhythms to conclude their sung exchange ("And as silent as an old Sahaira Spink!"). More significantly, Julie's dotted rhythms return when Billy reprises "You're a queer one" after Carrie's "Mister Snow" and Julie repeats her dotted jumpy melodic line to the words "I reckon that I keer t' choose t' stay."

In the closing moments of the first act Billy's imaginary daughter, appropriately enough, will share Julie's restlessness and her dotted rhythms. By the time Billy sings the "My little girl" portion of his "Soliloquy," dotted rhythms have acquired a strong association with Julie, and by extension her as-yet-unborn daughter, Louise. Thus when Billy imagines his daughter as "half again as bright" and a girl who "gets hungry every night," Rodgers has the future father sing Julie's dotted rhythms. True to

Example 8.2. "Jumpy" rhythms in *Carousel* and *State Fair*
    (a) Julie and Carrie Sequence (*Carousel*)
    (b) Scene Billy and Julie (*Carousel*)
    (c) "It Might As Well Be Spring" (*State Fair*)
    (d) Julie and Carrie Sequence (*Carousel*)

her character, in the second act Julie's "What's the Use of Wondrin' " also makes persistent use of dotted rhythms. On this occasion, however, Rodgers captures Julie's newly acquired inner peace when he replaces with more sedate scales the jumpy melodic leaps that characterized her conversations with Carrie and Billy in act I, scene 1.

Rodgers also gives dramatic meaning to another distinctive rhythm in *Carousel*: the triplet. The main association between triplets and the principal lovers occurs when each attempts to answer what would happen if

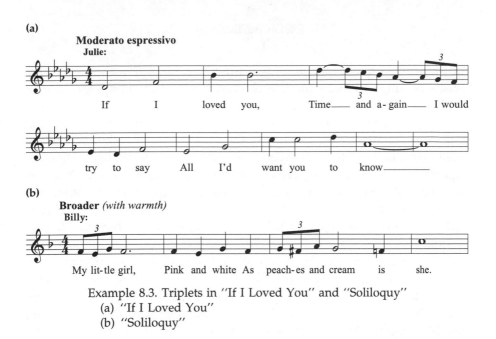

Example 8.3. Triplets in "If I Loved You" and "Soliloquy"
(a) "If I Loved You"
(b) "Soliloquy"

they loved the other in the song "If I loved you." The "hidden" triplets in their response to this subjunctive (Example 8.3a) reinforce the irreality and hesitation that matches the lines "Time and again I would try to say" and "words wouldn't come in an easy way." Not only do these words appear on the weak beats (second and fourth) of their measures—in marked contrast to the triplets in "Many a New Day" from *Oklahoma!* (Example 3.1b)—they are invariably tied to the stronger beats (first and third).

Of course, the imagined musical responses of Julie and Billy nevertheless reveal the truth that Julie is hiding from Billy and Billy from himself: the two misfits in fact are already in love. Although their desire for verbal communication is great ("Time and again I would try to say all I'd want you to know" or "Longing to tell you, but afraid and shy"), the pair must rely on music to express their deepest feelings. Words do not "come in an easy way." Most poignantly, as if to reflect the painful truth of the few words they do sing, within a few months Billy indeed will be leaving Julie "in the mist of day."

Just as Billy adopts Julie's dotted rhythms in his "Soliloquy," he will adopt in this central (and earliest-composed song) the triplets that he shared with Julie in "If I Loved You." In contrast to the hesitant tied triplets of his duet with Julie, however, Billy in his private "Soliloquy" sings "Many a New Day"-type triplets that stand alone when he envisions having a daughter (compare Example 8.3b with Example 3.1b).[20] After

Billy's death, triplets also provide a brief but distinctive contrast in the release of Julie's "What's the Use of Wondrin' " to the ubiquitous dotted rhythms of the main melody.

It makes musical sense, of course, for Rodgers to fill his prelude with waltzes to accompany the swirling of the carousel. But marches and polkas would be equally suitable. Rodgers knew, however, that waltzes, although capable of expressing a variety of meanings and emotions, had been associated with love ever since Viennese imports had dominated Broadway in the decade before World War I.[21] The most familiar waltz musical then and now was and is Lehár's *The Merry Widow*, the work that launched an operetta invasion on Broadway in 1907. But waltzes had also figured prominently in 1920s operetta. Several of these featured lyrics by Hammerstein himself, including "You are Love" in *Show Boat*. In *The King and I*'s "Hello, Young Lovers" and *South Pacific*'s "A Wonderful Guy" Rodgers gives Anna Leonowens and Nellie Forbush waltzes when they sing of love, and Nellie's temporarily rejected suitor Emile De Becque sings a waltz lamenting a lost love in "This Nearly Was Mine."

In *Carousel* waltzes are associated either with the carousel itself, as in the procession of the several sharply defined waltzes that make up the pantomimed prelude, or in the chorus of community solidarity that characterizes the main tune of "A Real Nice Clambake." Rodgers and Hammerstein therefore match the absence of directly expressed love between Billy and Julie by *not* allowing them to sing a waltz. Only when Billy sings his successions of triplets in his "Soliloquy" does Rodgers suggest a waltz (Example 8.4a), a suggestion that is reinforced with a melodic fragment identical to the melody of the final carousel waltz (Example 8.4b). Characteristically, Billy must keep his waltzes, as well as his expression of love, to himself.

Rodgers and Hammerstein and the Integrated Musical

As early as the 1920s Rodgers strove to create musicals in which songs were thoroughly integrated into a dramatic whole. In his finest efforts with Hart, including *On Your Toes* and *Pal Joey*, and in his first collaboration with Hammerstein, *Oklahoma!*, Rodgers often succeeded in making the songs flow naturally from the dialogue and express character. But it was not until *Carousel* that Rodgers created a thoroughly unified musical score which also achieved a truly convincing coordination (i.e., integration) be-

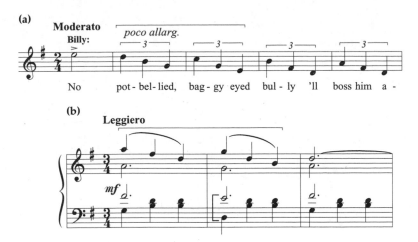

Example 8.4. "Soliloquy" and "The Carousel Waltz" (fifth waltz)
(a) "Soliloquy"
(b) "The Carousel Waltz" (fifth waltz)

tween music and dramatic action. Earlier, in *On Your Toes, Pal Joey,* and *Oklahoma!* Rodgers used the technique of thematic transformation for dramatic purposes, but the resulting musical unity did not always reinforce a drama generated by musical forces.

In *Carousel* many musical details, including the subtle reuse and transformation of rhythms that correspond to musical characters previously noted, frequently support dramatic details and generate dramatic themes. Some of these details serve more a musical rather than a dramatic purpose in their integration of disparate sections. For example, the parallelisms between the musical phrases that Carrie uses to describe Julie ("You are quieter and deeper than a well") and Mr. Snow ("He comes home ev'ry night in his round-bottomed boat") in the opening scene might be considered a musically meaningful but dramatically irrelevant unifying detail.

On the other hand, the primary accompaniment of "If I Loved You," in which three arpeggiated eighth notes follow an eighth rest, foreshadows the less breathless collection of four arpeggiated eighth notes that mark the first half of most measures of "Two Little People" (a melody which also not incidentally exhibits several prominent quarter-note triplets).[22] The musical link between the accompaniments of "If I Loved You" and "Two Little People" (Example 8.5a and b) shows up more clearly in the holograph manuscript on deposit at the Library of Congress, where the two songs share the key of C major.[23] Even those who refuse to see the accompaniment of "If I Loved You" as a foreshadowing of the accompaniment to "Two Little People" might acknowledge its connection with "You'll

(a)

Moderato espressivo

Julie:
p a tempo

If I loved you, Time— and a-gain— I would try to say

p a tempo

(b)

Moderato con moto

Billy *(speaks ad lib)* : Ain't much wind tonight. Hardly any.   Billy *(sings)* :

You

pp

℗ed.   ✱ *simile*

can't hear a sound, not the turn of a leaf, Nor the

Example 8.5. Arpeggiated accompaniments
(a) "If I Loved You"
(b) "Two Little People"

Never Walk Alone" (Example 8.5c). In this song the arpeggiated eighth-note figure is now continuous, not only for an entire measure but for nearly the entire song (Rodgers breaks the pattern in the final four measures). "If I Loved You" and "Two Little People" demonstrate the unity between Billy and Julie; "You'll Never Walk Alone" signifies musically as well as dramatically that neither of these star-crossed lovers will walk alone as long as Julie carries Billy in her memory.[24]

(c)

Moderato

Julie:

When you walk through a storm Keep your

mf legato *p*

chin up high, And don't be a - fraid of the

(Julie breaks off sobbing)

(c) "You'll Never Walk Alone"

Rodgers and Hammerstein also manage to convey a musical correspondence that matches the dramatic contrasts between two pairs of contrasting romantic leads (de rigueur in musicals for the next twenty years): Billy Bigelow and Julie Jordan on one end of the spectrum, Enoch Snow and Carrie Pipperidge on the other. In stark contrast to Billy (a baritone), Enoch (a tenor) is a man who plans ahead, whether he is building a fleet of herring boats or a fleet of children. With his irritating, self-satisfied laugh Enoch is reminiscent of Laurey's silly rival Gertie in *Oklahoma!* and embodies the negative as well as the positive consequences of conventionality and practicality.

When he gives Carrie flowers, Enoch, the builder and planner, gives her a package of geranium seeds to plant rather than the beautiful but ephemeral real thing. And when he tells Julie that he likes to "plant and take keer" of flowers, Julie replies that Billy "likes t' smell 'em," an impractical romantic trait that endeared the carousel barker to her in their first scene together. By the latter part of act II, Enoch has metamorphosed from an overbearing but essentially likable hard-working man with lofty plans for his sardine business and his family to an insufferable, condescending, and genuinely unsympathetic character. Unfortunately, his fleet of children are created in his image. Further, in opposition to Carrie's open appreciation for the less savory entertainments witnessed on their trip to New York, the pure-as-snow Enoch suggests that she discuss the Shakespeare play instead. Enoch's surreptitious visit to the burlesque house (where he runs into Carrie) adds hypocrisy to a growing list of negative characteristics, even if this action allows him a human vice that audiences might relate to.

In an age increasingly and justifiably less tolerant of wife-beating in any form and for any reason, Billy might be considered a much less wonderful guy than he was in 1945, even if Rodgers and Hammerstein's Billy is less abrasive than Molnár's Liliom. Although his predilection for violence is indefensible—to satisfy his fragile ego he hits Julie because she is on the right side of their arguments—it is significant that his blows do not *hurt* either Julie or later Louise. In fact, when he slaps his daughter it feels like a kiss.

Without condoning Billy's actions Hammerstein seems to be telling us that other forms of abuse might take an even greater toll. By the end of act II, Mr. Snow's verbal abuse and condescension have at least partially stifled his formerly spunky bride, whereas Julie Bigelow never fears to stand up to her husband. When Mr. Snow and Carrie glorify their conventional and quotidian life in their duet, "When the Children Are Asleep," it is difficult not to notice that Enoch's love for Carrie is based on her maintaining a conventional image as the "little woman." Billy and Julie may each lose their jobs within minutes of their meeting, certainly a bad omen for their future stability, but their inarticulate and unexpressed love contains a richness lacking in the conventional courtship and marriage of Enoch and Carrie.

On the surface Enoch and Carrie conclude their act I duet "When the Children Are Asleep" in a close harmony that befits their harmonious image of marital bliss. Nevertheless, this happiness depends in large part on Carrie's willingness to overlook the fact that Mr. Snow makes all the plans for the two of them. Snow also adds musical injury to emotional insult by interrupting Carrie's turn at the chorus, ironically with the words "dreams that won't be interrupted." Billy may be a surly bully who occasionally strikes his wife offstage, but he never interrupts Julie when they sing. Unlike Snow, Billy allows his future bride to complete her song.[25] Perhaps more significantly, when he sings by himself, Billy allows Julie's character—musically depicted by dotted rhythms and triplets—to infiltrate his thoughts and become a part of him. The pretentiousness of Mr. Snow and his fleet of nine offspring may cause many in the audience to take pity on Carrie for having so many children, one more than she had agreed to when Snow presented his blueprint in the verse of "When the Children Are Asleep." Given the choice of negatives, it is certainly possible that one might prefer the fuller albeit deeply troubled lives of Billy, Julie, and, after Billy's death, their daughter Louise, to the deceptively happily-ever-after, rudely interrupted American dream of Mr. and Mrs. Snow and their brood.

Since revivals say as much about directors and their audiences as they do about the works being revived, it is not surprising that the *Carousel* of the 1990s emphasizes the show's "dark side," which was very dark indeed for the 1940s. It is also not surprising that the primary means to convey this dark side and thereby establish the work's modernity and contemporary relevance is through staging. In a bold rethinking of the work, director Nicholas Hytner took the liberty of opening his *Carousel* at the Vivian Beaumont Theater in Lincoln Center on March 24, 1994, not with the amusement park but at the Bascombe Cotton Mill. In this new setting (underscored musically by the "moderato" introduction to the sequence of fast waltzes) audiences could for the first time watch the young women mill workers "gaze absentminded at the roof" and perhaps also at the large clock about to strike six o'clock. "As the waltz gains momentum," wrote Howard Kissel of the New York *Daily News,* "carousel horses begin circling the stage, the top of the carousel lowers into place, and the girls find release riding up and down under the admiring gaze of the handsome barker, Billy Bigelow. It takes your breath away."[26]

Reviewers were almost unanimous in praising "the most dazzling staging this musical is ever going to receive."[27] Two critics were even moved to repeat the old joke about leaving a show "humming the scenery." Others singled out the multiracial casting. Enoch and Carrie were a mixed-race couple in both the London and New York revivals; in a stylistic as well as a racial crossover, the role of Nettie was sung by the African American Shirley Verrett, a major opera star in the late 1960s and early 1970s.

Hytner's staging also intensified Billy's more sinister side. For example, no longer does Billy slap his daughter's hand when he returns to earth, he slaps her face. Thankfully, most critics, while rightly revulsed by a romanticized wife-beating hero who gains salvation (even though he does not get to sing his powerful musical plea, "The Highest Judge of All," in the second act), refused to confuse the message with the messenger. In the words of medieval scholar John Boswell, "To cite obscenity is not to be obscene."[28] In any event, Edwin Wilson concludes in the *Wall Street Journal* that "in the end, it is not Julie who can redeem Billy, but the musical alchemy of Richard Rodgers's score."[29]

In *Musical Stages* Rodgers speaks of a rhyming and rhythmic dialogue used in Mamoulian's films *Love Me Tonight* and *The Phantom President* in 1932 and the next year in *Hallelujah, I'm a Bum*. Rodgers, who preferred the term "musical dialogue" to describe the use of rhymed conversation with musical accompaniment, wrote that its purpose was "to affect a smoother transition to actual song" and to become "an authentic part of the action."[30] Twelve years later Rodgers transferred the device of "musical dialogue" to the stage to begin the Julie and Carrie sequence. In this new context the two friends begin each phrase with the rhythmic signature of Julie's name before it develops into a melodic theme, thus adding one additional layer to the dialogue-(spoken) verse-(musical speech) chorus (the main tune) progression from speech to song familiar from most theater songs of the 1920s and 1930s. By the time Billy arrives her motive underscores their conversation before they even begin to sing. In the course of the scene the rhythm of Julie's name becomes the foundation for a series of questions (three or four syllables each) that Billy asks her about her love life: "Where'd you walk?", "In the woods?", "On the beach?", and "Did you love him?"

Also in his autobiography Rodgers reveals his sensitivity to word painting. In the discussion of "It Might as Well Be Spring" noted earlier and illustrated in Example 8.2c, Rodgers concludes that, "since the song is sung by a young girl who can't quite understand why she feels the way she does, I deliberately ended the phrase ['I'm as jumpy as a puppet on a string"] on the uncertain sound of the F natural (on the word 'string') rather than on the more positive F sharp."[31]

Rodgers left it up to others to demonstrate how the musical details in *Carousel* support the lyrics and the libretto and create musical unity, and how such details create subtle correspondences between music, character, and drama. Nevertheless, his description of "musical dialogue" in *Love Me Tonight* and his analysis of his text-setting objectives in "It Might As Well Be Spring" reveal that Rodgers was fully conscious of how nuances can help a theater composer to achieve an artistic goal. In the light of his autobiography a discussion of how dotted rhythms, triplets, and arpeggiated accompanimental figures reveal greater dramatic truths appears to be grounded in reality.[32] Rodgers is the first to admit that a number of his musicals created with Hart do not even aspire to, much less achieve, the goals he first enunciated in the late 1920s with *Dearest Enemy* and *Peggy-Ann*. His primary desire throughout his extraordinary career, however, was to create a musical theater in which the songs belong to their characters and determine their place within the dramatic action, and a musical theater in which dialogue, song, and dance are unified and integrated.

These ideals did not suddenly appear with *Oklahoma!* and *Carousel*. After developing his vision and evolving technique as a dramatic composer with Hart, Rodgers found a collaborator who fully embraced the integrated ideal. Together Rodgers and Hammerstein were a winning combination that forged a living and posthumous legacy of popular commercial works and a critical stature unmatched by any other body of work in the history of the American musical.

After the death of his second collaborator, Rodgers, who had by necessity ghost-written lyrics for Hart, decided to write his own lyrics for an entire show. The result, the biracial romance *No Strings* (1962) with Diahann Carroll and Richard Kiley in the principal roles, turned out to be Rodgers's final success (580 performances), albeit a modest one by the standards of *Oklahoma!*, *Carousel*, *South Pacific*, *The King and I*, and *The Sound of Music*. His next show, a collaboration with Hammerstein's lyricist protégé Stephen Sondheim, produced the commercially and artistically disappointing *Do I Hear A Waltz?* in 1965 (220 performances).

Rodgers remained active to the end. In the 1970s he managed to mount three final shows on Broadway: *Two by Two* (1970), with lyrics by Martin Charnin and starring Danny Kaye as Noah (343 performances); *Rex* (1976), with lyrics by Sheldon Harnick and starring Nicol Williamson as Henry VIII (49 performances); and *I Remember Mama* (1979), with lyrics by Charnin and Raymond Jessel and starring Liv Ullmann and George Hearn (108 performances).[33] Less than four months after his fortieth and final musical closed, Rodgers died on December 30, 1979.

Because they float at the center of the mainstream, the convention-shattering features of Rodgers and Hammerstein's adaptations of literary sources with their carefully constructed subplots (*Oklahoma!*, *Carousel*, *South Pacific*, and *The King and I*) seem less apparent than their more experimental and less successful works with original books. Among the latter are *Allegro* (1947), with its Greek chorus and abstract sets, and the backstager *Me and Juliet* (1953), in which audiences could see on-and off stage events simultaneously.[34] Just as it is often difficult for present-day listeners to appreciate the iconoclasm of the less noisy modernists (for example, the revolutionary Debussy), it requires a special effort in the 1990s to understand just how unconventional and innovative Rodgers and Hammerstein musicals really were. Here is a glimpse of what was innovative (if not unprecedentedly new) in three of their shows, a body of work which helped to establish future conventions:

OKLAHOMA! (1943) eschews the usual opening chorus (or singer accompanied by an orchestra) and instead opens with a woman churning butter alone on stage and the hero singing "Oh, What a Beautiful Morning" (without even a piano to back him up) off stage. It also presents perhaps the first genuine, albeit pathetic, villain who dies in a struggle with a hero, and its full-length dream ballet moves several steps beyond *On Your Toes* in its integration of dance into the plot.

SOUTH PACIFIC (1949) offers the first major middle-aged romantic hero played by the first major defector from the Metropolitan Opera (Ezio Pinza). The younger romantic secondary male character dies, and the central romantic leads sing "Twin Soliloquies" to themselves "silently." The drama is conveyed through rapid and seamless scene shifts, and, most provocatively, the musical seriously explores the causes of racial prejudice in the song "Carefully Taught."

THE KING AND I (1951), based at least loosely on a true story and real people, is the first major musical in which the characters (if not the cast) are mostly Asian, a foreign language is conveyed by instruments rather than by speech, the principals never kiss and touch only once, when they are dancing, and the central male character dies at the end (and, unlike Billy Bigelow, stays dead).

Carousel (1945) was no less daring. It revolves around an unsympathetic character (unless he is singing) who hits his wife, sings a "Soliloquy" for nearly eight minutes before attempting a robbery, dies by suicide, and hits his daughter when he returns to earth (from purgatory) fifteen years later. Musicals of various types after *Oklahoma!* and *Carousel* would continue to be remembered by their songs, of course, but from now on their revivability would usually depend on integrated books. Although by no means did they invent the integrated Broadway musical (often referred to as the "sung play"), more than anyone else Rodgers and Hammerstein can be praised (or blamed) for demonstrating in their optimistic, homespun, and sentimental shows the commercial potential of this artistic ideal.

CHAPTER NINE

KISS ME, KATE

The Taming of Cole Porter

Two Tough Acts to Follow

Act I: Rodgers and Hammerstein

In the years following the success of *Anything Goes* in 1934 only Rodgers and Hart surpassed Porter in producing musical hits on Broadway. The Gershwins were unable to complete any more Broadway shows between *Porgy and Bess* in 1935 and George's death two years later, and Kern managed only one more new Broadway show, *Very Warm for May* (1939) in a final decade spent mainly in films. As Gershwin and Kern ebbed, Porter flowed for the remaining years of the 1930s with one successful (albeit now nearly forgotten) musical after another filled with unforgettable songs: "Begin the Beguine" and "Just One of Those Things" from *Jubilee* (1935); "It's De-Lovely" from *Red, Hot and Blue!* (1936); "Most Gentlemen Don't Like Love" and "My Heart Belongs to Daddy" from *Leave It to Me* (1938); "Well, Did You Evah!" and "Friendship" from *DuBarry Was a Lady* (1939).

In the mid-1940s, however, two successive failures, *Seven Lively Arts* (1944) and *Around the World in Eighty Days* (1946), prompted Porter and his backers to question the commercial vitality of the pre–Rodgers and Hammerstein–type musical. Earlier in 1944 Porter had produced his sixth successive Broadway hit, *Mexican Hayride*, a musical that would have been perhaps more at home in the previous decade. But the tides had turned, and the examples of Rodgers and Hammerstein's second musical, *Carousel* (1945), Berlin's *Annie Get Your Gun* (1946), and Porter's own *Kiss Me, Kate* (1948) bear testimony to the power that *Oklahoma!* now exerted. Even these two old dog songwriters now felt the urgency of learning the new trick of writing integrated musicals.

Before the historic collaboration of Rodgers and Hammerstein was launched in 1943, both Berlin and Porter had achieved universal recognition as songwriters. Even today, as many of their shows drift into oblivion, these illustrious composer-lyricists unquestionably remain the most widely known and revered of their generation. After four decades of composing revues Berlin was persuaded in 1946 to compose a full-fledged book show that paralleled the new objectives established in *Oklahoma!* and *Carousel*. Two years later Porter attempted his first integrated musical. The results, Berlin's *Annie Get Your Gun* and Porter's *Kiss Me, Kate*, remain the only musicals with unaltered books by these great songwriters that occupy a firm position in the Broadway repertory. Abandoned by his supporters and forced to sell his new work in degrading auditions, Porter celebrated his resurrection by creating one of the most highly regarded and popular musicals of all time.[1]

Shortly before his death in 1964 Porter publicly acknowledged the difficulty posed by the intimidating example of Rodgers and Hammerstein: "The librettos are much better, and the scores are much closer to the librettos than they used to be. Those two [Rodgers and Hammerstein] made it much harder for everybody else."[2] The specter of "those two" would haunt Porter for his remaining creative years. To add injury to insult they even managed to partially overshadow *Kiss Me, Kate* by depriving Porter of Mary Martin (the rising star of Porter's *Leave It To Me* ten years earlier and, more recently, the star of *One Touch of Venus*), who had auditioned for the lead but instead accepted the role of Nellie Forbush in *South Pacific*, which opened three months after Porter's classic.[3]

In a *New York Times* interview that he gave during the composition of *Can-Can* in 1953, Porter reveals that Rodgers and Hammerstein remained under his skin: "They [the songs] didn't come out of the book so much as now. Really, until Rodgers and Hammerstein, if you needed to change a scene, a girl could come out in front of the curtain and sing or dance or anything. But with *Can-Can*, I have worked since last June."[4]

Additional evidence that Porter suffered anxiety from the influence of *Oklahoma!* and *Carousel* appears amidst the extensive unpublished manuscript material for *Kiss Me, Kate* housed in the Music Division of the Library of Congress in a packet labelled "Unfinished Lyrics."[5] Although some of these lyrics are in fact unfinished and others only barely begun, including one tantalizing title, "To Be or Not to Be," most lyrics in this packet are alternate versions of known *Kiss Me, Kate* songs. One such draft belongs with the song "Bianca," a late addition to the show. In the staged (and published) verse of this song Bill Calhoun the Baltimorean and, as Lucentio, the Shakespearean suitor of Lois Lane/Bianca, sings the following lyric: "While rehearsing with Bianca, / (She's the darling I adore), / Offstage I found / She's been around / But I love her more and more; / So I've written her a love song / Though I'm just an amateur. / I'll sing it through / For all of you / To see if it's worthy of her. / Are yuh list'nin'?"

In the "Unfinished Lyrics" the private Porter can be observed working with an alternate idea: Bill Calhoun himself as an aspiring Broadway lyricist. Porter's surrogate lyricist, however, is not merely a suitor for the fair Lois/Bianca in this version. Porter has given his still-anonymous poet additional importance as "the dog who writes incog" for the great Berlin. In this alternative scenario "Bianca" is one of the songs Bill has composed on behalf of Mr. Berlin.

Despite this subterfuge, Porter's draft labelled "Bianca 2nd Verse" on the second page arguably reveals more about Porter than it does about Bill Calhoun: "Ev'ry night I write for Irving [Berlin] / 'Til I nearly bust my bean / 'Cause Irving fears / Two rival peers / Known as Rodgers and Hammerstein. / I shall now repeat my ballad / Then I'll rush to Irving quick / And if he thinks / My ballad stinks / He'll sell it to Oscar [Hammerstein II] and Dick [Richard Rodgers] / Are you list'nin? (repeat refrain)."[6]

All available witnesses corroborate the story that it was not an easy task for Bella Spewack, herself only a recent convert to the somewhat heretical notion of setting Shakespeare's *Taming of the Shrew* musically, to convince her former collaborator on *Leave It to Me* that a Shakespeare musical would not be "too esoteric, too high-brow for the commercial stage."[7] In contrast to his *modus operandi* in *Anything Goes* and his other pre–Rodgers and Hammerstein musicals in which an often tenuous relationship existed between the songs and the librettos, the extant manuscript evidence reveals that from the time he began work on *Kiss Me, Kate* Porter was greatly concerned with creating a musical that integrated music with the book.

Also in contrast to *Anything Goes*, whose second act was barely a gleam in the eyes of Howard Lindsay and Russel Crouse at the time of their first rehearsal and with deletions and substitutions continuing into the Broadway run, *Kiss Me, Kate* could boast a completed book by the end of May 1948 before auditions would begin the following month.[8] Although much would be altered during the months of auditions and rehearsals (between

May and November), by the Philadelphia tryouts on December 2, *Kiss Me, Kate* as we know it today was nearly set. As Spewack reports:

> I knew Cole had come through brilliantly. I knew what I had done and what Sam [colibrettist and spouse Samuel Spewack] had done was right. We had nothing to change. I knew it so I didn't have to be superstitious. In the history of American musicals this is the only one where they didn't have to touch a scene or a song. In rehearsals, changes were made. I wrote three versions, but I knew eventually we'd go back to the first one—and we did. There were disagreements over "Why Can't You Behave?" and over "Bianca," but the disagreements were all ironed out before we left town.[9]

After four weeks to "rehearse and rehearse," *Kiss Me, Kate* opened at the New Century Theatre on December 30, 1948, with nearly unequivocal endorsements from New York City reviewers.

When discussing the dramatic merits of *Anything Goes* (chapter 3) it was proposed that since Sir Evelyn Oakleigh does not sing, he does not deserve a woman like Reno Sweeney (Ethel Merman) who sings such hits as "I Get a Kick out of You," "You're the Top," "Anything Goes," and "Blow, Gabriel, Blow." At the very least, Sir Evelyn's nonsinging status created a dramatic problem that future revivals tried to assuage. In *Kiss Me, Kate* the musically silent character does not get the girl. Fred Graham's rival, the powerful Washington diplomat Harrison Howell who, like Sir Evelyn, remains songless, gets caught napping and ends up barefoot on Fred's wedding day. Petruchio/Fred, who sings more songs than Kate/Lilli Vanessi, not only deserves to get a tamed Katherine at the end of the *Shrew* play, he also gets a reformed spouse in real life.

It was also previously noted that Porter attempted to convey character musically in *Anything Goes*. Not only does Porter characterize his star Reno (Merman) with catchy syncopations and uncomplicated harmonies, he also conveys her spunky disregard for convention by having her sing triplets that clash with her duple meter, first and most consistently in "I Get a Kick Out of You" and later in "Blow, Gabriel, Blow." Once he makes this association, Porter then demonstrates how Hope Harcourt becomes more like the star when she adopts Reno's rhythmic signature in her own "Gypsy in Me."

Not surprisingly, in the wake of Rodgers and Hammerstein's *Oklahoma!* and *Carousel* Porter made a still greater effort in *Kiss Me, Kate* to channel music's power to establish character. He does this most noticeably by dis-

(a)

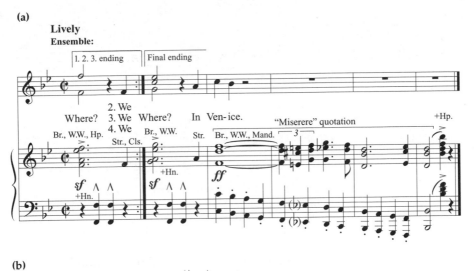

(b)

Example 9.1. "We Open in Venice" (closing orchestral tag)
and "Miserere" from Verdi's *Il Trovatore* (act 4)
(a) "We Open in Venice" (closing orchestral tag)
(b) "Miserere" from Verdi's *Il Trovatore* (act 4)

tinguishing the *Shrew* players from the Baltimore players. The former are given musical characteristics loosely associated with music of the Italian Renaissance. Bianca and her suitors are given an a cappella pseudo-madrigal in "Tom, Dick or Harry," the bluesy "Why Can't You Behave?" is transformed into a Renaissance dance (the pavane), and several of the *Shrew* songs display the long-short-short figure (♩ ♪ ♪) characteristic of the sixteenth-century Italian canzona.[10]

Porter's Italian evocations are not confined to the Renaissance. One nineteenth-century appropriation occurs in the orchestral tag to "We Open in Venice" (Example 9.1), where he quotes the opening of the "Miserere" from Verdi's *Il Trovatore* (act 4). Perhaps Porter intended a musical pun (the "misery" of an endless road tour and its associations with Verdi's fourteenth-century Spanish troubadour, Manrico) or perhaps he simply wanted to link a classic playwright with a classic Italian opera composer.[11] Porter adopts a more contemporary Italian flavor in "I Sing of Love" and "Where Is the Life That Late I Led?" and a more generalized Latin beguine character in "Were Thine That Special Face," again to distinguish the *Shrew*

183

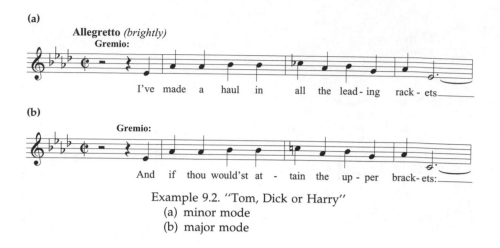

(a)

Allegretto *(brightly)*
Gremio:

I've made a haul in all the lead-ing rack-ets____

(b)

Gremio:

And if thou would'st at-tain the up-per brack-ets:____

Example 9.2. "Tom, Dick or Harry"
(a) minor mode
(b) major mode

numbers from the more recognizably American Baltimore numbers. Representative American vernacular characteristics include the show biz quality of "Another Op'nin', Another Show," the jazzy "Too Darn Hot," the satire of Bowery waltzes in "Brush Up Your Shakespeare," and the thirty-two-bar song form of a popularly styled ballad, "So In Love."

In his analysis of *Kiss Me, Kate* Joseph P. Swain notes Porter's technique of moving from the major mode to the minor mode or vice versa to distinguish the Padua songs from their Baltimore counterparts.[12] Indeed, with one exception ("I'm Ashamed That Women Are So Simple") the texted songs sung in Padua juxtapose major and minor in dramatically purposeful ways. In "Tom, Dick or Harry" Porter distinguishes each suitor's past accomplishments from their rosy description of Bianca's future if she were to marry one of them by the simple juxtaposition of minor and major mode (Example 9.2). Similarly, Petruchio at the conclusion of "Were Thine That Special Face" moves from the minor to the major mode to capture the optimism of "then you'll be mine, all mine" that concludes the song. In Petruchio's "Where Is the Life That Late I Led?" Porter contrasts the life of the carefree bachelor in the main chorus (major mode) with a mixture of minor and major modes that conveys his bittersweet nostalgia for the women he must now relinquish as a married man. Thus in the slower second portion of the song Momo and Rebecca stir memories in the minor mode and Alice and Lucretia in the major, while memories of Carolina and Fedora contain elements of the two.

Porter lessens the dramatic contrast between Padua and Baltimore, however, when he contrasts major and minor modes in the latter songs as well. In fact, it might be said that this device (widely and effectively used by Schubert) not only serves as Porter's way of demonstrating parallels between the *Shrew* numbers and the Baltimore numbers. In the end it functions primarily as a unifying musical device that shapes a musically

(a)

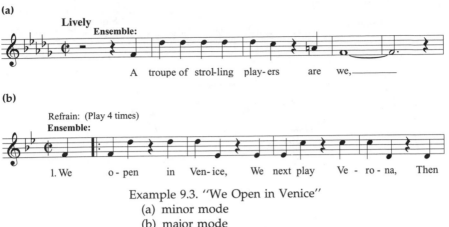

A troupe of strol-ling play-ers are we,——

(b)

Refrain: (Play 4 times)

Ensemble:

1. We o - pen in Ven- ice, We next play Ve - ro - na, Then

Example 9.3. "We Open in Venice"
(a) minor mode
(b) major mode

integrated score. The Paduan "We Open in Venice," for example, was certainly intended to parallel "Another Op'nin', Another Show" in Baltimore. In the Padua excerpts (Example 9.3) the players sing in the minor mode when describing themselves and in the major mode when they relate their circular itinerary. Conversely, "Another Op'nin' " opens in the major mode (E♭ major) and moves to G minor in the release (the B section) to convey the anxiety of the four weeks that lead to this opening ("Four weeks you rehearse and rehearse / Three weeks and it couldn't be worse"). Even a song as far removed from the drama as "Too Darn Hot" demonstrates a prominent move from minor (the "too darn hot" portion) to major (the "Kinsey report" portion).

Although the degree to which *Kiss Me, Kate* employs the major-minor juxtapositions is perhaps unprecedented in a Porter show, the roots of this idea can be found in Porter's pre–Rodgers and Hammerstein musical *Anything Goes*. We have already observed that the verse of the title song in his earlier musical (Example 3.2, p. 58) clearly contrasts the past (minor mode) with the present (major mode). In another example the sea chantey "There'll Always Be a Lady Fair" juxtaposes the modes to distinguish the hardships of a sailor's life in the verse (minor mode) from the fair ladies waiting on land (major mode). The intimidation by Rodgers and Hammerstein may have inspired Porter to explore additional and increasingly subtle ways to capture nuances in his characters and in their texts, but he did not suddenly discover textual realism or the dramatic potential of music after attending a production of *Oklahoma!*

Porter's efforts to demonstrate even more thematic unity for the purposes of dramatic credibility, however, does distinguish *Kiss Me, Kate* from Porter's pre–Rodgers and Hammerstein shows, including *Anything Goes*. It also arguably surpasses *Oklahoma!*, if not *Carousel*, in this respect. Some musical material such as the reappearance of the repeated fourth that

Example 9.4. "Why Can't You Behave?" transformed in the Pavane
(a) "Why Can't You Behave?"
(b) Pavane

marks the opening of the main tune of "Another Op'nin'" as the vamp in the following "Why Can't You Behave?" (Example 9.4a, mm. 5–6) helps to create a smooth musical linkage between the first two numbers without conveying a comparable dramatic meaning.[13] But most connections do serve dramatic purposes. Bill and Lois, for example, share improper be-

Kiss Me, Kate, act I, finale. Patricia Morison and Alfred Drake in the center (1948). Photograph: Eileen Darby. Museum of the City of New York. Gift of Harold Friedlander.

havior. Bill is a shiftless yet likeably dishonest gambler who signs an I.O.U. with Fred Graham's name; Lois is a shameless and fickle (and equally endearing) flirt who, in the role of Bianca, will mate with any Tom, Dick, or Harry and, as herself, date any man who asks her out for "something wet." It therefore makes sense that the verse of "Why Can't You Behave?" returns in "Always True To You in My Fashion." The transformation of "Why Can't You Behave?" (Example 9.4a) from the first act, when it is sung by Lois to Bill, into an orchestral pavane in act II (Example 9.4b) reinforces the commonality between Lois and Bill. At the same time it further identifies Lois and Bianca as the same character and clarifies the usurpation of the "Behave" theme in "Fashion."[14]

Another musical figure that links several songs first occurs in "I Sing of Love."[15] Not only does this song display a $\frac{6}{8}$ meter that evokes popular Italian tarantellas such as "Funiculi, Funiculà," it also presents a melodic and harmonic shift from C major to F minor (on the words "We sing of [C major] love" [F minor]) that will resurface in two songs from act II. With only insignificant alterations this exotic, pseudo-Renaissance juxtaposition of major and minor harmonic shifts returns in the verse of "Where Is the Life That Late I Led?" (also in $\frac{6}{8}$ meter). Here Petruchio describes the awakening of his desire and occasionally love for the opposite sex many

Example 9.5. Transformation of act I finale into act II finale
(a) March
(b) Waltz

years before ("Since I reached the charming age of [C major] puberty" [F minor]). In "Bianca" the progression appears in reverse, F minor to C major, when Bill as Poet expresses his love for Bianca in the verse of the song that bears her name ("While rehearsing with Bianca, / She's the darling I a- [F minor] dore" [C major]). In each case love underlies the harmony and links the musical material.

Also dramatically motivated are the thematic recurrences between the finales of act I and act II. At the end of act I Petruchio, accompanied by "all singing principals (except Hattie) and chorus," serenades his shrewish new bride, who shrieks "No! Go! Nay! Away!" before breaking character and shouting "Fred!" The verbal battle between Kate/Lilli and Petruchio/Fred that ensues is supported appropriately enough by a military march with dotted rhythms of a martial nature (Example 9.5a) before Kate sings a "quasi cadenza angrily" and the chorus concludes the act with a syncopated variant of "Another Op'nin'."

Porter signifies his intent to parallel this ending when, at the outset of the second-act finale, he offers an unmistakable melodic transformation in triple meter of Petruchio's act I duple-metered serenade. Instead of insults Kate/Lilli now interjects various terms of endearment in Italian. Petruchio's words, like Petruchio himself, remain unchanged from one act finale to the other, while Kate's dramatically contrasting response reinforces the significant change she had revealed moments before in her final song, "I Am Ashamed That Women Are So Simple."[16] Finally, the second melody of the act I finale (the march, Example 9.5a) returns transformed into a waltz, the dance of love (Example 9.5b). The transformation from a militaristic march to a romantic waltz succeeds simply but effectively in establishing musical equivalences for the dramatic changes that have taken place in the dynamics between Kate/Petruchio and Lilli/Fred.[17]

Act II: Shakespeare

After Rodgers and Hammerstein, the second tough act for Porter and his collaborators Bella and Sam Spewack to follow was "the bard of Stratford-on-Avon" himself, Shakespeare. As Bella Spewack writes in the introduction to the published libretto, "We hated to cut Shakespeare."[18] But when she received an unexpected and unwelcome new song from Porter, "Brush Up Your Shakespeare," both Spewacks acknowledged that they would have to adjust to the unpleasant idea that Shakespeare would be playing second fiddle to the demands of Broadway. Bella tells it this way in her introduction to the published libretto:

> We realized that according to the classic standards of Broadway it ["Brush Up"] was a "boff" number—a show-stopper, if you please. Perhaps not a New Art Form, but definitely a must for the male patron. So instead of any throat-cutting [Porter had written that "Belle will probably cut her throat when she gets this"], we dropped the final scene (all Shakespeare) and a beautiful dance for which the stairs had been built. We had exactly three minutes left in which to finish our show.[19]

According to Porter biographer George Eells, Porter's decision to add another song, "Bianca," for Harold Lang (Lucentio/Bill Calhoun) precipitated a strained correspondence between the Spewacks and the composer-lyricist.[20] Since Lang, then known primarily as a dancer, was not yet the star he would become four years later as the lead in Rodgers and Hart's *Pal Joey* revival, he was not given a solo when Porter and the Spewacks were planning their scenario. Patricia Morison, the original Kate/Lilli, recalls, however, that Lang "had it in his contract that he had to have a song in the second act" and "pulled a snit" until Porter decided "to write something that's going to be so bad they won't keep it in."[21] Silly and parodistic of the old Gillette razor jingle ("Look Sharp") as it is, "Bianca" added a great song and dance number to the show. In any event, without "Bianca," Bill Calhoun would only sing "Gee, I need you kid" near the end of "Why Can't You Behave?" and a verse of "Tom, Dick or Harry," and would remain virtually indistinguishable in musical importance from Bianca's other suitors.[22]

Bella Spewack fought and won a battle with the producers to retain "Were Thine That Special Face" and persuaded Porter himself to leave "Tom, Dick or Harry" in the show. Nevertheless, the libretto that the Spewacks originally sent to Porter contained far more of Shakespeare's *The Taming of the Shrew* than audiences would eventually see in *Kiss Me, Kate*. Most notably, the May libretto included Shakespeare's lines in act IV, scene 5, when Kate capitulates to Petruchio and agrees that the sun is the moon or vice versa according to his whim, and Kate's complete final speech in act V, scene 2.[23] Porter would collaborate with the bard on an abbreviated version of this latter speech to produce "I Am Ashamed That Women Are So Simple." Gone entirely from the May libretto is the Induction (often cut from Shakespeare productions as well). Also removed from Shakespeare is the character of the Widow, the woman who eventually marries Bianca's suitor, Hortensio. The Widow's departure led to the demise of her counterpart in the Baltimore company as well, Angela Temple.[24]

The major dramatic departure from Shakespeare's play, however, occurred after the May libretto draft. In May, when Lilli learns from Fred that she is no longer under the custody of the two gunmen and therefore free to abandon the *Shrew* play, she informs her ex-husband (Fred), without hesitation, that she will *not* desert:

FRED: Well, Miss Vanessi, you may leave now.
LILLI: I am not leaving!
FRED: Sleeping Beauty [Harrison] waits in your dressing room.
LILLI: Let him NAP!
FRED: Don't tell me the bloom is off (HE *sneezes*)—the rose?[25]

A few lines later Fred and Lilli reprise "We Shall Never Be Younger," a song that would soon be discarded. The two had sung a portion of this song together to conclude their duet in act I, scene 1, "It Was Great Fun the First Time," and Lilli sang the whole song alone in her dressing room two scenes later. Although the two stormy actors are not yet fully reconciled, an audience could reasonably infer from the reprise of their shared song that Fred and Lilli are on the verge of starting a happier third act together.

By December the Spewacks made a significant alteration in the dialogue to set up Fred's reprise of the newly added "So In Love" to replace "We Shall Never Be Younger" in act I:

FRED: You're free to go. You don't have to finish the show. . . . Aren't you taking Sleeping Beauty with you?

LILLI: Let him sleep.

FRED: Don't tell me the bloom is off—the rose? . . . Lilli, you can't walk out on me now.

LILLI: You walked out on me once.

FRED: But I came back.

(LILLI *hesitates*)

DOORMAN: (*From his cubbyhole*) Your cab's waiting, Miss Vanessi!

(LILLI *leaves*.)

After Lilli has walked out on both Fred and her sleeping (and, more significantly, nonsinging) fiancé, Harrison Howell, Fred, "alone, reprises 'So In Love'." In the May libretto Lilli decides to stay in the show, the Spewacks were able to maintain their fidelity to Shakespeare, and Petruchio wins his wager in the last scene. In the revised libretto, however, Lilli leaves. What can Petruchio say if his offstage counterpart knows that he will lose the wager? Petruchio replies to Kate's father: "I know she will not come. / The fouler fortune mine and there an end." In contrast to both Shakespeare and the May libretto Lilli's reappearance in December as a tamed Kate who will follow Petruchio's bidding comes as much of a surprise to Petruchio as it does to the other Shrew players. To clarify the impact of her return the stage directions tell us that Fred becomes "really moved, forgetting Shakespeare" and then utters a heartfelt "Darling" before returning to his Paduan character.

The circumstances that led to the addition of "So In Love" sometime between June and November remain a mystery. Neither Spewack nor any Porter biographer has anything to say about its appearance during auditions, and Morison recalled in 1990 only that " 'So In Love' was finished after I came into the show."[26] It is known, however, that "So In Love"—along with "Bianca" and "I Hate Men," the last songs to be added to the show—replaced "We Shall Never Be Younger," a song which all involved in the production agreed was a beautiful song but "too sad for a musical."[27] Like the song it superseded, the setting of "So In Love" is Lilli's dressing room in act I (after Fred's exit), and Lilli sings the song to herself unheard by her former husband. But the new song, unlike "We Shall Never Be Younger," is unknown to Fred as well as unheard. The once-married couple (the show opens on the first anniversary of their divorce) had sung a few lines of the sad earlier song as a mood-changing coda to their earlier duet, "It Was Great Fun" (also dropped after May). In the May libretto Fred does not hear Lilli sing her confession and remains oblivious of her hope that "my darling might even need me," but at least he knows the song that he has shared with his former romantic partner.[28]

In chapter 5 it was noted that in the original 1936 production of *On Your Toes*, Sergei Alexandrovitch and Peggy Porterfield sing the reprise of "There's a Small Hotel." Audiences were thus asked to accept a convention in which characters somehow know songs introduced privately by others, in this case Phil Dolan II and Frankie Frayne. In 1983 Sergei and Peggy sing a reprise of "Quiet Night" instead, a song that they have actually heard. Nevertheless, modern audiences still are expected to accept the idea that the entire cast can manage to learn "There's a Small Hotel" well enough to sing it the finale.

In *Kiss Me, Kate* Porter continues the tradition of characters singing songs they're not really supposed to know. Certainly the most significant example of this practice can be observed when Porter does not allow Lilli and Fred the opportunity to sing even a portion of "So In Love" together (as he did with the discarded "We Shall Never Be Younger"). Thus Porter removes the means by which his characters can establish associations and connections with a song. When Fred reprises "So In Love" in act II, audiences might justifiably ask how he came to know it. Was he eavesdropping on Lilli when she sang it in act I?

In contrast to Rodgers and Hammerstein's powerful reuse of "If I Loved You" in *Carousel*, the reprise of "So in Love" puts the song above the drama, so that it becomes, as Joseph Kerman might say, a reprise "for the audience, not the play."[29] The dramatic impact of Billy Bigelow's reprise of "If I Loved You" in *Carousel* stems at least in part from the audience's memory of a shared interchange between Billy and Julie Jordan. The song belongs to them, they know it, and the audience knows that they know it. In this isolated but telling dramatic detail in *Kiss Me, Kate* Porter returns to the era he himself had done so much to establish: once again a great song (and its reprise) takes precedence over the dramatic integrity of a book. Despite this criticism, it might also be said that Fred's reprise of "So In Love" demonstrates a credible bond and a communication with Lilli and serves a theatrical if not a literal truth.[30]

Kiss Me, Kate *and the Broadway Heroine*

In the revised ending Lilli (and, by extension, her *Shrew* counterpart, Katherine) willingly joins Fred and Petruchio in the final scene. She is free to leave both Fred (the frame of the musical) and his show (the musical within a musical). Although this ending took Porter and the Spewacks further away from their Shakespearean source, it also brought them perhaps a little closer to a modern view of the world. Lilli and Katherine return to their men as free agents, not as tamed falcons.

Nevertheless, Katherine's final Shakespearean speech, only "slightly altered by Cole Porter with apologies," creates a serious challenge to a feminist interpretation.[31] Katherine freely comes to Petruchio, but she then sings a speech almost invariably construed as degrading to women. Is *Kiss Me, Kate* therefore a sexist musical that should be banned, or at least restaged?

Long before feminism became part of the mainstream of intellectual thought and social action in the late 1960s and early 1970s, critics have been put off by Shakespeare's ending. For example, in 1897 George Bernard Shaw came to the following conclusion:

> The last scene is altogether disgusting to modern sensibility. No man with any decency of feeling can sit it out in the company of woman without feeling extremely ashamed of the lord-of-creation moral implied in the wager and the speech put into the woman's own mouth. Therefore the play, though still worthy of a complete and efficient representation, would need, even at that, some apology.[32]

Nearly seventy years later Robert B. Heilman wrote that "the whole wager scene falls essentially within the realm of farce," and assumes that Shakespeare accepted the idea that women are subservient to men even if modern theater-goers do not: "The easiest way to deal with it is to say that we no longer believe in it, just as we no longer believe in the divine right of kings that is an important dramatic element in many Shakespeare plays."[33] In the 1990s David Thornburn, during a panel discussion on "The

Remaking of the Canon," asked a conference speaker rhetorical questions that implicitly accused the Bard of harboring antediluvian views:

> Isn't it true that Shakespeare actually believes that women are subservient to men in *The Taming of The Shrew?* Now it is incumbent on people who offer the reified conception of the canon, as you, Professor [Gertrude] Himmelfarb, do, to explain how you can justify or defend texts whose obvious, explicit themes are so deeply offensive to what you as a thinker and as a moral person would regard as acceptable.[34]

Shakespeare has few modern defenders from the ranks of those who accept Katherine's speech at face value. But one unexpected apology might be noted—Germaine Greer's pioneering book on feminism, *The Female Eunuch:*

> The submission of a woman like Kate is genuine and exciting because she has something to lay down, her virgin pride and individuality: Bianca is the soul of duplicity, married without earnestness or good will. Kate's speech at the close of the play is the greatest defense of Christian monogamy ever written. It rests upon the role of a husband as protector and friend, and it is valid because Kate has a man who is capable of being both.[35]

Other critics offer interpretations that bring the apparently sexist playwright closer to modern feminism. As Martha Andresen-Thom writes: "Extraordinary individuals learn to play with wit and wisdom the roles of sex and class that at once bind them and bond them. Subordination of woman to man, in this view, is an opportunity for a brilliant and worthy woman to transform limitation into an incentive for play."[36] The "play" interpretation is supported in Shakespeare's text by the zeal with which Katherine takes the ball from Petruchio's court and pretends that Lucentio's elderly father Vincentio is a "young budding virgin, fair, and fresh, and sweet" (act IV, scene 5). At that moment Kate does not seem to be motivated by exhaustion and a realization that she cannot win, but by her newfound inspiration that play-acting can be fun rather than demeaning.[37]

Evolving sensitivities towards white and African-American racial relations have been explored briefly when discussing the history of *Show Boat* and *Porgy and Bess.* Two Rodgers and Hammerstein musicals introduced during the period of the present survey deal with relations between whites and Asians, *South Pacific* and *The King and I* (albeit on white terms), and the reworked books of *Anything Goes* revivals discussed in chapter 3 demonstrate a progressively less stereotypical approach towards Chinese Americans.

A discussion of sexism in *Kiss Me, Kate* opens the door to a broader discussion of how women featured in the present survey have fared. *Show Boat*'s Julie LaVerne and Magnolia Ravenal, *Carousel*'s Julie Jordan, and *West Side Story*'s Maria lose their men at some point in the musicals. *Porgy*'s Bess not only becomes a drug addict and a prostitute, she never gets to sing an aria by herself, even if she does have her own theme. The rich and powerful female executive in *Lady in the Dark*, Liza Elliott, must relinquish her post as head of a prestigious fashion magazine if she is to restore her lost glamor, femininity, and happiness, and complete her song, "My Ship." Liza Elliott has merely exchanged her unpleasant dreams for a living nightmare of submission to a sexist man, Charley Johnson, the advertising manager of Liza's magazine and her prosecuting attorney in the Circus Dream.

Compared to what happens to most nineteenth-century tragic European opera heroines, however, Broadway's women manage pretty well.[38] In contrast to her operatic sisters none of these heroines dies, although Julie LaVerne is reduced to alcoholism and almost certainly a premature death (offstage) in response to the loss of her man. Before *Miss Saigon* in the 1990s many Cinderellas but no Madame Butterflys inhabited Broadway musicals. Even Maria, unlike her Shakespearean counterpart, survives and is thereby presumably able to effect societal changes that will lead to a less violent world. After losing her man, Magnolia gains national fame as an actress, while Julie Jordan demonstrates enormous strength of character before and after Billy's death. Anna holds her own with the King of Siam and her actions lead to democratic reforms.

Among our musical heroines Adelaide (*Guys and Dolls*) and Eliza Doolittle (*My Fair Lady*) perhaps do the least to placate modern sentiments. Adelaide's saga of her fourteen-year engagement to Nathan Detroit ("Adelaide's Lament") and her advice to Sarah Brown to "marry the man today and change his ways tomorrow" might disappoint some. But audiences by and large have successfully distanced themselves from this cartoonish Runyonesque world and have been attending the Broadway and countless other revivals of this show in record numbers in the 1990s. And although we shall see in chapter 11 that it is admittedly a tough call who Eliza should end up with (in the epilogue to Shaw's *Pygmalion* she marries Freddy), her decision to return to the barely repentant misogynist Higgins in *My Fair Lady* might cause many to cringe in their seats. Porter and Spewack's Katherine may, like Shakespeare, put her hand at Petruchio's feet, but at least she is not asked to fetch his slippers.

Porter never surpassed the brilliance or the popularity of *Kiss Me, Kate*. Two years later he completed *Out of This World*, a show that, before it was dropped during tryouts, included the now-perennial favorite "From This Moment On" (later interpolated by Ann Miller in the 1953 film version of *Kiss Me, Kate*). After *Out of This World* Porter created two successful Broadway shows, *Can-Can* (1953) and *Silk Stockings* (1955), and he would complete his illustrious career with two film musicals, *High Society* in 1956 (which included "True Love," introduced by Bing Crosby and Grace Kelly in her final Hollywood role) and *Les Girls* in 1957. The next year Porter's last eight songs appeared in the television production *Aladdin* (scripted by *One Touch of Venus* librettist S. J. Perelman). His creative spirit broken after the deaths of his mother and his wife and the amputation of a leg (he had already suffered more than thirty operations since 1937 when a horse he was riding crushed both his legs), Porter spent the remaining years before his own death in 1964 in self-imposed isolation.

CHAPTER TEN

GUYS AND DOLLS
AND *THE MOST*
HAPPY FELLA

The Greater Loesser

For once nostalgia rings true. As Broadway and London revivals so frequently remind us, the 1950s were truly a glorious decade for the American musical. Following in their own luminous footsteps of the 1940s (*Oklahoma!, Carousel,* and *South Pacific*), Rodgers and Hammerstein continued to present their felicitous dramatic integrations of happy talk and happy tunes when they opened the new decade with their unprecedented fourth major hit musical, *The King and I* (1951), and closed it with a final hit collaboration, *The Sound of Music* (1959). In 1956 Lerner and Loewe presented *My Fair Lady,* a universally praised musical that eventually eclipsed *Oklahoma!* as the longest-running Broadway musical. One year later the Laurents-Sondheim-Bernstein trilogy brought to Broadway *West Side Story.* But in a decade that introduced many critical and popular successes, musicals like *Wonderful Town* (lyrics by Betty Comden and Adolph Green, music by Bernstein), *Kismet* (music and lyrics by Robert Wright and George Forrest with more than a little help from the nineteenth-century Russian composer Alexander Borodin), *Pajama Game* and *Damn Yankees* (music and lyrics by Richard Adler and Jerry Ross), *The Music Man* (music, lyrics, and book by Meredith Willson), *Fiorello!* (lyrics by Sheldon Harnick, music by Jerry Bock), and *Gypsy* (book by Laurents, lyrics by Sondheim, and music by Jule Styne), two 1950s classics by Frank Loesser, *Guys and Dolls* (1950) and *The Most Happy Fella* (1956), remain the toast of Broadway in the 1990s.

Even those who love to hate Broadway musicals make an exception for *Guys and Dolls* and consider this show one of the most entertaining and perfect ever. Although Gershwin's *Porgy and Bess* and perhaps Bernstein's *Candide* would later overshadow Loesser's next show in popularity or critical approbation, *The Most Happy Fella* continues to boast the longest initial run, 678 performances, of any Broadway work prior to the 1980s that might claim an operatic rubric. As a tribute to its anticipated appeal as well as its abundance of music, its cast album was the first to be recorded in a nearly complete state, on three long-playing records.

In contrast to the instant and sustained appeal and unwavering stature of *Guys and Dolls,* however, the popularity and stature of *The Most Happy Fella* has evolved more slowly and less completely. In one prominent sign of its growing popularity and acclaim in the United States, the 1990–1991 Broadway season marked the appearance (with generally positive critical press) of two new productions, one with the New York City Opera and one on Broadway.[1] Despite lingering controversy regarding its ultimate worth, *The Most Happy Fella* is clearly gaining in both popular acclaim and critical stature and is even receiving some attention in American scholarly journals.[2]

Like fellow composer-lyricist Stephen Sondheim two decades later, Loesser (1910–1969) gained initial distinction as a lyricist.[3] Unlike Sondheim, who had been writing music to complement his lyrics since his teens, only after a decade of professional lyric-writing could Loesser be persuaded to compose his own music professionally. He scored a bull's eye on his very first try, "Praise the Lord and Pass the Ammunition" (1942), one of the most popular songs of World War II. Earlier he wrote his first published song lyrics, "In Love with the Memory of You" (1931), to music composed by William Schuman, the distinguished classical composer and future president of the Juilliard School and the Lincoln Center for the Performing Arts. In an unusual coincidence Loesser made his Broadway debut (as a lyricist) for the same ill-fated revue, *The Illustrator's Show* (1936), that marked the equally inauspicious Broadway debut of Frederick Loewe, twenty years before *My Fair Lady* and *The Most Happy Fella.*

Loesser began a decade of film work more successfully the next year with his song, "The Moon of Manakoora." Film collaborations with major Hollywood songwriters would soon produce lyrics to the Hoagy Carmichael chestnuts, "Heart and Soul" and "Two Sleepy People" (both in 1938), and song hits with Burton Lane and Jule Styne who, like Loesser, would soon be creating hit musicals on Broadway beginning in the

Frank Loesser. © Al Hirschfeld. Drawing reproduced by special arrangement with Hirschfeld's exclusive representative, The Margo Feiden Galleries
Ltd. New York.

late 1940s.[4] After "Praise the Lord," Loesser, a composer-lyricist in the
tradition of Berlin and Porter, would go on to compose other World War
II popular classics, including "What Do You Do in the Infantry" (in
"regulation Army tempo") and the poignant "Rodger Young," and later
a string of successful film songs that culminated in the Academy
Award–winning "Baby, It's Cold Outside," featured in *Neptune's Daughter* (1947).

Clearly, by the late 1940s Loesser was ready for Broadway. Drawing on
the star status of Ray Bolger and the experience of George Abbott (the
writer-director of Rodgers and Hart's *On Your Toes,* also starring Bolger,
and the director of *Pal Joey*), fledgling producers Ernest Martin and Cy
Feuer were prepared to take a calculated risk on Loesser's music and lyrics
with Abbott's adaptation of Brandon Thomas's still-popular comedy, *Charley's Aunt* (1892). Unlike other musical settings of popular plays—including
Loesser's *The Most Happy Fella*, adapted from Sidney Howard's Pulitzer
Prize–winning but now mostly forgotten play, *They Knew What They
Wanted* (1924)—*Where's Charley?* (1948) never managed to surpass its progenitor. Nevertheless, this extraordinary Broadway debut became the first
of Loesser's four major hit musicals during a thirteen-year Broadway career (1948–1961). In the end the composer-lyricist and one-time librettist

would earn three New York Drama Critics Circle Awards (*Guys and Dolls,
The Most Happy Fella,* and *How to Succeed in Business Without Really Trying*),
two Tony Awards (*Guys and Dolls* and *How to Succeed*) and one Pulitzer
Prize for drama (*How to Succeed*).[5]

Where's Charley? was a well-crafted, old-fashioned Broadway show with
sparkling Loesser lyrics and melodies. In order to show off a wider spectrum of Bolger's talents, the character of Lord Fancourt Babberley (who
impersonated Charley's aunt in Thomas's play) was excised, and much of
the comedy revolved around Charley's switching between two roles, Charley and his aunt, throughout the musical. Working against type, the opening duet between the central character, Charley Wykeham (Bolger) and
Amy Spettigue, "Make a Miracle," was a comic number rather than a love
song. More typically, Charley's formal expression of love, "Once in Love
With Amy," was a show-stopper directed not to Amy but to the audience,
which Bolger asked to join in his public tribute.

Two years before Rodgers and Hammerstein offered a serious subplot
with Lt. Joseph Cable and Liat in *South Pacific,* the lyrical principals of
Where's Charley? were the secondary characters, Jack Chesney and Kitty
Verdun, who sing the show's central love song, "My Darling, My Darling."
Despite this less conventional touch, at the end of the farce Charley (Bolger), without any dramatic justification other than his stature, was allowed
to reprise and usurp his friend's "My Darling, My Darling." Such conces-
sions were a small price to pay for a hit, even as late as 1948.

Guys and Dolls: *Life in Runyonland*

Although *Where's Charley?* was one of the most popular Broadway book
musicals up to its time, the show hardly prepared critics and audiences
for Loesser's next show two years later.[6] Reviewers from opening night to
the present day have given *Guys and Dolls* pride of place among musical
comedies. Following excerpts from nine raves, review collector Steven Sus-
kind remarks that "*Guys and Dolls* received what might be the most unan-
imously ecstatic set of reviews in Broadway history."[7] In contrast to most
musicals where some perceived flaw was manifest from the beginning
(e.g., libretto weaknesses in *Show Boat,* the disconcerting recitative style in
Porgy and Bess, the unpalatable main character in *Pal Joey*), *Guys and Dolls*
was problem free. John McClain's epiphany in the *New York Journal–
American* that this classic was "the best and most exciting thing of its kind
since *Pal Joey*" is representative.[8] Indeed, after *Pal Joey* in 1940 Loesser's
Guys and Dolls exactly ten years later is arguably the only musical comedy

(as opposed to operetta) prior to the 1950s to achieve a sustained place in the Broadway repertory with its original book intact.

Although virtually no manuscript material is extant for *Guys and Dolls*, there is general agreement about the main outlines of its unusual genesis as told by its chief librettist Abe Burrows thirty years later.[9] After securing the rights to adapt Damon Runyon's short story "The Idyll of Miss Sarah Brown" (and portions and characters drawn from several others, especially "Pick the Winner"), *Where's Charley?* producers Feuer and Martin commissioned Hollywood script writer Jo Swerling to write the book, and Loesser wrote as many as fourteen songs to match. Feuer and Martin then managed to persuade the legendary George S. Kaufman to direct. In a scenario reminiscent of *Anything Goes* and *One Touch of Venus*, where new librettists were brought in to rewrite a book, all of the above-mentioned *Guys and Dolls* collaborators concurred that Swerling's draft of the first act failed to match their vision of Runyonesque comedy. Burrows was then asked to come up with a new book to support Loesser's songs. As Burrows explains:

> Loesser's songs were the guideposts for the libretto. It's a rare show that is done this way, but all fourteen of Frank's songs were great, and the libretto had to be written so that the story would lead into each of them. Later on, the critics spoke of the show as "integrated." The word "integration" usually means that the composer has written songs that follow the story line gracefully. Well, we did it in reverse. Most of the scenes I wrote blended into songs that were already written.[10]

The legal aspects of Swerling's contractual obligations has generated some confusion regarding the authorship of *Guys and Dolls*. The hoopla generated by the Tony Award–winning 1992 Broadway revival of *Guys and Dolls* reopened this debate and other wounds.[11] When novelist William Kennedy credited Burrows as "the main writer" in a feature article in the *New York Times*, he inspired a sincere but unconvincing letter from Swerling's son who tried to explain why the "myth" about Burrows's sole authorship "just ain't so."[12]

Although the full extent of Kaufman's contribution remains undocumented, his crucial role in shaping *Guys and Dolls* cannot be overlooked or underestimated. Just as his earlier partner in riotous comedy, Moss Hart, would work intensively with Lerner on the *My Fair Lady* libretto several years later and may be responsible for a considerable portion of the second act, the uncredited Kaufman had a major hand in the creation as well as the direction of the universally admired *Guys and Dolls* libretto. Even more than most comic writers Kaufman was fanatically serious about the quality and quantity of his jokes, and under his guidance Burrows removed jokes that were either too easy or repeated. In addition, Burrows followed Kaufman's advice to take the necessary time to "take a deep breath and set up your story."[13] Burrows recalls that even six weeks after the show opened to unequivocally positive notices Kaufman "pointed out six spots in the show that weren't funny enough."[14]

In contrast to *Pal Joey*, with its prominent melodic use of a leading tone that obsessively ascends one step higher to the tonic (e.g., B to C in "Bewitched") as a unifying device, *Guys and Dolls* achieves its musical power and unity from the rhythms associated with specific characters. The "guys" and "dolls," even when singing their so-called "fugues," display a conspicuous amount of syncopation and the half-note and quarter-note triplet rhythms working against the metrical grain and illustrated also by Reno Sweeney in *Anything Goes* (Example 3.1, p. 56), Venus and Whitelaw Savory in *One Touch of Venus* (Example 7.2, p. 152), and Tony in *West Side Story* (on the words "I just met a girl named Maria" in Example 12.2b, p. 251).

The clearest and most consistently drawn rhythmic identity occurs in Adelaide's music. Even when "reading" her treatise on psychosomatic illness in "Adelaide's Lament," this convincing comic heroine adopts the quarter-note triplets at the end of the verses ("Affecting the upper respiratory tract" and "Involving the eye, the ear, and the nose, and throat"). By the time she translates the symptoms into her own words and her own song, the more common, rhythmically conventional eighth-note triplets are almost unceasing.[15]

In order for Loesser to convince audiences that Sarah Brown and Sky Masterson are a good match, he needed to make Sarah become more of a "doll" like Adelaide; conversely, he needed to portray Sky as more gentlemanly than his crapshooting colleagues. He accomplishes the first part of this task by transforming Sarah's rhythmic nature, giving the normally straitlaced and rhythmically even "mission doll" quarter-note triplets in "I'll Know" and syncopations in "If I Were a Bell."[16]

Sarah must also cast aside her biases against the petty vice of gambling and learn that a man does not have to be a "breakfast eating Brooks Brothers type" to be worthy of her love. In her first meeting with Sky she discovers a person who surpasses her considerable knowledge of the Bible

(Sky emphatically points out that the Salvation Army sign, "No peace unto the wicked" is incorrectly attributed to Proverbs [23:9] instead of to Isaiah [57:21]). Soon Sky will reveal himself to be morally sound, genuinely sensitive, and capable of practicing what the Bible preaches. Not only does he refuse to take advantage of her physically in act I, he will even lie to protect her reputation in act II.

After audiences learn from his dialogue with Sarah that Sky's interest in and knowledge of the Bible sets him apart from the other "guys," his music tells us that he is capable of singing a different tune. His very first notes in "I'll Know" may depart from Sarah's lyricism, metrical regularity, and firm tonal harmonic underpinning, but after Sarah finishes her chorus, audiences will discover that Sky shares her chorus and verse as well as chapter and verse. Following Sarah's more "doll-like" acknowledgment of her changing feelings toward Sky in "If I Were a Bell," Sky is almost ready to initiate their second duet, "I've Never Been in Love Before." But first he needs to tell Sarah in "My Time of Day" (predawn) that she is the first person with whom he wants to share these private hours. The metrical irregularity, radical melodic shifts, and above all the harmonic ambiguity which mark his world before he met Sarah capture the essence of Sky's dramatic as well as musical personality.

The twenty measures of this private confession (the opening and closing measures are shown in Example 10.1) is stylistically far removed from any other music in *Guys and Dolls*. After the first chord sets up F major, Sky's restless nature will not allow him to find solace in a tonal center. By the end of his first phrase on the words "dark time," he is already singing a descending diminished fifth or tritone (D to A♭) which clashes with the dominant seventh harmony on C (C-E-G-B♭) that pulls to F major. Only when Sarah becomes the first person to learn Sky's real name, the biblical Obediah, will the orchestra—as the surrogate for Sky's feelings—return the music to F major. But now F is reinterpreted as a new dominant harmony instead of a tonic and serves to prepare a new tonal center, B♭ major, and herald a new song, "I've Never Been in Love Before."

Even when Sky sings his own music rather than Sarah's, he shows his closeness to her by avoiding much of the metrical, melodic, and harmonic conventionality and syncopated fun of the other "guys." In his song for the souls of his gambling colleagues in act II, "Luck Be a Lady," syncopation is reserved for the end of phrases, and his music, compared to the music of the tinhorns Rusty, Benny, and Nicely-Nicely, is contrastingly square. The marriage of Sarah and Sky at the end of the show is thus made

(a)

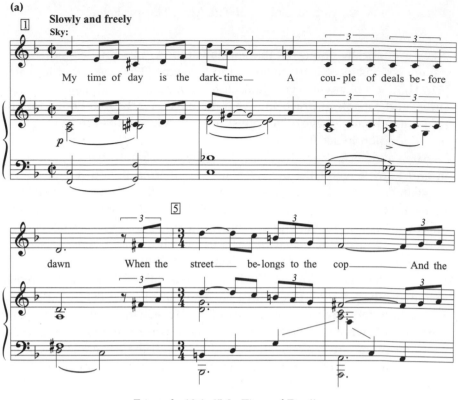

Example 10.1. "My Time of Day"
(a) opening

possible (and believable) by the compromising evolution of their musical personalities. Just as Sarah becomes more like Sky and his world, Sky moves closer to Sarah's original musical identity.

Before their individuality is established Sky and Sarah are introduced more generically in their respective worlds in one of the most perfect Broadway expositions, an opening scene that includes "Runyonland," "Fugue for Tinhorns," "Follow the Fold," and "The Oldest Established." The ancestor of "Runyonland" was Rodgers and Hammerstein's *Carousel*, which opened with an inspired pantomimed prologue (in contrast to *Guys and Dolls*, which contained an independent overture) that set up an ambiance and allowed audiences to place Julie Jordan's subsequent denial of her feelings in perspective. As we have seen in chapter 8, the *Carousel* pantomime focused on establishing the relationships between the central characters, Julie and Billy Bigelow, and the jealousy their romance will arouse in the carousel proprietress, Mrs. Mullin.

The musical component of the pantomimed "Runyonland" is a medley

(b) closing

of the title song, "Luck Be a Lady," and " Fugue for Tinhorns" in various degrees of completeness and altered tempos. Inspired by Kaufman's admonition to "take a deep breath and set up your story," the opening devotes itself entirely through narrative ballet and mime to capturing the colorful world of Runyon's stories. The scene description in the libretto and the published vocal score details an intricate comic interaction of con artists, pickpockets, a man who pretends to be a blind merchant, naive tourists, bobby soxers, and a prizefighter who is inadvertently knocked down by the unimposing Benny Southstreet, the only named character to appear in this elaborate sequence. At the end of "Runyonland" we meet two other tinhorns, Rusty Charlie and Nicely-Nicely Johnson, the latter of whom will emerge, after Sky, as the leading male singer of the evening. In a transition that literally does not skip a beat, the trio introduce the first song of the show, "Fugue for Tinhorns."

Tinhorns are gamblers who pretend to be wealthier than they are. Burrows's and Loesser's tinhorns match this description with their pretense to a verbal and musical sophistication they do not possess. The verbal pretensions are evident throughout their dialogue, the musical ones are most

Guys and Dolls, Crap game in the sewer in act II. Robert Alda throwing the dice, Stubby Kaye kneeling to the left, Sam Levene to the right (1950). Museum of the City of New York.

clearly revealed in their opening song. Even the word "fugue" is pretentious, referring to a musical form associated with J. S. Bach in which similar melodic lines, introduced at the outset in staggered entrances of a principal melody (known as the fugue subject), are then heard simultaneously. True to type, what Rusty, Nicely-Nicely, and Benny sing is in fact not a fugue at all but a form that pretends to be a fugue, the lowlier round, known to all from "Three Blind Mice" and "Row, Row, Row Your Boat."

In the first of many departures from a fugue, the participants in a round begin by singing the identical (rather than a similar) musical line, albeit also in staggered entrances. The whole tune of Loesser's "fugue" consists of twelve measures of melody, with the final eight measures containing additional repetition. Despite their relative simplicity, rounds are tricky to create, since they must be composed vertically (the harmonic dimension) as well as horizontally (the melodic dimension). In "Fugue for Tinhorns" Loesser therefore has constructed his twelve-bar tune so that it can be subdivided into three four-bar phrases (one complete phrase is shown in Example 10.2); each phrase is constructed so that it can be sung simultaneously with any of the others. In order to squeeze a horizontal twelve-bar melody comfortably into a vertical four-bar straitjacket, the harmony must not change. The entire musical content therefore consists of repetitions of harmonically identical four-bar phrases, alternated among the three participants, each of whom argues in favor of their chosen horse, Paul Revere, Valentine, and Epitaph.

Even though Loesser does not produce a real fugue, he does offer a degree of real counterpoint that is unusual in a Broadway musical, especially a musical comedy. In fact, the only substantial use of counterpoint among earlier musicals surveyed in this volume occurs, not surprisingly, in *Porgy and Bess* (a technique also demonstrated in earlier Gershwin shows not discussed here, perhaps most notably in "Mine" from *Let 'Em Eat Cake*). Prominent but relatively isolated additional examples can be found in Blitzstein's *The Cradle Will Rock* (scene 10) and Bernstein's *Candide* ("The Venice Gavotte") and *West Side Story* (the "Tonight" quintet). After 1970 this device would become more prominent in Sondheim (e.g., the combination of "Now," "Later," and "Soon" in *A Little Night Music*). Even straightforward harmonization between two principals is exceptional in the musicals of Kern, Rodgers, Porter, and Loewe. Interestingly, the only Broadway composer to rival Loesser at the counterpoint game was Berlin, another lyricist-composer with less formal musical training than the other composers discussed in the present survey, Loesser included. In songs that ranged throughout his career, most famously "Play a Simple Melody" from *Watch Your Step* (1914), "You're Just in Love" from *Call Me Madam* (1950), and his final hurrah as a composer, "An Old-Fashioned Wedding" from the 1966 revival of *Annie Get Your Gun,* Berlin created extraordinary pairs of melodies that could be sung simultaneously.

Loesser's predilection for counterpoint can be observed as early as "Baby, It's Cold Outside." In *Where's Charley?* Loesser used counterpoint prominently in "Make a Miracle," and he would continue to present simultaneous melodies in ingenious new ways in more than a few songs in *Hans Christian Andersen, The Most Happy Fella,* and *How to Succeed.* Since it is usually hard to sing simultaneous melodic lines (or even harmony), actor-oriented musicals, especially those inhabiting musical comedy stages, use counterpoint relatively rarely, at least before Sondheim.

After the unison cadence that concludes "Fugue for Tinhorns," the orchestra is instructed to hold their final D♭ until the "Mission Band starts playing on Stage" one half-step lower on C major. In this next number, "Follow the Fold" (Example 10.3), the Save-a-Soul Mission Band and a quartet of missionaries led by Sarah provide a rhythmic and textural contrast to "Fugue for Tinhorns" that could hardly be more extreme. The

Example 10.2. "Fugue for Tinhorns" (one complete statement of three-part round)

tinhorns inhabit a world of syncopation, counterpoint, and lots of sharps and flats, while one jarring half-step lower the missionaries occupy a rhythmically unsyncopated, homophonic, C-majorish musical realm. The only conspicuous common denominator between these contrasting musical worlds is a shared underlying harmonic simplicity. In the fugue a measure

March tempo

The Citizens gather

Sarah: Fol-low the Fold and stray no more, stray no more, stray no more.

Agatha: Fol-low the Fold and stray no more, stray no more, stray no more.

Arvide: Fol-low the Fold and stray no more, stray no more, stray no more.

Corporal: Fol-low the Fold and stray no more, stray no more, stray no more.

(Orch.)

Example 10.3. "Follow the Fold" (opening)

of dominant harmony alternates with a measure of tonic harmony; the mission march also employs these two basic harmonies exclusively.[17] "Follow the Fold" also illustrates a rare "appropriate" use of a hymnlike style in Loesser's work. The concluding a cappella harmonies of the next song, "The Oldest Established," is far more typical of Loesser's predilection to translate the religious fervor of secular emotions with mock musical religiosity: gambling as a religious experience. In *Where's Charley?* Loesser had inserted a cadence (marked *"religioso"*) in several places to mark the miracle in "Make a Miracle." Later, in *How to Succeed*, J. Pierrepont Finch's faith in himself would inspire Loesser to musical religiosity and prayer at the punchline of "I Believe in You." In all stages of his career Loesser would revisit the secular religiosity of his first hit, "Praise the Lord and Pass the Ammunition."

In addition to the touches inspired by Kaufman, the casting of the show also led to considerable changes of emphasis. This was not new. Earlier it was noted that the will of a star, Ethel Merman, lead to the rejection of one song and a reprise of another in *Anything Goes*. Within the next five years, the songs of *My Fair Lady* would be composed *after* the non-singing Rex Harrison had been cast, and written accordingly. Strangely enough, with *Guys and Dolls* it was not discovered until casting Sam Levene as Nathan Detroit that the creative team had cast a star who would make Harrison sound like Ezio Pinza.[18]

Guys and Dolls follows the Rodgers and Hammerstein integrated model with the careful insertion of a comic subplot, in Loesser's show the fourteen-year engagement of Nathan and Adelaide and the debilitating psychosomatic symptoms brought about by this delay (described in "Adelaide's Lament"). Indeed, Nathan's role is truly a large one. Even much of "The Oldest Established [Permanent Floating Crap Game in New York]" is sung in his praises: "Why it's good old reliable Nathan, / Nathan, Nathan, Nathan Detroit.—/ If you're looking for action he'll furnish the spot.—/ Even when the heat is on it's never too hot, / Not for good old reliable Nathan."

But all that the musically unreliable Nathan is given to sing in act I is speech-like chant in the verse to this song, rhythmically set almost exclusively to quarter-note triplets and virtually monotonal (all but three pitches are Cs): "And they've now got a lock on the door—/ Of the gym at Public School Eighty-four" and a couple of lines later, "And things being how they are, / The back of the Police Station is out." Later in act I Levene as Nathan was not only deprived of leading the title song, he was specifically instructed not to sing along.

In act II Nathan is finally—in number twenty-seven out of the thirty-two numbered selections in the vocal score—allowed to "sing" his waltz of love, "Sue me, Sue me, / What can you do me? / I love you." But before Kaufman & Co. discovered that Levene had meant what he said when he told them he could not sing, Nathan had also been designated to lead the song "Sit Down, You're Rockin' the Boat" at the prayer meeting.[19] Although this challenging song came to be indelibly associated with Stubby Kaye on stage and film in the expanded role of Nicely-Nicely Johnson, the reassignment of Nathan's music on the surface lessens his dramatic stature as well as his credibility as a romantic lead.

In any event, Nathan's romance with Adelaide certainly has a less comic side. How often must a major character undergo the indignity of a fourteen-year engagement (and fourteen years of a psychosomatic cold) and engage in a perpetual series of lies to her mother about her alleged husband's promotions and their inexorably growing family? To add insult to illness, on the one occasion she is aroused to anger, Adelaide remains the last to know that Nathan is for once telling the truth. Her fiancé is indeed on his way to attend a prayer meeting, Sky having successfully gambled to obtain his presence. After he reluctantly agrees to accept the inevitable deprivation of his freedom and mobility and marry Adelaide (now of course cured), Nathan expresses his feelings about this turn of events by appropriating his fiancée's former symptoms. Thus, after Adelaide describes the new Nathan "sitting there, beside me, every single night," he discharges an "enormous sneeze."

Adelaide and even Sarah are not above deceit and pretense. In the song that precedes Nathan's sneeze, "Marry the Man Today," the conniving pair reveal themselves as "dolls" who desire to change (in midstream) their chosen horses. A conspicuous and dramatically suitable resemblance to the pseudo-fugue tinhorn trio that opened the show is readily evident in the simple and static counterpoint of the following lines: "Marry the man today / Rather than sigh and sorrow, / Marry the man today / And change his ways tomorrow."

As we have observed, future book doctors of *Anything Goes* rightly questioned the 1934 premise in which a nonsinging Sir Evelyn Oakleigh gets the girl. Their solution in the 1962 and 1987 revivals was to interpolate songs from other Porter shows. But Nathan's inability to sing as extensively as other secondary leads in other musicals (especially in the first act) should not be cause for alarm. Fortunately, by the end of the evening and faced with the imminent loss of Adelaide (no longer willing to be taken for granted), Nathan can and does finally demonstrate his love for his long-suffering fiancée when he breaks into song ("Sue Me"). In the Runyon story, "Pick the Winner," Cutie Singleton, a nom de plume for Adelaide, leaves Nathan for Professor Woodhead after a ten-year engagement and lives happily ever after with her new beau in their country house. By the simple but powerful act of singing, Nathan convinces us that Loesser's Adelaide need not have followed Cutie's example.

The Most Happy Fella: *"A Musical With a Lot of Music"*

During the long *Guys and Dolls* run Samuel Goldwyn persuaded Loesser to compose the music for *Hans Christian Andersen* (1952), a Goldwyn-produced film starring Danny Kaye. In addition to its tuneful score, the movie is notable for its screenplay by Kaufman's former collaborator, Moss Hart. After his second consecutive Broadway success, Loesser was otherwise free to grow at his own pace and in his own way and to pursue his ambitious new Broadway show.

By the end of 1952 Loesser was simultaneously drafting sketches for his libretto, lyrics, and music in the first of sixteen sketchbooks of *The Most Happy Fella*. For more than the next three years he would work single-mindedly on his "musical with a lot of music" (calling it an opera would be the kiss of death).[20] His only other major creative project during these years was the composition of three new songs for the film version of *Guys and Dolls* (1955), also produced by Goldwyn.[21]

In contrast to the sparse documentary evidence for the compositional process of *Guys and Dolls*, *The Most Happy Fella* offers a cornucopia of dated and labelled material, all housed in the Music Division of the New York Public Library. These manuscripts shed some light on the embryonic mysteries and gestation of nearly every portion of the finished musical.[22] The sketchbooks tell us that Loesser had begun most of the major songs (i.e., the twenty-one musical numbers in the published vocal score and libretto (indicated by small capital letters in Appendix O), before September 1954. Most of these numbers would require additional work during the next fifteen months. In a striking demonstration of creative economy, Loesser managed to use nearly every scrap of sketchbook material (more than one hundred entries) usually in the final score, but at least in the unexpurgated version that opened in Boston.

From the sketchbooks we learn that Loesser's initial vision of the work allowed for even less spoken dialogue than the approximately fifteen minutes that would remain in the finished work. By far the most dramatically important material replaced by dialogue is the dramatic and climactic confrontation near the beginning of act III, when Rosabella tells Tony, the man she had come to love in act II, that she was willing to be seduced by his hired hand, Joe, at the end of act I. Relatively late in the compositional process (September and December 1955), in sketches marked "Angry Tony," Loesser revealed that the dialogue of this scene initially contained powerful and dissonant underscoring.[23]

The sketches also show that Loesser's titles for musical numbers, both large and small, were the generating force for the music to follow and that these titles generated rhythms (often indicated by X's) before the rhythms led to melodies. Those who admire Loesser's impeccable declamation of titles with strong profiles such as "The New Ashmolean Marching Society and Students' Conservatory Band" in *Where's Charley?* and "The Oldest Established" (the abbreviated title of "The Oldest Established Permanent Floating Crap Game in New York") in *Guys And Dolls* can observe first hand how the melody of a song such as "Happy to Make Your Acquaintance" evolved from sketches which share the rhythmic rather than the melodic profiles of the finished product.

The Most Happy Fella, act I, scene 2. Robert Weede (1956). Photograph: Vandamm. Museum of the City of New York. Gift of Harold Friedlander.

Without the sketchbooks the process by which Loesser expanded arioso
passages into full-scale arias would go undetected, nor would we understand how simple sequential musical patterns served Loesser as essential
starting points of so many of the songs in this show. The sketchbooks
reveal the creative effort that went into such nuances as the important
elongated emphasis on the word "full" in Tony and Rosabella's big love
duet, "My Heart Is So Full of You," after numerous compositional digres-
sions over a ten-month period. The sketchbooks also help to identify one
of the striking unifying musical features in *The Most Happy Fella*: Loesser's
ubiquitous use of the melodic sequence, i.e., short melodic phrases of symmetrical lengths repeated a step higher or lower. In *Guys and Dolls* melodic
sequences are displayed prominently only in the title song and in "I'll
Know"; in *Fella*, sequences appear prominently in nearly every song. The
first three phrases of "Happy to Make Your Acquaintance" (Example 10.4)
open with a clear and representative example of a thrice-ascending melodic
sequence in Rosabella's part.

Not surprisingly, the sketchbooks reveal something about the process
by which Loesser worked out ways to combine melodies. What is

213

Example 10.4. Melodic sequence and counterpoint in "Happy
to Make Your Acquaintance"

seemingly less explicable is that Loesser took the trouble early in his
compositional work to notate the familiar English round, "Hey Ho, Nobody Home" on a sketch entry labelled "Lovers in the Lane" ("Hi-ho
lovers in the lane" is how Loesser's text opens).[24] In the duet portions
of "How Beautiful the Days" Tony and Rosabella alternate entrances of
the same melody much as Charley and Amy shared their tune in
"Make a Miracle." When it came to "Abbondanza," the trio in which
Tony's servants take stock of the wedding feast, Loesser could not decide whether he wanted exact melodic imitation in triple meter ($\frac{3}{4}$ time)
or a freer melodic counterpoint in duple meter ($\frac{2}{4}$ time).[25] Eventually he
opted for the freer counterpoint and triple meter found in the published vocal score.

Loesser also included several songs that featured two simultaneous
statements of independent but equally important melodies (nonimitative
counterpoint). As "I Like Ev'rybody" for Herman and Cleo attests, Loesser
did not reserve such contrapuntal complexity for his central romantic characters. When the song is introduced in act II, scene 4, Cleo starts it off with
her tune. Then Herman sings the "main" tune against Cleo's tune, now
moved to the bass, where it was located in Loesser's sketchbook.[26] At the
reprise of the song late in the show (act III, scene 1) the now-compatible
Herman and Cleo simultaneously sing their compatible melodic lines (Example 10.5).

Example 10.5. Two-part counterpoint in "I Like Ev'rybody"

In a short essay in the Imperial Theatre playbill Loesser described his initial resistance to the idea of adapting Howard's play *They Knew What They Wanted*.[27] Before long, however, he realized that he could delete "the topical stuff about the labor situation in the 1920's, the discussion of religion, etc."[28] Loesser continues: "What was left seemed to me to be a very warm simple love story, happy ending and all, and dying to be sung and danced."[29] Throughout his compositional work Loesser never lost sight of this central dramatic focus: the developing love and eventual fulfillment between the central protagonists, Tony and Rosabella.

In keeping with the generally warmer and fuzzier expectations of a Broadway musical, Loesser added Cleo, Rosabella's partner in waitressing drudgery in San Francisco, who receives a sitting job in Tony's Napa Valley to rest her tired waitressing feet. He also gives Cleo a partner not found in Howard's play, Herman, the likable hired hand who will win Cleo when he learns to make a fist. Cleo and Herman, like their obvious prototypes, Ado Annie and Will Parker in *Oklahoma!*, serve their function faithfully (in contrast to Adelaide and the relatively unsung Nathan in *Guys and Dolls*). They also make admirable comic lightweights (albeit with sophisticated counterpoint) to contrast with the romantic heavyweights, Tony and Rosabella.

Gone from the musical are not only the lengthy discussions about religion, but even the character of Father McGee, the loquacious priest who opposes the marriage between Tony and Amy (in the play Tony is in love with Amy rather than Rosabella). In Howard's play, Father McGee shows no apparent concern about their age differences, nor is he motivated by the jealousy that motivates his newly created counterpart in the musical, Marie, Tony's younger sister. Howard's Father McGee responds negatively to the marriage for religious reasons: Tony's mail-order bride is not a Catholic.

Other differences between the musical and the somewhat darker play might be briefly noted. Howard has Tony seek a mate outside his Napa Valley Community because all the single women have slept with Joe, and he attributes Tony's accident to drunkenness rather than fear of rejection. In the play, but not the musical, we learn that Tony's fortune in the grape business stemmed from illegal earnings acquired during Prohibition. The play also contains a striking politically incorrect plot discrepancy. Only after the doctor tells Joe first that Amy (Rosabella) is pregnant does Joe tell Amy. In Howard's play Joe offers to marry Amy and take her out of the Napa Valley; in Loesser's adaptation Joe and Rosabella sing their private thoughts in the beginning of act II, but they never sing (or speak) directly after act I, and Joe leaves the community without knowing Rosabella's condition.

In his obituary for his friend and collaborator, Burrows recalled an exchange that took place after *The Most Happy Fella* premiere on May 3, 1956: "I came out of the theater in great excitement, dashed up to Frank and began chattering away about the marvelous, funny stuff. Songs like 'Standing on the Corner Watching All the Girls Go By.' 'Abbondanza,' 'Big D.' Suddenly he cut me off angrily. 'The hell with those! We know I can do that kind of stuff. Tell me where I made you cry.'"[30] Not content with the triumph of *Guys and Dolls*, Loesser wanted to do more in a musical than to entertain and write hit songs. He wanted to make audiences cry. And although the critical praise for Loesser's most ambitious show about the Napa wine grower and his mail-order bride was far more equivocal than that enjoyed by *Guys and Dolls*, the view espoused here is that the achievement of *The Most Happy Fella* is equally impressive and the work itself arguably even greater Loesser.[31]

Several New York tastemakers praised the show lavishly when it opened at the Imperial Theatre. Robert Coleman headed his review in the *Daily Mirror* with the judgment, " 'Most Happy Fella' Is a Masterpiece" and subtitled this endorsement with "Loesser has performed a truly magnificent achievement with an aging play."[32] John McClain of the *New York Journal-American* encapsulated his reaction in his title, "This Musical Is

Great," and underlying caption, "Loesser's Solo Effort Should Last as One of Decade's Biggest."[33]

In contrast to the unequivocal acclamation of *Guys and Dolls* and *My Fair Lady* (which opened less than two months before *Fella*), however, other New York critics then (and now) would respond negatively to the work's operatic nature, its surfeit of music, and especially its stylistic heterogeneity, much as they had two decades earlier with *Porgy and Bess*. Predictibly, some New York theater critics wanted a musical to be a traditional musical comedy or a Rodgers and Hammerstein sung play—anything but an opera in Broadway garb.

For these critics a Janus-faced musical was a sin in need of public censure. Walter Kerr's remarks in the *New York Herald Tribune* embody this distaste for works that combine traditional Broadway elements with features associated with European opera:

> Still, there's a little something wrong with "Most Happy Fella"— maybe more than a little. The evening at the Imperial is finally heavy with its own inventiveness, weighted down with the variety and fulsomeness of a genuinely creative appetite. It's as though Mr. Loesser had written two complete musicals—the operetta and the haymaker—on the same simple play and then crammed both into a single structure.[34]

Writing in the *New York Post*, Richard Watts Jr. notes the appropriateness of Loesser's decision that "most of the music . . . suggests the more tuneful Italian operas."[35] Nevertheless, Watts is grateful that "the composer has wisely added numbers which, without losing the mood, belong to his characteristic musical comedy manner, and these struck me as the most engaging of the evening." By the end of his review Watts is urging Loesser to return to "his more successful American idiom." George Jean Nathan, another critic who regularly expressed disdain for operatic pretensions in a musical, wrote in the *New York Journal-American* that Loesser "is more at home on his popular musical playground and that the most acceptable portions of his show are those which are admittedly musical comedy."[36] Even *New York Times* theater critic Brooks Atkinson, who praised the "great dramatic stature" and "musical magnificence" of the show, voiced "a few reservations about the work as a whole" and concluded that the work "is best when it is simplest," namely the songs that most clearly reveal Loesser's "connections with Broadway."[37]

Several weeks later the music critic Howard Taubman evaluated the work in the *New York Times*.[38] While he found much to praise in Loesser's score, including the operatic duet "Happy to Make Your Acquaintance" and the quartet "How Beautiful the Days," Taubman criticized in stronger terms than his theater colleague Loesser's failure "to catch hold of a lyrical expression that is consistent throughout." He also found fault with the composer-lyricist's capitulation "to the tyranny of show business" in such numbers as "Standing on the Corner" and "Big D." In the end Taubman defends his refusal to characterize *The Most Happy Fella* as an opera: "If it [music] is the principal agent of the drama, if the essential points and moods are made by music, then a piece, by a free-wheeling definition, may be called opera." Taubman writes that in a music column "it is not considered bad manners to discuss opera," but he agrees with Loesser's disclaimer. For Taubman, *"The Most Happy Fella* is not an opera."

Times have changed. Thirty-five years and one less-than-ecstatically received production (1979) later, Conrad Osborne, in an essay published several days before its 1991 New York City Opera debut, singled out *The Most Happy Fella* as one of three operatic musicals—the others were *Porgy and Bess* and *Street Scene*—that "have shown a particular durability of audience appeal and a growing (if sometimes grudging) critical reputation."[39] Like his predecessors in 1956 Osborne observed "a tension between 'serious' musicodramatic devices and others derived from musical comedy or even vaudeville," and noted perceptively that "this tension has been responsible for much equivocation about 'Fella.' "[40]

Rather than be disturbed by this clash between opera and Broadway, however, Osborne attributes "much of the fascination of the piece" to the same stylistic discrepancies that proved so disconcerting to Atkinson and Taubman.[41] Osborne also praises "Loesser's melodic genius," his "ability to send his characters' voices aloft in passionate, memorable song that will take hold of anyone," and contends that among musicals *The Most Happy Fella* ranks as "one of the few to which return visits bring new discoveries and richer appreciation."[42]

More frequently than not, heterogeneous twentieth-century classical music, especially American varieties, has been subjected to similar criticism. Music that combines extreme contrasts of classical and popular styles, of tonality and atonality, of consonance and dissonance, as found in Mahler, Berg, and Ives, often disturbs more than it pleases listeners who enjoy the more palatable stylistic heterogeneity of Mozart's *Magic Flute*. Before the 1970s most critics and audiences found *Porgy and Bess*, with its hybrid mix of popular hit songs and seemingly less-melodic recitative, at least partially unsettling. In the following chapter it will be suggested that even in *My Fair Lady* one song, the popular "On the Street Where You Live," whether or not it was inserted as a concession to popular tastes, clashes stylistically with the other songs in the show.

Similarly, the colliding styles of nineteenth-century Italian opera ("Happy to Make Your Acquaintance") and Broadway show tunes ("Big D") practically back-to-back in the same scene provoked strong negative reaction. What Loesser does in *The Most Happy Fella* is to use a popular Broadway style to contrast his Italian or Italian-inspired characters (and the operatic temperament of Tony's eventual match, Rosabella) with their comic counterparts and counterpoints, Rosabella's friend Cleo and her good-natured boyfriend Herman. Between the extremes of "How Beautiful the Days" and "Big D" lie songs like the title song and "Sposalizio," which are more reminiscent of Italian popular tarantellas such as "Funiculi, Funiculà" than of Verdian opera. Even those who condemn Loesser for selling out cannot fault him for composing songs that are stylistically inappropriate.

Nor will the accusation stick that Loesser undermined operatic integrity by inserting unused "trunk songs" from other contexts. The sixteen sketchbooks tell a different story. In fact, among all of the dozens of full-scale songs and ariosos only one song, "Ooh! My Feet," can be traced to an earlier show.[43] The sketchbooks reveal that Loesser conceived and developed the more popularly flavored "Standing on the Corner" and "Big D" exclusively for his Broadway opera (what Loesser himself described as a "musical with a lot of music"). In the case of the latter, the solitary extant draft of "Big D" is a rudimentary one from March 1954 (two years before the Boston tryout) that displays most of the rhythm but virtually none of the eventual tune.[44] Early rudimentary sketches for "Standing on the Corner" appear in the first sketchbook (August 1953) and continue in several gradual stages (December 1953 and February, May, and June 1954) before Loesser found a verse and chorus that satisfied him.[45]

In "Some Loesser Thoughts," another playbill essay, the composer notes his "feeling for what some professionals call 'score integration'," which for Loesser "means the moving of plot through the singing of lyrics."[46] Significantly, Loesser acknowledges that his comic songs do not accomplish this purpose when he writes in his next sentence that "in 'The Most Happy Fella' I found a rich playground in which to indulge both my 'integration' and my Tin Pan Alley leanings." His final remarks fan the fuel for those who would accuse Loesser of selling out by making "LOVE" the principal emphasis of his adaptation. For Loesser, not only is love "a most singable subject," it remains a subject "which no songwriter dares duck for very long if he wants to stay popular and solvent."

Loesser's judgment that the Tin Pan Alley songs do not contribute to the "moving of plot" shortchanges the integrative quality of songs such as Cleo's "Ooh! My Feet" and Herman's "Standing on the Corner," which tell us much about the characters who will eventually get together. Since one prefers to sit and the other to stand, even the concepts behind their songs reveal their complementariness. As a showstopper in the literal sense, "Big D" ranks as perhaps the sole (and welcome) exception to the work's stature as an integrated musical.

The principal characteristics that unify *The Most Happy Fella* musically do not always serve dramatic ends. The first of Loesser's most frequent melodic ideas, the melodic sequence defined earlier (Example 10.4) provides musical unity without dramatic meaning.[47] With only a few small exceptions, however, Loesser consistently employs another melodic unifier. This second melodic idea serves as the basis of a melodic family of related motives, melodies in which a descending minor or major second (a half-step or a whole-step) is followed by a wider descending leap that makes forceful dramatic points. A small but representative sample of this ubiquitous melodic stamp is shown in Example 10.6. Loesser's keen dramatic instincts can be witnessed as the growing intensification of this large family of motives expands throughout the evening from "Benvenuta" (Example 10.6a) to "How Beautiful the Days" (Example 10.6b) and "Warm All Over" (Example 10.6c) to Rosabella's heartfelt arioso, "I Love Him," when a minuscule minor second twice erupts into a full and uninhibited octave (Example 10.6d).

Loesser introduces a less familial and more individually significant musical motive after Tony has asked Joe for his picture (see the "Tony" motive in Example 10.7a). Convinced by his sister Marie that he "ain't young no more," "ain't good lookin'," and "ain't smart," the not-so-happy fella has the first of several chats with his deceased Mamma (act I, scene 2): "An' sometime soon I wanna send-a for Rosabella to come down here to Napa an' get marry. I gotta send-a Joe's pitch'."[48] The music that underscores Tony's dialogue with his mother consists of a repeated "sighing" figure composed of descending seconds on strong beats (appoggiaturas), a familiar figure derived from eighteenth and nineteenth-century operatic depictions of pain and loneliness, underneath a sustained string tremolo that contributes still further to the drama of the moment.[49]

In act II, Marie again feeds her brother's low self-image despite Rosabella's assurance that Tony makes her feel "Warm All Over" (in contrast to the "Cold and Dead" response she felt after sleeping with Joe). Consequently, the still-unhappy central character "searches the sky for 'Mamma' and finds her up there," and the original form of his "sighing"

Example 10.6. The family of motives in *The Most Happy Fella*
(M = major; m = minor; d = diminished; A = augmented;
P = perfect)
(a) "Benvenuta"
(b) "How Beautiful the Days"
(c) "Warm All Over"
(d) "I Love Him"

returns to underscore a brief monologue. Tony then sings a sad reprise of his sister's didactic warning, "Young People," with still more self-flagellating lyrics: "Young people gotta dance, dance, dance, / Old people gotta sit dere an' watch, watch, watch. / Wit' da make believe smile in da eye. / Young people gotta live, live, live. / Old people gotta sit dere an' die."[50]

After the potent dramatic moment in the final scene of act II, Rosabella finally convinces Tony that she loves him, not out of pity for an aging

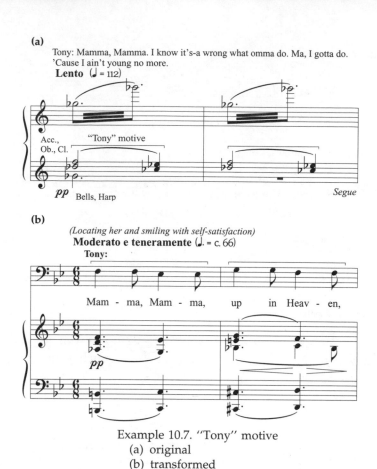

(a)

Tony: Mamma, Mamma. I know it's-a wrong what omma do. Ma, I gotta do.
'Cause I ain't young no more.

Lento (♩ = 112)

Acc.,
Ob., Cl.   "Tony" motive

pp Bells, Harp   *Segue*

(b)

(Locating her and smiling with self-satisfaction)
Moderato e teneramente (♩. = c. 66)
Tony:

Mam - ma, Mam - ma,   up   in Heav - en,

pp

Example 10.7. "Tony" motive
(a) original
(b) transformed

invalid but "like a woman needs a man." To celebrate this long-awaited
moment Tony and Rosabella sing their rapturous duet, "My Heart Is So
Full of You." Tony announces that the delayed wedding party will take
place that night, and everyone spontaneously dances a hoedown.

The newfound joy of this May-September mail-order romance is short-
lived. Rosabella faints from the strain, discovers that she is pregnant with
Joe's baby, and asks Cleo for advice. Tony, with a new self-confidence and
overcome by love (he is also somewhat oblivious to Rosabella's internal
anguish), again communicates with his mother over the returning string
tremolo and the "sighing" "Tony" motive (Example 10.7a). This time,
however, when Tony sings to his mother, Loesser ingeniously converts the
"sighing" motive into a passionate arioso of hope and optimism, "Mamma,
Mamma" (Example 10.7b). Tony's sighing motive will return briefly in the
final scene of the show on the words "have da baby," as Tony, "reflecting
sadly," decides to accept Rosabella's moment of infidelity as well as its
consequences. And as he did in "Mamma, Mamma" at the end of act II,

Tony successfully converts a motive that had previously reflected sadness, loneliness, and self-pity into positive emotions throughout the ten passionate measures of the abbreviated aria in act III, "She gonna come home wit' me."[51]

Just as Rosabella comes to express her growing love for Tony with ever-expanding intervals, Tony learns to channel the self-pity expressed in his sighing motive. By the end of the musical the "Tony" motive has been transformed into a love that allows him to put the well-being of another person ahead of himself and to understand how Rosabella's mistake with Joe was the consequence of Tony's own error when he sent Rosabella Joe's picture rather than his own. As part of this metamorphosis Tony finally stands up to his sister. When Marie once again points out his age, physical unattractiveness, and lack of intelligence, the formerly vulnerable Tony responds to the final insult in this litany in underscored speech: "No! In da head omma no smart, ma, in da heart, Marie. In da heart!"[52]

Loesser's *The Most Happy Fella,* smart in the head as well as in the heart, has managed to entertain and move audiences as much as nearly any musical that aspires to operatic realms (Loesser's denials notwithstanding). Although it lacks the dazzling and witty dialogue, lyrics, and songs of its more popular—and stylistically more homogeneous—Broadway predecessor *Guys and Dolls,* Loesser's musical story of Tony and his Rosabella offers what Burrows described as "a gentle something that wanted to 'make them cry'."[53] *The Most Happy Fella* makes us cry.

Four years later Loesser himself was crying over the failure (ninety-seven performances) of the bucolic *Greenwillow* (1960). The show contained an excellent score, the best efforts of Tony Perkins in the leading role, and a positive review by Brooks Atkinson in the *New York Times.* Despite all this, Donald Malcolm would ridicule the show's tone in the *New Yorker* when he wrote that the village of *Greenwillow* "makes Glocca Morra look like a teeming slum" and a village where "Brigadoon could be the Latin Quarter."[54]

The following year Loesser, again with *Guys and Dolls* librettist Burrows, succeeded in a more traditional urban musical comedy, *How to Succeed in Business Without Really Trying* (1961). Unlike Tony in *The Most Happy Fella,* whose vulnerability and humanity, if not age, appearance, and intelligence, distinguishes him from other Broadway protagonists, the hero of Loesser's next (and last) Broadway hit, J. Pierrepont Finch, is a boyish and aggressively charming Machiavelli who sings the show's central love song to himself ("I Believe in You").

223

As its well-received 1995 Broadway revival starring Matthew Broderick further demonstrated, *How to Succeed* deserves recognition as one of the truly great satirical shows. In how many musicals can we laugh so uproariously about nepotism, blackmail, false pretenses, selfishness, and the worship of money, among many other human foibles. One example of Loesser's comic originality and imagination in song is "Been a Long Day." In this number, which might be described as a trio for narrator and twin soliloquies, a budding elevator romance is described in blow-by-blow detail through a third party before the future lovebirds manage to express their privately sung thoughts directly.

For his remaining eight years Loesser was unable to bring a work to Broadway. *Pleasures and Palaces,* a show about Catherine the Great, closed out of town in 1965, and Loesser died before he could fully complete and begin to tryout *Señor Discretion.* But Loesser's legacy remains large, and in his thirteen years on the Broadway stage he fared far better than Runyon's 6-5 odds against. As Loesser's revivals have shown, Broadway audiences, collapsing under the weight of the musical spectacles of the 1980s and early 1990s, are revelling in the musicals of Loesser, the composer-lyricist who continues to give audiences and even musical and theater historians and critics so much to laugh (and cry) about and so little to sneeze at.

CHAPTER ELEVEN

MY FAIR LADY

From Pygmalion to Cinderella

My *Fair Lady* was without doubt the most popularly successful musical of its era. Before the close of its spectacular run of 2,717 performances from 1956 to 1962 it had comfortably surpassed *Oklahoma!*'s previous record of 2,248.[1] And unlike the ephemeral success of the wartime Broadway heroines depicted in *Lady in the Dark* and *One Touch of Venus,* librettist-lyricist Alan Jay Lerner's and composer Frederick "Fritz" Loewe's fair lady went on to age phenomenally well. Most remarkably, over eighteen million cast albums were sold and profits from the staged performances, albums, and 1964 film came to the then-astronomical figure of $800 million. Critically successful revivals followed in 1975 and 1981, the latter with Rex Harrison (Henry Higgins) and Cathleen Nesbitt (Mrs. Higgins) reclaiming their original Broadway roles. In 1993 the work returned once again, this time with television miniseries superstar Richard Chamberlain as Higgins, newcomer Melissa Errico as Eliza, and Julian Holloway playing Alfred P. Doolittle, the role his father, Stanley, created on Broadway on March 15, 1956.

As with most of the musicals under scrutiny in the present survey, the popular and financial success of *My Fair Lady* was and continues to be matched by critical acclaim. Walter Kerr of the *Herald Tribune* told his readers: "Don't bother to finish reading this review now. You'd better sit down and send for those tickets to *My Fair Lady*."[2] William Hawkins of the *World-Telegram & Sun* wrote that the show "prances into that rare class of great

My Fair Lady. George Bernard Shaw and his puppets, Rex Harrison and Julie Andrews (1956). © Al Hirschfeld. Drawing reproduced by special arrangement with Hirschfeld's exclusive representative, The Margo Feiden Galleries Ltd. New York.

musicals" and that "quite simply, it has everything," providing "a legendary evening" with songs that "are likely to be unforgettable."[3] In what may be the highest tribute paid to the show, Harrison reported that "Cole Porter reserved himself a seat once a week for the entire run."[4]

Opening night critics immediately recognized that *My Fair Lady* fully measured up to the Rodgers and Hammerstein model of an integrated musical. As Robert Coleman of the *Daily Mirror* wrote: "The Lerner-Loewe songs are not only delightful, they advance the action as well. They are ever so much more than interpolations, or interruptions. They are a most important and integrated element in about as perfect an entertainment as the most fastidious playgoer could demand. . . . A new landmark in the genre fathered by Rodgers and Hammerstein. A terrific show!"[5]

Many early critics noted the skill and appropriateness of the adaptation from George Bernard Shaw's *Pygmalion* (1912). For *Daily News* reviewer John Chapman, Lerner and Loewe "have written much the way Shaw must have done had he been a musician instead of a music critic."[6] Hawkins wrote that "the famed *Pygmalion* has been used with such artfulness and taste, such vigorous reverence, that it springs freshly to life all over again."[7] And even though Brooks Atkinson of the *New York Times* added the some-what condescending "basic observation" that "Shaw's crackling mind is still the genius of *My Fair Lady*," he concluded his rave of this "wonderful show" by endorsing the work on its own merits: "To Shaw's agile intelligence it adds the warmth, loveliness, and excitement of a memorable theatre frolic."[8]

Lerner (1918–1986) and Loewe (1901–1988) met fortuitously at New York's Lambs Club in 1942. Before he began to match wits with Loewe, Lerner's marginal writing experience had consisted of lyrics to two Hasty Pudding musicals at Harvard and a few radio scripts. Shortly after their meeting Loewe asked Lerner to help revise *Great Lady*, a musical which had previously met its rapid Broadway demise in 1938. The team inauspiciously inaugurated their Broadway collaboration with two now-forgotten flops, *What's Up?* (1943) and *The Day Before Spring* (1945).

Documentation for the years before Loewe arrived in the United States in 1924 is sporadic and unreliable, and most of the frequently circulated "facts" about the European years—for example that Loewe studied with Weill's teacher, Ferruccio Busoni—were circulated by Loewe himself and cannot be independently confirmed. Sources even disagree about the year and city of his birth, and the most reliable fact about his early years is that his father was the famous singer Edmund Loewe, who debuted as Prince Danilo in the Berlin production of Lehár's *The Merry Widow* and performed the lead in Oscar Straus's first and only Shaw adaptation, *The Chocolate Soldier*.[9]

As Loewe would have us believe, young Fritz was a child prodigy who began to compose at the age of seven and who at age thirteen became the youngest pianist to have appeared with the Berlin Philharmonic. None of this can be verified. Lerner and Loewe biographer Gene Lees also questions Loewe's frequently reported claim to have written a song, "Katrina," that managed to sell two million copies.[10] Loewe's early years in America remain similarly obscure. After a decade of often extremely odd jobs, including professional boxing, gold prospecting, delivering mail on horseback, and cow punching, Loewe broke into show business when one of his songs was interpolated in the nonmusical *Petticoat Fever* by operetta star Dennis King. Another Loewe song was interpolated in *The Illustrators Show* (1936).[11] The *Great Lady* fiasco (twenty performances) occurred two years later.

After their early Broadway failures Lerner and Loewe produced their first successful Rodgers and Hammerstein–type musical on their third Broadway try, *Brigadoon* (1947), a romantic tale of a Scottish village that awakens from a deep sleep once every hundred years. By the end of the musical the town offers a permanent home to a formerly jaded American who discovers the meaning of life and love (and some effective ersatz-Scottish music) within its timeless borders. The following year Lerner wrote the book and lyrics for the first of many musicals without Loewe, the modestly successful and rarely revived avant-garde "concept musical" *Love Life* (with music by Weill). Lerner and Loewe's next collaboration, the occasionally revived *Paint Your Wagon* (1951) was less than a hit on its first run. Also in 1951 Lerner without Loewe wrote the Academy Award–winning screenplay for *An American in Paris*, which featured the music and lyrics of George and Ira Gershwin. By 1952 Lerner, reunited with Loewe, was ready to tackle Shaw.

My Fair Lady *and* Pygmalion

It may seem inevitable that someone would have set *Pygmalion*, especially when considering the apparent ease with which Lerner and Loewe adapted Shaw's famous play for the musical stage. In fact, much conspired against any musical setting of a Shaw play for the last forty years of the transplanted Irishman's long and productive life. The main obstacle until Shaw's death in 1950 was the playwright himself, who, after enduring what he considered to be a travesty of *Arms and the Man* in Straus's *The Chocolate Soldier* (1910), wrote to Theatre Guild producer Theresa Helburn in 1939 that "nothing will ever induce me to allow any other play of mine to be degraded into an operetta or set to any music except its own."[12] As early as 1921, seven years after the English premiere of his play, Shaw aggressively thwarted an attempt by Lehár to secure the rights to *Pygmalion*: "a Pygmalion operetta is quite out of the question."[13] As late as 1948

Shaw was rejecting offers to musicalize *Pygmalion*, and in response to a request from Gertrude Lawrence (the original heroine of *Lady in the Dark*) he offered his last word on the subject: "My decision as to Pygmalion is final: let me hear no more about it. This is final."[14]

Much of our information on the genesis of *My Fair Lady* comes from Lerner's engagingly written autobiography, *The Street Where I Live* (1978), more than one hundred pages of which are devoted to the compositional genesis, casting, and production history of their Shaw adaptation.[15] Additionally, Loewe's holograph piano-vocal score manuscripts in the Music Division of the Library of Congress offer a fascinating glimpse into some later details of the compositional process of the songs.

From Lerner we learn that after two or three weeks of intensive discussion and planning in 1952 the team's first tussle with the musicalization of Shaw's play had produced only discouragement. Part of the problem was that the reverence Lerner and Loewe held for Shaw's play precluded a drastic overhaul. Equally problematic, their respect for the Rodgers and Hammerstein model initially prompted Lerner and Loewe to find an appropriate place for a choral ensemble as well as a secondary love story. While a chorus could be contrived with relative ease, it was more difficult to get around the second problem: Shaw's play, "had one story and one story only," and the central plot of *Pygmalion*, "although Shaw called it a romance, is a non-love story."[16] In a chance meeting with Hammerstein, the great librettist-lyricist told Lerner, "It can't be done. . . . Dick [Rodgers] and I worked on it for over a year and gave it up."[17]

Lerner and Loewe returned to their adaptation of Shaw two years later confident that a Shavian musical would be possible. As Lerner explains:

> By 1954 it no longer seemed essential that a musical have a subplot, nor that there be an ever-present ensemble filling the air with high C's and flying limbs. In other words, some of the obstacles that had stood in the way of converting Pygmalion into a musical had simply been removed by a changing style. . . . As Fritz and I talked and talked, we gradually began to realize that the way to convert *Pygmalion* to a musical did not require the addition of any new characters. . . . We could do *Pygmalion* simply by doing *Pygmalion* following the screenplay [of the 1938 film as altered by director Gabriel Pascal] more than the [stage] play and adding the action that took place between the acts of the play.[18]

Instead of placing Higgins as a professor of phonetics in a University setting in order to generate the need for a chorus of students, Professor

Higgins used his home as his laboratory and a chorus comprised of his servants now sufficed. Since the move from a tea party at the home of Higgins's mother to the Ascot races provided the opportunity for a second chorus, it seemed unnecessary to insert a third chorus at the Embassy Ball. Although they did not invent any characters, Lerner and Loewe did provide a variation of a Rodgers and Hammerstein–type subplot by expanding the role of Alfred P. Doolittle, Eliza's father.[19] Despite these changes and other omissions and insertions that alter the tone and meaning of Shaw's play, Lerner's libretto follows much of the *Pygmalion* text with remarkable tenacity. In contrast to any of the adaptations considered here, Lerner and Loewe's libretto leaves long stretches of dialogue virtually unchanged.

By November 1954 Lerner and Loewe had completed five songs for their new musical. Two of these, "The Ascot Gavotte" and "Just You Wait," would eventually appear in the show. Another song intended for Eliza, "Say a Prayer for Me Tonight," would be partially salvaged in the Embassy Ball music and recycled in the film *Gigi* (1958).[20] Also completed by November 1954 were two songs intended for Higgins, "Please Don't Marry Me," the "first attempt to dramatize Higgins' misogyny," and "Lady Liza," the first of several attempts to find a song in which Higgins would encourage a demoralized Eliza to attend the Embassy Ball.[21] Rex Harrison, the Higgins of choice from the outset, vigorously rejected both of these songs, and they quickly vanished. The casting of Harrison, the actor most often credited with introducing a new kind of talk-sing, was of course a crucial decision that affected the musical characteristics of future Higgins songs.[22] A second try at "Please Don't Marry Me" followed in 1955 and resulted in the now familiar "I'm an Ordinary Man." "Come to the Ball" replaced "Lady Liza" and stayed in the show until opening night. Lerner summarizes the compositional progress of their developing show: "By mid-February [1955] we left London with the Shaw rights in one hand, commitments from Rex Harrison, Stanley Holloway, and Cecil Beaton [costumes] in the other, two less songs than we had arrived with ["Please Don't Marry Me" and "Lady Liza"] and a year's work ahead of us."[23]

Earlier Lerner reported that a winter's journey around the frigid Covent Garden had yielded the title and melody of "Wouldn't It Be Loverly." The genesis of Eliza's first song demonstrates the team's usual pattern: title, tune, and, after excruciating procrastination and writer's block, a lyric.[24] The lyricist details the agony of creation for "Wouldn't It Be Loverly," a process which took Loewe "one afternoon" and Lerner weeks of delay and psychological trauma before he could even produce a word. Six weeks "after a successful tour around the neighborhood with 'Wouldn't It Be

Loverly?' " they completed Higgins's opening pair of songs, "Why Can't the English?" and "I'm an Ordinary Man."[25] These are the last songs that Lerner mentions before rehearsals began in January 1956.

Lerner's chronology accounts for all but four *My Fair Lady* songs: "With A Little Bit of Luck," "The Servants' Chorus," "Promenade," and "Without You." All Lerner has to say about "With a Little Bit of Luck" is that it was written for Holloway sometime before rehearsals.[26] But although Lerner's autobiography provides no additional chronological information about the remaining three songs, we are not reduced to idle speculation concerning two of these. On musical evidence it is apparent that the "Introduction to Promenade" was adapted from "Say a Prayer for Me Tonight," one of the earliest songs drafted for the show.[27] It will also be observed shortly that the principal melody of "Without You" is partially derived from Higgins's "I'm an Ordinary Man," completed nearly a year before rehearsals.[28] Loewe's holograph piano-vocal score manuscripts of *My Fair Lady* songs verify Lerner's remark that this last-mentioned song underwent "one or two false starts."[29] Harrison described one of these as "inferior Noël Coward."[30] (In other differences with the published vocal score the holograph of "You Did It" contains a shortened introduction and a considerable amount of additional but mostly repetitive material.[31])

Of great importance for the peformance practice of Higgins's role was the decision to allow the professor to talk his way into a song or a new phrase of a song. In "I'm an Ordinary Man," "A Hymn to Him," and "I've Grown Accustomed to Her Face," audiences have long been accustomed to hear Higgins speak lines that are underscored by orchestral melody; the pitches are usually indicated in the vocal part by X's, recalling the notation of Schoenberg's *Sprechstimme* in *Pierrot Lunaire*. The first of many examples of this occurs at the beginning of "I'm an Ordinary Man." This move from song to speech probably occurred during the course of rehearsals. In any event, the holograph scores almost invariably indicate that these passages were originally meant to be sung.[32]

In their most significant departure from their source Lerner and Loewe altered Shaw's ending to allow a romantic resolution between Higgins and Eliza Doolittle. Shaw strenuously argued against this Cinderella interpretation, but he would live to regret that his original concluding lines in 1912 allow the *possibility* that Eliza, who has metamorphosed into "a tower of strength, a consort battleship," will return to live with Higgins and Pickering as an independent woman, one of "three old bachelors together instead of only two men and a silly girl."[33] While in his original text Shaw expresses Higgins's confidence that Eliza will return with the requested shopping list, for the next forty years the playwright would quixotically try to establish his unwavering intention that Higgins and Eliza would never marry.[34] Here are the final lines of Shaw's play:

> MRS. HIGGINS I'm afraid you've spoilt that girl, Henry. But never mind, dear: I'll buy you the tie and glove.
>
> HIGGINS (*sunnily*) Oh, don't bother. She'll buy 'em all right enough. Goodbye.
>
> (*They kiss.* MRS. HIGGINS *runs out.* HIGGINS, *left alone, rattles his cash in his pocket; chuckles; and disports himself in a highly self-satisfied manner.*)

Despite Shaw's unequivocal interpretation—and long before Pascal's *Pygmalion* film in 1938 or the *My Fair Lady* musical in 1956—the original Higgins, Beerbohm Tree, had already taken liberties that would distort the play beyond Shaw's tolerance. In reporting on the 1914 London premiere to his wife Charlotte, Shaw wrote: "For the last two acts I writhed in hell. . . . The last thing I saw as I left the house was Higgins shoving his mother rudely out of his way and wooing Eliza with appeals to buy ham for his lonely home like a bereaved Romeo."[35] Mrs. Patrick Campbell, for whom Shaw created the role of Eliza, urged the playwright to attend another performance "soon—or you'll not recognize your play."[36]

When he summoned enough courage to attend the hundredth performance, Shaw was appalled to discover that "in the brief interval between the end of the play and fall of the curtain, the amorous Higgins threw flowers at Eliza (and with them Shaw's instructions far out of sight)."[37] To make explicit what he had perhaps naively assumed would be understood, Shaw published a sequel to *Pygmalion* in 1916, in which he explained in detail why Eliza and Higgins could not and should not be considered as potential romantic partners.

Considering his strong ideas on the subject, it is surprising that Shaw permitted Pascal to further alter the ending (and many other parts) of Shaw's original screenplay for the 1938 *Pygmalion* film in order to create the impression that Higgins and Eliza would in fact unite. Perhaps Shaw was unaware that Pascal had actually filmed two other endings, including Shaw's. In 1941 Penguin Books published a version of Shaw's screenplay, which included reworked versions of five film scenes that were not part of the original play:

1. Eliza getting in a taxi and returning to her lodgings at the end of act I;
2. Higgins's housekeeper, Mrs. Pearce, giving Eliza a bath in the middle of act II;
3. Eliza's lessons with Higgins at the end of act II;
4. The Embassy Ball at the end of act III (this scene is based on the Embassy Ball in the film—another Cinderella image—that replaced the ambassador's garden party, dinner, and opera that took place offstage in the play);
5. Eliza's meeting with Freddy when she leaves Higgins's residence at the end of act IV.

In his book on Shaw's films, *The Serpent's Eye*, Donald P. Costello carefully details and explains how the printed screenplay departs from the actual film.[38] Perhaps not surprisingly, the most dramatic departure between what was filmed and the published screenplay occurred at the work's conclusion. This is what filmgoers saw and heard in the film:

> *Eliza's voice is heard coming out of the phonograph:*
> ELIZA'S VOICE. Ah-ah-ah-ah-ow-ow-oo-oo!! I ain't dirty: I washed my face and hands afore I come, I did.
> HIGGINS'S VOICE. I shall make a duchess of this draggletailed guttersnipe.
> ELIZA'S VOICE. Ah-ah-ah-ow-ow-oo!
> HIGGINS'S VOICE. In six months . . . (*Higgins switches off the phonograph. Close-up of Higgins's sorrowful face.*) *Eliza enters the room, unseen by Higgins. He hears her voice, speaking with perfect lady-like diction, soft, gentle, lovingly.*
> ELIZA. I washed my face and hands before I came.
> *As Higgins turns to look at Eliza, the ballroom theme begins once more. Higgins looks at Eliza tenderly. Cut to a close-up of Eliza, looking back at him. Higgins just begins to smile; then he recollects himself, and says sternly, as the camera looks only at the back of his head:*
> HIGGINS. Where the devil are my slippers, Eliza?
> *As the ballroom theme swells into a crescendo, a fade-out from the back of Higgins's head. The lilting music of the ballroom waltz is heard as "The End" and the cast are flashed upon the screen.*[39]

Before the 1941 publication of the screenplay (as altered by Pascal), however, Shaw managed to have the last word. It appeared in a letter of corrections from August 19, 1939:

MRS. HIGGINS. I'm afraid you've spoilt that girl, Henry. I should be
uneasy about you and her if she were less fond of Colonel Pickering.

HIGGINS. Pickering! Nonsense: she's going to marry Freddy. Ha ha!
Freddy! Freddy!! Ha ha ha ha ha!!!!! (*He roars with laughter as the
play ends.*)

After submitting this final ending, Shaw parenthetically inserted the following remark: "I should like to have a dozen pulls of the corrected page
to send to the acting companies."[40]

When asked in an interview why he acquiesced to a "happy" ending
in Pascal's film, Shaw replied somewhat archly that he could not "conceive
a less happy ending to the story of 'Pygmalion' than a love affair between
the middle-aged, middle-class professor, a confirmed old bachelor with a
mother-fixation, and a flower girl of 18."[41] According to Shaw, "nothing
of the kind was emphasised in my scenario, where I emphasised the escape
of Eliza from the tyranny of Higgins by a quite natural love affair with
Freddy." Shaw even goes so far as to claim that Leslie Howard's "lovelorn
complexion . . . is too inconclusive to be worth making a fuss about." Despite Shaw's desire to grasp at this perceived ambiguity and despite the
fact that audiences of both film and musical do not actually see Eliza fetch
Higgins's slippers, most members of these audiences will probably conclude that Freddy is not a romantic alternative.

Shaw's denial to the contrary, the romanticization of *Pygmalion* introduced by Beerbohm Tree during the initial 1914 London run of the play
was complete in the 1938 film. As Costello writes: "What remains, after a
great deal of omission, is the clear and simple situation of a Galatea finally
being fully created by her Pygmalion, finally asserting her own individual
soul, and, becoming independent, being free to choose. She chooses Higgins."[42]

The stage was now set for *My Fair Lady*, where the phonetics lesson
introduced in the film would be developed still further, Alfred P. Doolittle
would be observed on his own Tottenham Court Road turf (and given two
songs to sing there, one in each act), and a new and more colorful setting
at Ascot would replace Mrs. Higgins's home (act III of Shaw). Again following the film, *My Fair Lady* deleted many of Doolittle's lines, especially
his philosophical musing on middle-class morality.[43]

If Lerner and Loewe did not invent a romantic pairing between Henry
Higgins and Eliza Doolittle, they succeeded in contradicting Shaw still
more completely (albeit more believably), a task made difficult by Higgins's extraordinary misogyny, rudeness, and insensitivity in Shaw's orig-

inal play. Using the Pascal film as its guide, the Broadway *Pygmalion* therefore made Higgins less misogynist and generally more likable and Eliza less crude, more attractive, and more lovable than their counterparts in Shaw's play and screenplay and Pascal's film. Perhaps more significantly, Lerner and Loewe prepared the eventual match of Higgins and Eliza when they created two moments in song that depict their shared triumph, "The Rain in Spain" and Eliza's gloriously happy "I Could Have Danced All Night" that shortly follows.

Lerner and Loewe would also go beyond the film with several liberties of omission and commission to help musical audiences accept the unlikely but much-wished-for romantic liaison between the antagonistic protagonists. More important, not only did Lerner remove all references to Higgins's "mother fixation," he gave Higgins compassion to match his brilliance. In order to achieve Higgins's metamorphosis from a frog to a prince, Lerner added a speech of encouragement—a song would be overkill—not found in either the film or published screenplay. Significantly, it is this newly created speech that leads directly to Eliza's mastery of the English language as she finally utters the magic words, "the rain in Spain stays mainly in the plain" with impeccable and lady-like diction.[44]

In this central speech Higgins, in contrast to the play and screen versions, demonstrates an awareness of what his subject might be feeling and suffering: "Eliza, I know you're tired. I know your head aches. I know your nerves are as raw as meat in a butcher's window." After extolling the virtues of "the majesty and grandeur of the English language," Higgins for the first time offers encouragement to his human experiment: "That's what you've set yourself to conquer, Eliza. And conquer it you will. . . . Now, try it again."[45]

A Cinderella Musical with an Extraordinary Woman

After conveying Higgins's humanity by the end of act I Lerner and Loewe tried in their second act to make musically explicit what Shaw implies or omits in his drama. Not only does Eliza now possess the strength and independence of "a consort battleship" admired by Higgins in Shaw's play. After the Embassy Ball in *My Fair Lady* the heroine now in fact has the psychological upper hand as well. Clearly, Lerner and Loewe romanticized, and therefore falsified, Shaw's intentions. At the same time they managed to reveal Eliza's metamorphosis as Higgins's equal through lyrics and music more clearly than either Shaw's play or screenplay and Pascal's

My Fair Lady, act I, scene 5. Julie Andrews and Rex Harrison ("In Hertford, Hereford, and Hampshire, hurricanes hardly happen.") (1956). Museum of the City of New York. Gift of Harold Friedlander.

film. The playwright lets Higgins express his delight in Eliza's newfound independence, but he does not show how Eliza surpasses her creator (in this case Higgins) in psychological power other than by allowing Higgins to lose his composure (*"he lays hands on her"*). Lerner and Loewe accomplish this volte-face by taking advantage of music's power to reveal psychological change. Simply put, the Broadway team reverse the musical roles of their protagonists.

In act I of *My Fair Lady* Eliza, in response to her initial humiliation prompted by her inability to negotiate the proper pronunciation of the letter "a" and to Higgins's heartless denial of food (recalling Petruchio's method of "taming" Kate in *Kiss Me, Kate*), sputters her ineffectual dreams of vengeance in "Just You Wait" (Example 11.1a).[46] Eliza sings a brief reprise of this song in act II after Higgins and the uncharacteristically inconsiderate Pickering display a callous disregard for Eliza's part in her Embassy Ball triumph ("You Did It"). Eliza will also incorporate the tune at various moments in "Without You," for example, when she sings "And there still will be rain on that plain down in Spain" (Example 11.1b).

Example 11.1. "Just You Wait" and selected transformations
  (a) "Just You Wait"
  (b) "Without You"
  (c) "I'm an Ordinary Man"
  (d) "I've Grown Accustomed to Her Face"

The opening phrase of the chorus in "Without You," Eliza's ode to independence, consists of a transformation into the major mode of "Just You
Wait." Its first four notes also inconspicuously recall Higgins's second song
of act I, "I'm an Ordinary Man," when he first leaves speech for song on
the words "who desires" (Example 11.1c). By this subtle transformation
audiences can subliminally hear as well as directly see that the tables have
begun to turn as Eliza adopts Higgins's musical characteristics. At the same
time Higgins transforms Eliza into a lady, by the end of the evening Eliza

237

(and her music) will have successfully transformed Higgins into a gentleman.

To reinforce this dramatic reversal, Higgins himself recapitulates Eliza's "Just You Wait" material in both the minor and major modes of his final song, "I've Grown Accustomed to Her Face" (Example 11.1d). At this point in the song Higgins is envisaging the "infantile idea" of Eliza's marrying Freddy.[47] The verbal and dramatic parallels between Higgins's and Eliza's revenge on their respective tormentors again suggest the reversal of their roles through song.

Higgins's "I've Grown Accustomed to Her Face" in act II also offers a musical demonstration of a dramatic transformation needed to convince audiences that Eliza's return is as plausible as it is desirable. In the fast sections of "I'm an Ordinary Man" in act I Higgins explains the discomforting effect of women on his orderly existence (Example 11.2a). Higgins's dramatic transformation in his final song is most clearly marked by tempo and dynamics, but the melodic change is equally significant if less immediately obvious.[48] As shown in Example 11.2b, no longer does Higgins move up an ascending scale to reach his destination like a "motor bus" (Eliza's description in Shaw's act V). For one thing, the destination of the opening line, "She almost makes the day begin," is the fourth degree of the scale (F in the key of C) on the final syllable rather than the first degree. For another, Higgins now precedes the resolution with the upper note G to soften the momentum of the ascending scale. Thus a lyrical Higgins, who sings more and talks less, conveys how he misses his Eliza. Eventually within the song this lyricism (to be sung *con tenerezza* or tenderly) will conquer the other side of his emotions, embodied in his dream of Eliza's humiliation.

The reuse of "Just You Wait" and the transformation of the "but let a woman in your life" portions of "I'm an Ordinary Man" into "I've Grown Accustomed to Her Face" provide the most telling musical examples of Higgins's dramatic transformation. The far less obvious transformation of "I'm an Ordinary Man" into "Without You" mentioned earlier (Example 11.1c) provides additional musical evidence of the power reversal between Higgins and Eliza in the second act of *My Fair Lady*.[49]

Although they lack the immediate recognizability of these melodic examples, the most frequent musical unities, however, are rhythmic ones, with or without attendant melodic profiles. The middle section of "Just You Wait," for example, anticipates the rhythm of "Get Me to the Church on Time" (Example 11.3a). The eighteenth-century Alberti bass in the accompaniment of this section, which suggests the propriety of classical mu-

(a)

Allegro molto vivo
Higgins:

Oh, let a wom - an in your life

(b)

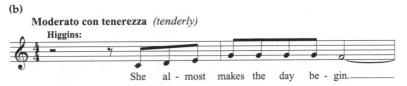

Moderato con tenerezza *(tenderly)*
Higgins:

She al - most makes the day be - gin.

Example 11.2. "I'm an Ordinary Man" and "I've Grown
Accustomed to Her Face"
(a) "I'm an Ordinary Man"
(b) "I've Grown Accustomed to Her Face"

sic, is also paralleled in the second act song of Eliza's father when he decides to marry and thereby gain conventional middle-class respectability.

It is possible that Lerner and Loewe intended to link the central characters rhythmically by giving them songs that begin with an upbeat. In act I both parts of Higgins's "Ordinary Man," the main melody of Doolittle's "A Little Bit of Luck," and Eliza's "I Could Have Danced All Night" all begin with three-note upbeats. Eliza's "Just You Wait," Freddy's "On the Street Where You Live," and "Ascot Gavotte" each open with a two-note upbeat and "The Rain in Spain" employs a one-note upbeat.

Dramatic meaning for all these upbeats may be found by looking at the two songs in act I that begin squarely on the downbeat, "Why Can't the English?" and "Wouldn't It Be Loverly?" Significantly, these songs, the first two of the show, are rhetorical questions sung by Higgins and Eliza respectively before their relationship has begun. Clearly Higgins, in speaking about matters of language and impersonal intellectual matters plants his feet firmly on solid ground. Similarly, the strong downbeats of Eliza's opening song demonstrate her earthiness and directness. Once Higgins has encountered Eliza in his study and sings "I'm an Ordinary Man," Lerner and Loewe let us know that Higgins is on less firm territory and can no longer begin his songs on the downbeat. After Eliza begins her lessons with Higgins, she too becomes unable to begin a song directly on the downbeat. As Doolittle becomes conventional and respectable, he too will begin respectably on the downbeat in his second-act number, "Get Me To the Church On Time."[50]

Although Eliza transforms Higgins's "Ordinary Man" in "Without You," complete with upbeat, moments later she manages to demonstrate

(a)

(b)

Example 11.3. "Just You Wait" and "Get Me to the Church on Time"
(a) "Just You Wait" (middle section)
(b) "Get Me to the Church on Time" (opening)

to Freddy that she can once again begin every phrase of a song on the downbeat, as she turns the Spanish tango of "The Rain in Spain Stays Mainly in the Plain" into the faster and angrier Latin rhythms of "Show Me." Tellingly, Higgins never regains his ability to begin a song on the downbeat. Especially revealing is his final song, "I've Grown Accustomed to Her Face," which retains the three-note upbeat of his own "Ordinary Man" ("but let a woman in your life") and Eliza's euphoric moment in act I, "I Could Have Danced All Night."

During the New Haven tryouts a few songs continued to present special problems. One of these songs, "Come to the Ball," Lerner and Loewe's second attempt to give Higgins a song of encouragement for Eliza prior to the Embassy Ball, was dropped after one performance.[51] Although Lerner never seemed to accept its removal, his more objective collaborators, Loewe and especially director Moss Hart, understood why the show works better for its absence: while it endorses Eliza's physical beauty, it simply does not offer her any other reason to attend the ball. Despite the current predilection of reinstating deleted numbers from Broadway classics, it seems unlikely that audiences will soon be hearing "Come to the Ball" in its original context.

The crucial role of Hart (the librettist of *Lady in the Dark*) in the development of Lerner's book should not go unnoticed. Even if the full extent of his contribution cannot be fully measured, Lerner readily acknowledged that the director went over every word with the official librettist over a four-day marathon weekend in late November 1955.[52] Several of Hart's major suggestions during the rehearsal and tryout process can be more accurately gauged. In addition to requesting the deletion of "Come to the Ball," we know from Lerner's autobiography that Hart persuaded Lerner and Loewe to remove "a ballet that occurred between Ascot and the ball scene and 'Say a Prayer for Me Tonight'."[53] To fill the resulting gap near the end of act I Lerner "wrote a brief scene which skipped directly from Ascot to the night before the ball."[54]

The other major song marked for extinction after opening night in New Haven was "On the Street Where You Live." In both his autobiography and his recorded presentation of songs from *My Fair Lady*, Lerner discussed the negative response to this song, his own desire to retain it, his failure to understand why it failed, and his solution to the problem several days later.[55] For Lerner, the "mute disinterest" that greeted this song was due to the fact that audiences were unable to distinguish Freddy Eynesford-Hill from the other gentlemen at Ascot.[56] Lerner's autobiography relates how he gave Freddy a new verse to help audiences remember him; in his live performance Lerner explains a revision in which for the sake of clarity Freddy has the maid ask him to identify himself by name. In Lerner's view the positive response to this change was vindication enough. Certainly "On the Street Where You Live" remains the most frequently performed song outside the context of the show.

The rich afterlife of "On the Street Where You Live" as an independent song may provide a clue as to why everyone else concerned with the show (other than Lerner) was willing, even eager, to cut this future hit after it failed to register on its opening night audience. Lehman Engel, an astute and sensitive Broadway critic and a staunch proponent of the integrated musical, writes that when he sees a musical for the first time "the highest compliment anyone can pay" is to not be conscious of the songs."[57] The absence of such awareness "indicates that all of the elements worked together so integrally that I was aware only of the total effect."

Engel's reaction to *My Fair Lady* expresses the problem clearly:

> I had a similar response to *My Fair Lady* the first time [that like *Fiddler On the Roof*, the elements worked integrally], but I did hear "On the Street Where You Live" and I believe this happened for two reasons. In the first place, nothing else was going on when the song was sung; the singing character was simply (and intentionally) stupid—nothing complex about that.[58] But secondly I heard the song because I disliked it intensely. (I love everything else in the score. But this song, to me, did not fit.) It was the picture that shoved its way out of the frame with a bang. Suddenly there was a "pop" song that had strayed into a score otherwise brilliant, integrated, with a great sense of the play's own style and a faithful, uncompromising exposition of characters and situations.

Although much of *My Fair Lady* departs from Shaw's play, its Cinderella slant nevertheless constitutes an extraordinarily faithful adaptation to Pascal's filmed revision of Shaw's original screenplay. Moreover, the music of *My Fair Lady* for the most part accurately serves most of Shaw's textual ideas. Additionally, the songs themselves, which are carefully prepared and advance the action in the Rodgers and Hammerstein tradition, convey the dramatic meaning that underlies this action.

One critical quandary remains. Just as Higgins neglects to consider the question of what is to become of Eliza, Lerner and Loewe's popular adaptation of *My Fair Lady* poses the problem of what is to become of Shaw's *Pygmalion*, a play which noted literary critics, including Harold Bloom, consider to be the playwright's masterpiece.[59] The relative decline of Shaw's *Pygmalion* in the wake of *My Fair Lady* seems especially lamentable.[60]

But even measured by Shavian standards, Lerner and Loewe's classic musical is by no means overshadowed on artistic grounds. Readers of Shaw's play know, as Shaw knew, that Higgins would "never fall in love with anyone under forty-five."[61] Indeed, marrying Freddy might have its drawbacks, but marrying Higgins would be unthinkable. It is the ultimate achievement of Lerner and Loewe's *My Fair Lady* that the unthinkable has become the probable.

Two years after *My Fair Lady* Lerner and Loewe completed *Gigi*, the Academy Award-winning film adaptation of a Colette novella. Not wishing to argue with success, *Gigi*, like *My Fair Lady*, tells the story of a young woman who ends up with an older man—Cinderella revisited. The final Broadway collaboration appeared two years later, *Camelot* (1960), a partially successful attempt to recycle a production team (director Hart and Julie Andrews as Guenevere, as well as a new, acclaimed, nonsinging actor in the Harrison tradition, Richard Burton, as King Arthur). The box office magic of the *My Fair Lady* "team" and a long televised segment on the Ed Sullivan Show helped *Camelot* (the positive associations with President Kennedy came later) to survive its extraordinarily bad critical press, growing tensions between Lerner and Loewe, and Lerner's hospitalization for bleeding ulcers. Perhaps the most devastating blow of all was Hart's sudden heart attack and hospitalization, which forced the director to assume the unaccustomed role of patient rather than that of play doctor, a role he had performed so irreplaceably on *My Fair Lady*.

Even those who feel that Eliza should have gone off into the sunset (or the fog) with Freddy rather than the misogynist Higgins might have second thoughts about Guenevere's decision to abandon her likable and desirable husband Arthur for the younger but boorish and egotistical Lancelot. As Engel writes: "It is not lack of fidelity that makes for our dissatisfaction but an unmotivated, rather arbitrary choice that seemed to make no sense."[62]

After *Camelot*, Lerner and Loewe would adapt *Gigi* for Broadway in 1973 (it ran for only three months). One year later they would work together on new material one last time in the film *The Little Prince*. With the exceptions of these brief returns, Loewe, who had collaborated exclusively with Lerner ever since *What's Up?* in 1943, retired on his laurels and died quietly in 1988. The more restless Lerner, who as early as the 1940s had teamed up with Weill on *Love Life* one year after *Brigadoon*, would collaborate with Burton Lane within five years after *Camelot* to create the modestly successful *On a Clear Day You Can See Forever*.

For his last twenty years Lerner without Loewe—and, in some respects equally unfortunately, without Hart, who died in 1961—would produce one failure after another. Not even the star quality of Katharine Hepburn in *Coco* (1970) could help this show with music by André Previn to run more than a year. A potentially promising collaboration with the brilliant Leonard Bernstein in *1600 Pennsylvania Avenue* (1976) closed within a week out of town. Other short-lived post-*Camelot* musicals included *Lolita, My*

Love (1972), *Carmelina* (1979), and *Dance a Little Closer* (1983) with music composed by John Barry, Lane, and Charles Strouse, respectively. At the time of his death in 1986, the indefatigable librettist-lyricist had drafted much of a libretto and several lyrics for yet another musical, this time based on the classic 1936 film comedy, *My Man Godfrey*.[63]

CHAPTER TWELVE

WEST SIDE STORY

The Very Model of a
Major Musical

West Side Story, a collaboration of four extraordinary individuals—
Jerome Robbins (choreographer and director), Arthur Laurents
(librettist), Leonard Bernstein (composer), and Stephen Sondheim (lyricist)—premiered on Broadway on September 26, 1957, and ran for
734 performances.[1] After a national tour that lasted a year, it returned to
Broadway for an additional 249 performances. A bona fide hit but not a me-
gahit like *Oklahoma!* or *My Fair Lady*, *West Side Story* eventually logged in as
the twelfth longest-running show of the 1950s (see Appendix B, p. 314).[2]

In its initial run *West Side Story* received mostly favorable and respectful
notices from our by-now familiar cast of critics. John McClain was the only
critic who assessed the show as "the most exciting thing that has come to
town since 'My Fair Lady.'"[3] Walter Kerr focused his attentions on the
dancing, "the most savage, restless, electrifying dance patterns we've been
exposed to in a dozen seasons," to the near exclusion of everything else,
and concluded his review with a tribute to Robbins: "This is the show that
could have danced all night, and nearly did. But the dancing is it. Don't
look for laughter or—for that matter—tears."[4] Brooks Atkinson praised
the blend and unity of the work and production and the authors for "pool-
ing imagination and virtuosity" to create "a profoundly moving show that
is as ugly as the city jungles and also pathetic, tender and forgiving."[5]
Robert Coleman and John McClain predicted that the show would be a
hit, and, in what was perhaps the most laudatory critical response, John

Chapman opened his review in the *Daily News* by exclaiming that "the American theatre took a venturesome forward step" to present "a bold new kind of musical theatre."[6] Nevertheless, it was not until 1961, with the release of the Academy Award–winning film starring the glamorous box-office draw Natalie Wood (her singing dubbed by the ubiquitous Marni Nixon), that *West Side Story* finally became a certified blockbuster, with a soundtrack that Stephen Banfield reports "remains the longest ever number 1 on *Billboard*'s album charts."[7]

In the years since the film, *West Side Story* has appeared in popular revivals both at Lincoln Center's New York State Theater in 1968 (89 performances), on Broadway in 1980 (333 performances), and in innumerable productions outside of New York. *West Side Story* has also acquired serious respect and attention from both theater and music historians and critics. While it shares with some of the other musicals in this survey a complex score rich in organicism and motivic and other musical techniques associated with the nineteenth-century European operatic ideal, as well as some songs that eventually become standards, it surpasses its European and Broadway predecessors in its reliance on dance and movement to depict dramatic action.

Like *Carousel*, the Bernstein-Sondheim-Laurents-Robbins collaboration contains a dream ballet and a mimed prologue that creates a backdrop for the story to follow. More than perhaps any previous book musical, *West Side Story* uses dance for many additional purposes, not only in musical numbers where characters would be expected to dance (the "Dance at the Gym" and "America"), but in more stylized choreographic settings for several of the show's crucial dramatic events ("The Rumble" and "Taunting Scene"). The creators of *West Side Story* also managed to take a canonic and extremely well-loved Shakespeare play and adapt it for 1950s audiences while remaining faithful to the spirit of the original. Most significantly, the adaptation both provides dramatically credible and audible musical equivalents of Shakespeare's literary techniques and captures his central themes.

The Making of a Masterpiece

Prior to its 1957 premiere only Sondheim (b. 1930) among the principal creators of *West Side Story* had yet to distinguish himself on Broadway (Sondheim's career will be surveyed in chapter 13). More than a decade earlier librettist Laurents (b. 1918) had written the critically lauded *Home of the Brave* (1945). Between Robbins's 1949 initial conception of a *Romeo and Juliet* musical with lots of dance and its working out, Laurents wrote his most successful play, *The Time of the Cuckoo* (1952).

In 1944 Robbins (b. 1918) collaborated with Bernstein (1918–1990) on both the ballet *Fancy Free* (as featured dancer and choreographer) and its inspired Broadway offspring later that same year, *On the Town*. Beginning with *High Button Shoes* in 1947 (lyrics by Sammy Cahn and music by Jule Styne) Robbins choreographed a quartet of musical comedies, mostly hits: Hugh Martin's *Look Ma, I'm Dancin'* (1948), Berlin's *Miss Liberty* (1949) and *Call Me Madam* (1950), and Rodgers and Hammerstein's *The King and I* (1951), with its innovative narrated ballet-pantomime "Small House of Uncle Thomas." As codirector with Abbott, Robbins helped to create Adler and Ross's *The Pajama Game* (1954); as director-choreographer he brought to life two shows with lyrics by Comden and Green and music by Styne, *Peter Pan* (1954) and *Bells Are Ringing* (1956), the latter one year before *West Side Story*.

Bernstein, like Gershwin, came to the piano at a relatively late age, in Bernstein's case, ten. He followed his undergraduate years as a music major at Harvard (class of 1939) with studies in orchestration, piano, and conducting at the Curtis Institute in Philadelphia. In 1941 he began his private studies with Boston Symphony conductor Serge Koussevitzky. While an assistant to Artur Rodzinski (then conductor of the New York Philharmonic), Bernstein gained instant (and permanent) recognition when he filled in for ailing guest conductor Bruno Walter and conducted the orchestra on a national broadcast in November 1943.

Within the next three months Bernstein's first "serious" classical works were performed in New York: the song cycle *I Hate Music*, the "Jeremiah" Symphony, the ballet *Fancy Free*, and, by the end of 1944, when the composer was twenty-six, his first Broadway hit, *On the Town*. Between *On the Town* and *West Side Story* the phenomenally eclectic composer, conductor, pianist, and educator composed three major theater works of enduring interest: *Trouble in Tahiti* (1952; with his own libretto and lyrics), *Wonderful Town* (1953; book by Joseph Fields and Jerome Chodorov and lyrics by Comden and Green), and *Candide* (1956; book by Lillian Hellman, lyrics by Richard Wilbur, John Latouche, Dorothy Parker, Hellman, and Bernstein).

Several published personal remembrances help sort out the complicated genesis of *West Side Story*. The first recollection was recorded in 1949 in "Excerpts from a *West Side Story* Log," the year Robbins introduced his concept to two of his future collaborators, Laurents and Bernstein. Bernstein's log, which originally appeared in the *West Side Story Playbill*, identifies major events and ideological turning points between Robbins's initial idea and the opening night tryout in August 1957.[8] Nearly thirty years later the foursome (Robbins, Laurents, Bernstein, and Sondheim) met in 1985 as a panel to discuss their creation before an audience of the Dramatists Guild.[9] Valuable information on the genesis of *West Side Story* can also be found in excerpts from published interviews with those involved in the original production, a number of which appear in Craig Zadan's *Sondheim & Co.*[10] Other important sources on the compositional process are contained in Bernstein's letters to his wife, Felicia, who was visiting her family in Santiago, Chile during the rehearsals and Washington tryouts, Sondheim's "Anecdote" published in the song book *Bernstein on Broadway*, and a Bernstein interview with theater critic Mel Gussow published shortly after the composer's death in 1990.[11]

Despite some minor discrepancies in their 1985 recollection of *West Side Story*'s genesis, the four collaborators shed a great deal of light on the evolution of their masterpiece.[12] Moreover, their memory of compositional changes is almost invariably vindicated by the eight libretto drafts and various lyric sheets housed among the Sondheim papers in the State Historical Society of Wisconsin. The first of the libretto drafts is dated January 1956, two months after Sondheim joined the entourage, and the last was completed on July 19, 1957, approximately midway through the unprecedentedly long eight-week rehearsal schedule (twice the usual length).[13] Earlier versions of Bernstein's holograph piano-vocal scores are also available both in Wisconsin and in the Music Division of the Library of Congress.

From Bernstein's log we learn that Robbins's original "noble idea" in January 1949 was "a modern version of *Romeo and Juliet* set in slums at the coincidence of Easter-Passover celebration."[14] Over the next four months Laurents drafted four scenes, and the original trio of collaborators discussed the direction of what was then known as *East Side Story*. Bernstein recorded that their goal was to write "a musical that tells a tragic story in musical-comedy terms . . . never falling into the 'operatic' trap," a show that would not "depend on stars" but must "live or die by the success of its collaborations."

The next log entries appear six years later when Robbins-Laurents-Bernstein returned to their dormant idea. On June 7, 1955 Bernstein reported that the group remained excited and hypothesized that "maybe I can plan to give this year to Romeo—if *Candide* gets in on time." By August 25 the trio had "abandoned the whole Jewish-Catholic premise as not very fresh," replacing Jews and Catholics with rival gangs, the newly arrived

Puerto Ricans (the future Sharks) and the "self-styled 'Americans' " (the Jets). *East Side Story* had metamorphosed into *West Side Story*.

Since Robbins's balletic conception entailed an unusually extensive musical score, Bernstein, who until then thought he could handle the lyrics himself, decided that he needed a lyricist after all. On November 14 he wrote that they had found "a young lyricist named Stephen Sondheim," and described him as "ideal for this project."[15] In the 1985 symposium Sondheim added that when he was signed on as "co-lyricist" (in an unspecified month in 1955) Laurents "had a three-page outline."[16]

In the sole entry of 1956 (March 17) Bernstein announced that *Romeo* would be "postponed for a year" to make way for *Candide*.[17] Not unlike *Candide*'s Professor Pangloss, Bernstein tried to put the best possible face on this delay. He then described the "chief problem" of the new "problematical work": "To tread the fine line between opera and Broadway, between realism and poetry, ballet and 'just dancing,' abstract and representational," and to "avoid being 'messagy'."[18]

On February 1, 1957 Bernstein noted briefly that with *Candide* "on and gone . . . nothing shall disturb the project." In the next entry (July 8), shortly after rehearsals had begun, Bernstein confirmed the wisdom of 1949 in not casting " 'singers,' " since "anything that sounded more professional would inevitably sound more experienced, and then the 'kid' quality would be gone." On August 20, one day after the opening-night tryout in Washington, Bernstein made his final entry. With great enthusiasm and pride he assessed the successful artistic collaboration ("all writing the *same* show"). Together the quartet had created a work which possessed a "theme as profound as love versus hate, with all the theatrical risks of death and racial issues and young performers and 'serious' music and complicated balletics."[19]

Shortly before his death Bernstein revealed that the melody of "America," portions of "Mambo" from "The Dance at the Gym" (both derived from a never-completed Cuban ballet called *Conch Town* begun in 1941), and the centrally important "Somewhere" and "Maria" were among the first musical ideas conceived.[20] Regarding the origins of "Somewhere" Bernstein explained: " 'Somewhere' was a tune I had around and had never finished. I loved it. I remember Marc Blitzstein loved it very much and wrote a lyric to it just for fun. It was called 'There Goes What's His Name'."[21] Larry Kert (the original Tony) placed Bernstein's recollection about "Somewhere" more precisely when he remembered that "Somewhere" was "written about the time of *On the Town*" (1944), which would make this song the earliest musical antecedent of the future *West Side Story*.[22] Of equal importance is Bernstein's recollection that at the time the

Stephen Sondheim (at piano) and Leonard Bernstein rehearsing *West Side Story* (1957). Museum of the City of New York.

musical was still *East Side Story* he "had already jotted down a sketch for a song called 'Maria,' which was operable in Italian or Spanish."[23] Not only did Bernstein's sketch have a "dummy lyric," it "had those notes . . . the three notes of 'Maria' [that] pervade the whole piece—inverted, done backward."[24]

In the light of their contribution to the organic unity of the work, the knowledge that "Somewhere" and "Maria" were the first two songs drafted provides invaluable historical confirmation of the analytical conclusions that follow. Also striking, even if perhaps coincidental, is the fact that both of these pivotal songs bear unmistakable resemblances to music of Bernstein's predecessors. The opening five pitches and rhythms of "Somewhere" (Example 12.1a) correspond closely to the fifth and six measures of the second movement of Beethoven's E♭ major Piano Concerto, op. 73, known as the "Emperor" (Example 12.1b).[25] More significantly, the thrice-repeated three-note motive in the cello part at the conclusion of Tchaikovsky's *Romeo and Juliet* Overture (Example 12.1c) is identical to the first three notes of Bernstein's melody. Intended or not, "Somewhere" seems to begin where Tchaikovsky's overture leaves off. Unlike borrowed material in other shows, a number of Bernstein's central classical borrow-

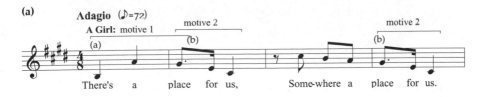

Example 12.1. "Somewhere" in Beethoven and Tchaikovsky
(a) "Somewhere"
(b) Beethoven: Piano Concerto No. 5, op. 73 ("Emperor")
(c) Tchaikovsky: *Romeo and Juliet*

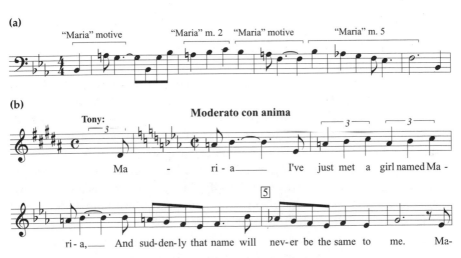

Example 12.2. Blitzstein's *Regina* and "Maria"
(a) *Regina*, Introduction to act I
(b) "Maria"

ings were apparently chosen for their programmatic and associative meaning.[26]

The main tune of "Maria" is more obviously indebted to an aria from the opera *Regina* (based on Hellman's *The Little Foxes*), composed by Bernstein's mentor and friend, Marc Blitzstein (Example 12.2).[27] Perhaps not coincidentally, *Regina* premiered in 1949, the year Robbins conceived his "noble idea." The exceedingly strong melodic, harmonic, and rhythmic similarities between "Maria" and the introductory music to act I of Blitzstein's lesser-known opera should be readily evident, even to those previously unfamiliar with the model.

Before intensive collaborative work began in 1956, several months after the entrance of Sondheim, the tangible evidence of *West Side Story* included a draft of several scenes, an outline of the remaining scenes, and substantial compositional work on two dramatically and musically central songs, "Somewhere" and "Maria." The cross-fertilization between *West Side Story* and *Candide* of the previous year is also evident. In 1956 the comic duet now indelibly associated with Candide and Cunegonde, "Oh, Happy We," had been considered for the bridal shop scene in *West Side Story*, and the song that was eventually placed there, "One Hand, One Heart," was originally intended for *Candide*.[28] Until at least 1957, however, this future bridal shop song was located in the balcony scene, after which it was replaced by "Tonight." Another version of an unused *Candide* song, "Where Does It Get You in the End?", served as the basis for "Gee, Officer Krupke," a song that was not added until rehearsals in July.[29]

By the end of 1956 Laurents had completed his fourth libretto draft (out of eight), and much of the eventual version was fixed. The most significant additions and revisions in the months prior to and during the rehearsal schedule from mid-June to mid-August 1957 were the addition of two songs, "Something's Coming" and "Gee, Officer Krupke," and considerable revamping of the opening Prologue. Also in 1957 more dance numbers would be added to the "Dance at the Gym" (only the "Mambo" was indicated for this section at the end of 1956); Tony's and Maria's "One Hand, One Heart" on the tenement balcony had still not been replaced by "Tonight."[30]

The Prologue and first scene, which had already undergone a number of changes in the first four librettos (all in 1956), required considerable revision before it achieved its revolutionary final version in the summer months of 1957. Although Bernstein exaggerates the ease with which he and his collaborators worked out the solution to the complex problems posed by this opening, the libretto and musical score drafts support his recollection in 1985 that the Prologue was originally intended to be sung: "It didn't take us long to find out that it wouldn't work. That was when

Vocal passages from "Up to the Moon" reused in "Prologue" and "Jet Song"

Example 12.3. Vocal passages from "Up to the Moon" reused
in Prologue and "Jet Song"
(a) "How long does it take"
(b) "Gettin' sweet and shined up"
(c) "Carazy, Daddy-O"

Jerry [Robbins] took over and converted all that stuff into this remarkable thing now known as 'the prologue to *West Side Story*,' all dancing and movement."[31]

The three sung themes of "Up to the Moon" (Example 12.3) found their way into the instrumental Prologue and the instrumental portions of the "Jet Song" as we know it. A fourth theme (and much of the text) from "Up to the Moon" was salvaged in the eventual Broadway version of the "Jet Song," when the Jets sing "Oh, when the Jets fall in at the cornball dance, / We'll be the sweetest dressin' gang in pants!"[32] In Laurents's fourth libretto (Winter 1956) the opening scene had shifted from a clubhouse to an alleyway, but it is not until the similar fifth and sixth librettos (April 14 and May 1, 1957) that the first scene—none of the eight librettos indicate a Prologue distinct from a first scene—begins to resemble the final version shown in Appendix Q, pp. 341–42.[33]

Sondheim recalled in the 1985 Dramatists Guild symposium that *West Side Story* "certainly changed less from the first preview in Washington to the opening in New York than any other show I've ever done, with the exception of *Sweeney Todd*, which also had almost no changes."[34] In *Sondheim & Co.* he comments further on the extent of these alterations: "Our total changes out of town consisted of rewriting the release for the 'Jet Song,' adding a few notes to 'One Hand,' Jerry *potchkied* with the second-act ballet, and there were a few cuts in the book."[35]

Again, the evidence from the music manuscripts and libretto drafts sub-
stantiates Sondheim's recollection on all these points. Bernstein's early piano-vocal score reveals the rejected release for the "Jet Song" and two
versions of "One," the original one-note-per-measure version and the familiar three-notes-per-measure version.[36] And in what is perhaps the most
significant *potch* of the dream ballet sequence, "Somewhere" was originally
intended to be danced rather than sung, at least until its conclusion when
Tony and Maria reprise the final measures.

Sondheim also remembered Robbins's preoccupation during the tryouts
with a number that would be eventually rejected:

> Jerry had a strong feeling that there was a sag in the middle of
> the first act [scene 6], so we wrote a number for the three young
> kids—Anybodys, Arab, and Baby John. It was called "Kids Ain't"
> and was a terrific trio that we all loved, but Arthur gave a most
> eloquent speech about how he loved it also but that we shouldn't
> use it, because it would be a crowd-pleaser and throw the weight
> over to typical musical comedy which we agreed we didn't want
> to do. So it never went in.[37]

During the July rehearsals Robbins & Co. had taken steps to remedy the
lack of a comic musical number caused by the removal of "Kids Ain't."
Although there had been a comic exchange between Officer Krupke and
the Jets in act II, scene 2 in the four 1956 libretto drafts, no song had yet
appeared in this space. Only in the final libretto draft did a recycled
"Where Does It Get You in the End?" from *Candide* materialize as "Gee,
Officer Krupke." Sondheim recalled that Robbins staged this number "in
three hours by the clock, three days before we went to Washington."[38] At
the time Sondheim thought that "Officer Krupke" would be better placed
in act I, since its presence detracted from the serious developments in the
drama. After viewing the 1961 film in which "Krupke" and "Cool" were
reversed "and weren't nearly as effective," Sondheim came to accept Robbins's directorial decision and to acknowledge that "Krupke" "works wonderfully" in act II on the basis of its "theatrical truth" rather than its "literal
truth."[39] Since its comic intent was meant to provide dramatic contrast and
relief from the mostly tragic theme based on tritones and "Somewhere"
motives (to be discussed), the absence of the latter and the softening of the
former in "Krupke" is understandable and dramatically plausible and welcome.

After "Krupke" one final song, not indicated even as late as the final
libretto draft of July 19, was added during rehearsals.[40] This song, newly

Jerome Robbins (second from left) rehearsing *West Side Story* (1957).
Museum of the City of New York.

composed to conclude act I, scene 2, after Tony promises Riff that he will attend the Settlement dance, is, of course, "Something's Coming." Bernstein describes the circumstances and motivation for this song:

> "Something's Coming" was born right out of a big long speech that Arthur wrote for Tony. It said how every morning he would wake up and reach out for something, around the corner or down the beach. It was very late and we were in rehearsal when Steve and I realized that we needed a strong song for Tony earlier since he had none until "Maria," which was a love song. We had to have more delineation of him as a character. We were looking through this particular speech, and "Something's Coming" just seemed to leap off the page. In the course of the day we had written that song.[41]

At Robbins's suggestion Laurents added the meeting between Tony and Riff in front of the drugstore, and in the course of the Washington tryouts the song "Something's Coming" replaced much of the dialogue.[42] Sondheim's recollection that the song ended with its eventual title is partially borne out by the Winter 1956 libretto, which concludes with the following exchange:

> TONY: Now it's right outside that door, around the corner: maybe being stamped in a letter, maybe whistling down the river, maybe—
>
> RIFF: What is?
>
> TONY: (*Shrugs*). I don't know. But it's coming and it's the greatest. . . . Could be. Why not?[43]

In contrast to "Gee, Officer Krupke," the purpose of which was to provide a respite from the surrounding tragedy, the motive behind "Something's Coming" was to introduce a main character and to link this character to the ensuing drama.[44] This is accomplished musically by allowing Tony to resolve a dissonant and dramatically symbolic interval (the interval of hate, a tritone) at the beginning and conclusion of his song.

From Verona to the Upper West Side

In order to understand the Romantic qualities inherent in *West Side Story* it may be helpful to recall that the nineteenth century, an age obsessed by the theme of idealized youthful passionate love that realizes its apotheosis only with premature death, was irresistibly drawn to Shakespeare's *Romeo and Juliet*.[45] Not only did this play—in various degrees of fidelity to Shakespeare—occupy the European stage throughout most of the nineteenth century, numerous musical settings also made their debut. Just as revisions of Shakespeare's play from the late-seventeenth through the nineteenth centuries frequently included a happy ending, most of the musical adaptations strayed conspicuously from the original. Gounod's still-popular *Roméo et Juliette* (1867), for example, introduces a major female role (Stephano) that has no Shakespearean counterpart.[46]

Although these operatic, orchestral, and balletic versions, unlike *West Side Story*, retain the names of the major characters and basic plot machinations, they more often than not distort Shakespeare's tragic intention with the insertion of either a happy ending (like many play performances) or an ending that enables the principals to sing (or dance) an impassioned love duet before their demise. Consider Prokofiev's ballet (1935–1936), one of the most popular of the twentieth century and most likely an inspiration for Robbins. After its premiere, Soviet Shakespearean scholars influenced censors to prohibit Prokofiev and his collaborators from allowing Romeo an extra minute in order to take advantage of his pyrrhic opportunity to witness Juliet alive. Prokofiev defended his original scenario: "The reasons that led us to such a barbarism were purely choreographic. Living people can dance, but the dead cannot dance lying down."[47]

Modern-day nonmusical versions of Shakespeare's play are similarly prone to alterations that can distort the meaning and tone of the Bard (or eliminate substantial portions of text), presumably for the sake of broader public palatability. The well-known 1968 film of *Romeo and Juliet* by director Franco Zeffirelli, probably the most popular film adaptation of Shakespeare ever made, serves as an instructive paradigm for the triumph of accessibility over authenticity introduced in chapter 1 (even though the eponymous principals die). One may acknowledge the need to make a Shakespeare movie cinematic and argue the artistic merits of Zeffirelli's considerable textual excisions, but the conclusion is nonetheless inescapable that Zeffirelli has succeeded more brilliantly in bringing himself rather than Shakespeare to a mass audience.[48]

Although it contains extensive transformational liberties, the tragic dramatic vision of *West Side Story* arguably corresponds more closely to Shakespeare than Zeffirelli's version or nineteenth-century musical adaptations that wear the garb of the Montagues and the Capulets. Robbins spoke of Laurents's achievement in following the "story as outlined in the Shakespeare play without the audience or critics realizing it," but most theatergoers familiar with the characters in Shakespeare's tale of "fair Verona" can easily recognize their West Side reincarnations.[49]

Most obviously, the warring gangs, the Jets and Sharks, parallel the warring families, the Montagues and Capulets.[50] Like Romeo at the outset of Shakespeare's play, Tony, a Jet, has disassociated himself from the violent members of his clan. His friend, Riff, shares the fate and much of the mercurial character of Romeo's friend, Mercutio. Maria appears as an older and therefore more credible Juliet for modern audiences. Bernardo's death has a greater impact because he is Maria's brother rather than a literal counterpart to Juliet's cousin Tybalt. By 1957 New York City teenagers were less likely to share intimacies with an aging nurse. Consequently, Anita, a woman only a few years older than Maria, serves as a more credible counterpart to Shakespeare's elderly crone, a confidante to Maria, and of course an agile dancing partner for her lover, Bernardo. Chino, Maria's unexciting but eventually excitable fiancé and Bernardo's choice for his sister, corresponds closely to Juliet's parentally selected suitor, the County Paris.

All these changes reflect societal changes that transpired between the 1590s and the 1950s. For similar reasons adult authority has been greatly reduced in the adaptation. Juliet's parents, who play a prominent role throughout the Shakespeare play (and in Laurents's early libretto drafts), are reduced to offstage voices in the musical; Tony's parents are represented metaphorically as dummies in the bridal shop where Tony and Maria marry themselves without benefit of clergy. Doc, a druggist who parallels the well-meaning but ineffectual Friar Laurence, serves far less as a catalyst for the plot than as an adult representative who can at least partially sympathize with troubled youth; Officer Krupke, although more abrasive than his counterpart, Prince Escalus, possesses less authority and earns even less respect.[51]

Other departures from Shakespeare's play were similarly motivated for the resulting accessibility. For example, in *Romeo and Juliet,* no Capulet or Montague can recall a specific cause for their senseless enmity.[52] *West Side Story* audiences learn that the Americans (the Jets) fear that the Puerto Ricans (the Sharks) are usurping jobs and territory.

Perhaps the most dramatic departure from Shakespeare also developed because the collaborators of *West Side Story* realized they needed a "believable substitute for the philter." Laurents speaks of his imaginative solution to this problem with justifiable pride: "The thing I'm proudest of in telling the story is why she [Anita] can't get the message through: because of prejudice. I think it's better than the original story."[53]

Thus, whenever dramatically possible, the youthful characters in *West Side Story* make their own mistakes and generate their own fate. Tony's form of suicide, his vociferous public invitation for Chino to shoot him, contrasts with Romeo's quiet decision to take the poison he has purchased for this purpose. In Shakespeare, a tragic coincidence (an outbreak of plague) prevented the news of Juliet's magic sleep from reaching Romeo; the sleep itself was induced by Friar Laurence's herbal potions, a well-meaning, albeit imprudent, adult action. A much-provoked Anita sets the stage for Tony's death with her deliberate lie to the Jets that Maria is dead. By letting Maria live, the creators of *West Side Story* allow her to assume the authority previously delegated to the patriarchal figures of the Capulet and Montague families and to inspire a reconciliation between the Sharks and Jets, who then carry Tony's body off the stage at the final curtain. Significantly, Maria leads the play's dramatic catharsis in front of adults as well as her peers.

Only the first two of Laurents's libretto drafts (January and Spring 1956) follow Shakespeare on this crucial dramaturgical point. Maria, thinking Tony dead, returns to the bridal shop and "sings passionately of her not wanting to live in a world without Tonio [at this point Tony was Italian-American], a world that has taken him from her." The scene description continues: "At the peak of this, she grabs up a pair of dressmaking shears and—with her back to us—plunges them into her stomach." Moments later Tony (Tonio) arrives and "cradling her in his arms, he starts to sing with her a reprise of their song from the marriage scene." The orchestra completes their song and after kissing her, Tony opens the door of the shop and cries out, "Come and take me! Come and take me too!"[54]

By the third draft (March 15, 1956), which also concludes at the bridal shop, Maria "tries to tear the wedding veil with her hands, cannot, picks up sewing shears and is about to cut the veil when a new thought [presumably suicide] enters her mind."[55] In this draft, as in the five others over the next sixteen months, a mortally wounded Tony finds Maria, and the lovers are able to share a few final moments together.

Robbins credits Rodgers for realizing how to "solve a problem like Maria" (two years before *The Sound of Music*'s Maria Von Trapp) and for keeping Maria alive: "I remember Richard Rodgers's contribution. We had a death scene for Maria—she was going to commit suicide or something, as in Shakespeare. He said, 'She's dead already, after this all happens to her'."[56] The final decision not to musicalize Maria's final impassioned speech came about by default rather than design after Bernstein had tried unsuccessfully "four or five times" to set Laurents's "dummy lyric for an aria for Maria, with flossy words about guns and bullets."[57]

Despite these liberties, the collaborators of *West Side Story* for the most part preserve the spirit of the original as well as what is perhaps Shakespeare's central theme: the triumph of youthful passionate love over youthful passionate hate, even in death. They also incorporate Shakespeare's literary device of foreshadowing, for similar dramatic and musical purposes, to inform audiences of the inevitable albeit mostly self-made destiny facing the young lovers. Tony's somewhat more optimistic premonition in "Something's Coming" early in the musical can be seen, for example, as a parallel to Mercutio's famous Queen Mab speech: "My mind misgives/ Some consequence, yet hanging in the stars, / Shall bitterly begin his fearful date / With this night's revels and expire the term / Of a despised life, closed in my breast, / By some vile forfeit of untimely death" (act 1, scene 4, lines 112–17).

Romeo's bittersweet, sorrowful premonitions in the first eleven lines of act V ("I dreamt my lady came and found me dead") clearly correspond to the Romantic message most clearly expressed in "Somewhere," introduced by an anonymous offstage "Girl" (opera stars Reri Grist on Broadway and Marilyn Horne on Bernstein's 1985 recording, handpicked by the composer) during the dream ballet sequence in act II.[58] By the end of Bernstein's musical counterpart to Shakespeare in the dream sequence, audiences know that the place and time for Tony and Maria will not be a flat on the Upper West Side. Rather, as in the tale of Tristan and Isolde, their passionate love will be fulfilled only after death. With great ingenuity Bernstein manages to discover a convincing musical equivalent to Shakespeare's foreshadowing of death, a musical transformation from youthful hate to youthful love.

A "Tragic Story in Musical-Comedy Terms"

As early as 1949 Bernstein, Laurents, and Robbins were consciously striving to write "a musical that tells a tragic story in musical-comedy terms" and to avoid "falling into the 'operatic trap'." At the same time they (mainly Bernstein as composer) borrowed freely from the European operatic and symphonic traditions.[59] The degree to which Broadway musicals could and should aspire to the condition of nineteenth-century tragic opera remains a controversial issue often vigorously and irreconcilably divided along party lines. Representing one side is Joseph P. Swain, who views Broadway generally as a series of "missed chances and unanswered challenges" that "made tragic drama in the American musical theater into an Olympus, beckoning beyond reach."[60] Not surprisingly for Swain, "Maria's last speech should indeed have been her biggest aria."[61] Similarly, in the *West Side Story* entry in *The New Grove Dictionary of Opera* Jon Alan Conrad considers Bernstein's "failure to find music for Maria's final scene" one of the "weak points."[62] Those who interpret the dramaturgy of musicals as a workable alternative, perhaps even a corrective, to opera might conclude with Stephen Banfield that "whatever fears Laurents may have had that it would turn into a 'goddamned Bernstein opera,' one of *West Side Story*'s greatest strengths is that it did not."[63] Accordingly, "Maria's final speech works perfectly well as dialogue."[64]

The analytical remarks that follow will show that Bernstein borrowed from his European predecessors as well as from his American present. Combining techniques and ideologies of nineteenth-century opera and American vernacular styles, Bernstein forged his own dramatic musical hybrid. While the connections to Latin dance rhythms and cool jazz are immediately apparent and even labelled, the European technical procedures require more explanation. Although motivic melodic analysis no longer serves as the central analytical paradigm, the crucial role motivic development plays in some musicals, most notably *Show Boat, Porgy and Bess,* and *West Side Story,* is virtually inarguable. More important, the principal motivic transformations are readily perceived (even to inexperienced listeners) and the more intricate melodic connections usually serve a demonstrable dramatic purpose.

Since the most famous exponent of nineteenth-century tragic drama was Wagner (his views were popular especially in the 1950s), it is not surprising that Bernstein, in setting the tragedy of Romeo and Juliet, borrowed melodic and harmonic elements most commonly associated with Wagner's operas (although certainly not limited to these works). The principal melodic technique is the pervasive use of leitmotivs (short themes that represent people, things, or abstract ideas) as source material for thematic transformation and organic unity.[65] Harmonically, Bernstein used the deceptive cadence, a sequence of chords in which a dominant fails to resolve to its tonic.[66] Also associated with Wagner and adopted by Bernstein is the technique of having the orchestra present an underlying dramatic commentary on the melodic line. Finally, the ensuing analytical discussion will suggest that Bernstein borrowed a central and specific leitmotiv from Wagner and used it for a related dramatic purpose.[67]

Bernstein's Wagnerian vision is most profoundly revealed in his use of the song "Somewhere," a song that, despite its early conception, did not achieve its vocal independence until a relatively late stage in the compositional process. As previously noted, until the production began its rehearsals in June, the piano-vocal score manuscript reveals that this song, eventually intoned by a woman off-stage, was to be entirely danced. Only after the "Procession and Nightmare" did Tony and Maria return to sing the final eight measures of "Somewhere."[68]

Nearly all of the musical material in "Somewhere" is based on one of three motives. The thirty-seven measures of this modified and expanded thirty-two-bar A-A-B-A song form can be outlined as follows:

A (8 measures)
   There's a place for us, (mm. 1–2)
   Somewhere a place for us. (mm. 3–4)
   Peace and quiet and open air (mm. 5–6)
   Wait for us Somewhere.—(mm. 7–8)
A' (8 measures)
   There's a time for us, (mm. 9–10)
   Some day a time for us, (mm. 11–12)
   Time together with time to spare, (mm. 13–14)
   Time to look, time to care, (mm. 15–16)

(a)

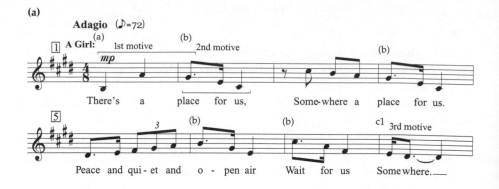

(b)

Example 12.4. "Somewhere" motives
(a) "There's a place for us" (motives *a* and *b*)
(b) "Some day! Somewhere" (motive *c*)

B   (8 measures)
    Someday!—Somewhere.—(mm. 17–18)
    We'll find a new way of living,—(mm. 19–20)
    We'll find a way of forgiving—(mm. 21–22)
    Somewhere. (mm. 23–24)

A"   (8 measures)
    There's a place for us, (mm. 25–26)
    A time and place for us. (mm. 27–28)
    Hold my hand and we're halfway there. (mm. 29–30)
    Hold my hand and I'll take you there (mm. 31–32)

B"   (5 measures)
    Somehow,—Some day,—Somewhere!—(mm. 33–37)

Despite its brevity, each motive shown in Example 12.4 contains a distinctive rhythmic or melodic profile. More important, each motive will be purposefully foreshadowed. The first motive (*a*) which opens the song on

"There's a place"—possibly derived from the second movement of Beethoven's "Emperor" Concerto or, more likely, from the final measures of Tchaikovsky's Fantasy-Overture on *Romeo and Juliet*—consists of three notes, a rising minor seventh (B up to A) followed by a descending half-step (A down to G#). Bernstein uses this motive in the vocal part to mark the principal statements of the tune on the words "There's a place" (mm. 1—2 and mm. 25—26) and "There's a time" (mm. 9—10) that initiate each A section.

Bernstein elides the last note of this *a* motive with a second motive, *b*, on "place for us," composed of intervals that form a simple descending minor or, less frequently, major triad. This second motive with its idiosyncratic rhythmic signature is usually paired with its predecessor and occurs nine times in the first sixteen measures of the song and another four thereafter. The most frequently stated (six times) descending minor triad, C-sharp minor (G#-E-C# or vi in E major as in m. 2) marks a deceptive and therefore ambiguous resolution. For most of the song Bernstein plays on our expectation that the B major dominant seventh implied in the first motive, which corresponds to the "place" for Tony and Maria, should be followed by the tonic chord, E major. Like many nineteenth-century composers, however, Bernstein does not allow his song to actually arrive on the tonic E until the final measures. It is tempting to make a connection between these deceptive cadences and Wagner's Prelude to *Tristan und Isolde,* where harmonic resolutions are similarly denied to make the dramatic point that nowhere on earth will there be a place to rest for Wagner's star-crossed lovers.

The minor seventh melodic interval of the first motive ("There's a place") and the dotted rhythm signature of the triadic second motive ("place for us") also permeates the orchestral underpinning of "Somewhere."[69] After the offstage "Girl" introduces the first motive vocally, the orchestra will repeat it until interrupted by the first appearance of the third (or "Somewhere") motive (c^1) at measure 8. The "place for us" motive gains in orchestral as well as vocal prominence after measure 8 as it frequently answers its vocal statements, occasionally straddling measures in the process.[70]

After its solitary appearance during the course of the first two A sections, the third "Somewhere" motive will emerge in the second half of the song as the principal rhythmic motive (with no less than eight statements). Bernstein introduces this third motive with a descending half-step (E to D#); thereafter the most emphasized melodic interval will be an ascending whole-step (c^2) to mark the modulation to C major on the words "Some day! Somewhere" (mm. 17 and 18). On three other occasions, "living," "–giving," and "Somewhere" (mm. 20, 22, and 23 respectively) he changes

Example 12.5. Orchestral foreshadowing of "Somewhere" at
the conclusion of the Balcony Scene ("Tonight")

the third motive more drastically with a descending perfect fifth (c^3). All
three melodic versions of this third "Somewhere" motive share the same
defining rhythmic identity.

At the outset of *Romeo and Juliet* the character known as the Chorus informs Shakespeare's audience of the destiny soon to befall the doomed
lovers.[71] The characters themselves, of course, are not allowed to know
this. Similarly, Romeo's dreams prepare audiences for the forthcoming
tragedy, but Romeo himself does not fully grasp their significance until
after the fact.

Bernstein borrows the theatrical device of foreshadowing when he suc-
cessively anticipates the three "Somewhere" motives in "Tonight," Tony
and Maria's impassioned love duet on the fire escape (Shakespeare's Ve-
ronese balcony) within minutes of their first meeting at the gym dance.[72]
As in Wagner's music dramas, the orchestra gives an alert audience clas-
sified information to which the principals are not privy. At the conclusion
of "Tonight" the idealistic lovers show their oneness by singing in unison
and the celestial heights of youthful optimistic love by singing and holding
high A♭'s. Meanwhile, back on earth, the omniscient orchestra warns audiences of their imminent doom (Example 12.5).

A second prominent foreshadowing of "Somewhere" occurs minutes
later during the dance between choruses of "Cool," when the Jets make
an energetic but ultimately fruitless attempt to achieve a calm before the

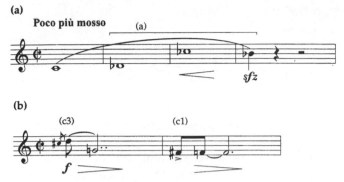

(a)

Poco più mosso   (a)

sfz

(b)

(c3)   (c1)

f

Example 12.6. "Somewhere" motives in "Cool" fugue
(a) first "Somewhere" motive (motive *a*)
(b) third "Somewhere" motive (motive *c*)

rumble. Here Bernstein uses the first "Somewhere" motive (without its usual second-motive continuation) as the first three notes of the fugue subject that introduces the "Cool" fugue, danced rather than sung by the Jets (Example 12.6a). Several measures later a slightly transformed version of the third "Somewhere" motive (Example 12.6b, c^3 and c^1) can also be heard.[73] Like the use of the three "Somewhere" motives presented in succession at the conclusion of the "Tonight" duet, the idea here is an orchestral one that can be interpreted as a foreshadowing of death, much in the way the orchestra at the conclusion of Wagner's *Das Rheingold* informs the audience, but not Wotan, of Siegfried's sword.[74]

More ingeniously, Bernstein finds a new use for the "There's a place" motive when Maria and Anita reconcile their anger and pain in "I have a love," the song which follows the "Somewhere" dream ballet. In this climactic scene the composer transforms the first "Somewhere" motive into a new context. As shown in Example 12.7, Bernstein preserves the melody but alters the rhythm to fit a new declamation on the words, "I love him, I'm his" and "I love him, we're one" sung by Maria to Anita, and in harmony with her friend on the words, "When love comes so strong."[75]

The "Procession and Nightmare" introduces a new important motive shown in Example 12.8a, a motive that will return to conclude the musical in the Finale. In contrast to the three "Somewhere" motives, the "Procession" motive is not foreshadowed in earlier portions of the work. Rather, this "Procession" motive itself foreshadows a new principal theme, set to "I have a love, and it's all that I have" and "I have a love and it's all that I need" (the opening is shown in Example 12.8b), where it alternates with a rhythmic transformation of the first "Somewhere" motive (compare Examples 12.4a and 12.7).[76] The "I have a love" motive also retains its symbiotic relationship with the three "Somewhere" motives, since it will

Ex. 12.7: *"Somewhere" motive in "I Have a Love"*

Andante sostenuto

Maria: 1st "Somewhere" motive

(a)   (a)

I love him; I'm his, And ev-'ry-thing he is I am

Example 12.7. "Somewhere" motive in "I Have a Love"

either adjoin or occur simultaneously with one or more of these "Some-where" motives whenever it is heard. The "Procession" motive also bears an uncanny and perhaps intended melodic, rhythmic, and symbolic con-nection with Wagner's "redemption" theme (Example 12.8c) first sung by Sieglinde in *Die Walküre* and later by Brünnhilde during the Immolation Scene that concludes *Die Götterdämmerung*.[77]

"Somewhere" and "Procession and Nightmare," with their foreshadow-ings and symbolic apotheoses, musically convey the principal dramatic message of *West Side Story*. But Bernstein also uses musical materials more directly by taking advantage of music's power to depict psychological states and by assigning appropriate musical equivalents to the driving emotions of passionate youthful hate and its counterpart in youthful love. Bernstein's principal musical accomplice to make this possible is the tritone or augmented fourth, a highly charged dissonant interval which figures prominently in the motive associated with the hate-filled gangs (Example 12.9a, F-B). It is possible but undocumented that the idea to make pervasive use of the intervals formed by these notes C-F-B (a rising perfect fourth followed by a rising tritone) as a central motive in *West Side Story*) was borrowed from Alban Berg's Piano Sonata, op. 1 (1907–1908), well known in Bernstein's circle (Example 12.9b, G-C-F♯). In any event, Bernstein's mo-tive clearly serves as a central unifying element. Although no one has spec-ulated on its possible connection with Berg's sonata, its appearance (in nearly every musical number of the show) was recognized as early as Jack Gottlieb's 1964 dissertation; the motive has been discussed in varying de-tail since then by Peter Gradenwitz, Larry Stempel, and Swain.[78] Gottlieb prefaces his discussion of the "hate" motive with the following statement:

It was in WEST SIDE STORY that the fullest expression of the interval as a progenitor of musical development came into effect. Unlike WONDERFUL TOWN (perfect fifth)[79] and CANDIDE (minor seventh),[80] the interval here was not used for melodic purposes only, but as a harmonic force also. The interval in question is the tritone (aug-mented fourth), the famous *Diabolus in Musica*, certainly an ap-propriate symbolism for this tragic musical drama.[81]

Example 12.8. "Procession" motive in "I Have a Love" and
Wagner's *Ring*
(a) "Procession" motive
(b) "I Have a Love" ("Procession" motive)
(c) Redemption motive in Wagner's *Die Walküre*

A summary of how Bernstein uses the "hate" motive for dramatic purposes follows.

Bernstein introduces the definitive form of the "hate" motive in the
Prologue shortly just after the stage directions "Bernardo enters."[82] Once
Bernstein associates his unresolved tritone motive with the hate-filled Jets,
he positions himself to convey dramatic meanings through its resolution
or attempted resolution. An example of the latter occurs in "Promenade,"

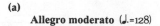

(a)

Allegro moderato (♩.=128)

(Bernado enters.)

pp

(b)

Mäßig bewegt

p

(c)

Solid and boppy (♩=96)

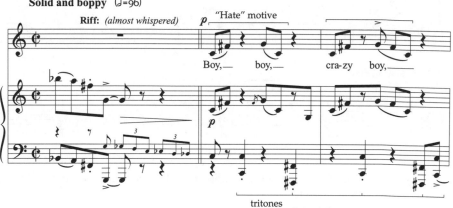

Riff: *(almost whispered)*   *p* ⸢"Hate" motive⸣

Boy,— boy,— cra-zy boy,—

p

tritones

(d)

Fast (♩=176)

Tony:

Could be!———— Who– knows?————

Tony's tritone resolution

Example 12.9. "Hate" in *West Side Story*
(a) "Hate" motive ("Prologue")
(b) "Hate" motive in Berg Piano Sonata
(c) "Hate" motive in "Cool" (attempted resolution)
(d) Resolution of the "Hate" motive in "Something's Coming"

(e)

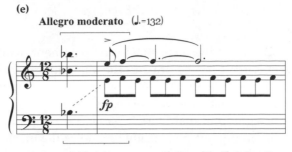

Maria's name as resolution of the "hate" motive

(e) Tony's resolution of the tritone and Maria's name as resolution of the "Hate" motive in The Dance at the Gym

when the social worker Glad Hand attempts to get the Sharks and Jets to mix amiably at the Settlement dance. Here the accented tritone dissonances in the bass (now spelled C-G♭), symbolically demonstrate the underlying tensions and resulting futility of attempts to resolve the animosity between the gangs. The drama reinforces this musical point when "Promenade" is interrupted by the "Mambo" and Bernardo and Riff circumvent their intended partners and heed Anita's subsequent dictum to associate exclusively with "their own kind."

As the song instructs, the Jets in "Cool" attempt to achieve a degree of calm prior to "The Rumble" (or after "The Rumble" in the film version).[83] The main tune of "Cool" consists of a tritone (spelled C-F♯) followed almost invariably by its upward resolution to the perfect fifth (G) (Example 12.9c). Underneath the main tune the definitive "hate" (or "gang") motive appears as an accompaniment, and tritones also provide a harmonic foundation. One might interpret the upward resolution as an easing of tension, a perfect fifth as a metaphor for a more perfect world. If so, the Jets' attempt to compose themselves in this song, like their attempts to mix at the Settlement dance, are also destined for musical failure, a failure borne out dramatically by the subsequent deaths of Riff and Bernardo.

Only the characters who represent the triumph of love over hate, Tony and Maria, can unambiguously and convincingly resolve the tritone tension embodied in the gang's signature motive. This happens as early as Tony's first song, "Something's Coming" (Example 12.9d). Tony's first words, "Could be!", outline a perfect descending fourth (D-A), and his next question, "Who knows?", establishes a second perfect fourth after an eighth-note digression to the tritone (D-G♯-A). By this immediate resolution Bernstein lets his audiences know, at least subliminally, that Tony, an ex-Jet, is a man capable of assuaging the tensions of his former gang as his musical line resolves its tritones. Throughout the entire first portion of

"Something's Coming," the orchestral accompaniment, which consists entirely of perfect fourths—in contrast to the alternating perfect fourths and tritones in the bass of "Promenade"—supports this important dramatic point: that Tony is a man who wants peace.

It is crucially significant that Maria's name (Example 12.2b) resolves the tritone and thus simply but powerfully embodies the musical antithesis of the unresolved "hate" motive. As with the first and third "Somewhere" motives, Bernstein foreshadows Maria's motive orchestrally before fully establishing her identity vocally. Reasonably attentive listeners can hear her motive for the first time at the outset of "The Dance at the Gym" (the introduction to "Blues") following Maria's explanation to her brother that "tonight" marks her debut "as a young lady of America!", where its upward resolution appears simultaneously with Tony's downward tritone (Example 12.9e). More obviously, Bernstein foreshadows the entire Maria tune in the "Cha-Cha" and brings it back appropriately as underscoring for her "Meeting Scene" with Tony.

The Maria motive of course dominates the next song, "Maria," where each repetition of the heroine's name conveys the message that Maria, to an even greater extent than her romantic counterpart, can resolve dramatic tensions. Maria's motive returns at other timely occasions during the remainder of the musical: throughout the orchestral underscoring which introduces the Balcony Scene that encompasses "Tonight"; in "Under Dialogue" as a cha-cha (a rare omission in Bernstein's "complete" 1985 recording); in the underscoring that marks the moment Tony and Maria declare themselves married directly prior to "One Hand, One Heart"; and at various other places in the orchestral accompaniment to this last-mentioned song. Thereafter the full three-note Maria motive becomes displaced by its dramatic (and musical) associate, the third "Somewhere" motive (c^3 in Example 12.4), which presents a readily apparent rhythmic association with the last two syllables of Maria's name.

The drama ends with a "real" death procession (in contrast to the dream procession earlier in the second act). At the end of this Bernstein presents three statements of the third "Somewhere" motive (c^2) with its customary rising whole-step (Example 12.10a). In the first two statements the bass answer to this C-major triadic resolution in the melody (C-E-G) is none other than the sinister tritone (F♯) for two statements. In the third and final statement, Bernstein allows an undiluted C major to stand alone.[84] Certainly it is possible to interpret the absence of a third F♯ as an optimistic ending, or at least more positive than if Bernstein had chosen to state the tritone the third time as well.

The screen version of *West Side Story* adds a *third* tritone to accompany

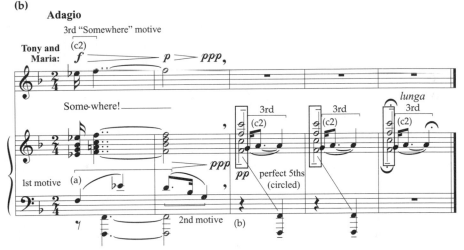

Example 12.10. "Finale" and "Procession and Nightmare"
(conclusions)
(a) Broadway ending ("Finale")
(b) Conclusion of "Procession and Nightmare" and the
film soundtrack

the end credits. The original movie soundtrack album, however, departs
both from the Broadway and the film ending in its musical resolution of
the drama. As shown in Example 12.10b it abandons tritones altogether
for all three statements of the "Somewhere" motive.[85] Why did the soundtrack do this? Here is one possible explanation. Despite the fact that the
film omitted the Dream Ballet Sequence (based on "Somewhere"), except
as underscoring at the beginning of act II, scene 3, the producers of the

soundtrack wanted to find a place for the song "Somewhere." When first released, the soundtrack therefore used the dream version of this song, but now sung by the principals rather than an offscreen "Girl," to conclude the recording. For this reason the original soundtrack concluded with an unambiguously positive major ending that avoids tritones entirely.[86]

To better depict an age when gang warfare is still rampant and exponentially more violent than it was on the West Side in 1957 or 1961, Bernstein, in his operatic recorded reinterpretation of the score he conducted in 1985, departs from his Broadway ending. This time he has the orchestra follow the third statement of the "Somewhere" motive with a third tritone as in the "End Credits" that followed the drama in the film. But even in the 1985 recording Bernstein allows a hopeful glimmer of C major to sound when he instructs the orchestra to quickly release the third tritone.

Maria lives, but Bernstein, despite numerous attempts, was unable to create an operatic aria for her that rang true. Thus in her most Wagnerian moment Maria does not sing. In an opera Maria, albeit "skinny—but pretty" and "delicate-boned" in contrast to the "fat lady" of operatic legend, would have no choice but to sing in order to inform audiences that the evening was over. Despite this conspicuous departure from operatic expectations, even requirements, *West Side Story* has been said to achieve genuine tragedy because "for the first time in a musical the hero sings while dying."[87] Perhaps more significantly, when Tony is carried off, the music of *West Side Story* has, metaphorically speaking, the last word. Audiences unaware of the musical relationships between death ("Procession") and love ("I Have a Love") and their mutual source in Wagner's "redemption" motive (Example 12.8a–c) nevertheless cannot fail to understand that the love of Tony and Maria, like that of Siegmund and Sieglinde, Brünnhilde and Siegfried, and of course Romeo and Juliet, has redeemed the tragedy of youthful death.

After *West Side Story* Bernstein failed to succeed on Broadway with a completely new musical, but a considerably revamped *Candide* directed by Hal Prince (which included Sondheim's newly created "Life is Happiness Indeed," a reworded "Venice Gavotte"), triumphed in 1974. Two years later Bernstein produced a musical with librettist-lyricist Alan Jay Lerner, *1600 Pennsylvania Avenue*. Although this promising but problematic show vanished after only seven Broadway performances, Bernstein managed to salvage portions of its score in his last compositions, and one song, the anthem "Take Care of This House" (originally sung by Abigail Adams in the White House), has since served as a talisman to protect many buildings, from houses of worship to the Kennedy Center. In 1983 Bernstein, who by then was focusing most of his creative energies on conducting, completed his final work for the musical stage, the opera *A Quiet Place*. A sequel to *Trouble in Tahiti* three decades later, *A Quiet Place* also recycled the former work (as a flashback) for a middle act.

Two years after *West Side Story* Robbins, Laurents, and Sondheim would again collaborate successfully on a new musical, *Gypsy*, with music by Styne. Without Robbins, Laurents and Sondheim worked together on two unsuccessful musicals in the next decade before they went on to work with other partners: *Anyone Can Whistle* (1964), a show without a literary source, and *Do I Hear a Waltz?* (1965), an adaptation of Laurents's own *The Time of the Cuckoo* (with the grudging musical collaboration of Rodgers). Meanwhile, Robbins and his new creative associates, lyricist Sheldon Harnick and composer Jerry Bock, would direct and choreograph his greatest popular triumph, *Fiddler on the Roof*, in 1964. After *Fiddler* Robbins virtually abandoned commercial theater. Laurents, without Sondheim, returned to Broadway in subsequent decades to direct Harold Rome's *I Can Get It for You Wholesale* (1962) and the Harvey Fierstein–Jerry Herman Tony Award–winning *La Cage aux Folles* (1983). Without Laurents in the 1970s, '80s, and '90s, Sondheim, the subject of the next and final chapter in this survey, would, like the descendant of painter Georges Seurat in act II of *Sunday in the Park With George,* continue to "move on" and in the process launch a new era in the Broadway musical.

CHAPTER THIRTEEN

HAPPILY EVER AFTER *WEST SIDE STORY* WITH SONDHEIM

Running Long on Broadway After 1960

By 1960 Broadway had nearly completed the changing of the old guard. Among the giants who contributed significantly to Broadway during the 1940s and 1950s only Loesser and Styne managed to produce a truly major popular Broadway success in the 1960s: Loesser's *How to Succeed in Business Without Really Trying* (1961) and Styne's *Funny Girl* (1964). Arguably more for economic than artistic reasons within the next several decades most of the long-running musicals featured in this volume would be at least partially eclipsed by new generations of ever-longer-running shows. In fact, only twelve of the musicals in the top forty shown in Appendix C made their debut before 1960.[1]

Not long after the barrage of (for the most part) critically as well as popularly well-received hits in the mid-1960s, *Fiddler on the Roof* and *Hello, Dolly!* in 1964, *The Man of La Mancha* in 1965, *Cabaret* and *Mame* in 1966, the differences between these two once-related criteria of success became increasingly pronounced.[2] *A Chorus Line*, at 6,137 performances the longest-running musical of all time (1975) (as of this writing *Cats* [1982] is scheduled to surpass this total on June 19, 1997), might be considered a special case, since it was initially lauded as an artistic breakthrough and won the prestigious Pulitzer Prize for drama as well as a Tony Award. Despite its extraordinary popularity and award-winning success, however, *A Chorus*

Line has not fared well over time with most music and theater critics. In the only serious critical study it has so far received, the critical nature of Joseph P. Swain's judgment of the work was so negative that its publisher, Wren Music Co., refused permission to reprint any music or lyrics.[3]

The disparities between popularity and critical acclaim in musicals after 1970 is most conspicuously embodied in the contrasting careers and achievements of Sondheim (b. 1930) and Andrew Lloyd Webber (b. 1948). The long runs of Lloyd Webber's *Evita* (1,567 performances) and the still-running *Cats* (5,944 performances) and *Phantom of the Opera* (3,542 performances) have firmly established this British import—collaborating respectively with lyricists Tim Rice, T. S. Eliot, and Charles Hart—as the most popular composer in Broadway history, the heir apparent to Rodgers and Hammerstein, Lerner and Loewe, Loesser, and Porter. Despite (or perhaps because of) Lloyd Webber's certifiable fame, critics—with several modest exceptions, most notably theater historian Martin Gottfried and *Time* theater reviewer and Lloyd Webber biographer Michael Walsh—have been relentlessly and stridently negative in their assessment of Webber's musicals.[4]

The response to Lloyd Webber's musicals is roughly analogous to the negative judgments as well as the condemnation and neglect by musical scholars of Sergei Rachmaninoff, the displaced romantic twentieth-century composer whose popularity with performers and audiences remains undiminished. Both are probably underrated, certainly underestimated and understudied. Sondheim's popular as well critical stock may continue to rise in the decades to come. Nevertheless, Lloyd Webber's musicals, like Carlotta in Sondheim's *Follies*, are "still here" (and apparently here to stay), and they merit more thoughtful and detailed attention than is possible in this survey.

In contrast to Lloyd Webber and his classical counterpart, Rachmaninoff, Sondheim's place in the Broadway firmament approximates that of Arnold Schoenberg in classical music of the early twentieth century. After composing popular and continuously accessible opening salvos, *Verklärte Nacht* (1899) and *A Funny Thing Happened on the Way to the Forum* (1962), respectively, both Schoenberg and Sondheim have so far proved relatively unpopular, if popularity is measured by number of performances or long first-runs on Broadway. Sondheim's musicals do, however, have an intensely loyal if relatively small popular following. Several have broken even or turned a profit with respectable runs (*Company, A Little Night Music, Sweeney Todd,* and *Into the Woods*), and *Forum* was a certifiable hit (the eleventh biggest of the 1960s and for the moment perching precariously as no. 40 in the top forty).[5] Nevertheless, even Sondheim himself concedes that his shows are "caviar for the General" rather than a regular diet for the masses. Moreover, while theater critics with rare dissent have long

Stephen Sondheim. © Al Hirschfeld. Drawing reproduced by special arrangement with Hirschfeld's exclusive representative, The Margo Feiden Galleries Ltd. New York.

considered his lyrics the equivalent in brilliance to Lorenz Hart and Porter, Sondheim's *music* has gained critical acceptance only gradually and less completely.[6]

Decade by Decade With Sondheim

Within two years after creating the lyrics to *West Side Story* (1957), Sondheim reluctantly but successfully wrote the lyrics to Styne's music for *Gypsy* (1959), a relatively popular musical in its time that has long-since demonstrated its revivability, perhaps even canonicity. Sondheim's next show, *Fo-*

rum (1962), his Broadway debut as a composer, won the Tony Award for best musical and at 964 performances would enjoy a far longer run than any future Sondheim show.[7] Despite these early associations with acclaim and popularity, however, Sondheim himself was relegated to the background, barely mentioned in the reviews of *West Side Story* and *Gypsy* and bypassed even as a nominee for his work on *Forum*. Perhaps the major achievement of his next musical, *Anyone Can Whistle* (1964), again with a libretto by *West Side Story* and *Gypsy* author Arthur Laurents, was that, despite a disappointing nine performances, Goddard Lieberson of Columbia Records produced a commercial recording. One year later Sondheim completed the trilogy of collaborations with composer legends begun with Bernstein and Styne when he wrote the lyrics for Richard Rodgers's *Do I Hear a Waltz?* (the fourth and final Laurents libretto), an unpleasant, occasionally acrimonious, experience for all concerned that led to a quickly forgotten musical.

After two successive flops and five fallow years Sondheim erupted on Broadway between 1970 and 1973 with a modernist explosion: *Company, Follies,* and *A Little Night Music*. From this trilogy *Company* has been most frequently singled out for its historic and artistic significance. Not atypical is the assessment by Thomas P. Adler in the *Journal of Popular Culture* that *Company* was "every bit as much a landmark musical as *Oklahoma!*"[7] In fact, Eugene K. Bristow and J. Kevin Butler conclude their essay on *Company* in *American Music* with a similar epiphany: "As *Oklahoma!* was the landmark, model, and inspiration for almost all musicals during the three decades that followed its opening, *Company* became the vantage point, prototype, and stimulus for new directions in musical theater of the seventies and eighties."[8]

Company and *Night Music* earned some profit despite relatively modest runs (the more lavish *Follies* lost $685,000 of its $800,000 investment), and Sondheim collected Tonys and Critics Circle Awards for all three musical scores. As part of the "nostalgia" revival that also included a successful revival of Vincent Youmans's *No, No, Nanette* (1925) in 1971, *Follies* even appeared on the cover of *Time*. Only *Night Music*, however, was spared the criticism that Sondheim was destined to share with another early twentieth-century modernist, Igor Stravinsky, who was accused of cynicism, coldness, and "bloodlessness." For a modernist such crimes are excusable, but they are serious accusations when addressed to a composer working in a genre whose clientele expects shows to appeal to the emotions—allegedly incompatible with the intellect. The career of Sondheim marks, perhaps for the first time, not only the consistent failure of a composer of the most highly regarded musicals of his generation to produce blockbusters on Broadway, but also the fact that even his award-winning shows have yet to produce a single major song hit (with the lonely exception of *Night Music*'s "Send in the Clowns").[9]

While the integrated musical remained very much alive after *West Side Story*, the next step in dramatic organicism, the so-called concept musical, where "all elements of the musical, thematic and presentational, are integrated to suggest a central theatrical image or idea," began to receive notoriety in the 1960s and 1970s.[10] Sondheim and his collaborators were very much in the forefront of this development. Musicals based more on themes than on narrative action were no more new in the 1960s than the integrated musicals were in the 1940s. Nevertheless, earlier concept musicals, including revues such as *As Thousands Cheer* in 1933 (arguably all revues are concept musicals) or book musicals from *Rose-Marie* (1924) and *Chee-Chee* (1928) to *Love Life* (1948)—like the integrated *Show Boat* and *Porgy and Bess* explored in the present survey—deviate from what Max Weber or Carl Dahlhaus would call an "ideal type."[11] In any event early concept musicals failed to inspire a flock of popularly successful followers. Perhaps more than any single individual, the inspiration in the move toward the concept musical ideal was Jerome Robbins, who early had established thematic meaning through movement and dance as the choreographer of *The King and I* (1951) and as the director-choreographer for Sondheim's first Broadway efforts, *West Side Story* and *Gypsy*. Robbins was notorious for going around asking "What is this show about?," a question that led to the late insertion of "Comedy Tonight" in *Forum* to inform audiences and prepare them for what they might expect in the course of the evening. Robbins's insistence on getting an answer to this probing question led to what is arguably the first full-fledged concept musical of the post-Rodgers and Hammerstein era, *Fiddler on the Roof* (1964), when the show-opener "Tradition" became, in addition to a song, the embodiment of an overriding idea (rather than an action) that could unify and conceptualize a show.

After *Fiddler* the concept musical was principally championed by Harold Prince, who had produced two of the above-mentioned Robbins shows (*West Side Story* and *Fiddler*) before going on to direct *Cabaret*, *Zorbá*, the considerably altered *Candide* 1974 revival, and no less than six Sondheim musicals from *Company* in 1970 to *Merrily We Roll Along* in 1981.[12] The use of a German cabaret as a metaphor for pre–World War II German decadence in *Cabaret* exemplifies Prince's continuation of the concept idea developed by Robbins. Arguably, the Sondheim-Prince standard of the concept musical (in the absence of a more meaningful term) throughout the 1970s, was less a revolution than a reinterpretation (using additional means to the same end) of the integrated musical.[13]

Sondheim's unique apprenticeships might serve as a Hegelian metaphor for his antithesis between and eventual synthesis of modernism and traditionalism, high-brow and low-brow. While still a teenager Sondheim had the opportunity to be critiqued at length by Hammerstein, who, by a fortuitous coincidence that would be the envy of *Show Boat*'s second act, happened to be a neighbor and the father of Sondheim's friend and contemporary, James Hammerstein. Sondheim never forgot Hammerstein's priceless lessons in how not to write a musical and in fact followed Hammerstein's advice to write four kinds of musicals to help him develop his craft and discover his own voice.[14]

Several years after Hammerstein's initial tutelage, Sondheim, who had majored in mathematics as well as music at Williams College, elected to use his Hutchinson Prize money to study with mathematician and avant-garde composer Milton Babbitt. At the same time he was teaching Sondheim traditional classical musical forms, Babbitt was pioneering a new stage of musical complexity known as "total serialization." While Schoenberg systematically arranged pitch according to various permutations of a twelve-tone series in his quest to systematically avoid a tonal center, his American protégé Babbitt serialized other parameters as well, including rhythm and tone color.[15]

Like Babbitt's total serialization, Sondheim's modernist musicals, aided and abetted by extraordinarily thoughtful and creative choreographers, directors, and scenarists such as Robbins, Prince, Michael Bennett, and James Lapine, expand on rather than discard the traditions established by earlier acknowledged masterpieces. Following the example of his mentor, Hammerstein, Sondheim in his songs continues to probe into the nuances of his increasingly complex characters and the meaning of his dramatic subjects.

Following an introduction to Sondheim's dramatic wedding of music and text in three songs, the present survey will examine one powerful idée fixe that serves as either a central or subtext for every Sondheim show since 1970: the need for and aversion against personal and artistic compromise. Although Sondheim has vigorously denied autobiographical elements in his shows, he might concede that the pressures to compromise faced by his characters are arguably analogous to those he faces himself as he creates their songs and responds artistically to the pressures of commercial theater. By the 1980s with *Sunday in the Park with George,* art and life, offstage and on, have become inextricably bound, but the lines and colors had been present for more than a decade.

Three Songs

Nearly any Sondheim song could serve as an example of his mastery of characterization, dramatic meaning, and integration. The three under scrutiny here, all from the pivotal years between 1970 and 1973, are "Now" from *A Little Night Music,* and "In Buddy's Eyes" and "Losing My Mind" from *Follies.* The latter pair are sung by the same character.

To display the lawyer Fredrik Egerman's educational achievements in "Now," heard near the outset of *Night Music,* Sondheim not only gives him rapid-fire and complex rhyme schemes, he also allows Egerman to present his song as if he were preparing a brief. In the course of his song, sung against a running spoken babble by his young wife, Anne, Egerman tries to decide whether to (A) ravish his virginal bride of six months or (B) nap. Deciding on the A alternative, Egerman must then decide between (A) charm and (B) physical force.

After rejecting B ("Removing her clothing / Would take me all day / And her subsequent loathing / Would turn me away—"), Egerman notes that there are two ways to exert his charm, (A) the suggestive and (B) the direct. Egerman continues with his elaborate rhymes and thoughts concerning the merits of the direct approach: "Say that I settle on B, to wit, / A charmingly / Lecherous mood . . . / A, I could put on my nightshirt or sit / Disarmingly, / B, in the nude . . ." Abandoning the "direct," Egerman also weighs the ramifications of the "suggestive." Then, "Though there are possibilities / Still to be studied," Egerman decides he "Might as well nap," the rejected B alternative from the beginning of the song.

Sondheim brilliantly portrays Egerman's intellectualization of his passions and his consequent inability to understand his feelings. The more Egerman intellectualizes the problem, the farther away he gets from the correct emotional solution. What Egerman does not know about himself is that Anne is the wrong match and that he still loves his former mistress, the actress Desirée Armfeldt. Only in his subconscious dreams does he utter her name out loud. It will take Egerman a whole evening to realize the implications of his subconscious.

The music Sondheim has given Egerman's lyrics effectively realizes with paradoxical simplicity the lawyer's intellectual complexity and lack of emotional awareness. Listeners may not detect that Egerman manages to open his song with an A♭, the fifth of the tonic D♭ major, D♭-F-A♭, or that until he arrives at the possibility of physical force, the lawyer is unable to begin or conclude his phrases with a note that belongs to the underlying harmony. But even a casual listener may note that Egerman's relentless but ultimately irrelevant logic is matched by incessantly even-note rhythmic values.[16]

Sally Plummer's two songs in *Follies* reveal additional ways that Sondheim captures character. In her first song, "In Buddy's Eyes," Sally tells her former and inextinguishable flame, the distinguished Benjamin Stone, about how her husband, Buddy, sees what Sally herself cannot see: "In Buddy's eyes, / I'm young, I'm beautiful. / In Buddy's arms, / On Buddy's shoulder, / I won't get older. / Nothing dies. / And all I ever dreamed I'd be, / The best I ever thought of me, / Is every minute there to see / In Buddy's eyes." In contrast to the sophisticated Egerman, the more emotionally transparent Sally sings deliberately, repeats words, and utters mostly simple one-syllable rhymes. Like her husband, Buddy, who is fated to love a woman who cannot return his love, Sally continues to carry the torch (and sing torch songs) for the unhappily married but emotionally unattainable Ben, who used her thirty years ago and will take advantage of her vulnerabilites at their reunion.

In the central chorus of her song Sondheim gives Sally an identical four-note syllabic melodic figure each of the six times she sings "in Buddy's eyes" (the last up an octave) and the one time she sings "in Buddy's arms." The figure turns in on itself down from F and back to F via D and E♭ above a static harmony that reflects her simplicity and Buddy's solidity and perhaps the boredom generated by Buddy's admiration. Significantly, the music Sondheim gives Sally to sing for this mantra, "in Buddy's eyes [or arms]," is the only music in sync with the underlying static harmony. It is also significant, perhaps a sign of her lack of self-awareness or her desire to avoid the root of her problems and her song, that when Sally moves from the third to the fifth of the tonic triad, she avoids singing the lowest and fundamental root note of this tonic so relentlessly repeated in the bass.

In her second song, "Losing My Mind," Sally sings openly about her unrequited love for Ben, the "folly" that has destroyed much of her contentment with her lot in life. Sondheim himself cited this song as one of his attempts in *Follies* "to imitate the styles of great songwriters of the times, and affectionately comment on them as well" by creating a George Gershwin song "with a Dorothy Fields lyric."[17] Although Sondheim was not more specific, a likely antecedent of "Losing My Mind" is Gershwin's classic ballad, "The Man I Love." The parallels are both obvious and subtle, since, although he follows its contours closely, Sondheim never actually quotes the Gershwin tune. He also takes the obsession of a woman ignored several steps farther than his "model" when he gives Sally an identical figure for each of the daily (and nightly) actions that remind Sally of Ben:

"the sun comes up," "the coffee cup," "the morning ends," "I talk to friends," "I dim the lights," and "spend sleepless nights."

As Sally shares the occurrences that remind her of her obsession—beginning each day, fittingly, one note per syllable with "the sun comes up," C-D♭-C-E♭—Sondheim has her sing a transformation of the three-note ascending figure that marked "in Buddy's eyes" (E♭-C-D♭-E♭ if transposed to fit the new song). By this simple device Sondheim retrospectively suggests that Sally is thinking of Ben even as she attempts to see herself through Buddy's eyes. But whether Sally sings "I think about you" or informs Ben how Buddy sees her, her obsessive personality comes through. Her repeated phrases recall another possible compositional model, "Bewitched," from *Pal Joey* (discussed in chapter 5), in which Rodgers and Hart use leading tones and repeated phrases to capture Vera Simpson's obsession for Joey.

The Art of Compromise

At the end of Sondheim's *Company*, Robert, the bachelor protagonist, has learned that compromise is an essential feature of marriage. The ambiguity that three of Robert's married male friends feel toward their wives and their marriages, expressed relatively early in the show in "Sorry-Grateful," culminates in Robert's final readiness for marriage, "Being Alive." It is widely known that "Being Alive" was Sondheim's fourth attempt at a final song for Robert.[18] "Marry Me a Little" expresses Robert's unwillingness to compromise, and the extraordinarily biting "Happily Ever After" describes a marriage that ends "happily ever after in hell." The marriage envisioned in "Being Alive" is far from perfect, but advocates of marriage can take heart that Robert has come to realize that "alone is alone, not alive." In his autobiography, *Contradictions*, Prince voiced his continued dissatisfaction with this final song, which he felt "imposed a happy ending on a play which should have remained ambiguous." Otherwise, Prince concludes his chapter on *Company* by saying that this show "represents the first time I had worked without conscious compromise." The producer in Prince was doubly pleased with its profit, however small, since "that is what commercial theatre must ask of itself."[19]

Follies, which explores the compromise of ideals in the lives of two unfulfilled married couples, lost most of its money for its own refusal to compromise and offer a lighter touch. The characters in Sondheim's (and Prince's) next musical, *A Little Night Music,* may need to discover their true feelings, but at least they do not have to compromise them. This time the compromises were artistic and occurred offstage, at least according to Prince, who wrote in his memoirs sardonically that "mostly *Night Music* was about having a hit."[20]

In *Pacific Overtures* (1976), generally perceived as a less compromising musical than *Night Music*, the formerly obedient feudal vassal Kayama forsakes ancient traditions in order to profit financially from his new Western trading partners. In act II Kayama sports "A Bowler Hat" and a pocket watch, pours milk in his tea, and smokes American cigars. The eponymous antihero in *Sweeney Todd* (1979) and the infamous historical murderers and would-be murderers in *Assassins* (1991) give up their moral decency for the sake of revenge or other misguided ideals. *Into the Woods* (1988) concludes with abandoned, deceived, and disillusioned fairy-tale characters who have compromised their innocence but learned that "No One Is Alone." Some, such as Martin Gottfried, find the moralizing tone of *Into the Woods* platitudinous, yet a critic as rigorous as Steven Banfield assesses this show as "Sondheim's finest achievement yet."[21]

In his first two shows of the 1980s, *Merrily We Roll Along* and *Sunday in the Park With George*, Sondheim directly confronts the issue of artistic compromise in his own work, an issue previously faced more obliquely by several of Broadway's spiritual fathers surveyed here. *On Your Toes* addresses the dichotomy between art music and popular music and *The Cradle Will Rock* offers a devastating attack on compromising artists, but *Merrily* and *Sunday* may be unprecedented in the degree to which they explore the creative process and commercial pressures on artists. *Merrily* tells the disconcerting story of a Broadway composer, Franklin Shepard, who has sold out his ideals and his artistic soul, the road pointedly not taken by Sondheim. *Sunday* presents two portraits of artists. In act I we meet a fictionalized but nevertheless once-real artist in 1884, the uncompromising painter Georges Seurat, who refused to sell out. In fact, Seurat reportedly never sold a painting in his lifetime. One hundred years later in act II, we meet his great-grandson, also an artist named George, a man who evolves from a compromising sculptor grubbing for grants and commissions to a genuine artist more like Seurat by the end of the evening.

Since *Merrily* is told in reverse, the disintegration of this Broadway Faust is all the more disturbing. When we first meet Franklin Shepard in 1980 as the graduation speaker of his former high school (a scene dropped from the 1985 revival), the once idealistic but now artistically sterile Broadway composer tells "young innocents a few realities" and introduces them to the two words that symbolize his abandoned ideals, "practical" and "compromise." The older Frank says "compromise is how you survive"; the younger Frank answers that compromise is "how you give up."

Twenty years earlier (but much later in the show) Franklin, his high school classmate and present collaborator Charley Kringas, and their friend Mary Flynn, an aspiring novelist, sing "Opening Doors." Even Sondheim acknowledged the autobiographical aspect to this song: "If there is one number that is really me writing about me, it is 'Opening Doors.' That was my life for a number of years. It is a totally personal number. Luckily it fits into the piece."[22] In this song Frank and Charley are creating their first show, auditioning the material, facing rejection and disappointment, and struggling to reject compromising alternatives. Charley is typing and Frank is composing "Good Thing Going," heard in its completed state earlier in the show when Frank and Charley sang it at a party in 1962.

Frank is having trouble going beyond the opening phrase, which, not incidentally, is the phrase that most clearly resembles the idealistic anthem that he and Charley composed for their high school graduation (both at the opening and toward the close of the musical in its original production).[23] When Mary calls to tell Frank that she is about to abandon her principles and her novel by taking commercial writing jobs, she sings this same opening phrase. Later in the song Charley and Frank audition the first several phrases of their future hit song for a wary producer, Joe Josephson.

Even without Sondheim's admission, it would be difficult to overlook the autobiographal component of Josephson's criticism, so closely does it correspond to the critical reactions which the modernist Sondheim, a close contemporary of the fictional Mr. Shepard, had by then been facing for more than two decades. Ironically, however, when Josephson tells them that "There's not a tune you can hum.—/ There's not a tune you go bum-bum-bum-di-dum" or that he will let them "know when Stravinsky has a hit," he sings Frank's tune. After this initial rejection, Charley and Frank continue to pitch their song. Josephson then abruptly dismisses them and sings his own: "Write more, work hard,—/ Leave your name with the girl.—/ Less avant-garde."

At this moment the ghost of Rodgers and Hammerstein returns to haunt Sondheim as well as Franklin Shepard. The "plain old melodee dee dee dee dee dee" that Josephson desires is none other than the chestnut "Some Enchanted Evening" from *South Pacific*. Characteristically, Josephson does not know the words to this familiar classic, and presumably does not even realize that he is trying to hum a Rodgers and Hammerstein song. In addition to several conspicuously incorrect pitches, Josephson also sings its opening musical phrase completely outside of its proper metrical foundation (a quarter-note quintuplet in $\frac{4}{4}$ time, one fifth of a beat too many for the measure).

Sondheim is reinforcing what we all know: that in 1958–1959 as well as in 1981 a Rodgers tune was and is the ideal Broadway theater song and the standard by which Shepard—and Sondheim—will be measured. But Charley and Frank refuse to alter their work and write a Rodgers and Hammerstein–type song, and instead join with Mary to produce a revue of their own. Within a few years the rejected song becomes a hit song in Frank's and Charley's new Broadway show, produced by Josephson. By the 1980s people were beginning to hum Sondheim's songs, too, and by the 1990s more and more could be heard out of their context in cabaret theaters, recordings, and television.[24] And although few if any, of his songs match the familiarity of "Send in the Clowns" and many songs of Rodgers, Sondheim's songs in the 1990s have belatedly begun to receive broader recognition.

By the end of Shepard's career, which real-life audiences witnessed with disappointment near the beginning of the show, the selling of an artistic soul is complete. At a party Frank tells Mary, now a critic (having forsaken her dream to write a great American novel), that he has not composed the music to his recent film. Frank has long since abandoned his creative partnership with Charley, who has become a distinguished playwright. Frank may be "Rich and Happy" in 1979, but he is also morally and artistically bankrupt and sad.

The fin-de-siècle classical modernists are rarely accused of compromising their ideals, but they are, like Sondheim and Franklin Shepard, still often chastized for writing unhummable melodies and, like Sondheim and Seurat, equally faulted for lacking artistic passion. Sondheim also shares with his modernist counterparts a profound awareness of his classic predecessors and self-consciously responds to his tradition in varied and profound ways. Just as the European modernists recreate the past in their own image, so Sondheim pays allegiance to and reinterprets his tradition and makes it his own.

At the center of this tradition are the integrated musicals of Rodgers and Hammerstein, Sondheim's one-time collaborator and long-time mentor, respectively. Sondheim's shows depart from the Rodgers and Hammerstein models stylistically and dramaturgically, especially in their subject matter and in their use of time and space. But at least from *Company* on they preserve the concept of the integrated musical. In this respect the earlier *Forum* stands out for the contradiction between song and story reminiscent of Brecht and Weill, a dissonance that Sondheim has acknowledged.[25] As with Rodgers and Hammerstein, the more-than-occasionally compromising characters in a Sondheim musical sing lyrics and music that reveal their essences and nuances and move the drama, narrative or non-narrative, uncompromisingly forward.

Sondheim and the Broadway Tradition: Follies *and* Sunday in the Park With George

Although Kern died before all the revisions were made, the 1946 revival of *Show Boat* (until the 1990s the only version regularly performed) gave Kern and Hammerstein an opportunity to rethink the work together in the light of a new present. Audiences accustomed to reworked versions of the pre–Rodgers and Hammerstein musical and to relatively fixed versions of musicals composed in the 1940s, '50s, and '60s, may be surprised to discover that the evolving nature of several Sondheim shows parallel the revival histories of several musicals treated in the present survey, including *Show Boat, Porgy and Bess, Anything Goes,* and *On Your Toes.*

The 1985 La Jolla Playhouse revival of *Merrily,* for example, dropped "Rich and Happy" and the high school scene. More radically, the 1987 revival of *Follies* in London's Shaftesbury Theatre precipitated a revised book with a new ending and both new and discarded songs.[26] Appendix R, p. 343, encapsulates the genesis of *Follies* from *The Girls Upstairs* in 1965 to the tryouts in 1971, and p. 345 lists the songs of the 1987 London *Follies.*

The *Follies* revival offers a striking recent example of a process that has much in common with the pre–Rodgers and Hammerstein musicals in the first part of this survey.[27] After a long gestation period that included the composition and production of *Company,* Sondheim & Co. were ready to return to a drastically revamped James Goldman script, *The Girls Upstairs.* originally drafted in 1965. According to Prince, the new *Follies,* begun in earnest 1970 after the completion of *Company,* could use only six of the songs from the earlier vision.[28] Prince biographer Carol Ilson summarizes the radical metamorphosis from *The Girls Upstairs* to *Follies:*

> The realistic and naturalistic *The Girls Upstairs* became the surrealistic *Follies.* Originally, Sondheim and Goldman wanted the show to be a backstage murder mystery with an attempted murder being planned. The idea was dropped. Prince, working with his collaborators, decided to use only the two couples that had been written to be the major characters, and to use the theatre locale. He encouraged the authors to utilize the younger selves of

the leading characters. Four new cast members would represent the leading characters as they had been thirty years earlier.[29]

All involved agree that it was Prince's concept to mirror the younger unmarried versions of the two unhappily married couples, Phyllis and Benjamin Stone and Sally and Buddy Plummer. The combined minds of codirectors Prince (stage director) and Michael Bennett (musical director) led to many additional dramaturgical changes, including an unusually large number of song replacements (nine) during rehearsals.

An opening montage (a medley of five songs, one of which was dropped during rehearsals) was abandoned, and two additional songs were replaced during tryouts.[30] The first of these songs, "I'm Still Here," was added because Yvonne De Carlo "couldn't do" the song originally intended for her, "Can That Boy Foxtrot!" Out of this necessity Sondheim invented a song that more closely fit the evolving concept.[31] De Carlo's character, Carlotta Campion, like De Carlo herself, was an actress who stayed in show business and endures against the ravages of time and age. Sondheim's conceit in the song is to have her sing an ascending major triad nearly every time she sings "I'm Still Here" (E♭-G-B♭). The device of repeating a simple motive parallels Sally's torch songs discussed earlier (which were by then already written) and would occur in other obsessive situations in subsequent shows, for example, when Seurat sings about "Finishing the Hat." Sally's song expresses a defeatist attitude toward and unrealistic view of life, exemplified by her inability to find a root or tonal center when she sings the oft-repeated "in Buddy's eyes" in her first song and her descending melodic phrase that matches "I think about you" in her second song. In bold contrast, Carlotta's mantra (a major triad) is triumphant and invariably ascending.

The last songs added were Phyllis's folly number, "The Story of Lucy and Jessie," a song which replaced "Uptown, Downtown," and Ben's folly song, "Live, Love, Laugh." Both of these were apparently composed and staged during a frenetic final week of rehearsals. In their published remarks Sondheim and Bennett disagree as to why "Uptown, Downtown" was discarded. Sondheim remembers that he wrote it after he had worked out Ben's breakdown number and gave it to Bennett one day before the Boston tryouts. Sondheim also recalls that Bennett resented being rushed, "turned against it," and asked for a new number: "I don't think there's really any difference between the numbers, but because he had more time to think about it, I think he liked it better."[32] Bennett remembered this part of the process somewhat differently: "I quite honestly don't understand why Steve had to write 'Lucy and Jessie' for Alexis [Smith] to replace the other number. I liked 'Uptown Downtown' so much better. It also lost me a phrase to hang her dance on. I was originally able to differentiate the character's two personalities by having half the phrase strutting up and the other half strutting down."[33]

In an intermediary view between these contrasting recollections, Prince commented tersely that "Uptown, Downtown" was "the right idea" but that "The Story of Lucy and Jessie" was "a better number."[34] Jeffrey Lonoff's jacket notes to *A Collector's Stephen Sondheim* offers a thoughtful comparison that places these disparate memories within a critical perspective:

> In the show we see two Phyllises—the young, open, vibrant girl and the cool, distant woman she carefully molds herself into. Her song in the Loveland section was to reflect her schizoid personality. But "Uptown, Downtown" presented Phyllis as a two-sided character whereas she was, as the show presented, really two separate people. It was dropped, and "The Story of Lucy and Jessie" was written to better portray this."[35]

Although Sondheim credits the influence of Cole Porter on "Lucy and Jessie," a more likely model might be Kurt Weill's and Ira Gershwin's "The Saga of Jenny" from *Lady in the Dark* (Example 7.1a, p. 146). Resemblances go beyond their respective titles and subject matter (a woman responding to the accusation that she cannot make up her mind), and include such musical details as the nearly constant dotted rhythms and frequent descending minor triads, a predilection for flatted (blue) fifths, and a general jazz flavor.[36]

Earlier it was observed that the successful cast recording of *Pal Joey* led to a Broadway revival that surpassed its initial run. The abbreviated and what was generally perceived as an (uncharacteristically) poorly produced original 1971 cast album of *Follies* generated the need for a recording that was both more complete and more felicitously engineered. Unfortunately, in contrast to the pre-production *Pal Joey* recording, the new *Follies* album with its all-star cast issued in 1985 substituted for a new staged performance. Although a revised staged *Follies* made a successful appearance in London two years later, a Broadway revival still seemed financially untenable.

James Goldman's original libretto for *Follies* was not only critically controversial, it provoked strenuous debate between the two visionary co-directors, Bennett and Prince. What mainly bothered Bennett was the absence of humor and the general heaviness of tone. When Prince vetoed the idea of bringing in a willing Neil Simon, master of the one-liner, Ben-

nett gave Goldman a joke book.[37] Although he remained embittered by
Follies's disappointing box office returns, Bennett felt that his judgment of
the book was vindicated by the show's box office failure.[38] Goldman agrees
that the show might have had a long run, but that "at the same time we
would have disemboweled it."[39] In retrospect, although Prince does not go
as far as to say that he *likes* the book, he thinks the book better than Bennett
thought and says he did not "hate the book at all."[40] Sondheim thought
the large number of pastiche numbers "hurt the book and subsequently
hurt the show" and that if they "had used fewer songs and had more book
the show would have been more successful."[41]

For the 1985 concert performance Herbert Ross, hired to stage the show,
asked Sondheim to change the ending: "I never liked the kind of hopelessness of the show's finale. . . . I think you never really believed that the
death of the theater was a sort of symbol for the death of these people's
lives. My view of it was that this was a celebration, and the original ending
was too downbeat and not appropriate for this event."[42] Eventually even
librettist James Goldman had second thoughts about the ending of his 1971
Follies: "The final scene of the show has always bothered me, I must admit.
There were all kinds of thoughts as to how we should have gone out at
the end. I was pleased with the ending that Buddy and Sally had. I think
it was honest and on target and about all you could do. I'm not so sure
that if I had it to write over again that I would have had Ben and Phyllis
together at the end."[43]

Two years later Goldman did have it to write over again when *Follies*
was staged in London. This time, however, Goldman produced a new and
still more upbeat book.[44] At the same time Sondheim's less acerbic new
songs showed that he too was not immune to the vicissitudes of the commercial marketplace.[45] Although Sondheim's new songs were expressly
composed for this revival rather than for other shows, the results are not
dissimilar. In fact, the 1987 London *Follies*, with a rewritten book and deleted, reordered, and new songs, is clearly analogous to the fate of Porter's
Anything Goes in its 1962 and 1987 reincarnations, and perhaps even more
closely akin to the changes in *Show Boat* between 1927 and 1946.

The principal casualties of the 1971 *Follies* (see Appendix R, p. 343) are
Ben Stone's philosophical "The Road You Didn't Take" and, perhaps significantly, the two latest additions to the earlier version, Phyllis's folly
song, "Lucy and Jessie," and Ben's folly song, "Live, Laugh, Love," that
pretty much ended the evening. Sondheim also created a new "Loveland"
to replace the 1971 song of the same name to open the quartet of follies
(one each for Benjamin and Phyllis Stone and Buddy and Sally Plummer)
that brought the earlier show to its depressing close. Perhaps not surpris-

ingly, the superficially successful Ben, who ultimately emerges as the most pathetic of the quartet in 1971, required the most surgery in 1987.

The first discarded song, Ben's "The Road You Didn't Take," is replaced two songs later with "Country House," a duet between Ben and Phyllis. This new song, although it conveys their poor communication skills and half-hearted attempts to work out their problems, also demonstrates a civil and resigned incompatibility rather than their earlier bitterness and hostility. Phyllis's new song, "Ah, but Underneath," like "Being Alive" in *Company*, provides another illustration of a final attempt to capture a difficult dramatic situation. It also marks a return to Phyllis's two-sided nature depicted in "Uptown, Downtown," discarded earlier from the 1971 *Follies* in favor of "The Story of Lucy and Jessie."

Ben's new folly song, like his new duet with Phyllis, constitutes the most radical change of tone between 1971 and 1987. Rather than breaking down as he did in "Live, Laugh, Love," with newly acquired equanimity Ben tells his 1987 audiences not "to disclose yourself" but to "compose yourself" as he sings "Make the Most of Your Music." Among the ironies of the song, with its instructions to "make the most of the music that is yours," is Sondheim's decision to begin Ben's song with a quotation from the opening of Edvard Grieg's Piano Concerto set to words in the vocal line; in the orchestra alone the related opening of Tchaikovsky's first Piano Concerto follows closely.[46] Ben initially considers himself "something big league" along with "Tchaikovsky and Grieg." Soon, however, he advises his admirers that even if they are unable to produce a work like Debussy's *Clair de Lune*, they can "make the most of the music that is yours" and eventually produce music that "soars." Whatever Sondheim is saying about the relative merits of Tchaikovsky, Grieg, and Debussy, Sondheim himself might be accused in this rare case of not practicing what his character preaches.

Just as the comic, even farcical, touches added to Bernstein's 1974 *Candide* (including Sondheim's own new lyric) no doubt contributed to its newfound success, perhaps at Voltaire's expense, the more upbeat 1987 *Follies* might eventually have found the audience it lost in 1971. As George says in *Sunday in the Park With George*'s "Putting It Together" (act II), "if no one gets to see it, it's as good as dead." Despite its relative grimness, however, the original 1971 *Follies* book has replaced the 1987 book in the 1990s. It is now the only version permitted to be distributed.[47]

If the history of *Follies* demonstrates the folly of viewing even the modern musical as a fixed entity unresponsive to changing social and artistic tastes, *Sunday in the Park* illustrates how the artistic product of an artist can shed light on its creator. The first act focuses on George's great-grandfather, the painter Georges Seurat, unlike Franklin Shepard a real historical figure and certainly one of the least compromising artists in any field of art. In this landmark show Sondheim and his new collaborator, James Lapine, who wrote the book and directed, explore the relationship between our artistic and our procreative legacies, the ephemeral cream pies of Louis the baker versus the immortality of an artistic masterpiece, and the contrasting legacies of children and art.[48] In his dedication to art Seurat has forsworn his relationship with his mistress, Dot, although through her he will leave a human legacy in their daughter Marie and, two generations later, another artist named George, whom we will meet in act II.

In the song "No Life" Sondheim again creates characters who voice criticisms that he has been subjected to himself throughout much of his career. When viewing a tableau vivant of Seurat's recently completed *Bathing at Asnières*, his rival, Jules, and Jule's wife, Yvonne, decry the passionless, lifeless, unlyrical, and inappropriate subject matter of Seurat's painting. Similarly, Sondheim himself has frequently been indicted for writing about cold, bloodless, neurotic, and frequently unlikable people, and for confronting unpalatable subjects ranging from the loss of youthful dreams to mass murder.

The contrast between accessible and difficult (and perhaps authentic) art is powerfully delineated in Dot's song, "Everybody Loves Louis." Louis the baker, a man who neither fathers a child nor sings a song in the show, is willing to take Dot and her child by Seurat to America. In vivid contrast to the unlovable, unpopular, and coldly intellectual painter, Louis is lovable, popular, and "bakes from the heart." "Louis' thoughts are not hard to follow," his "art is not hard to swallow," and, unlike George, the baker is "not afraid to be gooey." Also in contrast to George, Louis "sells what he makes." In return, Louis will perish without producing either art or children of his own.

In the final scene of act I the uncompromising Seurat completes his great painting *Sunday Afternoon on La Grande Jatte* after two years and many months of Sundays, an act marked musically by the completion of the opening horn fragment that represents Seurat's blank canvas. In stark contrast with the painter's exceptional meticulousness, his great-grandson is rapidly turning out a series of similar and risk-free high-tech sculptures known as chromolumes. The new George shares with his forefather an inability to connect the dots of human relationships, but unlike Seurat, the modern George has managed to successfully negotiate the politics of art and has gained all the trappings of success as well as the profit and fame denied the greater artist.

Like the characters in *Lady in the Dark* who appear metaphorically in Liza Elliott's dreams, many characters in Seurat's life and painting reappear in the life of the present-day George. Seurat's mistress, Dot, lives on as her daughter, the aged Marie; Seurat's unsympathetic rival, Jules, metamorphoses into Bob Greenberg, the director of the museum that now houses Chromolume #7. Perhaps most tellingly, the old lady who turns out to be Seurat's critical but supportive mother in act I returns in act II as the perceptive art critic Blair Daniels, who, like Seurat's mother, is able to see that the emperor has no clothes.

Nearly any Sondheim show can be used to demonstrate the realization of character through music. Most present simple but theatrically effective musical material that link the parts to the whole, for example, "Remember" (*Night Music*) "The Ballad of Sweeney Todd," and "Merrily We Roll Along." *Sunday in the Park With George* is especially rich in dramatically meaningful thematic transformations similar to *Show Boat*, *Porgy and Bess*, and *West Side Story*.

The Chromolume music is an electrifed version of the music that accompanies Seurat's "Color and Light." Dot returns at the end of act II to help the modern George to "Move On," and her music shares prominent motives from "We Do Not Belong Together" that Dot sang in act I, when she left the great painter and moved on to a new life in America with Louis. The gossips in the museum in act II are singing the same "I'm not surprised" motive in discussing the Chromolumes ("Putting It Together," part II) as Seurat's contemporaries in act I ("Gossip Sequence"). The obsessively repeated musical motive of "Putting It Together" is a slight variation on the motive associated with the words "Finishing the Hat." And these examples are only among the most prominent of a long list.[49]

Just as Seurat's mother evolves from a critical pose to an attitude of understanding and appreciation in act I, the childless Blair Daniels in act II rightly points out the meaningless and superficiality of recycling past successes and encourages the formerly vital artist to move on to something new. By the end of the drama young George returns to La Grande Jatte and meets Dot, a deus ex machina figure introduced to help George change and grow as an artist and "move on." Like the sadder-but-wiser characters in *Into the Woods*, George learns that he too is not alone, that he is part of a great tradition that includes the artistry of his great-grandfather and the wisdom of his maternal ancestors, and that his duty as an artist is to grow and develop his art and his humanity. The modern George has thus escaped the fate of Franklin Shepard Inc.

Sondheim, like Seurat and his modernist musical counterparts Schoenberg and Stravinsky, has long since demonstrated his ability to move on, to learn from the example of his mentor Hammerstein who wrote "You'll Never Walk Alone" and to give the Rodgers and Hammerstein tradition renewed life in "No One Is Alone." In works like *Follies* and *Sunday in the Park With George* Sondheim has successfully combined the musical trappings of musical modernism and arguably offered a broader dramatic range than his predecessors. But in a larger sense Sondheim's modernism might also be construed as a reinterpretation rather than a revolution, although his music is more dissonant and less tonal than his predecessors (with the possible exception of *West Side Story*) and his characters are usually more neurotic.

Also connecting him to the Broadway tradition he inherited as well as to Seurat and the modern George is Sondheim's willingness to reuse a legacy to say something new. The ingenious incorporation of past models explored in connection with "Losing My Mind" from *Follies* would reappear in subsequent shows, most extensively and literally in *Assassins*.[50] In this respect Sondheim's shows are very much analogous to *Show Boat, On Your Toes, The Cradle Will Rock,* and *West Side Story*, to name only the musicals discussed in the present survey that display popular and classical allusions prominently. Despite his successful attempt to move the Broadway musical on to a new phase through words and music supported by imaginative solutions to perennial dramatic problems, Sondheim's approach to the musical can be placed firmly in the great tradition from *Show Boat* to *West Side Story*. The Broadway musical from the 1920s to the 1950s could hardly ask for a worthier heir or more enchanted evenings.

SYNOPSES

Anything Goes

Reno Sweeney (Ethel Merman), an evangelist turned bar hostess, gets such a kick out of Billy Crocker (William Gaxton) that she boards a Europe-bound liner to dissuade him from pursuing Hope Harcourt (Bettina Hall). Although Billy dreams of Hope all through the night, Hope is determined to marry an English peer. Crocker has boarded without a ticket, so is forced to adopt a number of disguises. Also aboard is a wistful little man, the Reverend Dr. Moon (Victor Moore), whom J. Edgar Hoover has branded "Public Enemy 13." Moon's ambition is to rise to the top of Hoover's list. With a minister and former evangelist as passengers the captain hopes to cheer his Depression-ridden travelers with a revival meeting. Reno obliges with a rousing anthem directed at the archangel Gabriel. On landing, Hope discovers she has become an heiress. She drops her Englishman and consents to marry Billy. The Englishman turns his attention to Reno, while Moon, learning he has been judged harmless and dropped from the FBI list, walks away muttering nasty things about Hoover.

Carousel

When Billy Bigelow (John Raitt), a New England carnival barker, falls in love with Julie Jordan (Jan Clayton), he proves so shy that he can only convey his feelings by suggesting what might happen "If I Loved You." Nonetheless, by the time "June Is Bustin' Out All Over," he wins Julie. Later he discovers she is pregnant, so he agrees to join the scowling Jigger Craigin (Murvyn Vye) in a robbery to earn extra money. The plan misfires, and Billy kills himself rather than be caught. Before a heavenly judge, he pleads for another chance to return to earth, to redeem himself and see his daughter. But when the daughter refuses his gift of a star he has stolen from the sky he slaps her and must return to purgatory. The widowed Julie and her child are left to continue alone in the world, in stark contrast to her old friend Carrie Pipperidge (Jean Darling), who has made a prosperous marriage to the rich Mr. Snow (Eric Mattson). Julie's sole comforter, Nettie Fowler (Christine Johnson), assures her "You'll Never Walk Alone."

The Cradle Will Rock

Scene 1. Street Corner: In "Moll's Song" a prostitute (Olive Stanton) explains how the two dollars she earns on two days each week in Steeltown barely provides enough to eat for the five days her "efforts ain't required." A Gent enters, offers the Moll thirty cents, harasses her, and departs when a Dick comes to protect the Moll in exchange for sexual favors. A Cop instructed to pick up union workers mistakenly arrests the Liberty Committee, a group selected and cultivated by Mr. Mister (Ralph MacBane) to destroy the burgeoning attempts to form a union. The Liberty Committee and the Moll are taken to Night Court.

Scene 2. Night Court: The Liberty Committee explains how they were arrested as they were attempting to stop a union speech. Since they had gathered together for this purpose, and since Mr. Mister gave strict orders to "arrest anyone forming a crowd," the police arrested the Liberty Committee instead of Larry Foreman (Howard da Silva), "the man who made the speech." Significantly, the Moll and Harry Druggist (John Adair), the only nonmembers of the Liberty Committee to be arrested—the Moll for soliciting her body and the Druggist his soul—sing their exchange to the main theme from "Nickel Under the Foot." Harry explains that since "they won't buy our milkwhite bodies, / So we kinda sell out in some other way—to Mr. Mister." While waiting for the latter to arrive at Night Court and bail them out, Harry Druggist explains in flashbacks how each of the Liberty Committee has sold out.

Scene 3. Mission: In a flashback sequence that moves from 1915 to 1917, Reverend Salvation (Charles Niemeyer) changes his sermon from peace to war in response to the requests of Mrs. Mister (Peggy Coudray), who represents her husband's attempts to profit from World War I.

Scene 4. Lawn of Mr. Mister's Home: Junior Mister (Maynard Holmes) and Sister Mister (Dulce Fox), Mr. Mister's vapid children, sing "Croon-Spoon." Editor Daily (Bert Weston) arrives and capitulates to the demands of Mr. Mister, the paper's new owner ("The Freedom of the Press"), and agrees to print whatever his boss wants. After Junior and Sister wildly exhibit their boredom in "Let's Do Something," Editor Daily offers the bored Junior a post in "Honolulu" to get him out of the way of union trouble.

Scene 5. Drugstore: In a flashback Harry Druggist tells how he sold out to Mr. Mister six months earlier in order to keep the mortgage on his store, an act that led to the death of his son as well as the loving Polish immigrant couple, Gus and Sadie ("Love Song").

Scene 6. Hotel Lobby: The artists Yasha (Edward Fuller) and Dauber (Jules Schmidt) show nothing but loathing and contempt for "The Rich," but nevertheless eagerly accept Mrs. Mister's invitation for additional patronage ("Ask Us Again") and join Mr. Mister's Liberty Committee to obtain a free meal. Since they are apolitical artists who espouse "Art for Art's Sake," Yasha and Dauber do not even want to know the cause the Liberty serves.

Scene 7. Night Court: After the Moll sings a complete version of "Nickel Under the Foot," the Liberty Committee witnesses the long-awaited arrival of Larry Foreman, "the man who made the speech." Foreman explains to the Moll in "Leaflets" (an underscored rhythm song) how he has been formally charged with "Incitin' to Riot." He also asserts the power of the unions in the title song.

Scene 8. Faculty Room: President Prexie accedes to Mr. Mister's demand for compulsory military training in exchange for funding. Although the music is underscored almost throughout, this is the only scene without a musical number.

Scene 9. Dr. Specialist's Office: Dr. Specialist (Frank Marvel) lies in order to obtain his coveted research grants controlled by Mr. Mister. Ella Hammer (Blanche Collins) tells the press how her brother, Joe Hammer ("Joe Worker"), gets "gypped" and abused by a corrupt system.

Scene 10. Night Court: Larry Foreman refuses to be bought by Mr. Mister, the boilermakers agree to join the steel workers, and a union chorus reprises "The Cradle Will Rock."

Guys and Dolls

Nathan Detroit (Sam Levene), who runs the oldest established permanent floating crap game in New York, is hard up for money, a special problem since the biggest plunger of all, Sky Masterson (Robert Alda), is in town, ready to play. When Sky boasts that he can have any woman he wants, Nathan sees his chance. He wagers that Sky cannot win any woman Nathan points to. Sky takes the bet. At that moment, Sister Sarah (Isabel Bigley) of the Salvation Army comes marching by, and Nathan points to her. When Sky wins big at dice he forces the losers to attend a Salvation Army rally in order to help his pursuit of Sarah, whom he earlier had lured to Havana. In the end she converts him to her ways. Meanwhile Nathan agrees to wed Adelaide (Vivian Blaine), a night club singer with whom he has had a fourteen-year courtship.

Kiss Me, Kate

While cast members of a revival of *The Taming of the Shrew* celebrate "Another Op'nin', Another Show," the show's stars, Fred Graham (Alfred Drake) and Lilli Vanessi (Patricia Morison), celebrate the first anniversary of their divorce. They take time from their bickering to recall they had once sung "Wunderbar" in a long-forgotten operetta. Lilli receives a bouquet from Fred, leading her to believe he still loves her, and she confesses she is still "So In Love" with him, but when she learns the flowers are meant for someone else she determines to be revenged. Fred's problems are compounded when another member of the company, Bill Calhoun (Harold Lang), signs Fred's name to a gambling debt. Opening night is peppered by warfare between Fred and Lilli, and by demands by two comic hoods for payment of the debt. Fred convinces the hoods that they must force Lilli to perform. Bill's promiscuous girl, Lois (Lisa Kirk), helps him try to reform by promising she will be "Always True to You in My Fashion," and the hoods eventually leave when the debt proves no longer valid on a technicality. They decide it might be more profitable to "Brush Up Your Shakespeare." In the course of the evening, Fred and Lilli recognize they still do love each other.

Lady in the Dark

Liza Elliott (Gertrude Lawrence), a successful but greatly troubled fashion editor of a prestigious fashion magazine, reluctantly consults the psychiatrist, Dr. Brooks (Donald Randolph). In two sessions she relates musical dreams of a glamour girl (the Glamour Dream) and marriage (the Wedding Dream) that contrast markedly with the state of her waking life. In her dreams Liza is the toast of the town; in real life she dresses in dreary clothing and protects her emotional vulnerabilities in a dispassionate affair with a married man, Kendall Nesbitt (Bert Lytell). Her waking world unravels still further when Nesbitt offers to leave his wife and marry Liza. In her third dream, the Circus Dream, Liza goes on trial for her indecisiveness.

The people close to Liza appear metaphorically in her dreams. In the Circus Dream Nesbitt is the first witness for the prosecution, her nemesis Charley Johnson (MacDonald Carey) is the prosecuting attorney, the movie star Randy Curtis (Victor Mature) serves as the attorney in her defense, and the magazine's photographer Russell Paxton (Danny Kaye) appears as the Ringmaster. In a final session Dr. Brooks helps Liza understand the childhood trauma behind her fear of her femininity and success. As her repression vanishes, she is finally able to complete the song "My Ship," which has haunted her throughout the play. Having achieved this understanding as well as her feminine identity, Liza realizes that she really loves Johnson.

The Most Happy Fella

Rosabella (Jo Sullivan) comes to the Napa Valley expecting to marry a handsome young man who has sent her his picture and proposed by mail. She is certain that she has at last found "Somebody, Somewhere" to really love her. But she soon discovers the handsome man, Joe (Art Lund), is merely a hired hand, and that the man who proposed is actually an aging Italian vintner, Tony (Robert Weede). He had sent her Joe's picture, fearing one of himself would have disheartened her. He believes that she will quickly become reconciled and make him "The Most Happy Fella" in all of the valley. The shock, however, drives Rosabella into Joe's arms. Eventually she realizes that Tony is an honorable, loving man. Bit by bit, she and Tony admit that they are "Happy To Make Your Acquaintance." When he offers to accept not only her but the baby she is now pregnant with, she comes to love him.

My Fair Lady

Coming from a performance at Covent Garden, Professor Henry Higgins (Rex Harrison) meets a fellow scholar, Colonel Pickering (Robert Coote), and a somewhat raucous Cockney flower girl, Eliza Doolittle (Julie Andrews). Higgins casually mentions to Pickering that given a little time he could turn a flower girl into a lady, so when Eliza appears later at his residence asking him to make good on his boast, Higgins accepts Pickering's wager on the affair. It is a long, hard struggle, but by the time Eliza can properly enunciate "The Rain in Spain" and Higgins takes her to Ascot, her pronunciation is perfect—even if her conversation is not. Later she is successfully passed off as a lady at a ball, and she is so pleased that she confesses, "I Could Have Danced All Night." At one point Higgins must bribe Eliza's father, Alfred P. Doolittle (Stanley Holloway), to stay out of the girl's life. With his new-found wealth Doolittle recognizes that he must subscribe to middle-class morality by marrying, so he urges his friends to "Get Me to the Church on Time." But Higgins has no objections to rich, lovesick Freddy Eynsford-Hill (John Michael King) courting Eliza. So lovesick is Freddy he is happy merely to be "On the Street Where You Live." Nevertheless, Eliza recognizes she is too intelligent for the charming but vacuous young man, so casts her lot with the reluctant Higgins, who is appalled but admits "I've Grown Accustomed to Her Face." When Eliza returns Higgins can only respond, "Where the devil are my slippers?"

One Touch of Venus

Rodney Hatch (Kenny Baker), an unassuming barber, has come to shave Whitelaw Savory (John Boles). The latter, a prominent eccentric art collector, has recently acquired a statue of the Anatolian Venus for his Foundation of Modern Art, because it reminded him of a lost love. When Hatch is left alone, he foolishly puts the ring intended for his fiancée Gloria Kramer (Ruth Bond) on the statue's finger, and the statue of Venus (Mary Martin) comes to life ready to love the man who summoned her. After some initial resistance, Venus wins Hatch's affections and disposes of the shrewish Gloria. She also easily evades Savory's agents, who want to "Catch Hatch" for allegedly stealing the statue. When Venus comes to realize the quotidian nature of her monogamous future with Hatch, she returns to Mount Olympus and her statue returns to stone. As a parting gesture she arranges the descent of a more suitable partner for the prosaic but endearing barber.

On Your Toes

Junior Dolan (Ray Bolger), music professor and former child vaudeville star, presents his student's jazz composition, "Slaughter on Tenth Avenue," to the Russian Ballet. Prima Ballerina Vera Barnova (Tamara Geva) takes a fancy to Junior and sees to it that the ballet is produced with Junior dancing the male lead. Vera's former partner and lover, Konstantine Morrosine (Demetrios Vilan), becomes extremely jealous, and during a performance, tries to turn a stage killing into a real one. At the last minute, Junior is warned by his devoted student, Frankie (Doris Carson).

Pal Joey

Joey (Gene Kelly), a handsome, small-time dancer, begins his courtship of innocent Linda English (Leila Ernst) by proclaiming about her virtues, "I Could Write a Book." Joey himself is notably short on virtues, so when Vera Simpson (Vivienne Segal), a rich, callous, past-her-prime matron, finds herself "Bewitched" by him and offers to set him up in luxury with his own night club, he all but drops Linda. In time Joey's selfishness and egotism pall even for the tolerant Vera. Matters come to a head when Linda tells Vera of a plan to blackmail her by threatening to tell Mr. Simpson of the liaison. The women agree that as far as Joey is concerned they no longer want him, and the other can "Take Him." Having lost both women Joey wanders off into the night to find another romance.

Porgy and Bess

When Clara (Abbie Mitchell) fails to lull her baby to sleep with a lullaby about the languorous virtues of "Summertime," her husband, Jake (Edward Matthews), tries with "A Woman Is a Sometime Thing." One reason the baby has trouble sleeping is that Catfish Row is a noisy, dangerous place, where the menfolk are drinking and gambling. The men tease the crippled Porgy (Todd Duncan), who rides around in a goat-cart, about his love for Crown's girl, Bess (Anne Brown). Crown (Warren Coleman) himself gets into a fight with his fellow gambler, Robbins (Henry Dobbins), and stabs him to death. Robbins's wife, Serena (Ruby Elzy), is left to wail "My Man's Gone Now." Crown flees, leaving Porgy, who has been content to boast "I Got Plenty o' Nuttin'," free to court Bess. Aranging for her to get a divorce, he tells her, "Bess, You Is My Woman Now." The neighbors all go on a picnic where a glib drug peddler, Sportin' Life (John W. Bubbles), tells them of his cynical ideas about the Bible, insisting, "It Ain't Necessarily So." Crown suddenly appears, and he and Porgy fight, with Porgy killing Crown with Crown's own knife. Porgy is sent to jail. When he is released he learns that Sportin' Life has taken Bess to New York, so he sets out in his goat-cart to retrieve her.

Show Boat

When Cap'n Andy (Charles Winninger) and wife Parthy Ann (Edna May Oliver) bring their show boat *Cotton Blossom* into town for a performance, their daughter Magnolia (Norma Terris) meets a handsome professional gambler, Gaylord Ravenal (Howard Marsh). The youngsters fall in love at first sight, although they profess it is "Make Believe." Magnolia seeks advice on what to do from a black workhand, Joe (Jules Bledsoe), who tells her probably "Ol' Man River" alone can answer her but that the river "don't say nothin'." The show's leading lady, Julie (Helen Morgan), begins to understand Magnolia's situation and, recalling an old folk song, tells her how she too "Can't Help Lovin' Dat Man" of hers. But when Julie is accused of having Negro blood she is forced to leave the boat, taking the leading man with her. Magnolia and Gaylord are pressed into assuming the leads. Soon enough they are telling each other "You Are Love." They marry and head off. Years pass. At the Chicago World's Fair they seem amazed not only at the sights but at how their love has grown, and ask, "Why Do I Love You?" But eventually Gaylord's gambling costs him all his money, so he deserts Magnolia. She applies for a job singing at a night club where Julie, now a drunkard, is rehearsing her "Bill" number. Julie recognizes Magnolia and sacrifices what is left of her own career to help Magnolia begin hers. When Cap'n Andy finds his daughter there he persuades her to return to the *Cotton Blossom*. More years pass. One day an aging Gaylord returns. To his relief he is welcomed by Magnolia.

West Side Story

The story is set among two rival youth gangs in New York City in the 1950s, the longer-established Jets, led by Riff, and the Puerto Rican newcomers, the Sharks, led by Bernardo. Riff intends to meet Bernardo at a community dance—neutral territory—and challenge him to a fight for control of the neighborhood. Tony (Larry Kert), a former Jet and Riff's best friend, meets Maria (Carol Lawrence), Bernardo's sister, at the dance, and they fall immediately in love. They meet that night on her fire escape, and again the next day at the shop where she works, where they enact a mock wedding ceremony. Tony tries to intervene at the rumble but succeeds only in accidentally permitting Bernardo to kill Riff; in a rage, Tony himself kills Bernardo. Maria manages to forgive him and they decide to run away together. She sends a message to Tony who is in hiding with the Jets, by Bernardo's girlfriend Anita, but the gang so abuse her that she angrily tells them Maria is dead. Tony, in despair, runs through the streets begging to be killed; he discovers that Maria is alive just as a Shark shoots him. Maria in her grief manages to persuade everyone to let the retaliation stop, giving a hint of hope for reconciliation as the play ends.

DISCOGRAPHY

Selected Original, Revival, Film, and Studio Casts

Anything Goes

Composer and original cast (1934, 1935, and 1947): Cole Porter's "Anything Goes" in New York and London with the composer and members of the original 1934 cast. Ethel Merman, Jack Whiting, The Foursome, Jeanne Aubert, Sidney Howard, Porter (vocals and piano). Smithsonian American Musical Theater Series DPM1-0284 R 007. Contents: "I Get a Kick Out of You," "You're the Top," "Blow, Gabriel, Blow" (Merman), "All Through the Night" (Whiting), "Blow, Gabriel, Blow" (Aubert), "You're the Top" (Whiting and Aubert), "Sailor's Chanty," "Gypsy in Me" (The Foursome), "You're the Top," "Anything Goes," "Be Like the Bluebird" (Porter), and "Be Like the Bluebird" (Howard). Porter's rendition of "You're the Top" (October 26, 1934) was reissued on the compact disc *Showstoppers: Historic Victor Recordings* BMG 9590-2-R.*

Revival cast (1962): Hal Linden, Eileen Rodgers, Kenneth Mars, Ted Simons (conductor)†. Epic Footlight Series FLS 15100 (S); reissued on Time-Life P 15602 (S), set STL AM02 with *Kiss Me, Kate* and *Can-Can* (set title, *Cole Porter*). Missing: "Where Are the Men?"

*By the late 1980s all shows were issued in compact disc (the numbers given in this Discography) or tape formats. Many older long-playing cast recordings have also been reissued on CDs in recent years

†Throughout, no attempt is made to honor the distinctions between conductor, musical director, or musical supervisor. The term "conductor" is used exclusively.

Revival cast (1987): Patti LuPone, Howard McGillin, Bill McCutcheon, Edward Strauss (conductor). RCA 7769-4 RC.

Studio cast (1989): Kim Criswell, Cris Groenendaal, Jack Gilford, Frederica von Stade, John McGlinn (conductor). EMI/Angel CDC 7-49848-2.

Carousel

Original cast (1945): John Raitt, Jan Clayton, Jean Darling, Christine Johnson, Joseph Littau (conductor). Decca DLP-8003; reissue. MCA 2033. Missing: "Geraniums in the Winder" and some dance numbers.

Film cast (1956): Gordon MacRae, Shirley Jones, Barbara Ruick, Robert Rounseville, Cameron Mitchell, Alfred Newman (conductor). Capitol SW 694. Missing: "Geraniums in the Winder," "The Highest Judge of All," and some dance numbers.

Studio cast (1988): Barbara Cook, Samuel Ramey, Sarah Brightman, David Rendall, Maureen Forrester, and Paul Gemignani (conductor). MCA Classics MCAD 6209.

The Cradle Will Rock

Composer and original cast (1938): Olive Stanton, Charles Niemeyer, Bert Weston, Edward Fuller, Jules Schmidt, John Adair, Ralph MacBane, Peggy Coudray, Maynard Holmes, Dulce Fox, George Fairchild, Blanche Collins, Howard da Silva, Marc Blitzstein (narration and piano). Musicraft Records No. 18; reissued American Legacy T 1001. Nearly complete.*

Composer and studio cast (1957): *Marc Blitzstein Discuss His Theater Compositions.* Evelyn Lear, Roddy McDowall, Jane Connell, Alvin Epstein, Marc Blitzstein (piano). Spoken Arts 717. Spoken historical introduction by Blitzstein, "Nickel Under the Foot," and Hotel Lobby Scene.

Revival cast (1964): Jerry Orbach, Lauri Peters, Clifford David, Rita Gardner, Micki Grant, Hal Buckley, Nancy Andrews, Gershon Kingsley (musical director and pianist). MGM SE 4289-2 OC (complete on two records).

London cast (1985): Patti Lupone, Randle Mell, Michael Barrett (musical director and pianist). That's Entertainment Records ZC TED 1105 (complete).

Follies

Original cast (1971): Alexis Smith, Gene Nelson, John McMartin, Yvonne DeCarlo, Dorothy Collins, Mary McCarty, Ethel Shutta, Victoria Mallory, Fifi D'Orsay, Harold Hastings (conductor). Capitol SO 761.

*See Hummel, vol. 1, 32.

Concert cast (1985): Barbara Cook, Betty Comden, Adolph Green, Lee Remick, Mandy Patinkin, Licia Albanese, George Hearn, Phyllis Newman, Carol Burnett, Elaine Stritch, Paul Gemignani (conductor). RCA HBC2-7128.

Studio cast (1985): *A Collector's Sondheim*. Craig Lucas, Suzanne Henry, E. Martin Perry (conductor). Contents (dropped songs only): "All Things Bright and Beautiful," "Uptown, Downtown," "Who Could Be Blue?", "Little White House," "It Wasn't Meant to Happen," and "Can That Boy Foxtrot!" RCA CRL4-5359. With the exception of "Can That Boy Foxtrot!" all songs above appear in *Marry Me A Little* (1981) RCA ABL1-4159.

London cast (1987): Diana Rigg, Julia McKenzie, Daniel Massey, David Healy, Dolores Gray, Martin Koch (conductor). Geffen 24183-4.

Guys and Dolls

Composer and studio cast (c. 1950-1955): *An Evening With Frank Loesser: Frank Loesser Performs Songs From His Hit Shows*. DRG 5169 (CD). Contents: "Fugue for Tinhorns" (with Milton Delugg and Sue Bennett), "I'll Know," "Luck Be A Lady," "I've Never Been In Love Before," "Sit Down You're Rockin' The Boat," "Sue Me," "Traveling Light" (unused), and "Adelaide" (from 1955 MGM film).

Original cast (1950): Robert Alda, Vivian Blaine, Sam Levene, Isabel Bigley, Pat Rooney, Sr., Stubby Kaye, Irving Actman (conductor). Decca 8036; reissue MCA 2034. Missing: "Havana" and "Crapshooter" dances.

Film cast (1955): Marlon Brando, Frank Sinatra, Jean Simmons, Jay Blackton (conductor). Decca ED 2332. Added: "A Woman in Love," "Pet Me, Poppa," and "Adelaide."

Revival cast (1992): Peter Gallagher, Nathan Lane, Josie de Guzman, Faith Prince, Edward Strauss (conductor). RCA 09026-61317-2.

Kiss Me, Kate

Original cast (1949): Alfred Drake, Patricia Morison, Lisa Kirk, Harold Lang, Lorenzo Fuller, Harry Clark, and Jack Diamond, Pembroke Davenport (conductor). Columbia S 32609; reissued on Time-Life P 15602 (S), set STL AM02 with *Anything Goes* and *Can-Can* (set title, *Cole Porter*). Missing: "I Sing of Love," "Act I Finale," and some dance numbers.

Film cast (1953): Howard Keel, Kathryn Grayson, Ann Miller, Bobby Van, Tommy Rall, Keenan Wynn, James Whitmore, Bob Fosse, André Previn (conductor). MGM 3077. Added: "From This Moment On," dropped from *Out of This World*.

Original cast (1959): Alfred Drake, Patricia Morison, Lisa Kirk, Harold Lang, Lorenzo Fuller, Pembroke Davenport (conductor). Capitol STAO 126. Contents same as Original cast 1949.

Studio cast (1990): Josephine Barstow, Thomas Hampson, Kim Criswell, George Dvorsky, Damon Evans, David Garrison, John McGlinn (conductor). EMI/Angel CDS 54033-2.

Lady in the Dark

Original cast (1941): Gertrude Lawrence, MacDonald Carey, Donald Randolph, Maurice Abravenel (conductor). AEI 1146. Contents: "Oh Fabulous One," "One Life to Live," "Girl of the Moment," "It Looks Like Liza," "The Saga of Jenny," "My Ship," and dialogue from act I, scenes 1, 2, 4, and 5. Lawrence's "My Ship" (February 23, 1941) appears on *Showstoppers: Historic Victor Recordings*. BMG 9590-2 R (CD).

Studio recording (1950s): Arthur Winograd (conductor). MGM E 3334. Contents: "Dance of the Tumblers."

Original cast: *Danny Kaye Entertains*. Columbia CL 931. Contents: "Tschaikowsky."

Studio cast (1963): Risë Stevens, Adolph Green, John Reardon, Lehman Engel (conductor). Columbia OS 2390; reissued on Time-Life P 16374, set STL AM10 with *One Touch of Venus* and *The Threepeeny Opera* (set title, *Kurt Weill*); CD reissue MK44689. Missing: "Dance of the Tumblers."

A Little Night Music

Original cast (1973): Len Cariou, Harold Hastings (conductor). Columbia KS 32265.

Merrily We Roll Along

Original cast (1981): Jim Walton, Ann Morrison, Lonny Price, Paul Gemignani (conductor). RCA CBL1-4197.

The Most Happy Fella

Composer and studio cast (1953): *An Evening With Frank Loesser: Frank Loesser Performs Songs From His Hit Shows*. DRG 5169 (CD). Act I, Scene 1, vocals by Maxene Andrews as Cleo and unidentified singers (contains previously unreleased material). Contents: "Ooh! My Feet!", "How's About Tonight/House and Garden," "The Letter," and "Wanting To Be Wanted" (unused).

Original cast (1956): Robert Weede, Jo Sullivan, Art Lund, Susan Johnson, Shorty Long, Mona Paulee, Arthur Rubin, Herbert Greene (conductor). Columbia 03L 240; reissued on Columbia Special Products CO3L 240 (three LPs).

Revival cast (1992): Spiro Malas, Sophie Hayden, Scott Waara, Tim Stella (conductor). RCA 09026-61294-2 (two pianos).

My Fair Lady

Original cast (1956): Rex Harrison, Julie Andrews, Stanley Holloway, Robert Coote, Franz Allers (conductor). Columbia OL 5090 (M); reissued on Columbia Special Products AOL 5090 (M) and E/Philip RBL 1000 (M). Missing: "The Embassy Waltz."

Film cast (1964): Rex Harrison, Audrey Hepburn (sung by Marni Nixon), Stanley Holloway, André Previn (conductor). Columbia KOL 8000; reissued on Columbia JS 2600. Missing: "The Embassy Waltz."

Lyricist (1971): *An Evening with Johnny Mercer, Alan Jay Lerner and Sammy Cahn Singing Their Own Songs.* Contents (Lerner only): "Wouldn't It Be Loverly?," "Oh Come to the Ball," and spoken introduction to "On the Street Where You Live." Book-of-the-Month-Club Records 70-5240.

One Touch of Venus

Composer (1943): *Tryout: A Series of Private Rehearsal Recordings—Including Actual Performances by Kurt Weill and Ira Gershwin.* DRG 904 (CD). Contents: "West Wind," "Very Very Very," "Wooden Wedding," "Speak Low," "The Jersey Plunk" ("Way Out West in Jersey"), "The Trouble With Women" (quartet), and "That's Him."

Original cast (1943): Mary Martin, Kenny Baker, Maurice Abravanel (conductor). Decca DL 79122; reissued on AEI 1136; reissued on Time-Life P 16374, set STL AM10 with *Lady in the Dark* and *The Threepeeny Opera* (set title, *Kurt Weill*). Contents: "I'm a Stranger Here Myself," "Forty Minutes for Lunch (ballet)," "Speak Low," "West Wind," "Foolish Heart," "The Trouble with Women," "That's Him," "Wooden Wedding," and "Venus in Ozone Heights (ballet)."

Studio cast (mainly): *Ben Bagley's Kurt Weill Revisited.* Paula Lawrence (original cast), Arthur Siegel, Chita Rivera, Jo Sullivan. Painted Smiles PS 1375; reissued 1989 on Painted Smiles PSCD 108. Contents: "One Touch of Venus," "How Much Do I Love You," "Dr. Crippen," "Very, Very, Very," "Vive la différence" (cut), and "Love in a Mist" (cut).

On Your Toes

Original cast, revival cast, composer, studio cast (1936-1954).*

Original revival cast (1954): Vera Zorina, Bobby Van, Elaine Stritch, Ben Astar, Kay Coulter, Joshua Shelley, Nicholas Orloff, Jack Williams, George Church, Salvatore Dell'Isola (conductor). Decca DL 9015; reissued on Stet DS 15024. Missing: "La Princesse Zenobia Ballet."

Original revival cast (1983): Lara Teeter, George S. Irving, Dina Merrill, George De La Pena, Christine Andreas, John Mauceri (conductor). Polydor 813667-1 Y 1.

Pal Joey

Original cast, revival cast, and studio cast (1950): Vivienne Segal, Harold Lang, Barbara Ashley, Beverly Fite, Kenneth Remo, Jo Hurt, Lehman Engel (conductor) (1940s lyrics and orchestrations). Columbia ML 54364; reissued on Columbia Special Products COL 4364. Missing: "Chicago" and "The Flower Garden of My Heart."

Original revival cast, studio cast (1952): Helen Gallagher, Patricia Northrop, Elaine Stritch, Lewis Bolyard, Jane Froman, Dick Beavers, Max Meth (conductor) (1952 lyrics and orchestrations). Missing: Ballet ("Chez Joey"). Angel ZDM 0777-7-646962-2-1.

Film cast (1957): Frank Sinatra, Rita Hayworth (sung by Jo Ann Greer), Kim Novak (sung by Trudi Erwin), Morris Stoloff (conductor). Songs from original production: "Zip," "Chicago," "That Terrific Rainbow," "Pal Joey," and "Bewitched." Songs interpolated from other Rodgers and Hart shows: "There's a Small Hotel" (*On Your Toes* [1936]), "My Funny Valentine" and "The Lady Is a Tramp" (*Babes In Arms* [1937]), and "I Didn't Know What Time It Was" (*Too Many Girls* [1939]). Capitol W-912.

Porgy and Bess

Original cast (1935): *Gershwin Performs Gershwin Rare Recordings 1931-1935*. Musicmasters 5062-2 C (CD). *Porgy and Bess* rehearsal performance, July 19, 1935, conducted by Gershwin. Contents: "Introduction," "Summertime" (Abbie Mitchell), "A Woman Is a Sometime Thing" (Edward Matthews), Act I, scene 1: Finale, "My Man's Gone Now" (Ruby Elzy), and "Bess, You Is My Woman Now" (Todd Duncan, Anne Brown).

Studio cast (1936): *George Gershwin Plays George Gershwin*. Pearl Gemm CDS 9483 (CD). Lawrence Tibbett, Helen Jepson, Alexander Smallens (conductor). Selections

---

*See Hummel, vol. 1, 430.

from *Porgy and Bess,* November 1935 (originally issued on Victor 11878/81). Contents: "It Ain't Necessarily So," "The Buzzard Song," "Scene: Summertime/Crapgame/A Woman Is a Sometime Thing," "Bess, You Is My Woman Now," "I Got Plenty O' Nuttin'," "Where Is My Bess?," "Summertime," and "My Man's Gone Now." Lawrence Tibbett's "I Got Plenty o' Nuttin' " (October 23, 1935) appears on *Showstoppers: Historic Victor Recordings.* BMG 9590-2 R (CD).

Original cast (1940-1942): Todd Duncan, Anne Brown, Edward Matthews, Eva Jessye Choir, Alexander Smallens (conductor). Decca DL 9024; reissued on MCA 2035. Fourteen selections.*

Studio cast (1951): Lawrence Winters, Camilla Williams, Inez Matthews, Warren Coleman, Avon Long, J. Rosamond Johnson Chorus, Lehman Engel (conductor). Columbia OSL 163; reissued on Odyssey 32 36 0018 (nearly complete on three LPs).

Jazz recording (1957): Ella Fitzgerald, Louis Armstrong. Verve VE 2-2507.

Jazz recording (1958): Miles Davis, Gil Evans. Columbia PC 8085.

Studio cast (1963): Leontyne Price, William Warfield, McHenry Boatwright, John Bubbles, Skitch Henderson (conductor). RCA LSC 2679. Twelve selections.

Studio cast (1976): Willard White, Leona Mitchess, McHenry Boatwright, Florence Quivar, Barbara Hendricks, Cleveland Orchestra and Chorus, Lorin Maazel (conductor). London OSA 13116.

Opera production (1977): Clamma Dale, Donnie Ray Albert, Larry Marshall, Houston Opera Company. John DeMain (conductor). RCA ARL 3-2109.

Opera production (1986): Cynthia Haymon, Willard White, Damon Evans, Glyndebourne Festival Opera, Simon Rattle (conductor). EMI/Angel CDCC 49568.

Show Boat

Original cast (1928): Showstoppers: Historic Victor Recordings. BMG 9590-2 R (CD). Contents: "Ol' Man River" (Paul Robeson, March 1, 1928) and Bill'' (Helen Morgan, February 14, 1928).†

Original revival cast (1946): Jan Clayton, Carol Bruce, Charles Fredericks, Kenneth Spencer, Helen Dowdy, Edwin McArthur (conductor).‡

Film cast (1951): Kathryn Grayson, Howard Keel, William Warfield, Marge and Gower Champion, Ava Gardner, Adolph Deutsch (conductor). MGM E 3230.

*See Hummel, vol. 1, 462.
†See Hummel, vol. 1, 520–21 for a comprehensive listing of original Broadway and London cast excerpts between 1928 and 1936
‡Ibid., 522.

Original Lincoln Center revival cast (1966): Barbara Cook, Constance Towers, Stephen Douglass, David Wayne, William Warfield, Franz Allers (conductor). RCA LSO 1126.

London cast (1971): Cleo Laine, Thomas Carey, Lorna Dalla, Kenneth Nelson, Andrew Jobin, Ena Cabayo, Ray Cook (conductor). Stanyon Records 10048 (two LPs).

Studio cast (1988): Frederika von Stade, Teresa Stratas, Jerry Hadley, Paige O'Hara, David Garrison, Bruce Hubbard, John McGlinn (conductor). EMI/Angel CDS 7-49108-2.

Revival cast (1994): Rebecca Luker, Lonette McKee, Mark Jacoby, Elaine Stritch, Michel Bell, Gretha Boston, Robert Morse, Jeffrey Huard (conductor). Quality 257.

Sunday in the Park With George

Original cast (1984): Mandy Patinkin, Bernadette Peters, Charles Kimbrough, Barbara Bryne, Dana Ivey, Paul Gemignani (conductor). RCA HBC1-5042.

West Side Story

Original cast (1957): Larry Kert, Carol Lawrence, Chita Rivera, Max Goberman (conductor). Columbia OL 5230; reissued on Columbia S 32603. Missing: "Taunting."

Film cast (1961): Natalie Wood (sung by Marni Nixon), Richard Beymer (sung by Jim Bryant), Rita Moreno (sung by Betty Wand), Russ Tamblyn, George Chakiris, John Green (conductor). Columbia OS 2070; reissued with previously unreleased masters on Sony SK 48211 (1992).

Studio cast (1985): Kiri Te Kanawa, José Carreras, Kurt Ollmann, Tatiana Troyanos, Leonard Bernstein (conductor). Deutsche Grammophon 415253-1/4.

APPENDICES

Appendix A: *Sources, Published Librettos, and Vocal Scores*

Anything Goes *(1934)*

Source: Original book by Guy Bolton and P. G. Wodehouse, revised by Howard Lindsay and Russel Crouse

Published libretto: None (rental available from Tams-Witmark Music Library).

Published vocal score: Chappell & Co., and Harms (Broadway 1934); Vocal Selections Revival Edition, Warner Bros., 1988 (Broadway 1987).

Carousel *(1945)*

Source: *Liliom* (1921) by Ferenc Molnár (as adapted by Benjamin F. Glazer) (New York: Samuel French, 1945). [play]

Published libretto: *Six Plays by Rodgers and Hammerstein* (New York: The Modern Library Association, 1959).

Published vocal score: Williamson Music Co., 1945

The Cradle Will Rock *(1937)*

Source: Original book by Marc Blitzstein.
Published libretto: *The Cradle Will Rock* (New York: Random House, 1938); reprinted
in *The Best Short Plays of the Social Theatre*, ed. William Kozlenko, (New York:
Random House, 1939).
Published vocal score: None (rental available from Tams-Witmark Music Library)

Guys and Dolls *(1950)*

Source: "The Idyll of Miss Sarah Brown" and "Pick the Winner" by Damon Runyon. *Guys and Dolls*. Philadelphia: (J. B. Lippincott Company, 1931). [short
stories]
Published libretto: *The Guys and Dolls Book*. London: Methuen, 1982. [includes "The
Idyll of Miss Sarah Brown"]
Published vocal score: Frank Music Corp., 1949, 1950, 1951, 1953; renewed 1977,
1978, 1979, 1981.

Kiss Me, Kate *(1948)*

Source: *The Taming of the Shrew* by William Shakespeare (c. 1592). [play]
Published libretto: *Great Musicals of the American Theatre Volume One*, ed. Stanley
Richards (Radnor, Pa.: Chilton Book Company, 1973.
Published vocal score: Chappell & Co., 1951, 1967.

Lady in the Dark *(1941)*

Source: Original book by Moss Hart.
Published libretto: *Great Musicals of the American Theatre Volume Two*, ed. Stanley
Richards (Radnor, Pa.: Chilton Book Company, 1976).
Published vocal score: Chappell & Co, 1941.

The Most Happy Fella *(1956)*

Source: *They Knew What They Wanted* by Sidney Howard (New York: Doubleday,
Page & Company, 1925); reprinted in *Famous American Plays of the 1930s*, selected and introduced by Harold Curman (New York: Dell Publishing Co.,
1959). [play]
Published libretto: Frank Music Corp., 1956, 1957 [included with the vocal score];
reprinted in *Theatre Arts* October 1958), 26-53.
Published vocal score: Frank Music Corp., 1956, 1957

My Fair Lady *(1956)*

Source: *Pygmalion* (1913) by George Bernard Shaw; reprinted in *Pygmalion/My Fair Lady* (New York: Signet, 1975). [play]. See also published libretto.
Published libretto: *Pygmalion/My Fair Lady* (New York: Signet, 1975).
Published vocal score: Chappell & Co., 1956

One Touch of Venus *(1943)*

Source: *The Tinted Venus* (1885) by F. Anstey (Thomas Anstey Guthrie); reprinted in *Humour & Fantasy* (New York: Arno Press, 1978). [novel]
Published libretto: *Great Musicals of the American Theatre Volume One*, ed. Stanley Richards (Radnor, Pa.: Chilton Book Company, 1973).
Published vocal score: None (rental score available from the Rodgers and Hammerstein Theatre Library); Vocal selections, The Richmond Organization 1944; renewed by Hampshire House Publishing Corp. and Chappell & Co., 1972

On Your Toes *(1936)*

Source: Original book by Rodgers and Hart and George Abbott.
Published libretto: None (rental available from The Rodgers & Hammerstein Theatre Library).
Published vocal score: Chappell & Co., 1985 (Broadway 1983).

Pal Joey *(1940)*

Source: *Pal Joey* by John O'Hara; *Pal Joey: The Novel and The Libretto and Lyrics* (New York: Vintage, 1983). [novel based on short stories in the form of letters first published in the *New Yorker* from 1938 to 1940]. See also published libretto.
Published libretto: *Pal Joey: The Novel and the Libretto and Lyrics*.
Published vocal score: Chappell & Co, 1962

Porgy and Bess *(1935)*

Sources: *Porgy* by DuBose Heyward (New York: George H. Doran Company, 1925) [novel]; *Porgy, A Play in Four Acts* by DuBose and Dorothy Heyward (New York: Doubleday, Doran, 1928); reprinted in *Famous American Plays of the 1920s*, selected and introduced by Kenneth MacGowan (New York: Dell Publishing Co., 1959). [play]
Published Librettos: London OSA-13116 (1976); RCA ARL 3-2109 (1977); EMI/Angel CDCC-49568 (1986); Columbia OSL 162; reissued on Odyssey Stereo 32-

36-0018 (1951), also published in *Great Musicals of the American Theatre Volume One,* ed. Stanley Richards (Radnor, Pa: Chilton Book Company, 1973); see also the published vocal score.
Published vocal score: Gershwin Publishing Corp./Chappell & Co., 1935

Show Boat *(1927)*

Source: *Show Boat* by Edna Ferber (Garden City, N.Y.: Doubleday, 1926). [novel]
Published Librettos: Chappell, 1934 (London 1928); act I, scenes 1, 2, 4, 7, and 8, and act II, scene 3 [virtually complete] and scenes 4 and 9 [well represented] in EMI/Angel CDS-7-49108-2 (1988).
Published Vocal Scores: Harms Co., 1927 (Broadway 1927); Chappell & Co. and T. B. Harms Co., 1928 (London 1928); The Welk Music Group, 1927 (Broadway 1946).

West Side Story *(1957)*

Source: *Romeo and Juliet* by William Shakespeare (1595). [play]. See also published librettos.
Published librettos: *Romeo and Juliet/West Side Story* (New York: Dell Publishing Co., 1965); *Great Musicals of the American Theatre Volume One,* ed. Stanley Richards (Radnor, Pa.: Chilton Book Company, 1973).
Published vocal score: G. Schirmer and Chappell & Co., 1957 and 1959.

Appendix B: Long Runs

1920s–1980s

1920s

1. *The Student Prince in Heidelberg* (1924) (Romberg and Donnelly) 608
2. *Blossom Time* (1921) (Romberg and Donnelly) 592
3. **Show Boat (1927) (Kern and Hammerstein)*** 575
4. *Sally* (1920) (Kern, Bolton, and Grey) 570
5. *Rose-Marie* (1924) (Friml, Harbach, and Hammerstein) 557
6. *Good News* (1927) (Henderson, DeSylva, and Brown) 551
7. *Sunny* (1925) (Kern, Harbach, and Hammerstein) 517
8. *The Vagabond King* (1925) (Friml and Hooker) 511

*Musicals in boldface type are discussed in chapters 2–12.

9. *The New Moon* (1928) (Romberg and Hammerstein)   509
10. *Rio Rita* (1927) (Tierney and McCarthy)   494
11. *Wildflower* (1923) (Youmans, Stothart, Harbach, and Hammerstein)   477
12. *The Desert Song* (1926) (Romberg, Harbach, and Hammerstein)   471

1930s

1. *Of Thee I Sing* (1931)(G. and I. Gershwin)   441
2. ***Anything Goes* (1934) (Porter)**   **420**
3. *DuBarry Was a Lady* (1939) (Porter)   408
4. *The Cat and the Fiddle* (1931) (Kern and Harbach)   395
5. *Flying High* (1930) (Henderson, DeSylva, and Brown)   357
6. *Music in the Air* (1932) (Kern and Hammerstein)   342
7. *I Married an Angel* (1938) (Rodgers and Hart)   338
8. ***On Your Toes* (1936) (Rodgers and Hart)**   **315**
9. *The Great Waltz* (1934) (Johann Strauss Jr. and Carter)   298
10. *Roberta* (1933) (Kern and Harbach)   295
11. *I'd Rather Be Right* (1937) (Rodgers and Hart)   290
12. *Babes in Arms* (1937) (Rodgers and Hart)   289

1940s

1. *Oklahoma!* (1943) (Rodgers and Hammerstein)   2,212
2. *South Pacific* (1949) (Rodgers and Hammerstein)   1,925
3. *Annie Get Your Gun* (1946) (Berlin and H. and D. Fields)   1,147
4. ***Kiss Me, Kate* (1948) (Porter and B. and S. Spewack)**   **1,070**
5. ***Carousel* (1945) (Rodgers and Hammerstein)**   **890**
6. *Follow the Girls* (1944) (Shapiro, Pascal, and Charig)   882
7. *Song of Norway* (1944) (Wright and Forrest)   860
8. *Where's Charley?* (1948) (Loesser and Abbott)   792
9. *Gentlemen Prefer Blondes* (1949) (Styne and Robin)   740
10. *High Button Shoes* (1947) (Styne, Cahn, and Abbott)   727
11. *Finian's Ranbow* (1947) (Lane and Harburg)   725
12. *Bloomer Girl* (1944) (Arlen and Harburg)   654
13. *Brigadoon* (1947) (Lerner and Loewe)   581
14. ***One Touch Of Venus* (1943) (Weill, Nash, and Perelman)**   **567**

1950s

1. ***My Fair Lady* (1956) (Lerner and Loewe)**   **2,717**
2. *The Sound of Music* (1959) (Rodgers and Hammerstein)   1,443
3. *The Music Man* (1957) (Wilson)   1,375
4. *The King and I* (1951) (Rodgers and Hammerstein)   1,246
5. ***Guys and Dolls* (1950) (Loesser and Burrows)**   **1,200**
6. *Pajama Game* (1954) (Adler and Ross)   1,063

7. *Damn Yankees* (1955) (Adler and Ross) — 1,019
8. *Bells Are Ringing* (1956) (Styne, Comden and Green) — 924
9. *Can-Can* (1953) (Porter and Burrows) — 892
10. *Fanny* (1954) (Rome, Behrman and Logan) — 888
11. *Fiorello!* (1959) (Bock and Harnick) — 796
12. **West Side Story (1957) (Bernstein, Sondheim, and Laurents)** — **732**
13. *Gypsy* (1959) (Styne, Sondheim, and Laurents) — 702
14. *Li'l Abner* (1956) (de Paul and Mercer) — 693
15. **The Most Happy Fella (1956) (Loesser)** — **676**

1960s

1. *Fiddler on the Roof* (1964) (Bock, Harnick and Stein) — 3,242
2. *Hello, Dolly!* (1964) (Herman and Stewart) — 2,844
3. *The Man of La Mancha* (1965) (Leigh, Darion, and Wasserman) — 2,328
4. *Hair* (1968) (MacDermot, Ragni, and Rado) — 1,750
5. *Mame* (1966) (Herman, Lawrence, and Lee) — 1,508
6. *How to Succeed in Business Without Really Trying* (1961) (Loesser and Burrows) — 1,417
7. *Funny Girl* (1964) (Styne, Merrill, and Lennart) — 1,348
8. *Promises, Promises* (1968) (Bacharach, David, and Simon) — 1,281
9. *1776* (1969) (Edwards and Stone) — 1,217
10. *Cabaret* (1966) (Kander, Ebb, Masteroff) — 1,165
11. *A Funny Thing Happened on the Way to the Forum* (1962) (Sondheim, Shevelove, and Gelbart) — 964

1970s

1. *A Chorus Line* (1975) (Hamlisch, Kleban, Kirkwood, and Dante) — 6,137
2. *Grease* (1972) (Jacobs and Casey) — 3,388
3. *Annie* (1977) (Strouse, Charnin, and Meehan) — 2,377
4. *Pippin* (1971) (Schwartz and Hirson) — 1,944
5. *Magic Show* (1974) (Schwartz and Randall) — 1,920
6. *The Wiz* (1975) (Smalls and Brown) — 1,672
7. *The Best Little Whorehouse in Texas* (1978) (Hall, King, and Masterson) — 1,584
8. *Evita* (1979) (Lloyd Webber and Rice) — 1,567
9. *They're Playing Our Song* (1979) (Hamlisch, Sager, and Simon) — 1,082
10. *Shenandoah* (1975) (Geld, Udell, and Barrett) — 1,050
11. *Chicago* (1975) (Kander, Ebb, and Fosse) — 898
12. *Applause* (1970) (Strouse, Adams, Comden, Green) — 896
13. *I Love My Wife* (1977) (Coleman and Stewart) — 872
14. *No, No, Nanette* (1971) (revival) (Youmans, Caesar, and Shevelove) — 861
15. *Raisin* (1973) (Woldin, Brittan, Memiroff, and Zaltberg) — 847
16. *Candide* (1974) (revival) (Bernstein, Wilbur, Sondheim, et al., and Wheeler) — 740

17. *Jesus Christ Superstar* (971) (Lloyd Webber and Rice)   720
18. *Company* (1970) (Sondheim and Furth)   706

1980s

1. *Cats** (1982) (Lloyd Webber and Eliot)   5,944
2. *Les Misérables** (1987) (Boublil, Schönberg, and Kretzmer)   4,031
3. *Phantom of the Opera** (1988) (Lloyd Webber, Hart, and Stilgoe)   3,751
4. *42nd Street* (1980) (Warren, Dubin, Stewart, and Bramble)   3,486
5. *La Cage aux Folles* (1983) (Herman and Fierstein)   1,761
6. *Dreamgirls* (1981) (Krieger and Eyen)   1,522
7. *Me and My Girl* (1986) (revival) (Gay, Rose, and Furber)   1,412

Appendix C: The Forty Longest Running Book Musicals on Broadway

1920–1959

1. **My Fair Lady (1956)**[†]   **2,717**
2. *Oklahoma!* (1943)   2,212
3. *South Pacific* (1949)   1,925
4. *The Sound of Music* (1959)   1,443
5. *The Music Man* (1957)   1,375
6. *The King and I* (1951)   1,246
7. **Guys and Dolls (1950)**   **1,200**
8. *Annie Get Your Gun* (1946)   1,147
9. **Kiss Me, Kate (1948)**   **1,070**
10. *Pajama Game* (1954)   1,063
11. *Damn Yankees* (1955)   1,019
12. *Bells Are Ringing* (1956)   924
13. *Can-Can* (1953)   892
14. **Carousel (1945)**   **890**
15. *Fanny* (1954)   888
16. *Follow the Girls* (1944)   882
17. *Song of Norway* (1944)   860
18. *Fiorello!* (1959)   796
19. *Where's Charley?* (1948)   792
20. *Gentlemen Prefer Blondes* (1949)   740
21. **West Side Story (1957)**   **732**

*Running as of January 1, 1997.
†Musicals in boldface type are discussed in chapters 2–12.

22.	*High Button Shoes* (1947)	727
23.	*Finian's Rainbow* (1947)	725
24.	*Gypsy* (1959)	702
25.	*Li'l Abner* (1956)	693
26.	**The Most Happy Fella (1956)**	**676**
27.	*Bloomer Girl* (1944)	654
28.	*Call Me Madam* (1950)	644
29.	*The Student Prince in Heidelberg* (1924)	608
30.	*Wish You Were Here* (1952)	598
31.	*Blossom Time* (1921)	592
32.	*Kismet* (1953)	583
33.	*Brigadoon* (1947)	581
34.	**Show Boat (1927)**	**575**
35.	*Sally* (1920)	570
36.	**One Touch Of Venus (1943)**	**567**
37.	*Wonderful Town* (1953)	559
38.	*Rose-Marie* (1924)	557
39.	*Jamaica* (1957)	555
40.	*Good News* (1927)	557
41.	*Let's Face It* (1941)	547

1920–1996

1.	*A Chorus Line* (1975)	6,137
2.	*Cats** (1982)	5,944
3.	*Les Misérables** (1987)	4,031
4.	*The Phantom of the Opera** (1988)	3,751
5.	*42nd Street* (1980)	3,486
6.	*Grease* (1972)	3,388
7.	*Fiddler on the Roof* (1964)	3,242
8.	*Hello, Dolly!* (1964)	2,844
9.	**My Fair Lady (1956)**	**2,717**
10.	*Miss Saigon** (1991)	2,394
11.	*Annie* (1977)	2,377
12.	*The Man of La Mancha* (1965)	2,328
13.	*Oklahoma!* (1943)	2,212
14.	*Pippin* (1971)	1,994
15.	*South Pacific* (1949)	1,925
16.	*Magic Show* (1974)	1,920
17.	*La Cage aux Folles* (1983)	1,761
18.	*Hair* (1968)	1,750
19.	*The Wiz* (1975)	1,672
20.	*The Best Little Whorehouse in Texas* (1978)	1,584
21.	*Evita* (1979)	1,567

*Running as of January 1, 1997.

22.	*Dreamgirls* (1981)	1,521
23.	*Mame* (1966)	1,508
24.	*The Sound of Music* (1959)	1,443
25.	*How to Succeed in Business Without Really Trying* (1961)	1,417
26.	*Me and My Girl* (1986 revival)	1,412
27.	*The Music Man* (1957)	1,375
28.	*Funny Girl* (1964)	1,348
29.	*Promises, Promises* (1968)	1,281
30.	*The King and I* (1951)	1,246
31.	*1776* (1969)	1,217
32.	**Guys and Dolls (1950)**	**1,200**
33.	*Cabaret* (1966)	1,165
34.	*Annie Get Your Gun* (1946)	1,147
35.	*They're Playing Our Song* (1979)	1,082
36.	**Kiss Me, Kate (1948)**	**1,070**
37.	*Pajama Game* (1954)	1,063
38.	*Shenandoah* (1975)	1,050
39.	*Damn Yankees* (1955)	1,019
40.	*A Funny Thing Happened on the Way to the Forum* (1962)	964

Appendix D: Show Boat

Broadway 1927

Overture

(Based mainly on "Mis'ry's Comin' Around" and "Why Do I Love You?" Other musical material includes "Can't Help Lovin' Dat Man" and references to Magnolia's piano theme and "Ol' Man River"). [5 11]

Act I

Scene 1: The levee at Natchez, on the Mississippi—in the late eighteen eighties.
1. "Opening—Cotton Blossom" (Chorus) [12–44], "Cap'n Andy's Ballyhoo" (Captain Andy), "Where's the Mate for Me?" (Ravenal)
2. "Make Believe" (Ravenal and Magnolia) [45–53]
3. "Ol' Man River" (Joe) [54–65]
Scene 2: Kitchen pantry of the "Cotton Blossom"—a half-hour later.

Songs followed by an asterisk are not included in the McGlinn recording. Numbers in brackets refer to the Harms vocal score.

4. Orchestra: Parthy's theme, "Ol' Man River" (verse), Magnolia's piano theme, second "Mis'ry" theme [66–67]
5. "Can't Help Lovin' Dat Man" (Julie, Queenie, and Servants) [68–84]

Scene 3: Outside a waterfront gambling saloon. Simultaneous with scene 2.

6. Orchestra: "Life on the Wicked Stage," "Make Believe" (sections 5 and 2) [85–86]*
7. "Life on the Wicked Stage" (Ellie and Girls) [87–95]
8. "Till Good Luck Comes My Way" (Ravenal and Men) [96–104]

Scene 4. Auditorium and stage of the "Cotton Blossom"—one hour later.

9. "Mis'ry's Comin' Aroun'" (Queenie and Colored Chorus) [105–14]
   Underscoring: "Mis'ry" themes, "Where's the Mate for Me?", "If We Were on Our Honeymoon," "Make Believe" (A section) [115–25]

Scene 5: Box-office, on foredeck of the "Cotton Blossom"—three weeks later.

10. Introduction ("Cotton Blossom") [126–27]*
11. "I Might Fall Back on You" (Frank, Ellie, and Girls [128–37]
12. "C'mon folks" ("Queenie's Ballyhoo") (Queenie) [138–47]

Scene 6: Auditorium and stage of the "Cotton Blossom"—during the third act of the *The Parson's Bride*—that evening.

13. Incidental Music, played on the stage during the presentation of "The Parson's Bride" (Lange's "Blumenlied," Parson's Entrance, Villain's Entrance) [148–49]*
14. "Villain Dance" [150–51]

Scene 7: The top deck of the "Cotton Blossom"—later that night.

15. Introduction and Duet "You Are Love" ("Ol' Man River," "Can't Help Lovin' Dat Man," "Make Believe") [152–54]
16. "You are Love" (Ravenal and Magnolia) [155–61]

Scene 8: The levee—next morning.

17. Finale [Harms, 162–76]

Act II

18. Entrac'te ("Make Believe," "Ol' Man River") [177–78]*

Scene 1: The Midway Plaisance, Chicago World's Fair, 1893

19. "Opening—At the Fair" (Chorus) [179–92], Incidental (Fatima's 2nd Dance) [193]*
20. "Why Do I Love You?" (Magnolia and Ravenal) [193–205]
21. "In Dahomey" (Dahomey Villiagers and White Chorus) [206–19]

Scene 2: A room on Ontario Street, 1904. "Good Morning, Carrie" [Cecil Mack and Tim Brymn]*

22. Underscoring during Ellie's reading of Ravenal's letter ("Why Do I Love You?") [220]*

Scene 3: Rehearsal room of the Trocadero Music Hall, about 5 P.M. "The Washington Post March" (Sousa). [not in Harms]

23. "Bill" (Julie) [221–23]
24. "Can't Help Lovin' Dat Man" (Reprise) (Magnolia) [224–26]

Scene 4: St. Agatha's Convent—meanwhile.

25. Service and Scene music (includes "Alma Redemptoris Mater" [Nuns] and a reprise of "Make Believe" [Ravenal]) [227–34]

Scene 5: Corner of lobby of the Sherman Hotel, Chicago, 8 P.M. New Year's Eve, 1904.

26. Introduction ("Cotton Blossom," "Life Upon the Wicked Stage") [235]*

Scene 6: Trocadero Music Hall, New Year's Eve, 11:30 P.M., 1904.

27. "The Washington Post" (Sousa) [direction for performance only in 236]* "Apache Dance" [not included in Harms] "Goodbye, Ma Lady Love" (Howard) (Frank and Ellie) [236–38]
    Captain Andy's Entrance [239]* "After the Ball" (Harris) (Magnolia) [239–42]

Scene 7: In front of the office of "The Natchez Evening Democrat," 1927.

28. "Ol' Man River" (Reprise) (Joe) [243–44]

29. "Hey, Feller!" (Queenie and Chorus) [245–57]

Scene 8: Top deck of the new "Cotton Blossom," 1927. "Can't Help Lovin' Dat Man" (Radio broadcast/reprise)*

30. "You Are Love" (Reprise) (Ravenal) [258–60]

Scene 9: Levee at Natchez, the next night.

31. "Cotton Blossom" (Chorus) [261], "Why Do I Love You?" (Reprise) (Kim and Chorus) [262–63; Kim's imitations of her mother, Eccentric Dance, and Tap Dance not included in Harms or the McGlinn recording]

32. Finale ("Make Believe" and "Ol' Man River")

Principal Changes in Selected Stage Productions and Films (1928–1994)

1. May 3, 1928, Drury Lane, London (350 performances)[†]

ADDED

"How'd You Like To Spoon with Me?" (1905) (replaced "Good-by, Ma Lady Love")

"Dance Away the Night" (replaced Kim's reprise of "Why Do I Love You?") [Chappell, 219–25]

DELETED

Service and Scene Music with "Make Believe" reprise (No. 25) (not included in Chappell vocal score)

Apache Dance

"Hey Feller!" (No. 29)

Eccentric Dance and Tap Dance

[†]Based on Kreuger, *Show Boat*, 226–27.

2. *March 16, 1929, Universal Pictures, Paramount Theatre, Palm Beach, Florida⁺*

The first film version was distributed the day after the first Broadway production closed on May 4 (following a world premiere in Florida in March and a New York City premiere in April). Although mostly silent, this first of three filmed *Show Boat*s included five synchronized Kern songs ("C'Mon, Folks," "Can't Help Lovin' Dat Man," "Hey, Feller!" "Bill," and "Ol' Man River"). Its story line followed Edna Ferber's novel more closely than Hammerstein's librretto.

3. *May 19, 1932, Casino, New York (181 performances)⁺*

REINSTATED

Service and Scene Music with "Make Believe" reprise (No. 25)
"Good-bye, Ma Lady Love" ("How'd You Like to Spoon With Me?"
    interpolation from 1928 dropped)
"Hey, Feller!" (No. 29)
"Why Do I Love You!" reprise ("Dance Away the Night" from 1928
    dropped)
Eccentric Dance and Tap Dance

4. *May 14, 1936, Universal Film, Radio City Music Hall, New York⁺*

NEW SONGS

"I Have the Room Above Her"
"Gallivantin' Aroun' "
"Ah Still Suits Me"

DELETED

"Life on the Wicked Stage" (used as underscoring)
"Till Good Luck Comes My Way" (used as underscoring)
"I Might Fall Back on You"

5. *January 5, 1946, Ziegfeld, New York (418 performances)⁺*

ADDED

Dance: No Gems, No Roses, No Gentlemen
Dance: No Shoes

Cakewalk

"Nobody Else But Me" (replaced reprise of "Why Do I Love You?") (No. 31)

Dance 1927 (replaced Eccentric Dance)

DELETED

"Life on the Wicked Stage" (moved from No. 7 to No. 11 ["I Might Fall Back on You"] [No. 11])

"Till Good Luck Comes My Way" (No. 8)

"Dandies on Parade" ("When the sports of gay Chicago" from "At the Fair") (No. 19)

"Hey, Feller!" (No. 29)

Eccentric Dance

Tap Dance

6. *July 29, 1971, Adelphi, London (910 performances)*[†]

REINSTATED

"Mis'ry's Comin' Aroun' " (No. 9) (reinstated after being dropped during the tryouts in Washington, D.C.)

"I Might Fall Back On You" (No. 11) (reinstated after being dropped from the 1946 revival)

"How'd You Like to Spoon With Me?" (reinstated from London 1928)

"Dance Away the Night" (reinstated from London 1928 production)

DELETED

"Life on the Wicked Stage" (No. 7)

"In Dahomey" (No. 21)

Service and Scene and "Make Believe" reprise

Dance: No Gems, No Roses, No Gentlemen

Dance: No Shoes (Cakewalk is the only dance retained from 1946 revival)

"Nobody Else But Me" (retained from the 1946 production but placed in a new context and sung by Julie in act I)

7. *October 2, 1994, Gershwin, New York (951 performances)*[†]

REINSTATED AND ADDED

"Mis'ry's Comin' Aroun' " (dropped from 1927 production)

"I Have the Room Above Her" (from 1936 film)

"Alma Redemptoris mater" (Gregorian chant interpolation from 1927 production)

"Why Do I Love You?" (sung by Parthy instead of Magnolia and Ravenal)

DELETED

"In Dahomey"

DELETED (BUT USED AS UNDERSCORING)

"I Might Fall Back on You" (from 1927 production)
"It's Getting Hotter in the North" (dropped from Broadway 1927)
"Ah Still Suits Me" (1936 film)
"How'd You Like to Spoon with Me?" (interpolated song from 1905, used in London 1928 and London 1971)
"Dance Away the Night" (London 1928)
"Hey, Feller!" (1927 Broadway)
"The Washington Post" (by John Philip Sousa) (first interpolated in Broadway 1927)

Manuscript Sources for Ravenal's Entrance and Meeting with Magnolia

1. Before November 1927: Pre-tryout and tryouts
   Jerome Kern Collection Box 9 (Library of Congress) Manuscript material including an early typed script (26 pages) (Envelope 217) and two piano-vocal drafts (Envelope 245 [Draft 1] and Envelope 238 [Draft 2]).
2. November–December 1927: Tryouts
   Tryout libretto in Billy Rose Theatre Collection, New York Public Library.
3. December 27, 1927: Original New York production
   Libretto of New York Production (Hammerstein's personal copy given to Miles Kreuger on August 3, 1960). Substantial libretto portions published with the McGlinn EMI/Angel recording CDS 7–49108–2, pages 55–130. Vocal score published by T. B. Harms Co. in April 1928 (268 pp.).
4. May 3, 1928: London production
   Libretto published by Chappell in 1934.
   Vocal Score published by Chappell & Co. Ltd. in 1928 (229 pp.).
5. April 30, 1936: Universal film
   Screenplay by Oscar Hammerstein (unpublished)
6. January 5, 1946: New York revival
   Libretto of touring version distributed by Rodgers and Hammerstein. Vocal score based on touring version published by Welk Music Group (192 pp.).

Appendix E: *Anything Goes*

Broadway 1934

Act I

Scene 1: The Weylin Caprice Bar.
"I Get a Kick Out of You" (Reno)
Scene 2: The Afterdeck. Midnight sailing.
"Bon Voyage" (Boys/Girls)
"All Through the Night" (Billy/Hope/Sailors)
Scene 3: Mr. Whitney's and Dr. Moon's Cabins. The next morning.
"Sailor's Chanty" ("There'l Always Be a Lady Fair") (Four Sailors)
Scene 4: The Afterdeck. Same morning.
"Where Are the Men?" (1st & 2nd Girls/Girls' Chorus)
"You're the Top" (Reno/Billy)
Scene 5: Sir Evelyn's Cabin.
Reprise: "Sailor's Chanty" (Four Sailors)
Scene 6: The Deck.
"Anything Goes" (Reno/Four Sailors)
Reprise: "You're the Top" (Reno)

Act II

Scene 1: The Lounge. That Evening.
"Public Enemy Number One" (Four Sailors/ Passengers)
"Blow, Gabriel, Blow" (Reno/Company)
Scene 2: The Brig. Five Days Later.
"Be Like the Bluebird" (Moonface)
Reprise: "All Through the Night" (Hope/Billy)
"Buddie, Beware" (Reno) (replaced by a reprise of "I Get a Kick Out of
You" by the week of December 10)
Scene 3: Conservatory of Sir Evelyn's Home in England
"The Gypsy in Me" (Hope)
Reprise: "Anything Goes" (All)

Off-Broadway Revival 1962

Act I

Scene 1: Afterdeck of the Ship.
"You're the Top" (Billy/Reno)
"Bon Voyage" (Company)

Scene 2: On the Ship's Deck. Night.
"It's De-Lovely" (Billy/Hope/Company) (introduced in *Red, Hot and Blue*, by Ethel Merman and Bob Hope [October 29, 1936])

Scene 3: Two Cabins on the "A" Deck.
Reprise: "Bon Voyage" (Orchestra)

Scene 4: The Ship's Deck.
"Heaven Hop" (Bonnie/Girls) (introduced in *Paris* by Irving Aaronson and the Commanders [October 8, 1928])

Scene 5: The Ship's Deck.
"Friendship" (Billy/Reno/Moon) (introduced in *DuBarry Was a Lady* by Ethel Merman and Bert Lahr [December 6, 1939])

Scene 6: Evelyn's Stateroom.
Reprise: "Bon Voyage" (Orchestra)

Scene 7: The Ship's Deck.
"I Get a Kick Out of You" (Reno)

Scene 8: The Afterdeck.
"Anything Goes" (Reno/Chorus)

Act II

Scene 1: Ship's Lounge.
"Public Enemy Number One" (Chorus)
"Let's Step Out" (Bonnie/Chorus) (introduced in *Fifty Million Frenchmen* by Evelyn Hoey and Gertrude McDonald [November 27, 1929])
"Let's Misbehave" (Reno/Sir Evelyn) (written for *Paris* but replaced before the New York opening by "Let's Do It, Let's Fall in Love)
"Blow, Gabriel, Blow" (Reno/Chorus)

Scene 2: The Brig.
"All Through the Night" (Billy/Hope)
"Be Like the Bluebird" (Moon)
Reprise: "All Through the Night"
Reprise: "Bon Voyage" (Orchestra)

Scene 3: The Ship's Deck.
"Take Me Back to Manhattan" (Reno/Four Angels) (introduced in *The New Yorkers* by Frances Williams [December 8, 1930])
Reprise: "You're the Top" (Company)

Lincoln Center Revival 1987

Act I

Scene 1: A smokey Manhattan bar.
"I Get a Kick Out of You" (Reno)

Scene 2: The afterdeck of an ocean liner shortly before sailing.
"There's No Cure Like Travel" (Captain/Sailors) (dropped from original

production and replaced by "Bon Voyage")
"Bon Voyage" (Sailors/Passengers)

Scene 3: On Deck, that evening.
"You're the Top" (Reno/Billy)
"Easy to Love" (Billy) (dropped from original production and replaced by "All Through the Night"; introduced in *Born to Dance* by James Stewart, Eleanor Powell, and Reginald Gardiner [April 13, 1936])

Scene 4: Lights up on Whitney's Stateroom.
"I Want to Row on the Crew" (Whitney) (introduced in *Paranoia* by Newbold Noyes [April 24, 1914])

Scene 5: On Deck, mid-morning.
"Sailor's Chantey" (Sailors)
"Friendship" (Reno/Moon) (see act I, scene 5 of 1962 revival)

Scene 6: Evelyn's Stateroom.
no song

Scene 7: On Deck.
"It's De-Lovely" (Billy/Hope) (see act I, scene 2 of 1962 revival)

Scene 8: The same, early the following morning.
"Anything Goes" (Reno)

Act II

Scene 1: The Ship's Nightclub.
"Public Enemy Number One" (Company)
"Blow, Gabriel, Blow" (Reno/Chorus)
"Goodbye, Little Dream, Goodbye" (Hope) (dropped from *Born to Dance* and *Red, Hot and Blue* in 1936 before its introduction in the English production, *O Mistress Mine* [December 3, 1936])

Scene 2: The Brig.
"Be Like the Bluebird" (Moon)
"All Through the Night" (Billy/Hope/Sailors)

Scene 3: On Deck.
"The Gypsy in Me" (Evelyn)

Scene 4: The Brig.
no song

Scene 5: On Deck.
"Buddie, Beware" (Erma, new name for original Bonnie) (dropped from original 1934 production by the week of December 10)
Reprise: "Anything Goes"(Company)

Appendix F: *Porgy and Bess*: Songs, Arias, and Themes

Published Vocal Score
(Gershwin Publishing Corporation/Chappell & Co.)

Act I

Scene 1: Catfish Row, a summer evening (lyrics by Heyward).
"Introduction" (Catfish Row)
"Jasbo Brown Blues" (Catfish Row)
"Summertime" (Clara)
"A Woman Is a Sometime Thing" (Jake)
"Here Come De Honey Man" (Peter)
"They Pass By Singin' " (Porgy)
"Oh Little Stars" (Porgy)

Scene 2: Serena's Room, the following night (lyrics by Heyward).
"Gone, Gone, Gone" (Catfish Row)
"Overflow" (Catfish Row)
"My Man's Gone Now" (Serena)
"Leavin' For the Promise' Lan' " (Bess)

Act II

Scene 1: Catfish Row, a month later.
"It Take a Long Pull To Get There" (Catfish Row) (Heyward)
"I Got Plenty o' Nuttin' " (Porgy) (I. Gershwin and Heyward)
"Buzzard Song" (Porgy) (Heyward)
"Bess, You Is My Woman" (Porgy and Bess) (Heyward and I. Gershwin)
"Oh, I Can't Sit Down" (Catfish Row) (I. Gershwin)

Scene 2: Kittiwah Island, evening, the same day.
"I Ain' Got No Shame" (Catfish Row) (Heyward)
"It Ain't Necessarily So" (Sporting Life) (I. Gershwin)
"What You Want Wid Bess?" (Bess) (Heyward)

Scene 3: Catfish Row, before dawn, a week later.
"Oh, Doctor Jesus" (Catfish Row) (Heyward)
"Strawberry Woman" (Strawberry Woman) (Heyward)
"Crab Man" (Crab Man) (Heyward)
"I Loves You, Porgy" (Bess) (I. Gershwin and Heyward)

Scene 4: Serena's Room, dawn of the following day.
"Oh, Hev'nly Father" (Catfish Row) (I. Gershwin and Heyward)

"Oh, De Lawd Shake De Heavens" (Catfish Row) (Heyward)
"Oh, Dere's Somebody Knockin' At De Do' " (Catfish Row) (Heyward)
"A Red Headed Woman" (Crown) (I. Gershwin)

Act III

Scene 1: Catfish Row, the next night.
"Clara, Clara" (Catfish Row) (Heyward)
Scene 2: Catfish Row, the next afternoon.
"There's a Boat Dat's Leavin' Soon for New York" (Sporting Life) (I. Gershwin)
Scene 3: Catfish Row, a week later.
"Good Mornin', Sistuh!" (Catfish Row) (Heyward)
"Oh, Bess, Oh Where's My Bess" (Porgy) (I. Gershwin)
"Oh Lawd, I'm on My Way" (Porgy and Catfish Row) (Heyward)

Appendix G: On Your Toes: Broadway 1936 and Broadway Revival 1983

Act I

Scene 1: A Vaudeville Stage, sixteen years ago. [About 1920]
"Two a Day for Keith" (Phil II, Lil, and Phil III)
Scene 2: The Vaudeville Dressing Room.
Scene 3: A Classroom at Knockerbocker [Knickerbocker] University—W.P.A. Extension.
"The Three B's" ["Questions and Answers (The Three B's)] (Junior and the Ensemble)
"It's Got to Be Love" (Frankie and Junior)
Scene 4: Vera's Apartment, the next morning.
"Too Good for the Average Man" (Peggy and Sergei)
Scene 5: Central Park, night. [The Schoolroom as in scene 3]
"There's a Small Hotel" (Frankie and Junior)
Scene 6: A Green Room, Cosmopolitan Opera House.
[The Bare Stage, Cosmopolitan Opera House, the next evening]
"The Heart is Quicker Than the Eye" (Peggy and Junior) [placed in act II, scene 1 in the 1983 revival]
Scene 7: "La Princesse Zenobia" Ballet–Cosmopolitan Opera House.

Brackets include 1983 revival.

Act II

Scene 1: A Planetarium Roof Garden. [The Bare Stage, Cosmopolitan Opera House]
[“The Heart is Quicker Than the Eye” (Peggy and Junior)]
“Quiet Night” (Crooner) [placed in act II, scenes (2 and 4, in 1983 revival]
“Glad to Be Unhappy” (Frankie and Sidney)
Scene 2: The Stage of the Cosmopolitan Opera House. [The Classroom as in Act 1, scenes 3 and 5]
[“Quiet Night” (Hank and Three Girls)]
“On Your Toes” (Frankie, Junior, and the Ensemble)
Reprise: “There’s a Small Hotel” (Peggy and Sergei) [omitted from 1983 revival]
Scene 3: Stage Door. [The Bare Stage, Cosmopolitan Opera House]

1936

Scene 4: “Slaughter on Tenth Avenue” Ballet.
Scene 5: The Stage of the Cosmopolitan Opera House.
Reprise: “There’s a Small Hotel” (Frankie and Junior)

1983

[Scene 4: The Stage Door, Cosmopolitan Opera House.]
Reprise: “Quiet Night” (Sergei)]
[Scene 5: “Slaughter on Tenth Avenue” Ballet, Stage of Cosmopolitan Opera House.]
Reprise: “There’s a Small Hotel” (Frankie and Junior)]

Appendix H: Pal Joey Broadway 1940 and Broadway Revival 1952

Act I

Scene 1: Mike’s South Side Night Club. A September afternoon.
“Chicago [A Great Big Town]” (Joey)
“You Mustn’t Kick It Around” (Joey, Gladys, Agnes, The Kid, and Ensemble)
Scene 2: The Pet Shop. That evening.
“I Could Write a Book” (Joey and Linda)

Brackets include 1952 changes.

Scene 3: Mike's Night Club. An evening a month later.
Reprise: "Chicago" ["A Great Big Town"] (Ensemble)
"That Terrific Rainbow" (Gladys, Victor, and Ensemble)
Scene 4: (a) A Phone Booth. (b) Vera's Boudoir. The next afternoon.
"What Is a Man?" (Vera)
Scene 5: Mike's Night Club. After closing time that evening.
"Happy Hunting Horn" (Joey, Terry, and Ensemble)
Scene 6: The Tailor Shop. A few days later.
"Bewitched, Bothered and Bewildered (Vera)
"Pal Joey" (Joey)
Scene 7: Ballet.

Act II

Scene 1: Chez Joey. A few weeks later.
"The Flower Garden of My Heart" (Gladys, Specialty Dancer, and Ensemble) [Louis, Gladys, and Ensemble]
"Zip" (Melba Snyder)
"Plant You Now, Dig You Later (Lowell, Gladys, and Ensemble) [Gladys and Ensemble]
Scene 2: Joey's Apartment. The next morning.
"Den of Iniquity" (Vera and Joey)
Scene 3: Chez Joey. That afternoon.
Reprise: "Chicago (Morocco)" (Dance and song)
"Do It the Hard Way" (Lowell, Gladys, and Ensemble) [act II, scene 4, sung by Joey]
Scene 4: Joey's Apartment. Later that afternoon.
"Take Him" (Linda and Vera)
Reprise: "Bewitched" (Vera)
Scene 5: The Pet Shop. Later that evening.
Finale: "I Could Write a Book" (Joey)
["I'm Talking to My Pal" (Joey) dropped during Philadelphia tryouts]

Appendix I: The Cradle Will Rock: Broadway 1937

Scene 1: Street Corner.
"Moll's Song" (Moll)
Moll and Gent
Moll and Dick
Scene 2: Night Court.
Moll and Druggist
"Oh, What a Filthy Night Court" (Ensemble)

Scene 3: Mission.
          Mrs. Mister and Reverend Salvation
Scene 4: Lawn of Mr. Mister's Home.
          "Croon-Spoon" (Junior and Sister Mister)
          "The Freedom of the Press" (Mr. Mister and Editor Daily)
          "Let's Do Something" (Junior and Sister Mister)
          "Honolulu" (Editor Daily, Junior Mister, Mr. Mister, and Sister Mister)
Scene 5: Drugstore.
          Drugstore scene
          "Gus and Sadie Love Song" (Gus and Sadie)
Scene 6: Hotel Lobby.
          "The Rich" (Yasha and Dauber)
          "Ask Us Again" (Mrs. Mister, Yasha, and Dauber)
          "Art for Art's Sake" (Yasha and Dauber)

Act II

Scene 7: Night Court.
          "Nickel Under the Foot" (Moll)
          "Leaflets" (Larry Foreman)
          "The Cradle Will Rock" (Larry Foreman)
Scene 8: Faculty Room.
Scene 9: Dr. Specialist's Office.
          Doctor and Ella
          "Joe Worker" (Ella Hammer)
Scene 10: Night Court.
          "Finale: The Cradle Will Rock" (reprise) (Ensemble)

Appendix J: *Lady in the Dark*: Broadway 1941

Act I

1. Glamour Dream.
    "Oh Fabulous One" (Liza Elliott's Admirers)
    "Huxley" (Sutton and Liza)
    "One Life to Live" (Liza)
    "Girl of the Moment" (Liza Elliott's Admirers)
2. Wedding Dream.
    "Mapleton High Choral" (Boys and Girls of Mapleton High)
    "This Is New" (Randy and Liza)
    "The Princess of Pure Delight" (Liza)

Act II

3. Circus Dream.
   "The Greatest Show on Earth" (Ringmaster [Russell Paxton] and Paraders)
   Ballet: "Dance of the Tumblers"
   "The Best Years of His Life" (Ringmaster, Randy, and Liza)
   "Tschaikowsky" (Ringmaster)
   "The Saga of Jenny" (Liza)
4. Childhood Dream.
   "My Ship" (Liza and Charley Johnson)

Appendix K: One Touch of Venus: Broadway 1943

Act I

Scene 1: Main Gallery of the Whitelaw Savory Foundation of Modern Art.
"New Art Is True Art" (Savory and Students)
"One Touch of Venus" (Molly)
Scene 2: Rodney's Room.
"How Much I Love You" (Rodney)
Scene 3: Radio City Plaza.
"I'm a Stranger Here Myself" (Venus)
Scene 4: Arcade of the N.B.C. Building in Radio City.
Ballet: "Forty Minutes for Lunch"
"West Wind" (Savory)
Scene 5: Waiting room of Mid-City Bus Terminal.
"Way Out West in Jersey" (Mrs. Kramer, Rodney, and Gloria)
Scene 6: The Roof Garden of the Foundation.
"Foolish Heart" (Venus)
Scene 7: Rodney's Barbershop.
"The Trouble with Women" (Taxi, Stanley, Savory, and Rodney)
"Speak Low" (Venus)
Scene 8: The Roof Garden of the Foundation.
"Doctor Crippen" (Savory)

Act II

Scene 1: Savory's Bedroom.
"Very, Very, Very" (Molly)
Scene 2: The Tombs.
"Speak Low" (reprise) (Rodney and Venus)
Scene 3: The Sitting Room of a De Luxe Suite.
"That's Him" (Venus)

"Wooden Wedding" (Rodney)
Scene 4:   The Main Galley of the Foundation.
"Speak Low" (reprise) (Rodney)

Appendix L: Carousel: Broadway 1945

Prelude

An Amusement Park on the New England Coast. May.
"Carousel Waltz" (Orchestra)

Act I

Scene 1:   A tree-lined path along the shore. A few minutes later.
"You're a Queer One, Julie Jordan" (Carrie and Julie)
"Mister Snow" (Carrie)
"If I Loved You" (Billy and Julie)
Scene 2:   Nettie Fowler's Spa on the ocean front. June.
"June is Bustin' Out All Over (Nettie, Carrie, and Ensemble)
Reprise: "Mister Snow" (Carrie and Girls)
"When the Children Are Asleep" (Mr. Snow and Carrie)
"Blow High, Blow Low" (Jigger, Billy, and Men)
"Soliloquy" (Billy)
"Finale" (Billy, Jigger, Nettie, and Chorus)

Act II

Scene 1:   On an island across the bay. That night.
"A Real Nice Clambake" (Carrie, Nettie, Julie, Mr. Snow, and Ensemble)
"Geraniums in the Winder" (Mr. Snow)
"There's Nothin' So Bad for a Woman" (Jigger and Ensemble)
"What's the Use of Wond'rin' " (Julie)
Scene 2:   Mainland waterfront. An hour later.
"You'll Never Walk Alone" (Nettie)
Scene 3:   Up there.
"The Highest Judge of All" (Billy)
Scene 4:   Down here. On a beach. Fifteen years later.
Ballet (Louise, A Younger Miss Snow, The Brothers and Sisters Snow,
    Badly Brought Up Boys, A Young Man Like Billy, A Carnival Woman,
    Members of the Carnival Troupe)
Scene 5:   Outside Julie's cottage.
Reprise: "If I Loved You" (Billy)

Scene 6: Outside a schoolhouse. Same day.
Reprise: "You'll Never Walk Alone" (Company)

Appendix M: Kiss Me, Kate: Broadway 1948

Act I

Scene 1: Stage of Ford's Theatre, Baltimore.
"Another Op'nin, Another Show" (Hattie and Singing Ensemble. Danced by Dancing Ensemble.)

Scene 2: The corridor backstage.
"Why Can't You Behave?" (Lois Lane)

Scene 3: Dressing rooms, Fred Graham and Lilli Vanessi.
"Wunderbar" (Lilli and Fred)
"So In Love" (Lilli)

Scene 4: Padua.
"We Open in Venice" (Petruchio, Kathcrine, Bianca, Lucentio)

Scene 5: Street Scene, Padua.
Dance (Dancing Ensemble)
"Tom, Dick, or Harry" (Bianca, Lucentio, and the Two Suitors (Gremio and Hortensio)
Specialty Dance (Lucentio)
"I've Come to Wive It Wealthily in Padua" (Petruchio and Singing Ensemble)
"I Hate Men" (Katherine)
"Were Thine That Special Face" (Petruchio. Danced by Janet Gaylord and Dancing Girls)

Scene 6: Backstage.
Scene 7: Fred's and Lilli's dressing rooms.
Scene 8: Before the curtain.
"I Sing of Love" (Bianca, Lucentio, and Singing Ensemble)

Scene 9: Exterior church.
Tarantella (Danced by Bianca, Lucentio, and Dancing Ensemble)
Finale: "Kiss Me, Kate" (Katherine, Petruchio, and Singing Ensemble)

Act II

Scene 1: Theatre alley.
"Too Darn Hot" (Paul, Fred Davis, and Eddie Sledge. Danced by Fred Davis, Eddie Sledge, Bill Calhoun and Dancing Ensemble)

Scene 2: Before the curtain.
Scene 3: Petruchio's house.
"Where Is the Life That Late I Led?" (Petruchio)

Scene 4: The corridor backstage.
          "Always True to You in My Fashion" (Lois)
Scene 5: Lilli's dressing room.
Scene 6: The corridor backstage.
          "Bianca" (Bill Calhoun and Singing Girls. Danced by Bill Calhoun and
             Dancing Girls)
          Reprise: "So in Love" (Fred)
Scene 7: Before the asbestos curtain.
          "Brush Up Your Shakespeare" (First Man and Second Man)
Scene 8: Baptista's home.
          Pavane (Dancing Ensemble)
          "I Am Ashamed That Women Are So Simple" (Katherine)
          Finale (Petruchio, Katherine, and Company)

Spewack Libretto Draft (May 28, 1948)

Act I

Scene 1:   The bare stage of Ford's Theater, Baltimore.
Scene 2:   Connecting dressing rooms of Fred and Lilli.
           Background music: "Another Opnin'[Op'nin'], Another Show"
           "Wunderbar" (Fred and Lilli)
           "It Was Great Fun" [No. 2] (Fred and Lilli)
Scene 3:   Iron stairs and landing.
           "Why Can't You Behave?" (Lois and Bill)
Scene 4:   Exterior of Ford Theater.
           "Another Opnin', Another Show"
Scene 5:   Dressing rooms of Lilli and Fred.
           Background music: "Another Opnin', Another Show"
           "We Shall Never Grow Younger"
Scene 6:   Same.
           Background music: "We Shall Never Grow Younger" (Counterpoint, "It
              Was Great Fun")
Scene 7:   Shrew curtain.
           "We Open in Venice" (Shrew players)
           "If Ever Married I'm" (Bianca) [crossed out]
           "I Sing of Love" (Lucentio and Petruchio) [crossed out]
           "I've Come to Wive it Wealthily in Padua" (Petruchio) [crossed out]
           "Were Thine That Special Face" (Petruchio) [crossed out]
Scene 8:   Wings.
Scene 9:   Opposite wings.
Scene 10: On stage.
           Bill does his specialty with Ballet.
Scene 11: Exterior of Baptista's house and church.
Scene 12: Same.

Scene 13: Walled garden of Baptista's house.
"Tom, Dick or Harry" (Bianca and her suitors, Gremio, Tranio, and Lucentio) [crossed out]
Scene 14: Wings.
Scene 15: Garden.
Scene 16: Lilli's dressing room.
Scene 17: Exterior church.
Finaletto: "Kiss Me, Kate" (Petruchio, Katharine, Bianca, Lucentio, and Company) [lyrics yet to be written]

Act II

Scene 1: Theatre alley.
"Too Darn Hot" (Negroes) [crossed out]
Scene 2: Shrew curtain.
Background music: "Where Is the Life That Late I Led?"
Scene 3: Main room in Petruchio's house.
"Where Is the Life That Late I Led?" (Petruchio)
Scene 4: Back stage.
"I've Been Faithful to You, Darlin' in my Fashion" (Lois) [p. 2-4-16 missing in typescript]
Scene 5: Lilli's dressing room.
"A Woman's Career" (Fred) [p. 2-5-27 missing in typescript]
Scene 6: Iron staircase.
Reprise: "We Shall Never Be Younger"
Scene 7: Garden of Baptista's house.
Reprise: "I Sing of Love" (Shrew players) [no text included in typescript]
"I Am Ashamed That Women Are So Simple" [entirely spoken]
Reprise: "Were Thine That Special Face" [crossed out]
Reprise: Finaletto. First Act Finale. New lyrics.

Appendix N: *Guys and Dolls*: Broadway 1950

Act I

Scene 1: Broadway.
Opening (Runyonland) (Ensemble)
"Fugue for Tinhorns" (Nicely-Nicely Johnson, Benny Southstreet, and Rusty Charlie)
"Follow the Fold" (Sarah, Arvide, Agatha, and Mission Group)
"The Oldest Established" (Nathan, Nicely-Nicely, Benny, Brandy-Bottle Bates, and the Crapshooters)
Scene 2: Interior of the Save-A-Soul Mission.
"I'll Know" (Sarah and Sky)

Scene 3: A Phone Booth
Scene 4: The Hot Box, Nightclub.
"A Bushel and a Peck" (Adelaide and the Hot Box Girls)
"Adelaide's Lament" (Adelaide)
Scene 5: A Street Off Broadway.
"Guys and Dolls" (Nicely-Nicely and Benny)
Scene 6: Exterior of the Mission. Noon, the next day.
Scene 7: A Street Off Broadway.
Scene 8: Havana, Cuba—El Café Cubana.
Dance: Havana
Scene 9: Outside El Café Cubana. Immediately following.
"If I Were a Bell" (Sarah)
Scene 10: Exterior of the Mission.
"My Time of Day" (Sky)
"I've Never Been In Love Before" (Sky and Sarah)
Incidental music: The Raid

Act II

Scene 1: The Hot Box Nightclub.
"Take Back Your Mink" (Adelaide and Dolls)
"Adelaide's Second Lament" (Adelaide)
Scene 2: Forty-Eighth Street.
"More I Cannot Wish You" (Arvide)
Scene 3: Crap Game in the Sewer.
"Luck Be a Lady" (Sky and the Crapshooters)
Scene 4: A Street Off Broadway.
"Sue Me" (Adelaide and Nathan)
Scene 5: Interior of the Save-A-Soul Mission.
"Sit Down, You're Rockin' the Boat" (Nicely-Nicely and the Crapshooters)
Scene 6: Near Times Square.
"Marry the Man Today" (Adelaide and Sarah)
Scene 7: Broadway.
Reprise: "Guys and Dolls" (Ensemble)

Appendix O: *The Most Happy Fella*: Broadway 1956

Act I

OVERTURE
Scene 1: A restaurant in San Francisco; January, 1927.
"OOH! MY FEET!" (Cleo)
". . . I know how it is" (Cleo)

"...Seven million Crumbs" (Cleo)

"...I don't know" (Rosabella)

"...Maybe he's kind crazy" (Rosabella)

"SOMEBODY, SOMEWHERE" (Rosabella)

Scene 2: Main Street, Napa, California; In April.

"THE MOST HAPPY FELLA" (Townspeople)

"...A long time ago" (Marie)

"STANDING ON THE CORNER" (Herman, Jake, Clem, and Al)

"JOEY, JOEY, JOEY" (Joe)

"...Soon you gonna leave me, Joe" (Tony)

"ROSABELLA" (Tony)

Scene 3: Tony's barn; A few weeks later.

"ABBONDANZA" (Giuseppe, Ciccio, and Pasquale)

"...Plenty bambini" (Tony)

Scene 4: Tony's front yard.

"SPOSALIZIO" (Townspeople)

"...I seen her at the station" (Postman)

"BENVENUTA" (Giuseppe, Ciccio, and Pasquale)

"...Aren't you glad" (Rosabella)

"...No home, no job" (Rosabella)

"DON'T CRY" (Joe)

Act II

PRELUDE

Scene 1: The vineyards; In May.

"FRESNO BEAUTIES" (Vineyard Workers)

"...Cold and dead" (Joe and Rosabella)

"...Love and kindness" (Doc)

"HAPPY TO MAKE YOUR ACQUAINTANCE" (Rosabella and Tony)

"...I don't like this dame" (Cleo)

BIG D (Cleo and Herman)

Scene 2: Late in May.

"HOW BEAUTIFUL THE DAYS" (Tony, Rosabella, Marie, and Joe)

Scene 3: The vineyards; In June.

"YOUNG PEOPLE" (Marie)

"WARM ALL OVER" (Rosabella)

"...Old people gotta" (Tony)

Scene 4: The barn.

"I LIKE EV'RYBODY" (Herman)

Scene 5: The vineyards; In July.

"...I love him" (Rosabella)

"...I know how it is" (Cleo)

"...Like a woman loves a man" (Rosabella)

"MY HEART IS SO FULL OF YOU" (Tony and Rosabella)

"MAMMA, MAMMA" (Tony)

Act III

PRELUDE
Scene 1:   The barn; An hour later.
          "... Good-bye darlin' " (Cleo and Herman)
          "... I like ev'rybody" (Duet) (Cleo and Herman)
          "SONG OF A SUMMER NIGHT" (Doc and the Townspeople)
          "PLEASE LET ME TELL YOU" (Rosabella)
Scene 2:   Napa Station; A little later.
          "... Tell Tony and Rosabella good-bye for me" (Joe)
          "... She gonna come home wit' me" (Tony)
          "... Nobody's ever gonna love you" (Trio) (Marie, Tony, and Cleo)
          "... I made a fist!" (Herman)
          Finale (Ensemble)

Appendix P: My Fair Lady: Broadway 1956

Act I

Scene 1:   Outside the Opera House, Covent Garden. A cold March night.
          Overture and Street Entertainers (The Three Buskers)
          "Why Can't the English?" (Higgins)
          "Wouldn't It Be Loverly" (Eliza and Costermongers)
Scene 2:   A Tenement Section—Tottenham Court Road. Immediately following.
          "With a Little Bit of Luck" (Doolittle, Harry, and Jamie)
Scene 3:   Higgins's Study. The following morning.
          "I'm an Ordinary Man" (Higgins)
Scene 4:   Tenement Section—Tottenham Court Road. Three days later.
          "With a Little Bit of Luck" (reprise) (Doolittle and Friends)
Scene 5:   Higgins's Study. Later that day.
          "Just You Wait" (Eliza)
          "The Rain in Spain" (Higgins, Eliza, and Pickering)
          "I Could Have Danced All Night" (Eliza, Mrs. Pearce, and Maids)
Scene 6:   Near the Race Meeting, Ascot. A July afternoon
Scene 7:   Inside a Club Ten, Ascot. Immediately following.
          "Ascot Gavotte" (Spectators at the Race)
Scene 8:   Outside Higgins's House, Wimpole Street. Later that afternoon.
          "On the Street Where You Live" (Freddy)
Scene 9:   Higgins's Study. Six weeks later.
Scene 10: The Promenade of the Embassy. Later that night.
          "Promenade" (underscoring)
Scene 11: The Ballroom of the Embassy. Immediately following.
          "The Embassy Waltz" (Higgins, Eliza, Karpathy, and Guests)

Act II

Scene 1: Higgins's Study. 3:00 the following morning.
"You Did It" (Higgins, Pickering, Mrs. Pearce, and Servants)
"Just You Wait" (reprise) (Eliza)
Scene 2: Outside Higgins's House, Wimpole Street. Immediately following.
"On the Street Where You Live" (reprise) (Freddy)
"Show Me" (Eliza and Freddy)
Scene 3: Flower Market of Covent Garden. 5:00 that morning.
"Wouldn't It Be Loverly" (reprise) (Eliza and Costermongers)
"Get Me to the Church on Time" (Doolittle, Harry, Jamie, and Coster-
mongers)
Scene 4: Upstairs Hall of Higgins's House. 11:00 that morning.
"A Hymn to Him" (Higgins)
Scene 5: The Conservatory of Mrs. Higgins's House. Later that day.
"Without You" (Higgins and Eliza)
Scene 6: Outside Higgins's House, Wimpole Street. Immediately following.
"I've Grown Accustomed to Her Face" (Higgins)
Scene 7: Higgins's Study. Immediately following.

Appendix Q: West Side Story: Broadway 1957

Act I

Prologue: The Months Before
1. Prologue (Instrumental)
Scene 1: 5:00 P.M. The Street.
2. "Jet Song" (Riff and Jets)
Scene 2: 5:30 P.M. A Back Yard.
3. "Something's Coming" (Tony)
Scene 3: 6:00 P.M. A Bridal Shop.
Scene 4: 10:00 P.M. The Gym.
4. The Dance and the Gym (Instrumental)
5. "Maria" (Tony)
Scene 5: 11:00 P.M. A Back Alley.
6. Balcony Scene ("Tonight") (Maria and Tony)
7. "America" (Anita, Rosalia, and Girls)
Scene 6: Midnight. The Drugstore.
8. "Cool" (Riff and Jets)
The Next Day
Scene 7: 5:30 P.M. The Bridal Shop.
9. "One Hand, One Heart" (Tony and Maria)

Scene 8:   6:00 to 9:00 P.M. The Neighborhood.
           10. "Tonight" (Quintet) (Maria, Tony, Anita, Riff, and Bernardo)
Scene 9:   9:00 P.M. Under the Highway
           11. The Rumble (Instrumental)

Act II

Scene 1:   9:15 P.M. A Bedroom.
           12. "I Feel Pretty" (Maria and the Girls)
           13. Ballet Sequence (Instrumental, Tony, Maria and a Girl)
Scene 2:   10:00 P.M. Another Alley.
           14. "Gee, Officer Krupke" (Jets)
Scene 3:   11:30 P.M. The Bedroom.
           15. "A Boy Like That/I Have a Love" (Maria and Anita)
Scene 4:   11:40 P.M. The Drugstore.
           16. Taunting (Instrumental)
Scene 5:   11:50 P.M. The Cellar.
Scene 6:   Midnight. The Street.
           17. Finale (Maria and Tony)

Libretto Drafts 1 (January 1956) and 2 (Spring 1956)

Act I

Scene 1:   An Alleyway. Sundown.
           "Rumble Song" ["Mix" ?] (Jets and "Tonio")
Scene 2:   The Crystal Cave. Night.
           Mambo (Pantomime)
           "Maria" ("Tonio")
Scene 3:   Back of the Tenements. Night.
           "Maria" (second chorus) ("Tonio")
           "Love Song" ["One Hand, One Heart" ?] ("Tonio" and Maria)
           "Song for Anita and Girls" ["America" ?]
Scene 4:   Drugstore. Night.
           "Cool" (Riff and Jets)
Scene 5:   The Neighborhood. The Next Day.
           "Tonight" (Quintet) (Maria, Tony, Anita, Riff, and Bernardo)
Scene 6:   Bridal Shop. Late Afternoon.
           "Love Song" ["Oh, Happy We" from *Candide* ?] ("Tonio" and Maria)
           "Rumble Song" ["Mix" ?] (Instrumental)
Scene 7:   The Park. Sundown.
           "Rumble Song" ["Mix" ?] (Jets)

Act II

Scene 1: An Apartment. Early Evening.
         "I Feel Pretty" (Maria and Girls)
Scene 2: A Street. Night.
Scene 3: Police Station. Night.
         "Love Song" (reprise) ["One Hand, One Heart" ?] ("Tonio" and Maria)
Scene 4: Outside the Bridal Shop. Night.
         "Duet" ["I Have a Love" ?] (Anita and Maria)
Scene 5: Drugstore. Night.
         "Duet" (continuation) ["I Have a Love" ?] ("Tonio")
Scene 6: A Street. Night.
Scene 7: Bridal Shop. Night.
         "This scene will be almost entirely to music. MARIA comes in the back door, the music has brief theme of her love with Tonio" ["One Hand, One Heart" ?]

Appendix R: Follies: Broadway 1971 and London Revival 1987

Broadway* 1971

SCENE: A party on the stage of the Weismann Theatre
TIME: Tonight
There will be no Intermission

"Prologue" [Based on "All Things Bright and Beautiful" from *The Girls Upstairs*, second draft, preceding "Could I Leave You?" and "It Wasn't Meant to Happen," planned in 1966 as a second duet for Ben and Sally][1]

"Beautiful Girls" (Roscoe and Company) [*The Girls Upstairs*, first and second drafts][2]

"Don't Look At Me" (Sally, Ben) [*The Girls Upstairs*, second draft]

"Waiting for the Girls Upstairs" (Buddy, Ben, Phyllis, Sally, Young Buddy, Young Ben, Young Phyllis, Young Sally) [*The Girls Upstairs*, first and second drafts]

"Rain on the Roof" (The Whitmans) [*Follies*, January 2, 1971]

"Ah, Paris!" (Solange) [*Follies*, January 2, 1971]

"Broadway Baby" (Hattie) [*Follies*, January 2, 1971]

"The Road You Didn't Take" (Ben) [*Follies*, January 2, 1971; replaced in London *Follies* 1987 by "Country House"]

---

*Includes songs retained from *The Girls Upstairs* (1965).

"Bolero d'Amour" (Vincent and Vanessa) [added in 1971 rehearsal; cut in London *Follies* 1987]

"In Buddy's Eyes" (Sally) [*Follies,* January 2, 1971]

"Who's That Woman?" (Stella and Company) [Mirror Dance Routine in *The Girls Upstairs,* first and second drafts]

["Can That Boy Fox-trot!" in *The Girls Upstairs,* second draft, cut in 1971 rehearsals]

"I'm Still Here" (Carlotta) [replaced "Can That Boy Fox-trot!" during 1971 rehearsals]

[*"Pleasant Little Kingdom"* in *The Girls Upstairs,* first draft; cut in 1971]

"Too Many Mornings" (Ben, Sally) [*The Girls Upstairs,* first and second drafts]

["That Old Piano Roll" (Buddy) in *Follies,* September 1970 draft]

"The Right Girl" (Buddy) [added in 1971 rehearsals]

"One More Kiss" (Heidi, Young Heidi) [*The Girls Upstairs,* first and second drafts]

"Could I Leave You?" (Phyllis) [*The Girls Upstairs,* second draft]

LOVELAND

1. The Folly of Love

   "Loveland" (Sung by The Ensemble) [rewritten in London *Follies* 1987]

   The Spirit of First Love (Miss Kathie Dalton)

   The Spirit of Young Love (Miss Margot Travers)

   The Spirit of True Love (Miss Suzanne Briggs)

   The Spirit of Pure Love (Miss Trudy Carson)

   The Spirit of Romantic Love (Miss Linda Perkins)

   The Spirit of Eternal Love (Miss Ursula Maschmeyer)

2. The Folly Of Youth

   Scene—A Bower in Loveland.

   ["Who Could Be Blue?" and "Little White House"] [cut in 1971 rehearsals]

   "You're Gonna Love Tomorrow" (Sung by Mr. Ben Stone and Miss Phyllis Rogers) [added in 1971 rehearsals]

   "Love Will See Us Through" (Sung by Mr. Buddy Plummer and Miss Sally Durant) [added in 1971 rehearsals]

3. Buddy's Folly

   Scene—A Thoroughfare in Loveland.

   "The God-Why-Don't-You-Love-Me-Blues" (Sung and Danced by Mr. Buddy Plummer) (With the Assistance of Miss Suzanne Rogers and Miss Rita O'Connor) [added in 1971 rehearsals]

4. Sally's Folly

   Scene—A Boudoir in Loveland.

   "Losing My Mind" (Sung by Mrs. Sally Durant Plummer) [added in 1971 rehearsals]

5. Phyllis's Folly

   Scene—A Honky-Tonk in Loveland.

   "Uptown, Downtown" [cut in 1971 rehearsals]

   "The Story of Lucy and Jessie" (Sung by Mrs. Phyllis Rogers Stone) (Danced by Mrs. Stone and The Dancing Ensemble) [added in 1971 rehearsals; cut in London *Follies* 1987]

6. Ben's Folly
   Scene—A Supper Club in Loveland.
   "Live, Laugh, Love" (Sung by Mr. Benjamin Stone) (Danced by Mr. Stone and
   The Dancing Ensemble) [cut in London *Follies* 1987]

London 1987

PLACE: The stage of the Weismann Theatre, New York City
TIME: 1970

Act I

"Beautiful Girls" (Roscoe and Company)
"Don't Look At Me" (Sally, Ben)
"Rain on the Roof" (The Whitmans)
"Ah! Paris" (Solange)
"Broadway Baby" (Hattie)
"Waiting for the Girls Upstairs" (Buddy, Ben, Phyllis)
"Who's That Woman" (Stella and Company)
"In Buddy's Eyes" (Sally)
"Country House (Phyllis and Ben) [replaced "The Road You Didn't Take"]
"Too Many Mornings" (Ben, Sally)

Act II

"Social Dancing" (Company)
"I'm Still Here" (Carlotta)
"The Right Girl" (Buddy)
"Could I Leave You?" (Phyllis)
"One More Kiss" (Heidi, Young Heidi)
"Loveland" (Roscoe and Company) [rewritten in 1987]
"Love Will See Us Through" (Sung by Mr. Buddy Plummer and Miss Sally
   Durant) [revised as Double Duet in 1987]
"Buddy's Blues" (Sung and Danced by Mr. Buddy Plummer) (With the
   Assistance of Miss Suzanne Rogers and Miss Rita O'Connor)
"Losing My Mind" (Sung by Mrs. Sally Durant Plummer)
"You're Gonna Love Tomorrow" (Sung by Mr. Ben Stone and Miss Phyllis
   Rogers)
"Ah! But Underneath" (Sung by Mrs. Phyllis Rogers Stone) (Danced by
   Mrs. Stone and the Dancing Ensemble) [replaced "The Story of Lucy
   and Jessie"]
"Make the Most of Your Music" (Sung by Mr. Benjamin Stone) (Danced by Mr.
   Stone and the Dancing Ensemble) [replaced "Live, Laugh, Love"]
Double Duet (Young Sally, Young Ben, Young Phyllis, and Young Buddy)
   [revised "Love Will See Us Through"]

Notes

1. See Carol Ilson, 177–97; Mandelbaum, 66–78; Prince, 158–70; Sondheim, "Musical Theater," 231–32; and Zadan, 135–53.
2. Sondheim mentions a predecessor to "Beautiful Girls" called "Bring on the Girls" that Michael Bennett asked him to change when he "joined the show." See Mandelbaum, 71.

NOTES

Preface

1. *The Rodgers and Hammerstein Song Book* (New York: Simon & Schuster and Williamson Music Inc., 1956); *Six Plays by Rodgers and Hammerstein* (New York: The Modern Library Association, 1959).
2. Like other Broadway-loving families, especially those residing on the west side of the country, it took the release of the *West Side Story* movie with Natalie Wood for us to become fully cognizant of this show.
3. "The World of Stephen Sondheim," interview, "Previn and the Pittsburgh," channel 26 television broadcast, 13 March 1977.
4. A chronological survey of Broadway texts from the 1950s to the 1980s might include the following: Cecil Smith, *Musical Comedy in America* (New York: Theatre Arts Books, 1950; updated by Glenn Litton, 1981); Engel, *American Musical Theater*; Ewen *New Complete Book*; Mordden, *Better Foot Forward*; Abe Laufe, *Broadway's Greatest Musicals* (New York: Funk & Wagnalls, 1977); Martin Gottfried, *Broadway Musicals* (New York: Harry N. Abrams, 1979); S. Green, *World*; Richard Kislan, *The Musical* (Englewood Cliffs, N.J.: Prentice-Hall, 1980); Gerald Bordman, *American Musical Comedy, American Musical Theatre, American Musical Revue,* and *American Operetta*; Alan Jay Lerner, *The Musical Theatre: A Celebration* (London: Collins, 1986); and Mast.
5. See Bordman and Engel, n. 4.
6. Kreuger, *"Show Boat"*; Alpert. The literature on *Porgy and Bess* contains a particularly impressive collection of worthwhile analytical and historical essays by Richard Crawford, Charles Hamm, Wayne Shirley, and Lawrence Starr (see the Select Bibliography).
7. Swain; Banfield.
8. Kerman; Robinson.
9. Kivy.
10. Swain, 205.

347

11. Banfield, 6–7.
12. Ibid., 37. Quotation from Bernstein, 147. For a more detailed exploration of Swain and Banfield and the differences between opera and musicals see my review essay of Banfield in *Journal of the Royal Musical Association* 121/1 (1996): 20–27.

Chapter 1: Introduction

1. Book musicals contain a narrative and are represented by three discernible types: operas, operettas, and musical comedies. Operas, which come in various styles, including rock, are for the most part sung throughout. Musical comedies normally utilize contemporary urban settings with matching vernacular dialogue and music, the latter often incorporating jazz. Operettas are generally set in exotic locations, including early Americana (e.g., New England in the 1870s in *Carousel* and Oklahoma Territory "just after the turn of the century") and typically utilize appropriate regional dialects and such nineteenth-century European genres as waltzes and polkas or a nonjazz musical vernacular that somehow sounds American. The largest category of nonbook musicals are revues, which may possess a unifying theme, but only rarely a clearly delineated plot. In place of a book, most revues consist of a somewhat loose collection of skits (usually topical), along with dances and songs, often composed by a plethora of writers and composers.
2. Miles Kreuger, 'Some Words About 'Show Boat',' 18.
3. *A Trip to Chinatown* contained "Reuben and Cynthia," "The Bowery," and Charles K. Harris's "After the Ball"; *Little Johnny Jones* introduced "The Yankee Doodle Boy" and "Give My Regards to Broadway."
4. Both *Irene* and *No, No, Nanette* (670 and 321 performances, respectively, in their inaugural runs) enjoyed popular revivals in the early 1970s (*No, No, Nanette* in 1971 [861 performances] and *Irene* in 1973 [604 performances]).
5. The film version of *Naughty Marietta* (1935) starred Jeanette MacDonald and Nelson Eddy, and *The Student Prince* (1954) featured the voice of Mario Lanza dubbing for Edmund Purdom.
6. Included among these early hits are the following: Berlin (*Watch Your Step* [1914]); Kern (Princess Shows [1915–1918], *Sally* [1920], and *Sunny* [1925]); Porter (numerous interpolated songs in shows by other composers between 1919 and 1924 before making a hit with *Paris* in 1928); Hammerstein, *Wildflower* [1923], *Rose-Marie* [1924], *Sunny* [1925], and *The Desert Song* [1926]; George and Ira Gershwin (*Lady, Be Good!* [1924], *Oh, Kay!* [1926], and *Funny Face* [1927]); and Rodgers and Hart (*The Garrick Gaieties, Dearest Enemy,* [1925], and *A Connecticut Yankee* [1927]); and Weill (*Die Dreigroschenoper* [*The Threepenny Opera*] [1927]). Several months before the premiere of *Show Boat*, the team of Ray Henderson (music) and B. G. DeSylva and Lew Brown (lyrics) presented their first book musical hit, *Good News*.
7. The term "anxiety of influence" is borrowed from literary critic Harold Bloom's *The Anxiety of Influence: A Theory of Poetry* (Oxford: Oxford University Press, 1973).
8. R. Crawford, 87.
9. For a valuable perspective on the development of cultural hierarchies, authentic versus accessible approaches to Shakespeare, and "the sacralization of culture" in nineteenth-century America, see Lawrence W. Levine, *Highbrow Lowbrow: The Emergence of Cultural Hierarchy in America* (Cambridge, Mass.: Harvard University Press, 1988).
10. Charles Hamm, "Theatre Guild Production," 495–532.
11. Kerman. While under current attack for its elitism and narrow vision of dramatic worthiness, Kerman's study remains a central text for any exploration of the relationship between music and drama. Another excellent and less judgmental study of opera with concepts that can be applied to Broadway musicals is Robinson.

12. Kivy, 10–11.
13. Some exceptions are Banfield; Block, "Frank Loesser's Sketchbooks"; Hamm, "Theatre Guild Production"; Oja; and Shirley, *"Porgy and Bess"* and "Reconciliation."
14. The literature on gender studies in music is considerable and growing exponentially. The most influential work to appear is probably Susan McClary, *Feminine Endings: Music, Gender, and Sexuality* (Minneapolis: University of Minnesota Press, 1989).
15. The top forty also includes four musicals that premiered before *Show Boat* (29, 34, 37, and 39 in the 1920–1959 list) and four that first appeared after *West Side Story* (4, 5, 18, and 24 in the 1920–1959 list).
16. *West Side Story* (1980); *My Fair Lady* (1981, 1993) *Show Boat* (1983, 1994); *On Your Toes* (1983); *The Cradle Will Rock* (1983); *Porgy and Bess* (1983, 1986, 1989); *Anything Goes* (1987); *The Most Happy Fella* (1992); *Guys and Dolls* (1992–1994); and *Carousel* (1994).
17. The figure 467 is deceptively low since *Lady in the Dark* returned to Broadway after a tour for another 310 performances. The grand total of 777 performances would place this show as the ninth longest-running musical of the 1940s and no. 20 in the 1920–1959 list. See Symonette and Kowalke, eds., *Speak Low*, 274.
18. In any event *Pal Joey's revival* (542 performances) falls only five performances and one show below the top forty, and the combined number of performances of its two runs (916) would place it just below *Bells Are Ringing* at No. 13.
19. Before *Porgy and Bess* arrived at the Metropolitan Opera in 1986, no American opera had been performed there more than fifteen times. See Carl Johnson, "American Opera at the Met: 1883–1983," *The American Music Teacher* 35/4 (February–March 1984): 20–25. Virgil Thomson's and Gertrude Stein's *Four Saints in Three Acts* (1934), which premiered on Broadway one year before *Porgy and Bess*, lasted only forty-eight performances.
20. The composers, composer-lyricists, or teams that produced two or more musicals in Appendix C, pp. 317–19 include the following: Adler and Ross (*Damn Yankees, Pajama Game*); Arlen and Harburg (*Bloomer Girl, Jamaica*); Berlin (*Annie Get Your Gun, Call Me Madam*); Rome (*Fanny, Wish You Were Here*); Styne (*Bells Are Ringing, Gentlemen Prefer Blondes, Gypsy, High Button Shoes*); and Wright and Forrest (*Kismet, Song of Norway*). Also missing is Gene de Paul's *Li'l Abner* (with lyrics by Johnny Mercer) that debuted between the premieres of *Show Boat* and *West Side Story*. The contributions by Rudolf Friml, Ray Henderson, and Sigmund Romberg preceded *Show Boat*; Meredith Willson's *The Music Man* followed *West Side Story* by two months.
21. Since Rodgers and Hammerstein produced *Annie Get Your Gun*, this leaves *Kiss Me, Kate* as the only show among the top five musicals of the 1940s that was not created or produced by the ubiquitous team.
22. Engel, 35–36.
23. See Gänzl and Lamb; Kingman; and Herbert Kupferberg, *The Book of Classical Music Lists* (New York: Facts on File, 1985).
24. Similar criteria motivate Gänzl's criteria of selection: "Firstly, we chose those pieces which a theatre-goer would be likely to encounter on the currrent stages of . . . America, the hits of today and the hits of yesterday which have been brought back for the further enjoyment of the theatre-going public. Secondly, we chose those shows which had a notable success in their own times, those which have left a particular legacy of favourite songs, those which are significant historically or artistically and those which are just plain good and which deserve a reappearance on the modern stage. Thirdly, we added our own particular favourites among the shows of yesteryear which we hope, if we bring them to your notice, might become favourites of yours as well." Gänzl and Lamb, p. xii.
25. See Block, "Broadway Canon," 525–44.
26. Northrop Frye, *Anatomy of Criticism: Four Essays* (Princeton, N.J.: Princeton University Press, 1957), 4.

Chapter 2: Show Boat

1. Ronald Byrnside, Andrew Lamb, and Deane L. Root, "Jerome Kern," *The New Grove Dictionary of Music and Musicians*, ed. Stanley Sadie (London: Macmillan, 1980), vol. 10, 1–2; a slightly expanded version of this entry appeared in *The New Grove Dictionary of American Music*, ed. H. Wiley Hitchcock and Stanley Sadie (London: Macmillan, 1985), vol. 2, 623–26.
2. Byrnside, Lamb, and Root, 1.
3. The *New Grove* authors do not mention that the New York City Opera selected *Show Boat* perhaps more for financial than artistic reasons. See Martin L. Sokol, *The New York City Opera: An American Adventure* (London: Collier Macmillan, 1981), 126.
4. Kreuger, *"Show Boat."* Kreuger's volume offers a comprehensive comparative survey of Edna Ferber's novel, the New York 1927 premiere and revivals (1932 and 1946), and the three film versions (1929, 1936, and 1951).
5. The Secaucus materials discussed later in this chapter are identified in Appendix D, p. 324, no. 1.
6. Some reviewers of the album noted with admiration that the McGlinn reconstruction, which featured noted operatic crossover artists Frederica von Stade as Magnolia and Teresa Stratas as Julie, contained only ten minutes' less music than Wagner's *Die Walküre.*
7. Robert Coleman, *Daily Mirror*, 27 December 1927. Quoted in S. Green, *Rodgers and Hammerstein Fact Book*, 353.
8. Ibid. According to Gerald Bordman, *Show Boat* opened with a cast of *only* ninety-six chorus members (fifty-two white and thirty-two black) and twelve black dancers. Bordman, *Jerome Kern*, 286.
9. Percy Hammond, *New York Herald Tribune*, 8 January 1928; Brooks Atkinson, *New York Times*, 8 January 1928. Quoted in S. Green, *Rodgers and Hammerstein Fact Book*, 354–55.
10. Cecil Smith and Glenn Litton, *Musical Comedy in America* (New York: Theatre Arts Books, 1981), 158.
11. George Jean Nathan, *Judge*, 21 January 1928. Quoted in S. Green, *Rodgers and Hammerstein Fact Book*, 355.
12. Robert Garland, *New York Telegram*, n.d.; Alexander Woollcott, *New York World*, 15 January 1928. See also Robert Benchley, *Life*, 12 January 1928. Quoted in S. Green, *Rodgers and Hammerstein Fact Book*, 354–55.
13. Richard Traubner, *Operetta: A Theatrical History* (Garden City, N.Y.: Doubleday, 1983), 393.
14. Kreuger, "Some Words about 'Show Boat'," 17. In Ferber's novel Captain Andy becomes part of his beloved river when he is thrown overboard in a storm and drowns, Julie becomes a prostitute, and Ravenal and Magnolia are never reunited.
15. Engel, *American Musical Theater*, 13.
16. Ibid., 13. Two pages later Engel asserts his view that only *Porgy and Bess* (1935) and *The Boys from Syracuse* (1938) before *Pal Joey* (1940) have revivable books.
17. Ibid., 14. In a book published five years later Engel reiterates his 1967 perspective, but concedes *Show Boat*'s originality as well as the historical importance of its interweaving five couples: "Nothing as rich as this had happened before it in any other libretto, nothing as courageous in subject matter and nothing in America as opulent musically." Engel, *Words With Music;* 70.
18. Bordman, *Jerome Kern*, 23 and 25; Kern quotation on page 23.
19. Ibid., 150.
20. Ibid., 171.
21. Kern was already a proven commodity to Ziegfeld, who had produced the hit *Sally* (570 performances) in 1920. Rumors of Ziegfeld's lack of faith in *Show Boat* may be exaggerated.

22. Kreuger, "*Show Boat*," 26.
23. Appendix D offers an outline of the 1927 *Show Boat* (scenes and songs) as listed in a souvenir program for the week beginning Monday, October 28, 1928, by which time changes had long since been consolidated (the program is reproduced in Kreuger, "*Show Boat*," 68–69). For convenience, the outline is keyed to the show numbers as they appear in the original Harms vocal score. Songs listed in the Harms score (but not listed in the souvenir program) are placed in italics. The appendix also provides an encapsulated view of the most important subsequent productions.
24. EMI/Angel CDS 7-49108-2.
25. Kreuger, "*Show Boat*," viii-ix.
26. With the issuing of McGlinn's reconstructed recording, a libretto that is virtually complete for those scenes where underscored dialogue plays an important role (act I, scenes 1, 2, 4, 7, 8,) finally became widely available. Act II, scene 3 is also nearly complete and the text of act II, scenes 4 and 9 is well represented. The only previously published libretto is based on the 1928 London production (Chappell, 1934).
27. John McGlinn, "Notes on 'Show Boat'," 28.
28. McGlinn candidly concedes that his recording is not absolutely complete. He does not, for example, include the *Entr'acte* to act II or several "utility arrangements . . . which are in any case verbatim repeats of music recorded herein," and he notes also the omission of underscoring in act II, scene 2. McGlinn leaves unmentioned the unfortunate absence of the interpolated "Good Morning, Carrie" from the same scene and Gustav Lange's "Blumenlied" ("Flower Song"). The latter served Kern as the "Incidental Music, played on the Stage during the presentation of 'The Parson's Bride'" in act I, scene 6.
29. The dramatic changes are fully reflected in Chappell's published libretto of 1934, but the published vocal score, while it contains "Dance Away the Night" and omits "Good-bye, Ma Lady Love" and "Hey, Feller," does not include "How'd You Like to Spoon with Me?" and prints "Ol' Man River" in the original C major (to better feature Robeson's *basso profundo* the London "Ol' Man River" was transposed down a whole tone to Bb from its New York key of C major).
30. After 418 performances the 1946 revival would spawn two phenomenal national tours (fourteen cities and forty-five cities, respectively) that would last the better part of the next two years.
31. Kreuger, "*Show Boat*," 160–63. The legacy of the 1946 production is largely preserved in the Welk vocal score and the unpublished libretto distributed by the Rodgers and Hammerstein Theatre Library for those who would produce *Show Boat* over the next five decades. Missing, however, from both the Welk score and the acting edition of the 1946 libretto is Kim as an adult and her song "Nobody Else But Me." This was the song that replaced Norma Terris's impersonations and Edith Day's new song for the London production, "Dance Away the Night." Although he acknowledges that it was made "to facilitate travel and trim the running time to avoid overtime fees for the stage hands," Kreuger asserts that these changes "strengthen the reunion of Magnolia and Ravenal." Ibid., 170.
32. For Kreuger, the three scene cuts "were made to help trim the lengthy show to a more conventional running time," and, since "developments in scenic technology permitted speedier set changes than were possible in the 1920s," such "front" scenes (including act I, scene 3) were an unnecessary impediment to contemporary possibilities in stagecraft. Kreuger also defends another deletion when he writes that "although the replacement of one song for another in the same spot requires the sacrifice of 'I Might Fall Back on You,' the better of the two songs is retained; and the script probably benefits from far smoother action." Ibid., 160 and 162.
33. Ethan Mordden, "'Show Boat'," *New Yorker*, 3 July 1989, 83.
34. Ibid.

35. The London production that docked on July 29 at the Adelphi Theatre stayed afloat longer than any previous production, closing 910 performances later on September 29, 1973. Its legacy is preserved on a recording promoted somewhat inaccurately in the jacket notes as "the first and only complete recording containing all the lyrics and music." Stanyon Records 10048 (two LPs).

36. The first of these, "How'd You Like to Spoon with Me?" (Kern's first London success of 1905 with lyrics by Edward Laska) served in the 1971 London production as an interpolation to replace "I Might Fall Back on You." The second, "Dance Away the Night," which Kern had written as a new last song for the London Magnolia, Edith Day, in 1928, was transferred to Frank Schultz.

37. "Gallivantin' Aroun' " (sung by Irene Dunne in the film) was not used.

38. In both the *Playbill* ("Director's Notes") and in his Tony Award acceptance speech Prince gratefully acknowledged McGlinn's scholarship. Hal Prince, "Director's Notes," *Playbill* 95/11 (1994), n.p.

39. *Variety* critic Jeremy Gerard noted that these signs were "just about the only things that remain unchanged over the show's 40–year span"; reprinted in *New York Theatre Critics' Reviews* 55/13 (1994): 262.

40. Prince, "Director's Notes," n.p.

41. Ibid., n.p. Robeson's "Ah Still Suits Me" from the film was used as underscoring.

42. Kim's "It's Getting Hotter in the North," dropped after opening night in 1927, was restored as a dance number; Queenie's "Hey, Feller!" (gone since the 1928 London production) and "How'd You Like to Spoon with Me?" from London 1971 were relegated to underscoring.

43. Robert Simon, 24.

44. A precedent for this technique can be found in 1916, when to accompany the silent film, *Gloria's Romance*, Kern had composed "fifteen themes for specific characters and situations." Bordman, *Jerome Kern*, 128.

45. Not only do these motives avoid notes outside the scale, they capture the openness of the river as well as its simplicity and purity by avoiding the tensions inherent in half steps.

46. Bordman was perhaps the first to note "that the Cotton Blossom theme is essentially the beginning of 'Ol' Man River''s chorus played in reverse and accelerated" Bordman, *Jerome Kern*, 290. The relationship between the "Cotton Blossom," "Ol' Man River," and Captain Andy's themes is also mentioned by Ethan Mordden (" 'Show Boat' ").

47. Bordman writes that Kern "demonstrated the universality of some folk themes when he returned to his roots and used an old Bohemian melody for Captain Andy's entrance." Bordman, *Jerome Kern*, 291. Dvořák authority John Clapham notes a connection between Dvořák's theme and the spiritual "Swing Low, Sweet Chariot." Clapham, "The Evolution of Dvořák's Symphony 'From the New World'," *Musical Quarterly* 44 (April 1958): 175; see also Jean E. Snyder, "A Great and Noble School of Music: Dvořák, Harry T. Burleigh, and the African American Spiritual," in *Dvořák in America 1892–1895*, ed. John C. Tibbetts, (Portland, Ore.: Amadeus Press, 1993), 123-48, especially 131–32. Three years before *Show Boat* Kern quoted the openings of both the first movement and the even more well-known slow movement from Dvořák's symphony in the dance music of "Shufflin' Sam" (from *Sitting Pretty*), perhaps as a musical pun to support Sam's motto, "This old world's no place to cry and be glum in." Bordman attributes this last Dvořák reference to orchestrator Robert Russell Bennett. Bordman, *Jerome Kern*, 249.

48. It is more difficult to offer an unequivocal identification of the theme associated with Sheriff Vallon. Unlike the "Cotton Blossom," Captain Andy, and Parthy themes, which establish immediate associations, Vallon's theme, introduced immediately after the Overture, at first suggests a more generalized darker side of river life rather than a specific human representative of law and order. At its second appearance, where stage directions

tell directors to "enter Vallon," Kern makes a direct association between Vallon and his theme, an association that Kern will recall at the conclusion of "Make Believe" ("enter Vallon followed by Joe").

49. In the 1994 Broadway revival Captain Andy's theme is absent on both these occasions.

50. Not only does Kern adopt the B section of *The Beauty Prize* music as the B section of "Where's the Mate?" he also retains its unusual modulation from G major to F♯ major.

51. The three-note descending scalar fragment also returns prominently in the opening chorus (sung by whites) at the Midway Plaisance in Chicago (Harms, 181).

52. Julie's song "Bill," if not her fate, is also foreshadowed by the barker at the Chicago Fair (Harms, 186).

53. Also mm. 5–6, 9–10, and 15–16.

54. Stanley Green notes this reference to "Make Believe" in *The Rodgers and Hammerstein Story* (New York: The John Day Company, 1963), 58–59. Ethan Mordden and Deena Rosenberg provide two additional examples of thematic reminiscence. In "Why Do I Love You?" the orchestra plays the first eight measures of "I Might Fall Back On You" while a chorus sings "Hours are not like years, / So dry your tears! / What a pair of love birds!" Immediately thereafter Ravenal reprises the first eight measures of "Can't Help Lovin' Dat Man" to the words "I'll come home as early as I can, / Meanwhile be good and patient with our man." Mordden, " 'Show Boat'," 81, and Rosenberg, " 'Show Boat' Sails Into the Present," *New York Times*, 24 April 1983, sec. 2, 12.

55. *Show Boat* (Garden City, N.Y.: Doubleday, Page, 1926), 183–85.

56. The meeting scene portion of act 1, scene 1 is found in Harms, 37–53, Chappell, 36–52, and Welk, 31–46; the libretto appears in the McGlinn booklet of the EMI recording, 62–66.

57. This harmonic progression is known in classical theoretical parlance as a deceptive cadence (a B minor triad in the key of D major).

58. This chord, an augmented sixth chord on B♭ expands into a dominant A major triad to prepare circuitously the return to the tonal center of D.

59. It is similarly not an accident that Magnolia and Ravenal's declaration of love at the conclusion of the act will also be a waltz, "You Are Love." Considering the importance of this waltz section in "Make Believe," its omission in both the 1936 and 1951 film versions is regrettable.

60. The Library of Congress typescript (identified in Appendix D, pp. 324, no. 1) shows that before settling on "convention's P's and Q's" the line read, "There really is no cause to have the blues," a lyric that was removed before Kern's first musical draft of this scene. In the third section of the song, this same typescript shows that "the world we see" replaced "reality."

61. The 1951 MGM film version offers yet another division of this material before Magnolia and Ravenal profess their love together:

RAVENAL: Others find peace of mind in pretending
          Couldn't you?
MAGNOLIA: Couldn't I?
BOTH: Couldn't we:
RAVENAL: Make believe our lips are blending
          In a phantom kiss or two or three—
BOTH: Might as well make believe I love you—
          For, to tell the truth . . . I do.

62. In addition to the Library of Congress and New York Public Library libretto typescripts there are two substantial musical drafts for this scene housed in the Library of Congress

(designated Draft 1 and Draft 2 in Appendix D, p. 324, no. 1). All of the Library of Congress material was acquired from the Warner Brothers Warehouse in Secaucus, New Jersey.

63. In the Library of Congress typescript Frank appears before Ravenal has the opportunity to pick up Ellie's handkerchief.

64. The 1927 production offered two other exchanges between Ellie and Frank that succeeded in conveying the dynamics between them. The first of these opens act I, scene 3 (Outside a Waterfront Gambling Saloon) where Ellie explains to Frank that she "won't never marry no actor"; the second appears in scene 5 where she informs him that she might settle for Frank if nothing better comes along ("I Might Fall Back on You").

65. The dialogue in the New York Public Library typescript (Appendix D, p. 324, no. 2) goes like this:

> PARTHY (Off): Magnolia! (She enters lower deck.) Andy! Drat that man, he's never home—Magnolia! (Magnolia enters on top deck. Windy motions her to stand still where she is so that Parthy won't see her. Windy exits R. Parthy exits L.)
>
> RAVENAL (Ravenal resumes soliloquy): Who cares if my boat goes upstream?
>
> PARTHY (Off): Nola!
>
> RAVENAL: Or if the gale bids me go with the river's flow.

The Library of Congress typescript (Appendix D, p. 324, no. 1) originally had Magnolia's stage action occur after Ravenal sang this last line with corrections made in pencil.

66. Library of Congress typescript 1–21 and 1–22.

67. During the tryouts Kern and Hammerstein made still more changes in this scene. Shortly before its closing moments Draft 2 of the Library of Congress score had the lovers sing a reprise of the waltz (section 2) for fifteen measures, after which Kern indicated by arrows and hatch marks a direct move to the coda. Draft 2 also contained another six measures of "Make Believe" after the coda, which Kern deleted before the return of Vallon's theme. The underscored waltz of section 2 then led to a scene between Magnolia and Joe and "Ol' Man River."

In the earlier musical manuscript (Draft 1) Kern had Ravenal introduce the main chorus of "Make Believe" with a different text (beginning with "As the river goes so time goes"), and while the text is crossed out, the melody provides the underscoring between Ravenal and Vallon before the former sings the first A section of "Where's the Mate for Me?" Also in Draft 1 after Ravenal hears Magnolia's piano theme, a chorus of Girls rather than Ravenal himself repeats the theme. Kern's inspiration to have Magnolia's piano theme intrude upon Ravenal's song was apparently not part of the initial conception.

In contrast to Draft 2, a draft that clearly served as the model for the published vocal scores, Draft 1 does not show the third and fourth sections of "Make Believe," sections that provide much psychological nuance and musical richness to the scene. Instead, Draft 1 brings back the six measures of coda and the final confrontation between Ravenal and Vallon. As in Draft 2, the scene in Draft 1 concludes with Magnolia seeing Joe, and their dialogue (not given) is underscored by the opening strains of "Ol' Man River" and "Can't Help Lovin' Dat Man."

68. Included among this group of song hits are "When I Grow Too Old to Dream" from *The Night Is Young* (1935) with Romberg, and a trio of hits with Kern, "The Folks Who Live on the Hill" and "Can I Forget You?" from *High, Wide and Handsome* (1937), and the Academy Award–winning "The Last Time I Saw Paris" from *Lady, Be Good* (1941). Soon after he had begun working with Richard Rodgers, Hammerstein wrote "It Might as Well

Be Spring" and "It's a Grand Night for Singing" for *State Fair* (1945) with Rodgers and "All Through the Day" from *Centennial Summer* (1946) with Kern.

69. Beginnning with the first of three versions of *Show Boat* in 1929 Hollywood would adapt twenty-six of Hammerstein's Broadway shows for film.

70. Kern turned down Hammerstein's offer in 1942 to write a musical based on Lynn Riggs's play, *Green Grow the Lilacs* (1931). One year later the property was turned over to Rodgers. The result, of course, was *Oklahoma!*

71. The Annie Oakley property turned out to be Berlin's greatest book show, *Annie Get Your Gun*, in 1946 with a book by Herbert and Dorothy Fields.

72. The quotation is from Bordman, *Jerome Kern*, 294. The sensitive issues explored in *Show Boat* have hardly gone away. In reviewing the 1993 Toronto production of *Show Boat*, directed by Prince, theater critic John Lahr found it necessary to respond to the Coalition to Stop Show Boat, a group that tried to close the show for its alleged "racist, anti-African propaganda." According to Lahr "the past must be remembered for its sins as well as for its triumphs" and *Show Boat* admirably "chronicles slavery not to condone but to deplore it." "Mississippi Mud," *New Yorker*, 25 October 1993, 123–26; quotation on p. 126.

73. Ibid., 126.

Chapter 3: Anything Goes

1. Porter's original lyric, "I wouldn't care for those nights in the air / That the fair Mrs. Lindbergh went through," intended for the unproduced *Star Dust* (1931), was replaced in *Anything Goes* by the now familiar "Flying too high with some guy in the sky / Is my idea of nothing to do, / Yet I get a kick out of you." See Eells, 113, and Kimball, ed., *Complete Lyrics of Cole Porter*, 167 and 270.

2. Eells, 111; Kreuger, "Some Words About 'Anything Goes', " 13; and Davis, 329–36. Kreuger also points out that the Bolton-Wodehouse book was not really about a shipwreck. In fact, a fake bomb created a mood of terror that was eventually alleviated by a celebratory prayer, "Blow, Gabriel, Blow." Davis's more detailed survey of the early genesis of *Anything Goes* has the advantage of being based on a previously unknown first draft from 1934 in addition to Bolton's less reliable reconstruction of the still-missing second draft (the rejected draft) years later.

3. Richard G. Hubler, *The Cole Porter Story* 30.

4. Brooks Atkinson, "The Play: 'Anything Goes' as Long as Victor Moore, Ethel Merman and William Gaxton Are Present," *New York Times*, 22 November 1934, 26.

5. McGlinn, "The Original 'Anything Goes'," 30.

6. Mast, 194. Many thanks are due to Roberta Staats of The Cole Porter Musical and Literary Property Trusts for generously sending me a copy of Porter's twenty-nine-page will, and to trustee Robert H. Montgomery, Jr., for confirming its contents.

7. In the McGlinn recording "There's No Cure for Travel" is relegated to the appendix.

8. The McGlinn notes indicate that Merman's principal objection was the line "She made the maid who made the room," with its implied homosexuality. Ibid., 33. A similar line appears in act I, scene 2, when Billy asks if Reno made the boat and a character named Snooks replies: "Did she make the Boat? She made the Captain!" Perhaps because of its heterosexual implications this line was permissible and could be retained in the dialogue (see 1934 libretto, 1–2–13).

9. In this instance McGlinn was reluctant to perform an appendectomy so he inserted "What a Joy to Be Young" in the main body of his recording rather than its rightful place in his appendix beside "There's No Cure Like Travel," "Kate the Great," and "Waltz Down the Aisle."

10. Kreuger, "Some Words About 'Anything Goes', " 17.

11. Ibid., 17.
12. McGlinn, "The Original 'Anything Goes'," 33.
13. Perhaps because present-day late-arriving listeners usually come into the theater already whistling "I Get a Kick Out of You," McGlinn took the initiative of placing "Buddie, Beware" in the body of his recording rather than the appendix.
14. Weidman has also written two librettos for Sondheim musicals, *Pacific Overtures* (1976) and *Assassins* (1990).
15. Atkinson, "The Play: 'Anything Goes'," 26.
16. Ibid., 26.
17. Eells, 116.
18. Lewis Funke, "Theatre: 'Anything Goes' Revival of Musical Opens at Orpheum," *New York Times*, 16 May 1962, 35.
19. Ibid., 35.
20. Abbott, 187.
21. 1962 libretto, 1–8–59. Many thanks to Louis H. Aborn, President of Tams-Witmark, for graciously allowing me to examine the 1934, 1962, and 1987 *Anything Goes* librettos, and to John L. Hughes, Managing Director of Samuel French Limited in London, for generously supplying a reference copy of the 1935 London libretto.
22. Holden.
23. *New York Times*, 25 August 1987, C14. For *West Side Story*, librettist Arthur Laurents created a deliberately artificial and meaningless slang that would never become old-fashioned and require updating.
24. Kreuger, "The Annotated 'Anything Goes'," 133.
25. Ibid., 133–37. Despite Kreuger's best efforts, however, the full meaning of the reference, "Drumstick Lipstick," "is lost to the ages."
26. Eells, 124.
27. A more direct reference to Aimée Semple McPherson had occurred in Moss Hart's sketch on the headline "Gandhi Goes On Hunger Strike" in the 1933 revue *As Thousands Cheer* (music by Berlin).
28. "Son Helping to Update Crouse's 'Anything Goes'," *New York Times*, 25 August 1987, sec. 3, 14.
29. Ibid., 14.
30. Holden, 35.
31. 1934 libretto, 2–1–11.
32. Those concerned by this usurpation of Hope's role and her solo opportunity may be somewhat placated to learn that in 1987 she is given a new interpolation, "Goodbye, Little Dream, Goodbye" (act II, scene 1), and a duet with Billy and some sailors, "All Through the Night" (a song from the original 1934 version now transferred to act II, scene 2). Furthermore, she is allowed to retain her interpolated duet with Billy in act I, scene 7, "It's De-Lovely," which had been introduced in act I, scene 2, of the 1962 version (see Appendix E).
33. 1934 libretto, 1–6–71. Mrs. Wentworth is the owner of the Pomeranian canine that Billy turns into a Mexican hairless.
34. In 1962 Billy is Chinchilian. The phrase "putting on the dog" is making a comeback. Throughout the gestation of this book the *New Yorker* has regularly displayed ads for "Put on the Dog" T-shirts, the expected side of the shirt featuring drawings of the front or back of a dog.
35. "Preserving the Heritage: The Living Record," in *Musical Theatre in America*, ed. Glenn Loney (Westport, Conn.: Greenwood Press, 1984), 407.
36. From *Pal Joey*, "I Could Write a Book."
37. *The New Harvard Dictionary of Music* defines a triplet as "three notes of equal value to be played in the time normally occupied by two notes of the same value, indicated by the

figure 3." Don Randel, ed., *The New Harvard Dictionary of Music* (Cambridge, Mass.: Harvard University Press, 1986), 873.

38. "Everything's Coming Up Roses" (lyrics, Stephen Sondheim; music, Jule Styne) from *Gypsy* (1959), also written for Merman as the eccentric Rose, uses a variation of this idea on the title words.

39. In an early version of "Blow, Gabriel Blow," vastly different melodically but otherwise rhythmically identical to the familiar version, the triplets are absent. See the Cole Porter Collection, box 15, folder 121, Yale University, New Haven, Conn.

40. "Easy to Love," Billy's love song to Hope that was dropped because of its difficulty for William Gaxton, also retains Reno's half-note triplet in the midst of a chromatic line.

41. Porter harmonizes "if today" with a dominant seventh on C (C-E-G-B♭), a chord which also necessitates a change of key (F major) two measures later.

42. See Citron, 112.

43. Those responsible for choosing the interpolated songs either inadvertently or by design discovered two that fit in with the syncopated world of Reno and Billy, "Friendship" and "It's De-Lovely," both of which share melodic fragments in common with the original "Anything Goes" and, of course, many other Porter songs.

Chapter 4: Porgy and Bess

1. "Gershwin Gets His Music Cues For 'Porgy' on Carolina Beach," *New York Herald Tribune*, 8 July 1934, sec. 5, 2, and G. Gershwin; reprinted in Armitage, 72–77.

2. See Frederick S. Roffman, "At Last the Complete 'Porgy and Bess'," *New York Times*, 19 September 1976, sec. 2, 1+, and Woll, 165–66. Shortly before these exploratory negotiations the Met introduced Louis Gruenberg's opera *The Emperor Jones*. Although well received, Gruenberg's opera, which featured Lawrence Tibbett singing the title role in blackface, was performed only ten times in 1933 and 1934. African Americans were similarly excluded in most of the other important roles.

3. Jablonski, 194–96.

4. Two years after its Met debut the international reputation of *Porgy and Bess* as an opera was further enhanced in Glyndebourne. A third uncut recording generated by this production was released in 1990. See the Discography.

5. After Gershwin's *Pardon My English* Freedley (without Aarons) would produce four hits for Porter shows: *Anything Goes* (1934), *Red, Hot and Blue!* (1936), *Leave It to Me!* (1938), and *Let's Face It!* (1941).

6. See especially Alpert, 11–118; Ewen, *George Gershwin*, 218–65; Jablonski, 250–91; and Schwartz, 243–71.

7. Dorothy Heyward, "Porgy's Goat," *Harper's* 215 (December 1957): 37.

8. Jablonski, 255.

9. Appendix F designates the division of lyrical labor between DuBose Heyward and Ira Gershwin.

10. Gershwin began his orchestration with act I, scene 2, completing it in February 1935. In a letter to Schillinger (May 16) the composer wrote that he had completed act I, scene 1. Act II occupied Gershwin's attentions at least for the remainder of May and June, and on July 19 Gershwin conducted a run-through of acts I and II at the CBS studio. Completion dates for act III are carefully documented: scene 1 (July 22); scene 2 (August 4), scene 3 (August 23). Several weeks later Gershwin wrote on the first page of the orchestral score, "finished September 2, 1935."

11. Brooks Atkinson and Olin Downes, " 'Porgy and Bess,' Native Opera, Opens at the Alvin; Gershwin Work Based on DuBose Heyward's Play," *New York Times*, 11 October 1935, 30.

12. Atkinson and Downes, ibid.
13. Downes, ibid.
14. Atkinson, ibid.
15. Ibid.
16. Downes, ibid.
17. Ibid. Several days later the *New York Times* gave the composer an opportunity to respond at some length to his critics: "I chose the form I have used for 'Porgy and Bess' because I believe that music lives only when it is in serious form. When I wrote the 'Rhapsody in Blue' I took 'Blues' and put them in a large and more serious form. That was twelve years ago and the 'Rhapsody in Blue' is still very much alive, whereas if I had taken the same themes and put them in songs they would have been gone years ago." G. Gershwin, 1.
18. Jablonski, 264.
19. Thomson, "George Gershwin," 18.
20. Thomson, "Porgy in Maplewood," *New York Herald Tribune*, 19 October 1941; reprinted in Thomson, *The Musical Scene* (New York: Alfred A. Knopf, 1945), 167–69.
21 Vernon Duke, "Gershwin, Schillinger, and Dukelsky: Some Reminiscences," *Musical Quarterly* 33 (January 1947): 108.
22. Richard Rodgers, Foreword, *The Gershwins*, by Robert Kimball and Alfred Simon (New York: Atheneum, 1973), xiii.
23. Ibid.
24. Schwartz, 318.
25. G. Gershwin, 1–2. Interestingly, neither Atkinson nor Downes was bothered by Gershwin's songs. In fact, according to Atkinson it was their presence that made the "hour of formal music transitions" palatable. Similarly, Downes may have felt that there were a few songs too many "which hold back the dramatic development," but he undeniably shared Atkinson's view that "it is in the lyrical moments [i.e., songs] that Mr. Gershwin is most completely felicitous."

    Gershwin finds an ardent recent defender in Lawrence Starr, who observes that "for a nineteenth-century European like Verdi, it is acceptable—perhaps even appropriate and admirable—to have 'hit tunes' in an opera; for a twentieth-century American it is inappropriate and vulgar." Starr, "Gershwin's 'Bess'," 430.
26. G. Gershwin, 1.
27. R. Crawford, "Gershwin's Reputation, 259.
28. Hamm, "Theatre Guild Production," 495–532.
29. The following discussion of the "Buzzard Song" is excerpted (with some changes) from Block, "Gershwin's Buzzard."
30. The play by Dorothy and DuBose Heyward was originally published by Doubleday in 1927. Page references in this chapter correspond to the version of Porgy anthologized in *Famous American Plays of the 1920s* (New York: Dell, 1959), 207–307. The typescript of DuBose Heyward's libretto with George Gershwin's annotations is now housed in the Music Division of the Library of Congress, Washington, D.C. (Gershwin Collection, box 27, item 2).
31. Heyward, *Porgy*, 252.
32. Typescript libretto, 2–18.
33. Ibid.
34. Ibid., 2–14.
35. Armitage, 52.
36. Goldberg, 325.
37. Ewen, *George Gershwin*, 231.
38. Jablonski, 288.
39. The original 78-R.P.M. discs (Victor 11878/81) were reissued on long-playing records (RCA Camden CAL 500) and again on CDs (Pearl Gemm CDS 9483). At the same October 14

session, which took place only four days after the Broadway premiere, Tibbett also recorded "It Ain't Necessarily So" and, with Helen Jepson, "Bess, You Is My Woman Now." The selections sung by Tibbett and Jepson have also been reissued on Pearl Gemm CDS 9483. The baritone was the Met's most highly marketable commodity where new operas were concerned, and he had already portrayed a black man there (the title role of Louis Gruenberg's *Emperor Jones* in 1933). It was not until the administration of Rudolf Bing that black singers were welcomed at the Met (Marian Anderson was the first, in 1955).

40. A facsimile of the Los Angeles Gershwin program appears in Merle Armitage, *George Gershwin: Man and Legend* (New York: Duell, Sloan & Pearce, 1958), between pages 144 and 145. The Duncan recordings were issued on Decca DL-9024.

41. Columbia OSL 162; reissued on Odyssey Stereo 32–36–0018.

42. Armitage, *George Gershwin: Man and Legend*, 156–60.

43. The idiosyncratic Davis/Breen version became the second published version of the opera libretto. See Stanley Richards, ed., *Great Musicals of the American Theatre Volume One* (Radnor, Penn.: Chilton, 1973), 75–113.

44. G. Gershwin, 1–2.

45. *New York Herald Tribune*, 8 July 1934, sec. 5, 2.

46. Shirley, "Reconciliation."

47. Shirley, " 'Porgy and Bess'," 104.

48. Hamm, "Theatre Guild Production," 495–532. Samuel Spewack and Bella Spewack, *Kiss Me, Kate*, anthologized in Richards, 273.

49. Mellers, 402.

50. The video directed by Nunn was a Primetime/BBC and Homevale/Greg Smith Production, a Picture Music International Release, and was issued on EMI Records, Ltd., 1993.

51. Allen Woll explores the "irony" of *Porgy and Bess* as a black musical created by whites for a white audience, and David Horn shows how Gershwin's opera continues to pose "struggles over meaning" between various social and ethnic groups. See Woll, 154–75, and Horn.

52. Horn. Horn explores the ideological conflict in 1989 between the Royal Liverpool Philharmonic Society, who praised Gershwin for "forging a new musical language," and the Liverpool Anti-Racist and Community Arts Association, who condemned Gershwin for "wading into black culture."

53. Kreuger, "*Showboat*," 212.

54 Ira Gershwin writes that in preparation for the 1951 recording of the complete opera he went through the score and changed "some opprobrious terms in the recitatives—there were about twenty—to substitutes inoffensive to the ear of today." I. Gershwin, 83.

55. Thomson, "George Gershwin," 17.

56. Johnson.

57. Ibid., 24. Johnson made the following comment about Gershwin's recitatives: "We are confronted with a series of musical episodes which, even if they do not belong together, could be made to appear as if they do by a better handling of the musical connecting tissue."

58. Ibid., 25. Johnson also finds fault with Mamoulian's staging for its misperceptions about African Americans.

59. Ibid., 26. According to Johnson, it is incredulous that Sporting Life "could be so entirely liberated from that superstitious awe of Divinity which even the most depraved southern Negro never quite loses."

60. Ibid.

61. Ezra Bell Thompson, 54.

62. Ibid.

63. Harold Cruse, *The Crisis of the Negro Intellectual* (New York: Morrow, 1967), 100–01.

64. Ibid., 103.

65. Ibid., 102.
66. G. Gershwin, 1.
67. Edward Morrow, "Duke Ellington on Gershwin's 'Porgy," *New Theatre* (December 1935): 5–6; reprinted in Mark Tucker, ed., *The Duke Ellington Reader* (New York: Oxford University Press, 1993), 114–18 (quotation on page 115).
68. One important difference might be noted. In *Porgy and Bess* all six prayers are in the same key; in the African-American Pentecostal tradition each singer chooses his or her own key.
69. The relationship between perceived authenticity and critical approbation is explored by John Spitzer in "Musical Attribution and Critical Judgment: The Rise and Fall of the Sinfonia Concertante for Winds, K. 297b)," *Journal of Musicology* 5 (Summer 1987): 319–56.
70. Gates.
71. Gershwin's spiritual "It Take a Long Pull to Get There" also bears an uncanny resemblance to the Jewish folk song "(Haveynu) Shalom A'leychem," music and Hebrew lyrics by Shlomo Ben-Chaim (New York: Henseley, 1960).
72. "Gershwin Gets His Music Cues," 2, and Goldberg, 331.
73. Starr, "Toward a Reevaluation," 27.
74. Additional connections between Porgy's theme and other characters are charted in Rosenberg, 277, 279, 282, 285, and 294.
75. Gershwin enhances the blues flavor by supporting Porgy's melodic minor third (G♮) with a major harmony (G♯).
76. Again, Gershwin creates a harmonic clash with a G♯ against the G♮ in the melody. Note also the resemblance between this Porgy theme and Gershwin's Prelude No. 2 for piano composed in 1926.
77. The melodic as well as rhythmic profile of Porgy's "loneliness" theme also figures prominently in the River Family of themes in *Show Boat* shown in Example 2.2. It may not be too fanciful to speculate that Gershwin's choice for Porgy's motive, like Kern's choice for his River Family of motives, may owe something to Dvořák's "New World" Symphony and the African-American spiritual "Swing Low, Sweet Chariot" (see chap. 2, n. 47).
78. Starr, "Toward a Reevaluation," 36; see also Starr's extended analysis of a Gershwin song in "Gershwin's 'Bess'."
79. Examples include the following: "Oh, I Can't sit Down!" (the word *"down!"* at the outset, and in the middle section, *"Hap*-py *feel*-in'," *"a-steal*-in'," *"con-ceal*-in'," and many more); "It Take a Long Pull to Get There" (the frequently repeated *"get* there" and *"Lan' "* [the latter divided into two musical syllables]); and "I Got Plenty o' Nuttin'" (the repeated *"nut*-tin' " and *"plen*-ty").
80. Labelled by Gershwin in the typescript libretto 1–11. The presence of a separate "happy dust" theme was first noted by Shirley, " 'Porgy and Bess'," 106.
81. For two recent denials of a "Bess" theme see Rosenberg, 285, and Joseph P. Swain, 62.
82. Vocal score (New York: Gershwin Publishing Corporation/Chappell, 1935), 272.
83. Since Bess is Porgy's woman now, it makes some sense for him to appropriate her theme as well.
84. Vocal score, 533–36 and 559. The signature melodies for Porgy, Sporting Life (and his "happy dust"), Crown, and Bess do not exhaust the themes of the opera nor even those of act I, scene 2. Gershwin himself designated at least one other theme, the first fisherman theme used prominently in this and other scenes (see the beginning of act II, scene 1 [Vocal score, 189]). A second theme also introduced in act I is associated more specifically with the enterprising Jake; four measures before rehearsal no. 171 (Vocal score, 323) shows this theme as it opens act II, scene 3, shortly before Jake goes out into the storm that will take his life and that of his wife Clara. Finally, Gershwin assigns an orchestral motive to indicate the presence of the lawyer Frazier, who appears only in act II, scene 1, a descrip-

tive theme with a prominent dissonant syncopated leap of a major seventh (see rehearsal no. 41, [Vocal score, 214]).

85. Note that Peter's melody which follows Bess's recitative is rhythmically identical to "I Got Plenty o' Nuttin' " (Vocal score, 329–30).

86. To complete the cycle of reminiscence motives that began this scene Gershwin returns one last time to Jake's motive (Vocal score, 357–58) before new storm music takes over to conclude the scene (359–64). The short-long rhythm of the dirge that opens act III, scene 1 ("Clara, Clara") might also be interpreted as an augmentation of Porgy's loneliness theme.

87. Hitchcock, 205, and Hamm, *Music in the New World*, 450.

Chapter 5: On Your Toes *and* Pal Joey

1. Ewen, *Richard Rodgers*, 236 and 254.
2. Rodgers, 262.
3. Ibid., 71.
4. Ibid., 91. Stanley Green summarizes other innovations in *Peggy-Ann:* "No songs were sung within the first fifteen minutes, the scenery and costumes were changed in full view of the audience, and the first and last scenes were played in almost total darkness." S. Green, *Broadway Musicals Show by Show,*
5. Rodgers, 118.
6. Ibid., 118.
7. Pandro Berman, the man who dismissed the vaudeville-Russian ballet idea, produced in *Shall We Dance* (1937) a movie musical starring Astaire and Rogers (with a score and lyrics by the Gershwins) that bears more than a passing resemblance to Rodgers and Hart's rejected conception.
8. Brooks Atkinson, " 'On Your Toes', Being a Musical Show With a Book and Tunes and a Sense of Humor," *New York Times*, 13 April 1936, 14.
9. Atkinson, "On Your Toes," *New York Times*, 12 October 1954, 24.
10. Rodgers, 175.
11. Mordden, *Better Foot Forward*, 143.
12. *On Your Toes*, 1936 libretto, I-4–22. Special thanks to Tom Briggs of the Rodgers and Hammerstein Theatre Library for allowing me to examine the librettos of the 1936 and 1983 productions.
13. Ibid., I-4–30.
14. Ibid., II-2–13; 1983 libretto, 46.
15. 1936 libretto, I-5–34.
16. Ibid., II-2–13. In the 1983 libretto (30), Junior explains further: "I admit that basic off-beat appears in many cultures—but I would think that all would have to agree that American jazz has a very individual sound"; also, in the 1983 version Sergei expresses artistic as well as commercial motives for staging "Slaughter" when he acknowledges to Peggy that he finds the work "admirable." His primary question is "can we dance it?" The problem facing the Russian ballet in 1983 is not that jazz is demeaning but whether a classical ballet company can master the stylistic nuances and comparable challenges of an alien form.
17. Frank Rich, "Theater: 'On Your Toes', A '36 Rodgers and Hart," *New York Times*, 7 March 1983, C13.
18. Dudar.
19. Theodore S. Chapin, *On Your Toes* (vocal score) (New York: Chappell 1985), 4.
20. Quotation in Abbott, 177; see also, Rodgers, 174.
21. Abbott, 177–78, and Rodgers, 174.
22. Dudar.

23. *On Your Toes*, 1936 libretto, I-4–32.
24. Ibid., I-6–39.
25. Ibid., I-3–10.
26. 1983 libretto, 4.
27. 1936 libretto, I-3–8 and I-2–9.
28. The professor reveals the limitations of his own education and refinement, since it is he who misprounces Schubert's name. Professor Dolan also assigns the words "Dein ist mein Herz" to the wrong song. The correct answer is "Ungeduld" from Schubert's *Die schöne Müllerin*. It should also be noted that as late as 1983 the view that Schubert was gay was not yet widely held. Thus Frankie in both 1936 and 1983 is almost certainly thinking about Junior, not one of Schubert's male lovers. See Maynard Solomon, "Franz Schubert and the Peacocks of Benvenuto Cellini," *19th Century Music* 12 (Spring 1989), 193–206.
29. The opening of "Goodnight Sweetheart" by Ray Noble, Jimmy Campbell, and Reg Connelly, published in 1931, also bears an unmistakable resemblance to the opening of *Les Préludes*.
30. By a twist of fate, in 1943 Hart collaborated with Kálmán on an unproduced musical about the French underground in World War II, *Miss Underground*. See Hart and Kimball, 291.
31. *On Your Toes*, 1936 libretto, I-3–16 and 17. In 1983 the conclusion to the exchange that precedes "It's Got to Be Love" is as follows (7–8):

> JUNIOR: I'll tell you something—and I shouldn't say it—it's terribly personal— I'm very fond of you.
> FRANKIE: You are? Even with my derivative song?
> JUNIOR: Yes, Miss Frayne.
> FRANKIE: Well, in that case, why don't you call me Frankie?
> JUNIOR: All right—and you can call me Junior.
> FRANKIE: All right. Yesterday some of the kids were dancing to my song and they thought it was pretty good.
> JUNIOR: Well, gee Christmas, I'd like to hear it again.
> FRANKIE (Goes to bench. Gets music): O.K. That's a fair exchange. (JUNIOR crosses UP CENTER) I'll introduce you to Peggy Porterfield and you'll listen to my song. (She gives him the music)
> JUNIOR: All right, Frankie. (He goes to bench, below FRANKIE and sits)

32. Rodgers's sinking melody also conveys a new harmonic interpretation of an identical (albeit more extended) descending melody from the verse of the song (mm. 9–13) on the words, "color, Aquamarine or em'rald green. And . . ."
33. Mauceri.
34. By the time the audience witnesses the entire "Slaughter," one of its principal tunes has been heard on several previous occasions, always in an appropriate context, e.g., in act I, scene 3, when Junior's private rehearsal is interrupted by Frankie.
35. 1983 libretto, 19.
36. Rodgers, " 'Pal Joey': History of a Heel." *New York Times*, 30 December 1951, sec. 2, 1+.
37. Rodgers, 202.
38. O'Hara's letter was reprinted with Rodgers's jacket notes for the 1950 recording (Columbia 4364). Rodgers recalls receiving the letter in Boston in October 1939 during the tryouts of *Too Many Girls* (Rodgers, 198). The letter, however, is dated "early 1940." See *Selected Letters of John O'Hara*, ed. Matthew J. Bruccoli (New York: Random House, 1978), 158–59.
39. Stanley Green in his *Rodgers and Hammerstein Fact Book* (217), provides more comprehen-

sive information on *Pal Joey*'s unusual initial New York run in three theaters: Ethel Barrymore Theatre (December 25, 1940—August 16, 1941), Shubert Theatre (September 1—October 18, 1941), and St. James Theatre (October 21—November 29, 1941). Tryouts were held at the Forrest Theatre, Philadelphia, December 16–22, 1940.

40. Brooks Atkinson, "Christmas Night Adds 'Pal Joey' to the Musical Stage," *New York Times*, 26 December 1940, 22.

41. Burns Mantle, " 'Pal Joey' Smart and Novel," *Daily News*, 26 December 1940, reprinted in *New York Theatre Critics' Reviews*, vol. 1, 172.

42. Rodgers, 201.

43. John Mason Brown, " 'Pal Joey' Presented at The Ethel Barrymore," *New York Post*, 26 December 1940; reprinted in *New York Theatre Critics' Reviews*, vol. 1, 172.

44. Sidney B. Whipple, "Pal Joey Is a Bright Gay, Tuneful Novel Work," *New York World-Telegram*, 26 December 1940; reprinted in *New York Theatre Critics' Reviews*, vol. 1, 173.

45. Brooks Atkinson, "At the Theatre," *New York Times*, 4 January 1952, 17; reprinted in *New York Theatre Critics' Reviews*, vol. 13, 399.

46. Engel, *American Musical Theater*, 35–36.

47. Ibid. Engel places another four Rodgers musicals with Hammerstein among his top fifteen (*Oklahoma!*, *Carousel*, *South Pacific*, and *The King and I*).

48. "Plant You Now, Dig You Later," another duet between Gladys and Lowell in 1940—rendered by Harold Lang (Joey) on the prerevival recording—is sung solely by Gladys in 1952 (Glady's verse is not, however, included in the 1952 published libretto). Consequently, the comically sinister blackmailer Lowell becomes as ineffectual musically as he is dramatically (for example, his confrontation with Vera and her powerful police allies). One final change deprived Gladys of a fifth musical number (one less than Joey's six songs) when she is excluded from "You Mustn't Kick It Around." But unlike Lowell, Gladys as played by Helen Gallagher in 1952 remains as she was when played in 1940 by June Havoc (sister of the famous stripper Gypsy Rose Lee), i.e., third in musical prominence after Joey and Vera and the lead show singer both in Mike Spears's second-class nightclub in act I ("That Terrific Rainbow") and the chic Chez Joey in act II ("The Flower Garden of My Heart"). In this last named song the character Louis (the tenor), who sings the verse, first chorus, and recitations, was added in 1952.

49. For example, in O'Hara's Broadway transcript Joey does not sing the opening song, "Chicago," the first song of 1952. Similarly, Joey's audition number is nowhere to be found in the earlier script, only the words, "Joey has just finished singing." When it appears later in the show, slightly altered as "Morocco," it is sung by Michael Moore. See Hart and Kimball, 27. I am grateful to Chicago's Goodman Theatre for allowing me to see the unpublished typescripts of O'Hara's 1940s Broadway libretto and the preliminary script.

50. Gone from "Take Him" (act II, scene 4) in 1952 are both Linda's and Vera's verses. Vera's verses appear in the O'Hara Broadway typescript. See also Hart and Kimball, 275.

   Revisions in the 1952 book are more modest than those for the lyrics, although the absence of a reprise of "I Could Write a Book" from O'Hara's 1940 Broadway transcript must be considered a significant change. The dialogue that separates the refrains in "You Mustn't Kick It Around" was not present in 1940, and the transition lines to "Plant You Now" and "Do It The Hard Way" would later exclude Lowell. Perhaps the most substantial change in the 1952 book is the deletion of a page of dialogue between Joey and the manager of the apartment house, who dispassionately informs the anti-hero that he has until 6:00 P.M. to leave the building. Other changes in the 1952 book: Vera is now "over twenty-one" instead of "thirty-six," Gladys's interpretation of Lowell's brand of humor is an old lady hit by a trolley car (rather than a truck), and Joey no longer gets a good meal at the home of Linda's sister.

51. Abbott, 194–95.

52. In O'Hara's early typescript Joey meets Linda English, generically named Girl, at Mike Spears's club where she performs as a singer. Like other performers at the club Linda is initially repelled by Joey and what he stands for. In the final 1940 libretto, where Joey wins her over in front of the pet store with his fictitious story of his childhood dog Skippy, Linda acquired more sweetness. She also acquired more dialogue as a guest rather than a performer in Mike Spear's joint in act I, scene 3, and in a telephone exchange in scene 4.

Some additional distinctions: In O'Hara's original draft Lowell and Gladys actively solicit Linda's help in their plan to blackmail Vera, which in the later libretto Linda merely overhears. In both versions the generous Linda warns her rival. Nevertheless, the earlier and tougher Vera thwarts the blackmail attempt without the help of Police Deputy Commissioner O'Brien when she reproduces a photograph that shows her husband and Gladys in flagrante delicto. Not present in the earlier typescript are the angry final words between Joey and Vera following Vera's lie (that Joey frightened away the blackmailers), an exchange that credibly prepares Vera's reprise of "Bewitched."

In the preliminary typescript Vera was nine years older (Joey found Vera's name in the 1910 rather than the 1919 social register; see n. 50). Lowell's racket is more clearly explained, and Lowell participates in the song "Plant You Now, Dig You Later." The typescript also contains some additional dialogue for Joey, Mike, and Melba to create a smoother transition for "Zip." Following "Zip," Melba takes a costume away from a show girl and poses for photographs with Joey and another chorus girl for her newspaper. This scene is based on Joey's thirteenth letter to his successful bandleader friend Ted, "A Bit of a Shock." Finally, the preliminary typescript contained several pages of dialogue in which Joey is fitted for additional clothes and purchases an automobile before Linda arrives to warn Vera about the blackmail attempt.

53. Abbott, 195.

54. Rodgers biographer Frederick Nolan writes that "Larry Hart chortled with delight when he read those lines ['I love it / Because the laugh's on me''] over the phone to Joshua Logan and explained with glee that they meant Joey was actually *on* Vera Simpson." Frederick Nolan, *The Sound of Their Music: The Story of Rodgers and Hammerstein* (New York: Walker, 1978), 112–13. When the song was broadcast, these lyrics were changed to "the laugh's about me."

55. Rodgers, 45. Although Goetschius does not discuss this particular point, his *Exercises in Melody-Writing* (first published in 1900) offers a systematic approach to a subject of great interest to Rodgers. Percy Goetschius, *Exercises in Melody-Writing* (New York: G. Schirmer, 1928).

56. Stephen Sondheim, "Theater Lyrics," 84–85.

57. The half step also appears conspicuously in "Talking to My Pal," dropped during the out-of-town tryouts. Its presence, however, in "Plant You Now, Dig You Later," a duet between Gladys and gangster agent Ludlow Lowell in the 1940 version, places a considerable strain on the theory that Rodgers is making a dramatic statement or creating subtle associations through a musical interval.

58. Wilder. Two recent books that discuss popular song with more analytical rigor than Wilder appeared too late to be incorporated into the present survey. Allen Forte's study, *The American Popular Ballad of the Golden Era, 1924–1950* (Princeton, N.J.: Princeton University Press, 1995), surveys the songs of Kern, Berlin, Porter, Gershwin, Rodgers, and Arlen; Steven E. Gilbert offers a more specialized analytical study of Gershwin's songs in *The Music of Gershwin* (New Haven: Yale University Press, 1995).

59. Wilder, 216. In the essay cited above Sondheim clarifies why he is "down on" Hart. His principal objection was that the pyrotechnic lyricist created lyrics "so wrenching that the listener loses the sense of the line." Sondheim, "Theater Lyrics," 83.

60. Wilder, 164.

Chapter 6: The Cradle Will Rock

1. E. Gordon, 538.
2. Martin Esslin, *Reflections: Essays on Modern Theatre* (Garden City, N.Y.: Doubleday, 1969), 80. The Kurt Weill Foundation, however, still considers the Blitzstein version the only singable version of this work in English. After the 1976 Lincoln Center revival the Foundation no longer permitted Ralph Manheim's and John Willett's harder-edged, more literal translation to be staged. On the relative merits of the Blitzstein and Manheim-Willett productions see Kim H. Kowalke, " 'The Threepenny Opera' in America," *Kurt Weill: The Threepenny Opera*, ed. Stephen Hinton (Cambridge: Cambridge University Press, 1990), 78–119.
3. See, for example, Hitchcock, 225–27, and Engel, *American Musical Theater*, 146–50.
4. Aaron Copland, *The New Music 1900–1960* (New York: W. W. Norton, 1968), 139–44.
5. Wilfrid Mellers, *Music and Society* (New York: Roy Publishers, 1950), 211–20.
6. Mellers, *Music in a New Found Land*, 415–28.
7. Gordon. Despite its length, Gordon's study does not include an analytical component. See also the following: Hunter; Dietz, "Operatic Style" and "Marc Blitzstein"; Shout; and Oja.
8. Gordon, 141–46. Blitzstein's account of the premiere was recorded on *Marc Blitzstein Discusses His Theater Compositions*, published as "Out of the Cradle," and reprinted posthumously in the *New York Times*. For other eye-witness accounts of the events surrounding the first performance see Archibald MacLeish, Introduction to *The Cradle Will Rock* (New York: Random House, 1938), Howard Da Silva's jacket notes for *The Cradle Will Rock*, MGM SE 4289-2-0C (1964), and especially Houseman, 255–79.
9. John Houseman notes the irony of Blitzstein's troubles with Musicians' Local #802, which demanded that an orchestra be paid to remain silent during *Cradle*'s run at the Windsor, a commercial Broadway theater. As Houseman explains, "For thirteen weeks, eight times a week, twelve union musicians with their instruments and a contractor-conductor with his baton arrived at the theater half an hour before curtain time, signed in and descended to the basement where they remained, engrossed in card games and the reading of newspapers, while their composer colleague exhausted himself at the piano upstairs." 336.
10. *The Cradle Will Rock* (New York: Random House, 1938) and *The Best Short Plays of the Social Theatre*, ed. William Kozlenko (New York: Random House, 1939), 113–67. A microfilm of the original Random House publication is included in the Blitzstein Papers of the Wisconsin State Historical Society.
11. *The Cradle Will Rock*, Musicraft, album 18 (recorded April 1938) (reissued in a limited edition on American Legacy Records, T 1001 [December 1964]).
12. Virgil Thomson, "In the Theatre," 113. The deus ex machina ending, so clearly reminiscent of Brecht and Weill's *The Threepenny Opera*, may have further prompted for Weill to ask, "Have you seen my new opera?" See Minna Lederman, "Memories of Marc Blitzstein, Music's Angry Man," *Show* (June 1964): 18+.
13. Brooks Atkinson, "Marc Blitzstein's 'The Cradle Will Rock' Officially Opens at the Mercury Theatre," *New York Times*, 6 December 1937, 19.
14. Edith J. R. Isaacs, "An Industry Without a Product—Broadway in Review, *Theatre Arts Monthly* 22 (February 1938): 99.
15. George Jean Nathan, "Theater," *Scribner's Magazine* 103 (March 1938): 71.
16. That's Entertainment Records ZC TED 1105.
17. In citing the German premiere in Recklinghausen (1984), the first *Cradle* performance in continental Europe, Gordon notes that Gershon Kinsley, the director and pianist of the 1964 production and recording, "rescored it for chamber ensemble, including synthesizer." Gordon, 539.
18. Blitzstein, "Case for Modern Music," 27.

19. Ibid.
20. Blitzstein, "Case for Modern Music, II," 29.
21. Ibid.
22. Blitzstein, "New York Medley, Winter, 1935," *Modern Music* 13/2 (January–February 1936): 36–37.
23. Blitzstein, "Case for Modern Music, II," 29.
24. Minna Lederman, *The Life and Death of a Small Magazine (Modern Music, 1924–1946),* I. S. A. M. Monograph, no. 18 (Brooklyn, N.Y.: Institute for Studies in American Music, 1983), 67.
25. Its published text and original conception called for the ten scenes to form an unbroken chain. Despte this, it became traditional to divide the work into two acts with a break after scene 6, a division observed in the Tams-Witmark Music Library rental score.
26. Blitzstein, "Author of 'The Cradle'," 7.
27. The quotation is taken from Brecht's essay "On the Use of Music in an Epic Theatre." See Willett 85.
28. Brecht explores these ideas in "The Modern Theatre is the Epic Theatre (Notes to the opera *Aufstieg und Fall der Stadt Mahagonny*)." See Willett, 33–42.
29. The "Croon–Spoon" portion of Scene Four is found in *The Cradle Will Rock* (New York: Random House, 1938), 52–58 (the piano-vocal score for this song is included) and Kozlenko, *The Best Short Plays,* 132–33.
30. The word "nerts," another expression for "nuts" (as in "crazy") was, like spoon, also used in the early 1900s. *The New Dictionary of American Slang,* ed. Robert L. Chapman (New York: Harper & Row, 1975), 298.
31. In the event that devotees of Bing Crosby (1901–1977), perhaps the best-remembered and best-loved crooner, are reading this note, it should be mentioned that Crosby (and many other crooners) did not share Junior's poor sense of pitch. Blitzstein might be indicting the content of Crosby's songs and the legion of Crosby epigones, but not crooners in general or Crosby in particular. In fact, Gordon notes that Blitzstein had considered Crosby for the film *Night Shift* (1942) and that several years later he gladly worked with the crooner on the American Broadcasting Station in Europe. Gordon, 216, 250, 274.
32. At the risk of further complicating this analysis, it should be noted that the F melodic center of Mister Mister's A sections is neither major nor minor but in the Lydian mode (F major with a raised fourth degree of the scale or B♮ instead of B♭). The harmonizations often do not clearly support the melodic implications.
33. The harmony here begins by alternating between E major (the key in which Daily began his second B section) and D minor. After considerable harmonic maneuvering it ends up with a strong cadence back to D minor and circles back to the vamp that introduced Mr. Mister's first *a* section.
34. Hitchcock, 226–27. The rocking "Hawaiian guitar" accompaniment also serves as a relaxed and understated version of the accompaniment heard earlier in "Let's Do Something."
35. *Cradle,* 87–96 and Kozlenko, *The Best Short Plays,* 141–46.
36. Max Unger, Notes to Beethoven's *Overture to Goethe's "Egmont"* (New York: Eulenburg, 1936), ii (with a musical illustration for this measure). It is tempting to speculate that Blitzstein had Thayer's interpretation (reiterated in Unger's notes) fresh on his mind. In any event the popular Eulenburg edition appeared the same year that Blitzstein wrote his *Cradle.*
37. *Cradle,* 96, and Kozlenko, *The Best Short Plays,* 145–46.
38. In his survey of Blitzstein's theatrical work through 1941 Robert Dietz notes three recurring ideas in the midst of *Cradle*'s otherwise autonomous ten scenes: the multiple appearance of the Moll's music (scenes 1, 2, 7, and 10); the reprise of the title song, first sung in scene 7, to conclude the work three scenes later; and an ominous three-chord

motive in the orchestra. This last motive first appears in scene 5 to underscore Bugs's explanation to Harry Druggist how an explosion will kill Gus and Sadie, and reappears in scene 9 when Mr. Mister explains to Dr. Specialist that Joe Hammer's "accident" was due to drunkenness. Dietz, Operatic Style," 297–98.

39. Only the Moll, however, will sing the musical line first given to dreams in scene 7 (and repeated with new words to conclude the next two stanzas): "Oh, you can dream and scheme / and happily put and take, take and put . . . / But first be sure / The nickel's under your foot."

40. Quotation in Kingman, 458. For a recent example of negative criticism based at least in part on Blitzstein's political agenda see Samuel Lipman, *Arguing for Music—Arguing for Culture* (Boston: David R. Godine, 1990), 157–63.

41. In his memorial tribute Copland wrote that "the taxi driver, the panhandler, the corner druggist were given voice for the first time in the context of serious musical drama. . . . No small accomplishment, for without it no truly indigenous opera is conceivable." Copland, "In Memory of Marc Blitzstein (1905–1964)," *Perspectives of New Music* 2/2 (Spring–Summer 1964): 6.

42. Perhaps alone among recent assessments is Hitchcock's, that "it was not so much the message as the music that was significant in Blitzstein's art." Hitchcock, 227.

Chapter 7: Lady in the Dark *and* One Touch of Venus

1. To cite two recent examples, Gerald Mast, in his otherwise comprehensive *Can't Help Singin'* (1987), offers neither an explanation nor an apology for his conspicuous neglect of Weill, while Joseph P. Swain in *The Broadway Musical* (1990), a more selective study, remains similarly silent about Weill's American works.

2. See especially Ronald Sanders's interpretation of *Lady in the Dark*'s genesis in Sanders, 292–309, and Scott. Less judgmental in this respect is Schebera.

3. David Drew, "Weill, Kurt (Julian)," *The New Grove Dictionary of Music and Musicians*, ed. Stanley Sadie (London: Macmillan, 1980), vol. 20, 300–10. The ensuing quotations from this article are found on pp. 305 and 307–8; for a more recent assessment by Drew see *Kurt Weill: A Handbook*, 45–47.

4. Scott.

5. Engel, *American Musical Theater*, 61.

6. Robert Garland, "Mary Martin, John Boles, Kenny Baker Head Cast of New Comedy," *New York Journal-American*, 8 October 1943; quoted in Suskin, 525; reprinted in *New York Theatre Critics' Reviews*, vol. 4, 264.

7. Letter from Weill to Ira Gershwin, 27 February 1944, Music Division, Library of Congress.

8. Kurt Weill, Notes for the original cast recording of *Street Scene* (Columbia OL 4139).

9. Ibid. See also Larry Stempel, "*Street Scene*," 321–41.

10. Weill, Notes.

11. Ibid.

12. Letter from Weill to Ira Gershwin, 13 April 1944, Music Division, Library of Congress. Mast also perceives second-act weaknesses in Rodgers and Hammerstein musicals. See Mast, 204–5.

13. Letter to Ira Gershwin, 13 April 1944.

14. Malcolm Goldstein, *George S. Kaufman: His Life, His Theater* (New York: Oxford University Press, 1979), 343.

15. See Arlene Croce, *The Fred Astaire & Ginger Rogers Book* (New York: Vintage Books, 1972), 142, 144, and 146 on Ginger Rogers's film roles as women who cannot make up their minds (including the 1944 Paramount film version of *Lady in the Dark*). The idea of a future Mr. Right being able to complete a "dream" song is at least as old as Victor Herbert's "Ah, Sweet Mystery of Life" from *Naughty Marietta* (1910).

16. F. Anstey, *Humour & Fantasy* (New York: Arno Press, 1978), 288–468.
17. Crawford herself credits stage designer Aline Bernstein, who remains unindexed in the standard biographies of Weill; Ronald Sanders (who used Crawford as his major souce for the genesis of *One Touch of Venus*) attributes this suggestion to *Lady in the Dark* costume designer Irene Sharaff. Both Crawford and Sanders offer a date, the former in June 1942 and the latter November 1941. David Drew writes that "in February 1942 *The Tinted Venus* headed a list of fifteen possibilities he [Weill] was considering for Cheryl Crawford." C. Crawford, 116; Sanders, 322; and Drew, *Kurt Weill: A Handbook*, 328. See also Dorothy Herrmann, *S. J. Perelman: A Life* (New York: G. P. Putnam's Sons, 1986), 147.
18. Perelman had, however, contributed sketches to other Broadway revues beginning in 1931. Douglas Fowler, *S. J. Perelman* (Boston: Twayne, 1983).
19. C. Crawford, 121.
20. The role of Venus, originally intended for Marlene Dietrich, was Mary Martin's first starring Broadway role. After answering more than tentatively in the affirmative, Dietrich backed down from playing the sexy Venus, allegedly for the sake of her impressionable nineteen-year-old daughter. Martin, now mainly known from later roles as the wholesome Nellie Forbush (*South Pacific*) and Maria Rainer (*The Sound of Music*), earlier in her career had proven her sexual allure in Porter's "My Heart Belongs to Daddy" in *Leave It To Me* (1938).
21. Crawford and Kazan had also worked together on Weill's *Johnny Johnson* as producer and actor, respectively. Crawford continued to produce musicals, most notably Lerner and Weill's *Love Life* and Lerner and Loewe's *Brigadoon* (also with de Mille) and *Paint Your Wagon*; Kazan left musicals for theater and films after directing *Venus* and *Love Life*. According to Gerald Bordman, Kazan "was the most important American director of the late 1940s and the 1950s." Bordman, *Oxford Companion*, 394.
22. Virgil Thomson, "Plays With Music," *New York Herald Tribune*, 23 February 1941. Barlow writes the following about *Lady in the Dark*: "In this long score, there are not three minutes of the true Weill. And in this new medium, this new life, this new success, the promise has been buried under a branch of expensive but imitation laurel." Samuel L. M. Barlow, "In the Theatre," *Modern Music* 8/3 (March–April 1941): 189–93.
23. The *Lady in the Dark* playbill also included other highly distinguished collaborators: Sam H. Harris, who had earlier produced fifteen Cohan musicals, seven Berlin shows, the Gershwins' *Of Thee I Sing*, Porter's *Jubilee*, and Rodgers and Hart's *I'd Rather Be Right*; Hassard Short, director of production, lighting, and musical sequences, who had designed illustrious shows for two decades, including *The Band Wagon*, *Roberta*, and *Jubilee*; and Albertina Rasch, the choreographer of *The Band Wagon*, *The Cat and the Fiddle*, and *Jubilee*.
24. C. Crawford, 135.
25. Ibid., 138.
26. See mcclung, *"Psicosi per musica."* I am grateful to Mr. mcclung for sharing a typescript of this essay prior to its publication. See also mcclung, "American Dreams: Analyzing Moss Hart, Ira Gershwin, and Kurt Weill's *Lady in the Dark*," (Ph.D. diss., Eastman School of Music, University of Rochester, 1994).
27. Also until much later, Whitelaw Savory would sing the beautiful "Love in a Mist" in the place later reserved for "Westwind." "Love in a Mist" can be heard in *Ben Bagley's Kurt Weill Revisited Vol. II* (Painted Smiles PSCD 109).
28. Another song, "Who Am I?," which Savory sang in his bedroom early in act II before being surprised by the angry Anatolian Zuvetli, was also dropped after Weill had orchestrated it.
29. The typescript of *I Am Listening* is located at the State Historical Society in Madison, Wisconsin. The Weill-Gershwin correspondence and other Ira Gershwin documents are housed in the Music Division of the Library of Congress, and Weill's musical manuscripts are housed at Yale University. Copies of all Hart, Gershwin, and Weill materials for *Lady*

in the Dark are available for study at the Kurt Weill Foundation for Music in New York. I am grateful to all of the above institutions for making these materials accessible to me, especially Harold L. Miller (State Historical Society), Raymond A. White (Library of Congress), Victor Cardell and Kendall Crilly (Yale), and David Farneth (Kurt Weill Foundation). Thanks are also due to Tom Briggs of the Rodgers and Hammerstein Theatre Library for enabling me to examine the full orchestral score of *Lady in the Dark.*

30. Letter from Weill to Ira Gershwin, 2 September 1940, Music Division, Library of Congress.

31. Ibid.

32. Letter from Weill to Ira Gershwin, 14 September 1940, Music Division, Library of Congress. Since they had cut the Hollywood Dream (but not the Hollywood sequence) and Randy Curtis now had nothing to sing in the second act, all concerned were eager to have this character sing something. The problems with all of Curtis's music, however, stemmed from the disturbing discovery about the man they had cast in this role, Victor Mature. As Ira Gershwin expressed it in *Lyrics on Several Occasions,* "when handsome 'hunk of man' Mature sang, his heart and the correct key weren't in it" (144).

33. Ira Gershwin annotations (September 1967) to "The Third Dream Sequence Section 1," Music Division, Library of Congress; and *Lyrics on Several Occasions,* 207–8; reprinted in Kimball, ed., *Complete Lyrics of Ira Gershwin,* 291–92.

34. Gershwin annotations to "The Third Dream Sequence Section 2."

35. Ibid. In his annotations of November 3, 1967, appended to the texts for "Three Discarded Songs," Gershwin briefly explains their originally intended place in the show. "Unforgettable," recorded as "You are Unforgettable" on *Ben Bagley's Kurt Weill Revisited* (Painted Smiles PSCD 108) and "It's Never Too Late to Mendelssohn" were deleted from the second dream (some of the lyrics of the latter were retained). "Bats About You" "was written for a flash-back scene and supposedly was a song of the late Twenties, sung at a Mapleton High School graduation Dance." In *Kurt Weill: A Handbook,* Drew lists "Bats About You" and "You are Unforgettable" under unlocated songs.

36. I. Gershwin, *Lyrics on Several Occasions,* 187. Arthur and Francis were the given names of George and Ira's lesser-known younger siblings. The conclusion of the Wedding Dream (including the Mendelssohn Endelssohn and Lohengrin and Bear It material) is borrowed from another wedding song, "Bride and Groom," in the act I finale of Ira's collaboration with his brother George, *Oh, Kay!* (1926), starring Lawrence as Lady Kay.

37. Drew, *Kurt Weill: A Handbook,* 274. See also Drew, "Reflections," especially 243–48.

38. Drew, *Kurt Weill: A Handbook,* 220.

39. Michael Morley offers a possible "common denominator" between "In der Jugend Gold'nem Schimmer" and its reincarnations in *Marie Galante* and *One Touch of Venus.* See Morley, " 'I Cannot/Will Not Sing the Old Songs Now' ": Some Observations on Weill's Adaptation of Popular Song Forms," in Kowalke and Edler, 221.

40. Kowalke, *Kurt Weill,* 117.

41. Originally published as "Über den gestischen Charakter der Musik." Weill's article is translated by Kim H. Kowalke in *Kurt Weill,* 491–93 (the quotations in this paragraph are found on p. 493).

42. Ibid., 493.

43. Ibid., 494. The remaining quotations from Weill's essay are also found on this page.

44. Kowalke, *Kurt Weill,* 113–23.

45. *The New Harvard Dictionary of Music* defines the doctrine of affections as "the belief, widely held in the 17th and early 18th centuries, that the principal aim of music is to arouse the passions or affections (love, hate, joy, anger, fear, etc., conceived as rationalized, discrete, and relatively static states)." Don Randel, ed., *The New Harvard Dictionary of Music* (Cambridge, Mass.: Harvard University Press, 1986), 16.

46. mcclung, *"Psicosi per musica,"* 53–54.

47. Weill's self-borrowings parallel the controversial self-borrowings of Handel. See George

J. Buelow, "The Case for Handel's Borrowings: the Judgment of Three Centuries," in *Handel: Tercentenary Collection,* ed. Stanley Sadie and Anthony Hicks (Ann Arbor, Mich.: UMI Research Press, 1987), 61–82.

48. Lewis Nichols, " 'One Touch of Venus,' Which Makes the Whole World Kin, Opens At the Imperial," *New York Times,* 8 October 1943; review excerpted in Suskin, 526; reprinted in *New York Theatre Critics' Reviews,* vol 4, 264.

49. "September Song" from *Knickerbocker Holiday,* "My Ship" from *Lady in the Dark,* "Speak Low" from *One Touch of Venus,* "Green-Up Time" from *Love Life,* and the title song from *Lost in the Stars* are perhaps the best known song legacies from Weill's otherwise currently little-known Broadway shows.

50. Weill, Notes.

51. Ibid.

52. Ibid.

53. Rodgers explains his ideas about dramatic unity in *Chee-Chee* (1928) in his autobiography, *Musical Stages,* 118 (see also chapter 5, p. 87). Larry Stempel notes Rodgers's early attempt at an integrated musical and adds Hammerstein's *Rose-Marie* (1924) to the short list of integrated 1920s musicals (see Stempel, "*Street Scene,*" 324).

54. King.

55. In Bob Fosse's 1972 acclaimed film adaptation of the Weill-influenced *Cabaret* (1966), for example, the songs that took place outside the Kit Kat Club on Broadway were mostly removed, an artistic decision which deprived the central male character the inalienable right of any central character in a musical: the right to sing.

56. *Lady in the Dark* (Chappell, 1941). Hart dates his remarks March 18, 1941.

57. mcclung, "*Psicosi per musica,*" 242–45.

58. Ibid., 250–63.

59. Howard Barnes of the *New York Herald Tribune,* October 17, 1943, wrote that *Venus* was "the first integrated and joyous entertainment of the current theatrical semester."

60. Stanley Richards, ed., *Great Musicals of the American Theatre* (Radnor, Pa: Chilton Book Company), 128.

61. The subject of quarter-note (and half-note) triplets is introduced in the musical discussion of *Anything Goes* (see chapter 3, pp. 55–57).

62. Richards, *Great Musicals of the American Theatre,* 129.

63. Thanks to Robert M. Stevenson, Professor Emeritus at the University of California at Los Angeles, for this inspired simile.

64. Richards, *Great Musicals of the American Theatre,* 158.

65. Stanley Richards, ed., *Great Musicals of the American Theatre Volume 2* (Radnor, Pa.: Chilton Book Company, 1976), 98.

66. Ibid., 82.

67. Ibid., 79.

68. When Danny Kaye left the show and his role as Russell Paxton, his replacement proved difficult. Within two weeks after Gershwin wrote Weill that Rex O'Malley "is too lady-like for the lady-like characters and may make the character far too realistic," the production staff bought out his contract. See the letter from Ira Gershwin to Kurt Weill, 23 August 1941, Music Division, Library of Congress.

69. Richards, *Great Musicals of the Musical Theatre,* 157.

Chapter 8: Carousel

1. *New York Post,* 23 October 1944; cited in Frederick Nolan, *The Sound of Their Music: The Story of Rodgers and Hammerstein* (New York: Walker, 1978), 128. For the Gershwin reference see Rodgers, 238; for the Weill reference see Kowalke, "Formerly German," 50.

2. Oscar Hammerstein II, "Turns on a Carousel," *New York Times,* 15 April 1945, sec. 2, 1 and Rodgers, 238.

3. Ewen, *Richard Rodgers,* 236–37. Hammerstein also recalled that Molnár made a "valuable suggestion" during the New Haven tryouts, "which involved playing two scenes in one set—actually a more radical departure from the original than any change we had made" and "proved successful in pulling together a very long second act." See Hammerstein, "Turns on a Carousel," 1.

4. Norton, 80. Ewen credits Mamoulian for removing Mr. and Mrs. God from their New England living room and replacing them with a Starkeeper. Ewen, *Richard Rodgers,* 236.

5. "Guild Scores Again With Its 'Carousel'," *New York World-Telegram,* 20 April 1945; review excerpted in Suskin, 147; reprinted in *New York Theatre Critics' Reviews,* vol. 6, 226.

6. Ward Morehouse, " 'Carousel', Beguiling Musical Play With Lovely Score, Opens at Majestic," *New York Sun,* 20 April 1945; reprinted in *New York Theatre Critics' Reviews,* vol. 6, 226–27.

7. John Chapman, " 'Carousel' Is a Lovely, Touching Musical Drama Based on 'Liliom'," *Daily News,* 20 April 1945; quoted in Suskin, 144; reprinted in *New York Theatre Critics' Reviews,* vol. 6, 228.

8. Robert Garland, " 'Carousel' Makes Bow At Majestic Theatre," *New York Journal-American,* 20 April 1945; quoted in Suskin, 146; reprinted in *New York Theatre Critics' Reviews,* vol. 6, 227.

9. Brooks Atkinson, "The Theatre: 'Carousel'," *New York Times,* 3 June 1954, 32.

10. Rodgers, 243.

11. For another interpretation of the relationship between music and drama in *Carousel* see Larry Stempel's comparison between the aria "Somehow I Never Could Believe" from Weill's *Street Scene* and Billy's "Soliloquy." Stempel observes that Hammerstein's words and not Rodgers's music "indicate the basic emotional change he [Billy Bigelow] undergoes in thinking about being a father." "*Street Scene,*" 327.

12. Kern's shrewd decision to use Magnolia's piano theme for the release of Ravenal's song "Where's the Mate for Me?" (Example 2.4) lets audiences know immediately that Magnolia has entered Ravenal's consciousness and foreshadows their eventual union. At the end of Ravenal's song Magnolia appears as if in answer to the question posed in the song's title, and Ravenal is unable to complete his final words, "for me." After some underscored dialogue Ravenal admits within the song "Make Believe" that his love for Magnolia is not a pretense but a reality ("For, to tell the truth, I do"). Versions of *Show Boat* differ on whether or not Magnolia actually says the magic words "I do" at the conclusion of their duet, but no one in the audience can seriously doubt that after "Make Believe" her love for Ravenal is the real thing.

13. *Six Plays by Rodgers and Hammerstein* (New York: The Modern Library Association, 1959), 161–62.

14. Ibid., 176.

15. Ibid., 100.

16. Although the published vocal score (Williamson Music Co.) lists the scene between Julie and Billy as act I, scene 1 (following the pantomimed Prelude), the published libretto identifies the scene as act I, scene 2. See *Six Plays.*

17. Ibid., 93–94.

18. Quotation in Rodgers, 236. *State Fair* was released in August 1945, several months after the opening of *Carousel.*

19. Ibid.

20. The words "dozens of boys," "many a likely," "does what he can," "she has a few," and "fellers of two" also display these untied and metrically neutral eighth-note triplets. During the opening thoughts in the "Soliloquy" (when Billy imagines that he will be having a son), he sings metrically challenging quarter-note triplets tied to quarter notes (e.g.,

"The old man!" and "Of his Dad"). See the introduction of the quarter-note triplet in chapter 3, 55–57.

The eighth-note triplets that Billy and Julie sing do not go against the metrical grain as Reno Sweeney's half-note triplets do in "I Get a Kick Out of You" (the bracketed words and syllables in "Mere al-co-[hol doesn't thrill me at] all, / so [tell me why should it be] true" and Example 3.1a). Nevertheless, they do help to establish a distinct and slightly askew rhythmic plane (especially when preceded by ties in "If I Loved You"), just as Billy and Julie try unsuccessfully to thwart society's expectations. Four measures of triplets appear in succession in Billy's "Soliloquy" (in duple meter) on the words that describe the future Billy Jr. and Billy himself: "No pot-bellied, baggy-eyed bully'll boss him a round" (in Example 8.4a), later with the words, "No fat bottomed, flabby-faced, pot-bellied, baggy-eyed bastard'll boss him around."

21. David Ewen writes that the *Carousel* waltzes were taken from a work called *Waltz Suite* that Paul Whiteman had commissioned but never performed (Ewen, *Richard Rodgers,* 239). Rodgers, who in his autobiography recalls two other associations with Whiteman in 1935 and 1936, is silent on this point.

22. "Two Little People" does not appear as a separate title in the vocal score (Williamson Music Co., 43–47), but Hammerstein does so title this music in his *Lyrics,* 142. Also in *Lyrics* Hammerstein includes a stanza that does not appear in the published vocal score: "There's a feathery little cloud floatin' by / Like a lonely leaf on a big blue stream. / And two people—you and I—/ Who cares what we dream?" Hammerstein's stanza does appear, however, in the holograph manuscript in the Music Division of the Library of Congress where it is sung by Julie to music that is altered only on the words, "leaf on a big blue stream" (g-f-e♭-d-c-d). In his holograph score Rodgers entered a sketch labelled "2 little people" that does not correspond either to Hammerstein's text or to Rodgers's final version.

23. Aside from Julie's complementary stanza discussed in the previous note, the only major changes between Rodgers's holograph and the published vocal score are those of key and the absence of dotted rhythms in the D major sketch. Not only does Rodgers place "If I Loved You" in C Major in the holograph, he places the first page of "Scene Billy and Julie" in F♯ major and G major instead of G Major and A♭ major, 33; he also assigns the "mill theme" (Example 8.1) to D major in both of its appearances rather than G major and E♭ major as in the published score, 38–39 and 47–48 respectively.

24. The idea of retaining an accompaniment figure for the sake of musical unity rather than for a demonstrable dramatic purpose was earlier evident in *On Your Toes* ("There's a Small Hotel" and the principal tune of "Slaughter on 10th Avenue"). See chapter 5, pp. 101–2.

25. When in act II Carrie imitates one of the "hussies with nothin' on their legs but tights" that she saw in New York, her music also clearly echoes the music associated with Julie's name ("You're a queer one, Julie Jordan") that Carrie introduced early in act I ("I'm a Tomboy, jest a Tomboy"). Appropriately, the stage directions indicate that "Mr. Snow enters with Snow Jr. and interrupts song."

26. Howard Kissel, "*Carousel* is Music to Our Tears," *Daily News,* 28 March 1994; reprinted in *New York Theatre Critics' Reviews,* vol. 55, 6.

27. Frank Scheck, "Sharp New Staging Gives a Lift to Rodgers and Hammerstein," *Christian Science Monitor,* 25 March 1994; reprinted *New York Theatre Critics' Reviews,* vol. 55, 72.

28. This quotation was Boswell's adaptation of the medieval dictum, also appropriate in this context, "to cite heresy is not to be a heretic." John Boswell, *Christianity, Social Tolerance, and Homosexuality* (Chicago: University of Chicago Press, 1980), xvii.

29. Edwin Wilson, "The Music Makes It Soar," *Wall Street Journal,* 28 March 1994; reprinted in *New York Theatre Critics' Reviews,* vol. 55, 76.

30. Rodgers, 156.

31. Ibid., 236.
32. Joseph P. Swain discusses how augmented triads and modality also serve to establish an individual character and identity for *Carousel*. See Swain, 99–127.
33. *I Remember Mama* was based on the first play that Rodgers and Hammerstein produced on Broadway, John Van Druten's hit play of the same title, which opened its long run of 714 performances in 1944. In 1967 Rodgers wrote eight songs for a televised adaptation of Shaw's *Androcles and the Lion* that featured Norman Wisdom as Androcles, Geoffrey Holder as the Lion, and Noël Coward as Caesar.
34. Perhaps the least known of their adaptations, *Pipe Dream* (1955), based on John Steinbeck's *Sweet Thursday*, ended up as their major disappointment; despite an enthusiastic review from Brooks Atkinson in the *New York Times*, it ran only 246 performances, less than either *Allegro* (315) or *Me and Juliet* (358). Their final musicals, both adaptations, produced one modest success, *Flower Drum Song* in 1958 (600 performances), and their fifth major hit, *The Sound of Music* in 1959, at 1,443 performances the second-longest-running musical of the 1950s and the fourth-longest-running show before 1960. In addition to these stage shows Rodgers and Hammerstein wrote *Cinderella*, a ninety-minute musical for television starring Julie Andrews broadcast on March 31, 1957; a remake starring Lesley Ann Warren was broadcast on February 22, 1965.

Chapter 9: Kiss Me, Kate

1. According to Steven Suskin's "Broadway Scorecard," *Kiss Me, Kate* received eight "raves" and one "favorable" review and no reviews in the lower categories ("mixed," "unfavorable," and "pan"). See Suskin, 367. Of the musicals surveyed in this book only *Guys and Dolls* and *My Fair Lady* would receive no reviews lower than a "rave."
2. S. Green, *World of Musical Comedy*, 156. The first sentence of the Porter quotation appears in Hubler, *The Cole Porter Story*, 90; in the annotated Hubler interview Porter goes on to say without further explanation that Rodgers and Hammerstein "are, let us say, more musicianly."
3. The only known commodity in the *Kiss Me, Kate* cast was Alfred Drake (Fred Graham/ Petruchio), who had earlier achieved stardom as the original Curley in *Oklahoma!*
4. Eells, 279.
5. The Porter Collection also contains sketch material, the May libretto, and copies of the discarded songs.
6. *Kiss Me, Kate*, "Unfinished Lyrics," ("Bianca"), in the Cole Porter Collection, Music Division, Library of Congress. See also Citron, *Noel and Cole*, 218.
7. Eells, 239.
8. This book will be referred to as the Spewack libretto draft or the May libretto.
9. Eells, 248–49.
10. Citron cites addition borrowings "from native Italian dances, especially the Venetian boat song, and the canzones of Sorrento" in "Where Is the Life That Late I Led?" Joseph P. Swain mentions the use of the modal flat seventh degree, a typical melodic figure in Renaissance music (e.g., B♭ in the key of C) rather than the more tonal B♮ that marks most European music after 1600). See Citron, 307, and Swain, 133–34.
11. Citron notes another possible musical pun in the verse of "Where Is the The Life That Late I Led?": "And one cannot overlook Porter's use of the Neapolitan sixth chord 3 bars before the verse's end. Was Cole pulling our leg?" Citron, 309.
12. According to Swain, the Baltimore songs "have no structural consistency, and show instead Porter's vaunted and bewildering eclecticism." Swain, 138.
13. Perfect fourths also begin nearly every musical phrase in "Tom, Dick or Harry" and appear prominently in the finale to act I (see the vocal score published by Tams-Witmark, 118–20).

14. Among Porter's drafts are a "minuet" version labelled "Bianca's Theme," an eighteenth-century dance that would soon give way to Lois's song "Why Can't You Behave?" in act I and its transformation into a Renaissance pavane for Bianca in act II (Example 9.4). Several labelled drafts in piano score also reveal that Porter abandoned an earlier idea to characterize Petruchio and Katherine with musical signatures.

15. "I Sing of Love" was excluded from both the original cast album issued in 1949 and its stereo rerecording (with most of the original principals) ten years later. See Discography.

16. In the act II finale Porter returns to a guitar-like accompaniment (rather than a lute-like accompaniment as befits the Renaissance) that is similar to his first serenade to Kate in "Were Thine That Special Face," now altered to triple meter.

17. The consistency with which Porter tried to create musical linkages among the songs is further demonstrated in at least four songs that were removed before the Broadway opening. In "It Was Great Fun the First Time" Porter presents a melody that will anticipate the distinctive melodic figure with its turn to minor that will appear in "I Sing of Love" and "Where Is the Life?"; another phrase in the song foreshadows the verse of "Bianca" (at that point probably unwritten). "We Shall Never Be Younger" exhibits an emphasis on perfect fourths suggestive of "Another Op'nin" and "Why Can't You Behave?," and a phrase in "A Woman's Career" closely resembles a phrase in "Too Darn Hot" without any particular dramatic justification. Finally, the discarded "What Does Your Servant Dream About?", also with many perfect fourths, opens with a vamp that is nearly identical to the conclusion of "I've Come to Wive It Wealthily in Padua."

18. Spewack, xiii.

19. Ibid., xiii-xiv.

20. Eells, 248.

21. "Patricia Morison and Miles Kreuger Discuss the Deleted Songs July 5, 1990," Notes to *Kiss Me, Kate*, conducted by John McGlinn (EMI/Angel CDS 54033-2), 15.

22. Neither Spewack nor Eells has anything to say about the history of the two other songs that Porter added between June and November: "So In Love" and "I Hate Men." The only dated typescript of "I Hate Men" shows the late date November 18.

23. These Shakespeare passages can be found in the final scene of the May libretto, act II, scene 7.

24. Morison had the following recollection: "In the scripts that were given to me by Bella Spewack, the song ["A Woman's Career"] is performed by a character named Angela Temple, a friend and confidant of Lilli Vanessi" (Notes to *Kiss Me, Kate*, 15). In the May Spewack libretto, however, "A Woman's Career" was to be sung by Fred Graham to conclude act II, scene 5.

25. May libretto, act II, scene 6.

26. Morison interview, Notes to *Kiss Me, Kate*, 15. Robert Kimball writes that " 'So In Love' appears to have been composed as late as September 1948." Kimball, *Complete Lyrics of Cole Porter*, 399.

27. Eells, 244.

28. In addition to "It Was Great Fun the First Time" and "We Shall Never Be Younger," the May libretto included two other songs that would be dropped: "If Ever Married I'm" (sung by Bianca in act I, scene 7), and "A Woman's Career" (sung by Fred in act II, scene 5). Another two songs, also discarded before the Philadelphia tryouts, were probably introduced after the May libretto.

The first of these, "What Does Your Servant Dream About?" can be placed quite accurately, since Porter's draft indicated "Opening Act 2, Scene 3," and "Curtis and Lackeys." No such indication occurs in the May libretto, although Curtis and other servants do appear in the opening of the scene to the accompaniment of "Where Is the Life?" A Porter lyric typescript for "What Does Your Servant Dream About?" is dated July 10.

The chronology and placement of the other later addition (also soon to be deleted),

"I'm Afraid, Sweetheart, I Love You," is less clear, since neither Porter nor the Spewacks offer clues as to who should be singing this song and where. Presumably this song, too, came and went between June and November, perhaps around the time of Porter's August 7 typescript copy.

Lyrics to all of these songs are reprinted in *The Complete Lyrics of Cole Porter* and are included in John McGlinn's first complete recording of *Kiss Me, Kate* issued in 1990. Unfortunately, several of Morison's recollections (for example that "It Was Great Fun the First Time" and "If Ever Married I'm" were replaced by "Wunderbar" and "Tom, Dick or Harry" respectively) are at odds with the information provided by the May libretto. See note 17 for a summary of the musical similarities between the discarded songs and those retained.

29. The reprise of "E lucevan le stelle" in act III of Puccini's *Tosca*, an opera notoriously described by Kerman as a "shabby little shocker," offers a more publicized example of a similar problem. As Kerman wrote: "Tosca leaps, and the orchestra screams the first thing that comes into its head, 'E lucevan le stelle.' How pointless this is, compared with the return of the music for the kiss at the analogous place in *Otello*, which makes Verdi's dramatic point with a consummate sense of dramatic form. . . . 'E lucevan le stelle' is all about self-pity; Tosca herself never heard it. . . ." Kerman, 15.

Although Kerman's overall assessment of *Tosca*'s artistic worth has not gone unchallenged, even sympathetic Puccini scholars such as Roger Parker and Mosco Carner understand Kerman's "exasperation." Like Kerman, Parker concludes that "the theme is that of Cavaradossi's soliloquy earlier in the third act; Tosca has had no opportunity to hear it; what we see and what we hear seem out of joint." Roger Parker, "Analysis: Act I in perspective," in Mosco Carner, *Giacomo Puccini: "Tosca"* (Cambridge: Cambridge University Press, 1985), 138.

30. The terms "theatrical truth" and "literal truth" are used by Sondheim in his assessment in 1985 of the most effective placement of "Gee, Officer Krupke" in *West Side Story*. Guernsey, *Broadway Song & Story*, 50.

31. In adopting Shakespeare, Porter first uses the eight lines that begin with "I am ashamed that women are so simple" and ends with "should well agree with our external parts." He then replaces Shakespeare's "Then vail your stomachs, for it is no boot, / And place your hands below your husband's foot" with "So wife, hold your temper and meekly put / Your hand 'neath the sole of your husband's foot." Porter's final two lines agree with Shakespeare's external rhymes (although the composer adds a second "ready" in the last line).

32. Bernard Shaw, *Dramatic Opinions and Essays with an Apology* (New York: Brentano's, 1928), vol. 2, 364.

33. Robert B. Heilman, "The Taming Untamed, or the Return of the Shrew," *Modern Language Quarterly* 27 (June 1966): 159.

34. "The Remaking of the Canon," *Partisan Review* 58 (1991): 380.

35. Germaine Greer, *The Female Eunuch* (New York: McGraw-Hill, 1971), 206.

36. Martha Andresen-Thom, "Shrew-taming and other rituals of aggression: Baiting and bonding on the stage and in the wild," in *Women's Studies* 9 (1982): 121–43; quotation on 141.

37. I am indebted to my colleague Peter Greenfield, Professor of English at the University of Puget Sound, for pointing out the "play" interpretation.

38. See, for example, Catherine Clement's feminist indictment of the operatic tradition, *Opera, or the Undoing of Women* (Minneapolis: University of Minnesota Press, 1988), and Susan McClary, *Feminine Endings* (Minneapolis: University of Minnesota Press, 1991).

Chapter 10: Guys and Dolls *and* The Most Happy Fella

1. This last Broadway revival of *The Most Happy Fella* was again upstaged in the Best Revival category by the splashier and fully orchestrated revival of *Guys and Dolls* (the *Fella* revival offered only two pianos).
2. See Block, "Frank Loesser's Sketchbooks," and Stempel, "Musical Play Expands."
3. For profiles of Loesser's early career see Arthur Loesser, "My Brother Frank," *Notes* 7 (March 1950): 217–39 and Ewen, "He Passes the Ammunition."
4. Styne's *High Button Shoes* (1947) and *Gentlemen Prefer Blondes* (1949) and Lane's *Finian's Rainbow* (1947) were the earliest successes of these prominent Broadway composers.
5. Suskin, 275.
6. In his notes to the 1958 original London cast recording of *Where's Charley?*, Stanley Green noted that "at the time of its closing, its 792 performances made it the tenth longest-running musical in Broadway history" (Monmouth-Evergreen MES/7029).
7. Suskin, 275.
8. John McClain, "The Best Thing Since 'Pal Joey'," *New York Journal-American*, 25 November 1950; quoted in Suskin, 274; reprinted *New York Theatre Critics' Reviews*, vol. 11, 186.
9. Burrows. For additional material on the genesis of *Guys and Dolls* see Mann, 67–87.
10. Burrows, 41.
11. On June 29, 1994 this production became the longest-running revival in Broadway history.
12. William Kennedy, "The Runyonland Express Is Back in Town," *New York Times*, 12 April 1992, sec. 2, 1 and 26, and Jo Swerling, Jr., "Abe Burrows: Undue Credit?", *New York Times*, 3 May 1992, sec. 2, 4 (with a response from William Kennedy). Those familiar with the machinations of Hollywood screenplays will recognize the terms of Swerling's contract which allowed him to receive primary credit as the libretto's author, even if none of his work was used. It is difficult to credit the notion espoused by Swerling's son that Feuer, Martin, and stage manager Henri Caubisens conspired with Burrows to diminish Swerling's role in the *Guys and Dolls* drama. Burrows's account is also corroborated in S. Loesser, 101–2.
13. Burrows, 44.
14. Ibid, 47.
15. The quasi-triplets created by two groups of three eighth notes (in $\frac{6}{8}$ time) also pervade Adelaide's admonishment of Nathan in "Sue Me."
16. Late in the show when Sarah sings her duet with Adelaide, "Marry the Man Today," her evolution is complete and triplets (albeit of the common eighth-note variety) become the dominant rhythm.
17. Tonic (4 measures), dominant (2 measures), tonic (6 measures), dominant (2 measures), and tonic (1 measure).
18. A leading Italian bass at La Scala (1921–24) and the Metropolitan Opera (1926–1948) Pinza was introduced in chapter 8 as the first internationally known opera singer to star on Broadway (*South Pacific* [1949]).
19. Another song intended to feature Nathan and Sky, "Travelin' Light," was one of several songs dropped from the show. It is included in *An Evening with Frank Loesser: Frank Loesser Performs Songs from His Hit Shows* (DRG 5169).
20. F. Loesser, "Some Notes."
21. Ironically, one of these new songs, "Adelaide," was given to Nathan, played by Frank Sinatra.
22. Block, "Frank Loesser's Sketchbooks."
23. Loesser Collection, Music Division, New York Public Library, 3129–30.
24. Ibid., 2842. This undated sketch page is found sandwiched between other pages dated December 1953.
25. "Abbondanza" sketches (first sketched as "The Helps"), unlike the sketches for "Lovers

in the Lane," were dated precisely by Loesser in December 1953. Ibid., 2851 and 2859–62.

26. Ibid., 3006–07.
27. F. Loesser, "Some Loesser Thoughts."
28. Ibid. Loesser expresses the same sentiment in "Some Notes on a Musical."
29. F. Loesser, "Some Loesser Thoughts."
30. Abe Burrows, "Frank Loesser 1910–1969," *New York Times,* 10 August 1969, sec. 2, 3.
31. The phrase "Greater Loesser" in the present chapter title is borrowed from a *New York Times Magazine* profile by Gilbert Millstein, 20 May 1956.
32. Robert Coleman, " 'Most Happy Fella' Is a Masterpiece," *Daily Mirror,* 4 May 1956; review excerpted in Suskin, 455; reprinted in *New York Theatre Critics' Reviews,* vol. 17, 310.
33. John McClain, "This Musical Is Great," *New York Journal-American,* 4 May 1956; review excerpted in Suskin, 455–56; reprinted in *New York Theatre Critics' Reviews,* vol. 17, 310.
34. Walter F. Kerr, " 'The Most Happy Fella'," *New York Herald Tribune,* 4 May 1956; quoted in Suskin, 455; reprinted in *New York Theatre Critics' Reviews,* vol. 17, 308.
35. Richard Watts, Jr., "Arrival of 'The Most Happy Fella'," *New York Post,* 4 May 1956; reprinted in *New York Theatre Critics' Reviews,* vol. 17, 308.
36. George Jean Nathan, "Theatre Week: Fish nor Foul," *New York Journal-American,* 9 May 1956, 16.
37. Brooks Atkinson, "Theatre: Loesser's Fine Music Drama," *New York Times,* 4 May 1956, 20; reprinted in *New York Theatre Critics's Reviews* vol. 17, 311.
38. Howard Taubman, "Broadway Musical: Trend Toward Ambitious Use of Music Exemplified by 'Most Happy Fella'," *New York Times,* 10 June 1956, sec. 2, 7.
39. Osborne.
40. Ibid., 5.
41. Ibid.
41. Ibid., 17.
43. According to Abba Bogin, Loesser's musical assistant and rehearsal pianist in *Fella* and a reliable source of practical and anecdotal information, "Ooh! My Feet" was originally intended for Lieutenant Branigan in *Guys and Dolls*. See Block, "Frank Loesser's Sketchbooks," 77–78.
44. Loesser Collection, 3004. A transcription of this "Big D" draft appears in Block, "Frank Loesser's Sketchbooks," 65.
45. Loesser Collection, 2794, 2811, 2857–58, 2900–01, and 2915.
46. F. Loesser, "Some Loesser Thoughts."
47. In the previous chapter it was suggested that Porter deprived *Kiss Me, Kate* of dramatic nuance when he departed from his conceit that the Padua songs would distinguish themselves from the Baltimore songs through contrasting statements in the major and minor modes.
48. Vocal score and libretto (New York: Frank Music, 1956, 1957), 67.
49. Sometimes Loesser's melodic manipulations can be subtle to the point of inaudibility for most listeners. For example, a transformed version of the "Tony" motive (the seconds have now been inverted to become sevenths) can be detected during the final moments of act I, when Rosabella "overcomes her resistance" and willingly accepts Joe's sexual advances. During the course of their kiss the "Tony" motive returns to the "sighing" seconds that underscored Tony's imaginary conversation. Vocal score, 126.

   Moments later (near the beginning of act II) Loesser inserts another small musical detail that conveys a dramatic message. In the fleeting moment between choruses of the uplifting "Fresno Beauties" Joe and Rosabella sing their private thoughts in a duet that neither can hear. The interval that separates the one-night lovers is the same minor seventh that brought them together in the seduction music ending act I. Ibid., 133.
50. Ibid., 187–88.
51. Ibid., 252–53.

52. Ibid., 257.
53. Burrows, "Frank Loesser 1910–1969."
54. Donald Malcolm, "Nymphs and Shepherds, Go Away," *New Yorker*, 19 March 1960, 117–18.

Chapter 11: My Fair Lady

1. *My Fair Lady*'s performance run was not surpassed until nearly a decade later by *Hello Dolly!* in 1971.
2. Walter Kerr, " 'My Fair Lady'," *New York Herald Tribune*, 16 March 1956; quoted in Steven Suskin, 470–71 (quotation on 470); reprinted in *New York Theatre Critics' Reviews*, vol. 17, 346.
3. William Hawkins, " 'My Fair Lady' Is a Smash Hit," *New York World-Telegram* and *The Sun*, 16 March 1956; quoted in Suskin, 470; reprinted in *New York Theatre Critics' Reviews*, vol. 17, 347.
4. Harrison, 114. According to Gene Lees, Porter was one of the many who had turned down the *Pygmalion* adaptation (see n. 17). Lees, 88.
5. Robert Coleman, " 'My Fair Lady' Is A Glittering Musical," *Daily Mirror*, 16 March 1956; quoted in Suskin, 470; reprinted in *New York Theatre Critics' Reviews*, vol. 17, 345.
6. John Chapman, " 'My Fair Lady' a Superb, Stylish Musical Play with a Perfect Cast," *Daily News*, 16 March 1956; quoted in Suskin, 468 and 470 (quotation on 468); reprinted in *New York Theatre Critics' Reviews*, 17, 345.
7. Hawkins, " 'My Fair Lady'," 347; Suskin, 470.
8. Brooks Atkinson, "Theatre: 'My Fair Lady'," *New York Times*, 16 March 1956, 20; quoted in Suskin, 468. reprinted in *New York Theatre Critics' Reviews*, 17, 347.
9. Gene Lees and *The New Grove Dictionary of American Music* and *The New Grove Dictionary of Opera* annotator William W. Deguire give 1901 as the date for the composer's birth (some earlier sources say 1904). Although Lees remains curiously noncommittal in attributing the city of Loewe's birth (Berlin or Vienna), Berlin is the setting for all the biographical material that he offers for Loewe's early years. Lees, 12–16; and William W. Deguire, "Loewe, Frederick," *The New Grove Dictionary of American Music*, ed. H. Wiley Hitchcock and Stanley Sadie (London: Macmillan, 1985), vol. 2, 101–3, and *The New Grove Dictionary of Opera*, ed. Stanley Sadie (London: Macmillan, 1992), vol. 2, 1306.
10. Lees, 14.
11. It was noted in the previous chapter that the revue *The Illustrators Show*, which folded after five performances, also marked the Broadway debut of Loesser, who wrote the lyrics of several Irving Actman songs for this same show.
12. Dan H. Laurence, ed., *Bernard Shaw Collected Letters 1926–1950* (New York: Viking, 1988), 528.
13. Laurence, ed., *Bernard Shaw Collected Letters 1911–1925,* (New York: Viking, 1985), 730–31. It is clear from this letter, however, that Shaw's motives were as much financial as they were artistic.
14. Laurence, ed., *Collected Letters 1926–1950*, 817.
15. Lerner, 30–135. See also Stephen Citron, *Wordsmiths*, 261–64, and Keith Garebian, *The Making of "My Fair Lady"* (Toronto: ECW Press, 1993).
16. Lerner, 36.
17. Ibid., 38. In Lees's undocumented claim, Lerner and Loewe "knew that he [Pascal] had previously approached Rodgers and Hammerstein, Howard Dietz and Arthur Schwartz, Cole Porter, and E. Y. Harburg and Fred Saidy, all of whom had turned the project down as fraught with insoluble book problems." Lees, 88.
18. Lerner, 43–44.
19. In contrast to the Rodgers and Hammerstein prototype, in which the secondary characters

show some emotional or comic bond and sing to or about one another, *My Fair Lady* audiences never actually meet Doolittle's bride.

20. "Say a Prayer for Me Tonight" would be abandoned in the Broadway version of *Gigi* (1973).

21. Lerner, 50. Before it became *My Fair Lady*, *Lady Liza* was the show's working title.

22. Harrison attributed his idiosyncratic combination of speaking and singing to conductor Bill Low. According to Harrison, Low informed him that "there is such a thing as talking on pitch—using only those notes that you want to use, picking them out of the score, sometimes more, sometimes less. For the rest of the time, concentrate on staying on pitch, even though you're only speaking." Harrison, 108.

23. Lerner, 65. Harrison places his meeting with Lerner, Loewe, and their lawyer, Herman Levin, several months later "in the summer of 1955 . . . in the middle of the London run of *Bell, Book and Candle.*" Harrison, 106.

24. Lyricist-composers Porter and Loesser similarly gave their songs a title before composing a tune. Lerner also shared the frustrations suffered by fellow lyricist-librettist Hammerstein. While falling somewhat short of Rodgers's legendary speed (e.g., "Bali Ha'i" allegedly in five minutes, "Happy Talk" in twenty), the comparative ease and rapidity with which Loewe composed melodies was a fate that Lerner too had to endure.

25. Lerner, 70.

26. Lerner places the creation of "The Rain in Spain," his one "unexpected visitation from the muses," during a spontaneous ten-minute period after an audition (Lerner, 87). Harrison contradicts Lerner when he recalls hearing "The Rain in Spain" along with "Lady Liza" and "Please Don't Marry Me" at his initial London meeting with Lerner, Loewe, and Levin. Harrison, 107.

27. Just as "Say a Prayer" would return two years later in the film *Gigi,* the main theme of "Promenade" would return in both the film and subsequent stage versions of this show as "She Is Not Thinking of Me."

28. The chronology of "The Servants' Chorus" must remain conjectural. The most likely hypothesis is that it followed the inception of "The Rain in Spain" during rehearsals. The fact that the lyrics were added in pen in the Library of Congress holograph score suggests, but does not confirm, that they were a late addition.

29. Lerner, 70.

30. Ibid., 79. The earlier version of "Why Can't the English?," the lyrics of which Lerner discusses in his autobiography (79–80), can be found on the reverse sides of three song holographs in the Loewe Collection of the Library of Congress: "I Could Have Danced All Night," "Show Me," and "On the Street Where She Lives" (original title). Larry Stempel notes their presence and their "Coward touch," as exemplified in "Mad Dogs and Englishman," in the first two of these holograph scores. See Stempel, "Musical Play," 166, n. 18.

31. The holograph does not display a text over the underscoring as found on the vocal score (152 and 159) or the right-hand accompaniment figure that is prominently featured a little later (160 and 161). Also in the holograph the word "aren'" (to rhyme with "foreign") appears as "aren't."

32. A complete list for the spoken passages in the three mentioned Higgins songs follows: "I'm an Ordinary Man" ("I'm an ordinary man," "But let a . . ." [all three times], "I'm a very gentle man," and "I'm a quiet-living man") [the final spoken "Let a woman in your life" does not appear on the holograph in any form]; "A Hymn To Him" ("What in all of Heaven could have prompted her to . . ." [the next word "go" is sung] and "Why can't a . . ." [the next word "woman" is sung]; and "I've Grown Accustomed To Her Face" ("I can see her now," "In a . . . ," and "I'm a most forgiving man").

Despite this increased tendency to replace song with speech-song, the holograph indicates that some passages were originally spoken. For example: "A Hymn to Him"

("Why can't a woman be like that?," "Why can't a woman be like you?," and "Why can't a woman be like us?"); and "I've Grown Accustomed to Her Face" ("Damn!! Damn!! Damn!! Damn!!" and "I've grown accustomed to her face!" at the beginning of the song, and later the "quasi recitative" "Poor Eliza! How simply frightful! How humiliating! How delightful!"). It should also be noted that the holograph of the opening three syllables in Doolittle's "With A Little Bit Of Luck," "The Lord a-," indicates three sung pitches, a rising scale G-A-B leading to a C on "-bove."

33. *George Bernard Shaw Pygmalion/Alan Jay Lerner My Fair Lady* (New York: Signet, 1975), 88.

34. As late as February 23, 1948, ten years after the film version of *Pygmalion*, Shaw would write, "I absolutely forbid the Campbell interpolation ['What size'] or any suggestion that the middleaged bully and the girl of eighteen are lovers." Laurence, ed., *Collected Letters 1926–1950*, 815.

35. Laurence, ed., *Collected Letters 1911–1925*, 227.

36. Michael Holroyd, *Bernard Shaw, Volume II, 1898–1918, The Pursuit of Power* (New York: Random House, 1989), 339.

37. Ibid., 340.

38. Costello. Costello discusses each of the fourteen scenes that appear in the film but not its screenplay; he also offers a useful appendix, "From Play To Screen Play To Sound Track: A Textual Comparison Of Three Versions Of Act V of Shaw's Pygmalion."

39. Costello, 187–88.

40. Laurence, ed., *Collected Letters 1926–1950*, 532–33.

41. *Pygmalion/My Fair Lady*, 93–94. The remaining quotations in this paragraph can be found on p. 94.

42. Costello, 76.

43. Considering its indebtedness to the Pascal film, it is not surprising that on the title page of the *My Fair Lady* vocal score, Lerner and Loewe were requested to include the phrase "adapted from Bernard Shaw's 'Pygmalion' produced on the screen by Gabriel Pascal," and that Pascal would receive 1 percent of the *My Fair Lady* royalties. Costello, 68.

44. The exercises themselves appeared in the film (but not the published screenplay): "The rain in Spain stays mainly in the plain" for vowels and "in Hertford, Hereford, and Hampshire hurricanes hardly ever happen" for aspirate *h*'s. See the production photograph on p. 236.

45. *Pygmalion/My Fair Lady*, 140.

46. The opening notes of Loewe's melody are identical to the opening of Brahms's intermezzo for piano in C♯ minor, op. 117, no. 3. On the subject of musical quotation, Tosca's "Non la sospiri la nostra casetta" in act I of her opera bears an uncanny melodic resemblance to Doolittle's "With a Little Bit of Luck." In contrast to Blitzstein's and Bernstein's classical borrowings, neither of these possible *My Fair Lady* borrowings were apparently chosen to make a dramatic point.

47. Swain, 196.

48. Ibid., 199.

49. More remote and perhaps unintentional are the melodic correspondences between the opening A sections of "On the Street Where You Live" and "I've Grown Accustomed to Her Face." In any event, it makes sense that a dramatically transformed Higgins would sing a variation of Freddy's lovesick tune. After all, Higgins could easily have heard Freddy's song on any number of the many occasions Eliza's would-be suitor performed it under his window. Although the causes are less dramatically explicable, it is also arguable that "On the Street Where You Live" is melodically derived from "I Could Have Danced All Night."

50. It might be recalled that the rhythm of "Get Me to the Church on Time" was anticipated in the middle portion of "Just You Wait," where it was preceded by an upbeat.

51. The full text of "Come to the Ball" is located in B. Green, 109–10. Loewe's holograph score can be found in folder 15 of the Loewe Collection, Music Division, Library of Congress.
52. Lerner, 88–89.
53. Ibid., 106.
54. Ibid, 106–7. Lerner went on to explain how "quite unwittingly, the new scene also solved our one major costume problem." In contrast to the original ball scene when Eliza's elegant gown was unable to stand out from the splendor of the other gowns, "in the new scene she appeared at the top of the stairs in Higgins' house in her ball gown, and the audience broke into applause." Ibid., 108.
55. The original text of "On the Street Where You Live" appears in B. Green, 96. Lerner's remarks and the opening night version of this song were recorded on December 12, 1971, in a live performance (Book-of-the-Month Records 70–5240).
56. Shaw introduces Freddy and his ineffectual attempts to hail a cab as well as his sister Clara in act I; Lerner and Loewe do not present Freddy until Ascot, and they drop the role of Clara altogether.
57. Engel, *Words With Music*, 116. All quotations in this and the following paragraph can be found on p. 116.
58. In contrast to Engel, Lerner described "the flagrantly romantic lyric that kept edging on the absurd" as "exactly right for the character." Lerner, 106.
59. Harold Bloom, ed., *George Bernard Shaw's Pygmalion* (New York: Chelsea House, 1988), vii and 1–10.
60. The demise of Dorothy and DuBose Heyward's *Porgy*, Sidney Howard's *They Knew What They Wanted*, and even Ferenc Molnár's *Liliom*, and their displacement by *Porgy and Bess*, *The Most Happy Fella*, and *Carousel* has been accepted with equanimity by theater audiences and producers. Fortunately, Shakespeare's *The Taming of the Shrew* and *Romeo and Juliet* have so far been spared a similar fate.
61. *Pygmalion/My Fair Lady*, 43. The original Mrs. Patrick Campbell was a youthful forty-eight at the time she introduced the role of Eliza.
62. Engel, *Words With Music*, 87.
63. For all of Lerner's shows after *Camelot* see B. Green for Lerner's lyrics, and, in the case of *My Man Godfrey*, his outline and scenario.

Chapter 12: West Side Story

1. In his autobiography Harold Prince acknowledged that he closed the show six months prematurely. Prince, 39–40.
2. *West Side Story* was surpassed in first-run longevity by twenty book shows that premiered before 1960 (see Appendix C, pp. 317–19), including several concurrent hits that had not yet completed their initial runs: *Damn Yankees*, *The Pajama Game*, *Bells Are Ringing*, and, of course, *My Fair Lady*, which opened the year before. (If one were to take into account the return engagement that directly followed *West Side Story*'s tour, however, its place in the 1920–1959 list would rise to 12). Meredith Willson's *The Music Man*, which first paraded on Broadway two months after *West Side Story* and eventually ran for 1,375 performances, also eclipsed the *Romeo and Juliet* adaptation when it won the Tony for best musical of 1957. The London version of *West Side Story* was voted the Best Musical of the Year 1960.
3. John McClain, "Music Magnificent In Overwhelming Hit," *New York Journal-American*, 27 September 1957; quoted in Suskin, 696; reprinted in *New York Theatre Critics' Reviews*, vol. 18, 254.
4. Walter Kerr, " 'West Side Story'," *New York Herald Tribune*, 27 September 1957; quoted in Suskin, 695–96 (quotations on 696); reprinted in *New York Theatre Critics' Reviews*, vol. 18, 253.

5. Brooks Atkinson, "Theatre: The Jungles of the City," *New York Times*, 27 September 1957, 14; quoted in Suskin, 695; reprinted in *New York Theatre Critics' Reviews*, vol. 18, 253.

6. Robert Coleman, " 'West Side Story' A Sensational Hit!," *Daily Mirror*, 27 September 1957. *New York Theatre Critics' Reviews*, vol. 18, 254. John McClain, "Music Magnificent In Overwhelming Hit," and John Chapman, " 'West Side Story': A Splendid and Super-modern Musical Drama," *Daily News*, 27 September 1957; reprinted in *New York Theatre Critics' Reviews*, vol. 18, 252; the McClain and Chapman reviews are excerpted in Suskin, 695–96.

7. Quotation in Banfield, 39. *West Side Story* Oscars include: Best Picture; Direction (Robert Wise and Jerome Robbins); Supporting Actor (George Chakiris); Supporting Actress (Rita Moreno); Scoring of a Musical Picture (Saul Chaplin, Johnny Green, Sid Ramin, and Irwin Kostal); Cinematography; Art Direction; Costume Design; Sound; Film Editing; and an Honorary Award to Jerome Robbins "for his brilliant achievements in the art of choreography on film." There was also a nomination for the screenplay based on material from another medium. Other prestigious awards included the New York Film Critics Award for Best Picture, and the *New York Times* annual "Ten Best." Not until 1988 would a movie (*The Last Emperor*) capture as many Academy Awards.

8. Bernstein's log was reprinted in *Findings*, 144–47, and in 1985 with the jacket notes to Bernstein's recording, Deutsche Grammophon 4125253–1/4. References to this log will be keyed to the pagination in *Findings*.

9. Guernsey, ed., *Broadway Song & Story*, 40–54.

10. Zadan, 11–31.

11. Burton, 265–77; Sondheim, "An Anecdote," xi-xii; and Gussow. Stephen Banfield also discusses the genesis of *West Side Story* in *Sondheim's Broadway Musicals*, 31–38.

12. The manuscript evidence suggests that the discrepancies among the recollections are greatly exaggerated in Joan Peyser's relentlessly negative Bernstein biography, in which she accuses the collaborators of deliberate lying. See Peyser, 255–77.

13. The eight libretto drafts are dated as follows: (1) January 1956; (2) Spring 1956; (3) March 15, 1956; (4) Winter 1956; (5) April 14, 1957; (6) May 1, 1957; (7) June 1, 1957; and (8) July 19, 1957. I am grateful to Harold L. Miller and the State Historical Society of Wisconsin for making these and other *West Side Story* materials available to me.

14. All 1949 entries appear in Bernstein, 147.

15. All 1955 entries appear in Bernstein, 147–48.

16. Guernsey, ed., *Broadway Song & Story*, 41.

17. *Candide* would open the first of its disappointing seventy-three performances on December 1, 1956.

18. Bernstein, 148.

19. Bernstein's 1957 entries are located in Bernstein, 146–47.

20. "Mambo" was reprised on the drugstore juke box late in act II when the Jets are taunting Anita ("Taunting Scene"). Gussow.

21. Ibid.

22. Peyser, 267 and n. 20.

23. Gussow.

24. Ibid. The undeniable organicism of the work and Bernstein's awareness of musical technique makes one skeptical of the composer's remark that he "didn't do all this on purpose."

25. Peyser, 267.

26. Another possible melodic source for the opening of "Somewhere" is a prominent lyrical theme in Richard Strauss's youthful *Burleske* for piano and orchestra (1885–1886). See chapter 11, n. 46.

27. Peyser, 261. Despite its borrowed origins, Bernstein remembered that it "took longer to write that song ["Maria"] than any other" because "it's difficult to make a strong love song and avoid corn." See Zadan, 21.

The principal certain or possible borrowings are derived from Tchaikovsky's *Romeo and Juliet* (and perhaps Beethoven's "Emperor" Concerto), Blitzstein's *Regina* (previously discussed and illustrated with Bernstein's transformations in Examples 12.1 and 12.2), Berg's Piano Sonata, op. 1 (Example 12.9), and Wagner's "redemption" motive from *Die Walküre* (Example 12.8). Other possibilities include the following: "America" (Ravel's "Chansons romanesque" from *Don Quichotte* [1933] and Copland's *El Salón México* [1936], the latter a work which Bernstein had arranged for solo piano in 1941); "Tonight" (Quintet) (Stravinsky's *Symphony of Psalms*, third movement [1930]); and "I Feel Pretty" (Ravel's *Rhapsodie Espagnole* [1908]). The Stravinsky reference appears in Stempel, "Broadway's Mozartean Moment," 48. For another possible Beethoven borrowing see n. 73.

Gradenwitz overstates the musical resemblance between the opening measure of the Balcony Scene and the first four notes of Britten's "Goodnight Theme" from act I of *The Rape of Lucretia*, the recently published score of which Bernstein noticed in Gradenwitz's "modest private apartment." Peyser fixes a date (1946) to this occasion and adds that Bernstein was then attending rehearsals of the work prior to its premiere. Her statement that " 'Tonight' was derived from Benjamin Britten" similarly places far too great a burden on this four-note descending scale. See Gradenwitz, 193 and Peyser, 365–66.

28. The libretto drafts of January and Spring 1956 describe the bridal shop song as "light and gay," a description that fits "Oh, Happy We" but not "One Hand, One Heart," which until the Washington tryouts in August 1957 "had only a dotted half note to each bar." Zadan, 23 (see also n. 35).

29. According to Burton, "Where Does It Get You in the End?" was "annexed from the Venice scene in *Candide*." Burton, 269.

30. Other material would be altered or discarded in 1957. Instead of a Dream Ballet, the librettos before April 14 indicated a scene in a police station where the death of Bernardo and Riff, unknown to the Sharks and the Jets, would be announced. In the police station Tony and Maria would reenact their meeting at the dance and decide to elope, and Chino would utter the immortal words, "Life, liberty . . . and the pursuit of crappiness." In the drugstore scene before the climax of the drama in the final 1956 version Maria rather than Anita was taunted by the Jets. Not until the final months before rehearsals began did the creators of *West Side Story* succeed in finding a substitute for the philter.

31. Guernsey, ed., *Broadway Song & Story*, 44. The first two libretto drafts (January and Spring 1956) contained one song in an opening scene, the "Rumble Song." Judging from an earlier musical draft of the actual "Rumble," the "Rumble Song" of early 1956 and the song "Mix" were probably one and the same, but since no lyrics are given in the libretto, this conclusion cannot be established with certainty. In any event, by the third libretto draft (March 15), the concluding song of the scene is in fact labelled "Mix" (in the fourth libretto draft, however, "Mix" is not indicated). The early libretto drafts also suggest that two songs, "Up to the Moon" and "My Greatest Day," based on the eventual "Prologue" and "Jet Song," respectively, preceded "Mix."

32. Bernstein would reuse a melody from "Mix," also discarded from the "Prologue," in the "Blues" portion of "Dance at the Gym." A version of this idea (with some different lyrics) was retained in the published vocal score, 20–21, as part of the "Jet Song," and accompanied by a note that this material was cut in the New York production.

33. Laurents's fifth and sixth libretto drafts still indicate only one song in the "Prologue," "Mix"; the seventh and eighth drafts (June 1 and July 19) contain a song for the Jets called "We're the Greatest" and a reference in the dialogue to another ephemeral song, "This Turf Is Ours." Shortly before rehearsals "Mix" was finally dropped. Although it is more difficult to date the "new" Rumble, the rehearsal period certainly marks a terminal date for the replacement of a "Rumble" (based on "Mix") with the present version. Bernstein recalls in his interview with Gussow that "Mix" "wound up in 'The Chichester Psalms' in Hebrew." See Gussow, and *Chichester Psalms* II (Amberson/Boosey & Hawkes), 38–50.

34. Guernsey, ed., *Broadway Song & Story*, 45. Sondheim also confirms the reference to "This Turf Is Ours" in an interview reported in Zadan, 24: "Then we wrote a new opening because everyone felt the opening wasn't violent enough. The new opening was really violent and everyone thought it was too violent, so we went back to the 'Jet Song.' " Like "Mix," "This Turf Is Ours" resurfaced in another Bernstein work when it was incorporated in the *Fanfare for the Inauguration of John F. Kennedy* (January 19, 1961). Its opening motive is nearly identical to the "hate" motive (see Example 12.9a).

35. Zadan, 23–24. Sondheim also has more to say about the aptly titled "One": "I remember that the tune of 'One Hand, One Heart,' which Bernstein originally wrote for *Candide*, had only a dotted half note to each bar. I realized I couldn't set any two-syllable words to the song, it had to be all one-syllable words. I was stifled, and down in Washington, after my endless pleas, Lenny put in two little quarter notes so that I could put 'make of our' as in 'Make of our hearts one heart.' Not a great deal, but at least a little better." Ibid., 23.

36. The piano-vocal manuscript of "One Hand, One Heart" also reveals that some of its orchestral material was sung, and more significantly, that the instrumental foreshadowing of "Somewhere" introducing the song was not a late addition.

37. Zadan, 24. "Kids Ain't" is included among Bernstein's vocal manuscripts.

38. Guernsey, ed., *Broadway Song & Story*, 49.

39. Ibid., 49–50.

40. In a letter dated "8 Aug already!" Bernstein writes to his wife, Felicia, that he had written "a new song for Tony" the day before. Burton, 272.

41. Zadan, 21. Sondheim confirms that "Something's Coming" was indeed completed in a day. See Sondehim, "An Anecdote," xi-xii.

42. The locale of this scene changed several times. In the first two librettos "Tonio" appears in the opening scene with the Jets. In the two following libretto drafts, the scene takes place at the drugstore fountain; in the librettos of April 14 and May 1 the locale is the corner of a playground. The final drafts moves from Tony's bedroom (June 1) to an unspecified yard in (July 19).

43. The final libretto of July 19 concludes with a variation on the first words of the song, "Who knows? Could be. Why not?!" See also Guernsey, ed., *Broadway Song & Story*, 43, and Zadan, 21.

44. Bernstein describes his intentions further in his "8 Aug. already!" letter to Felicia: "It's really going to save his character—a driving $\frac{2}{4}$ in the great tradition (but of course fucked up by me with $\frac{3}{8}$ and whatnot)—but it gives Tony balls—so that he doesn't emerge as just a euphoric dreamer." Burton, 272.

45. The antecedents of the Romeo and Juliet legend go back at least as far as the Greek myth of Pyramus and Thisbe, who, like their Shakespearean counterparts, are forbidden from marrying by their parents, and who, mistakenly thinking the other dead, needlessly take their own lives. Variations on a related theme frequented Renaissance Italy and were adapted by French and English writers for more than a hundred years before Shakespeare drafted his play. Geoffrey Bullough and Kenneth Muir have surveyed these and other sources of this tale of woe, and it is now unquestioned that Shakespeare borrowed heavily from Arthur Brooke's once popular poem, "The Tragicall Historye of Romeus and Juliet" (1562), itself based on the Italian *Le Novelle del Bandello* (1554), adapted into French by Pierre Boisteau (1559) and translated into English by William Painter (1567). Muir demonstrates Shakespeare's fidelity to Brooke's poem, including unmistakable "verbal echoes," and notes "three occasions" where "the phrasing of the poem is repeated almost word for word."

  In performing his alchemy Shakespeare condensed the time frame of Brooke's leisurely romance (3,020 lines) from more than nine months to less than one week. Brooke even allows his Romeus and Juliet a month or two of marital bliss before the fatal duel in which Romeus, in self-defense, kills Tybalt. Muir argues that this striking increase in "speed and intensity . . . shows the passionate impulsiveness of the two lovers, and [that] it makes them consummate their marriage in the knowledge that they must separate on the morrow." Geoffrey Bullough, ed., *Narrative and Dramatic Sources of Shakespeare*, vol. I, *Early Comedies, Poems, Romeo and Juliet* (London: Routledge & Kegan Paul, 1973), 269–83; Kenneth Muir, *Shakespeare's Sources*, vol. I, *Comedies and Tragedies* (London: Methuen, 1957), 21–30 (quotation on 24).

46. Despite the vocal resources on hand, Berlioz in his "dramatic symphony" (1838–1839) uses the orchestra exclusively to portray the central dramatic events, the Balcony Scene and the Death of Romeo and Juliet. Tchaikovsky's Fantasy-Overture (1869, revised in 1870 and 1880) contains no vocal parts at all.

47. Harlow Robinson, *Sergei Prokofiev: A Biography* (New York: Viking, 1987), 302.

48. Most of the Zeffirelli's distortions can be attributed to his predilection to replace Shakespeare's dialogue with visual images, often with musical accompaniment. Act V exemplifies this approach. In scene 1 he replaces Romeo's soliloquy (a description of a dream that lasts approximately thirty seconds) with the visual image of Balthasar passing Friar John on the road to Mantua. Gone also from scene 1 is Romeo's poignant meeting with the Apothecary. Together these deletions reduce Shakespeare's eighty-five lines to a mere six. Gone entirely is the twenty-nine line second scene between Friar Laurence and Friar John.

In scene 3 Zeffirelli omits Paris and his duel with Romeo in front of Juliet's tomb, the dialogue between the watchmen, most of Prince Escalus's lines, and Friar Laurence's explanation of the tragic events. Capulet, Lady Capulet, and Montague are seen but not heard. Thus out of 310 lines Zeffirelli preserves only 160. The time he saves on Shakespeare's "extraneous" dialogue allows movie audiences to hear additional uninterrupted repetitions of Nino Rota's "Love Song from Romeo and Juliet." Ironically, when all is said and sung the nineteen minutes of Zeffirelli's act V occupies nearly as much total time as the marginally abbreviated B.B.C. version (twenty-two minutes).

49. Guernsey, ed.,*Broadway Song & Story*, 47.

50. Some of the parallels between Shakespeare's play and its musical adaptation described in the following paragraphs were derived from Houghton.

51. A rare "sugar coating" in the film version occurs when Doc's drugstore is metamorphosed into a candy store.

52. Isaac Asimov cites numerous textual details to support his assertion that the feud had lost most of its steam before the outset of the play. *Asimov's Guide to Shakespeare* (New York: Avenel Books, 1978), vol. 1, 474–98.

53. Guernsey, ed., *Broadway Song & Story*, 47.

54. *West Side Story* libretto drafts Nos. 1 and 2, 2–5–9.

55. *West Side Story* libretto draft No. 3, 2–5–23.

56. Guernsey, ed., *Broadway Song & Story*, 43.

57. Ibid., 44. Bernstein told Burton in an interview that he "tried giving all the material to the orchestra and having her [Maria] sing an *obbligato* throughout" and "a version that sounded just like a Puccini aria, which we really did not need." Even after numerous attempts, he "never got past six bars with it." Burton, 275.

58. Original cast, Columbia S 32603; studio cast, Deutsche Grammophon 415253–1/4.

59. In a letter to Felicia, dated July 23, 1957, Bernstein writes that "all the aspects of the score I like best—the big, poetic parts—get criticized as 'operatic'—and there's a concerted move to chuck them." Burton, 271.

60. Swain, 205.

61. Ibid., 245.

62. Jon Alan Conrad, "*West Side Story*," *The New Grove Dictionary of Opera*, ed. Stanley Sadie (London: Macmillan, 1992), vol. 4, 1146.

63. Banfield, 37. For a more extended comparison between the ideologies of Swain and Banfield see my review-essay of *Sondheim's Broadway Musicals*, 20–27.
64. Banfield, 37.
65. In chapter 2 the notion of a "river family" of motives in *Show Boat* was considered; a network of motives related to the principal characters of *Porgy and Bess* was explored in chapter 4.
66. The deceptive chord is usually the submediant or vi chord (e.g., A in the key of C). An earlier example of a deceptive cadence to the vi chord occurs in *Show Boat*'s "Where's the Mate for Me?", the first chord on the word "fancy" (see Example 2.5b).
67. See also the discussion of Blitzstein's meaningfully dramatic treatment of Beethoven's *Egmont* Overture in *The Cradle Will Rock* (chapter 6, pp. 129–31).
68. In the orchestral manuscript that followed shortly, Tony and Maria also sing the four preceding measures reserved for the orchestra in the vocal manuscript and the final version.
69. Bernstein also displaces the second note of "Somewhere" in mm. 3, 11, and 27 by raising it an octave.
70. See mm. 11, 13, 14–15, 27, 29, 31–32. When they reach the "open air" (m. 6) with "time to spare" (m. 14), the vocal part melodically outlines an E major triad (E-G♯-B), although Bernstein contradicts this latter tonic resolution with opposing harmony. The harmony which supports "time to spare" once again suggests C♯ minor (C♯-E-G♯). Bernstein further dilutes the impact of his first major triads associated with his second motive by immediately following each of its statements with a minor triad in the vocal line.
71. Shakespeare, much like a Greek tragedian, wanted his audiences to know in advance the fate of his "star-crossed lovers." In the event that they were unfamiliar with this popular and often-told tale, he provided a précis of the plot in the Prologue to act I told by a Chorus.
72. The scene that contains "Tonight" is designated the Balcony Scene in the published vocal score (New York: G. Schirmer and Chappell, 1957 and 1959).
73. In his introductory survey of music, Joseph Kerman concludes his discussion of *West Side Story* by pointing out that "Bernstein's fugue recalls the famous 'Great Fugue' by Ludwig van Beethoven" [the original final movement of the B♭ Major String Quartet, op. 130]. Joseph Kerman, *Listen*, 2d brief ed. (New York: Worth, 1992), 393. According to Banfield, "the 'Cool' twelve-note fugue seems as indebted to Beethoven's *Grosse Fuge* as does 'Somewhere''s melodic contour to his 'Emperor' Concerto and its sparse counterpoint to his late quartet." Banfield, 37.
74. In particular, the abrupt and explosive *sforzando* accent on the concluding third note of the first motive (*a*) and the strong accents on the first note of the third motive (*c¹* and *c³*) within a jazzy context depicts a convincing premonition of the inevitable outcome facing the Jets and Sharks as well as Tony and Maria.

    The remaining appearances of the first or "There's a place" motive from "Somewhere" (*a*) maintains its primary association with the principal lovers. For example, the orchestral introduction to "One Hand, One Heart"—which also incorporates additional melodic liberties in its statement of the "place for us" motive (*b*)—again prepares the future fate of Tony and Maria and in the process links a song to *West Side Story* that had been withdrawn from *Candide* the previous year. The upwardly striving "There's a place" motive acts as a musical symbol for a better place in another life for Tony and Maria. In a dramatically effective reprise, at the end of the "Nightmare" the elided first and second "Somewhere" motives ("There's a place" and "place for us") returns to the orchestra and Bernstein uses the second motive to support Tony's singing of "half-way there" and "take you there."
75. Like the "There's a place" motive, the third "Somewhere" motive (Example 12.4c) appears ubiquitously in the "Cool" fugue. It is most conspicuous, however, in earlier portions of

the "Dream Sequence" where an ascending half step—again as in Maria's name—appears in the orchestral underpinning of "Under Dialogue" (13) and "Ballet Sequence" (13a). The third "Somewhere" motive will again figure prominently in the "Finale" (17) directly after Tony's death as an inner melodic strand throughout the procession and in the three final statements that parallel the finale of the Dream Ballet as the last notes we hear. It also appears conspicuously but with less apparent dramatic justification throughout much of "America" (7).

76. Larry Stempel notes that the music of "I Have a Love" is a transformed version of Anita's music in the preceding "A Boy Like That," for example, on the words, "A boy who kills cannot love, / A boy who kills has no heart." Stempel, "Broadway's Mozartean Moment," 50.

77. Among *West Side Story* chroniclers only Banfield notes a possible Wagnerian reference when he writes that "one even senses a hint of *Tristan* in Tony's supplication for 'endless night'." Banfield, 34. Peyser, in noting the influence of Wagner in Bernstein's final opera, *A Quiet Place* (1983), concludes that Wagner was "an influence that had been nowhere apparent in Bernstein up to the late 1970s." Peyser, 457.

78. Gottlieb, 26–32; Gradenwitz, 185–202; Stempel, "Broadway's Mozartean Moment," 39–56; and Swain, 205–46. Gottlieb, a composer who acted as Bernstein's musical assistant and general factotum at the New York Philharmonic from 1958–1966, wrote articulate jacket notes for Bernstein's recordings and served as an editor of the composer's writings, including the Omnibus television lectures of the 1950s. Gradenwitz, a German musicologist who remained a personal friend of the composer, also wrote notes for Bernstein recordings.

79. In the underrated *Wonderful Town* (1953) perfect fifths also figure prominently in abbreviated thematic reminiscences that contribute to an "organic" musical unity, although these musical connections do not reinforce dramatic nuances as they will in *West Side Story*. Several melodies that emphasize perfect fifths reappear in other songs as well: the main tune of "A Little Bit in Love" serves as an introduction to "It's Love" and the main tune of "It's Love" forms the introduction to "A Quiet Girl." A second type of connection is thematic reminiscence, as for example, when the first measure of "Pass That Football"—most of the tune is musically and dramatically identical to "What a Waste"—returns in the first two measures of "A Quiet Girl." A third unifying element derives from the reuse of the dotted boogie-woogie accompaniments originally associated with the sisters Ruth and Eileen in "Ohio," Ruth in "One Hundred Easy Ways," and Eileen in "A Little Bit in Love," and distorted in Wreck's "Pass That Football," Ruth's "Swing!," and the sisters's "Wrong Note Rag."

80. The instrumental "Paris Waltz Scene" and its rhythmic transformation in the finale "Make Our Garden Grow" of *Candide* bears a strong resolution to the first "Somewhere" motive. In both the upward leap of a minor seventh is followed by descending half step (minor second). In the *Candide* finale, as in "Somewhere," Bernstein starts in E major and modulates to C (although *Candide* parts company with "Somewhere" with its intervening modulation to A♭ major and in its advoidance of a return to E). The overlapping compositional histories of *Candide* and *West Side Story* produced additional musical affinities that go beyond the exchanges among their songs discussed earlier in this chapter.

81. Gottlieb, 26.

82. Bernstein's manuscript for the "Prologue" opens with the "hate" motive (A♭-D♭-G), bracketed and labelled "optional curtain music." The Broadway cast album retains this introduction, and in the film version, the "hate" motive is used effectively at the outset and at other strategic moments as the Jet's warning whistle. The "hate" motive also appears unaltered in the "Cool" fugue where it joins the first and third "Somewhere" motives.

83. In the album jacket notes of the soundtrack Hollis Alpert makes the following point: "With the intermissions between acts eliminated, one rising line of tension, from begin-

ning to end, was required. The neatest solution, resulting in almost no change in the text, was the juxtaposition of musical numbers" (Columbia OS 2070). Thus, in dramatic contrast to most movie versions of hit Broadway shows, the makers of the *West Side Story* film made a valiant attempt to retain all of the music and to preserve the dramatic integrity, if not the ordering, of the Broadway original. Ironically, when *West Side Story* was first released, theaters, deprived of a B-movie second feature due to the length of the main event, thwarted the intentions of the film's creators by inserting an intermission as a concession to the concessioners. Following the numbers in the vocal score and Appendix Q, pp. 341-42, the order in the film version is as follows: Nos. 1–5, 7–6, 14, 12, 9–11, 13, 8, and 15–17.

84. The final measures of Bernstein's musical bears a striking—and identically pitched—resemblance to the apotheosis of the central character on the final notes of Stravinsky's *Petrushka* (1911).

85. The CD reissued in 1992 restores the Broadway ending in the previously unreleased "Finale" (Sony SK 48211).

86. In the reissued CD the previously released "End Credits" restored the three tritones that accompanied the film.

87. Swain, 243. See also Stempel, "Broadway's Mozartean Moment," 54.

Chapter 13: Sondheim

1. Appendix C excludes musical revues and Off-Broadway shows. In the former category are the *Oh, Calcutta* revival (1976), *Dancin'* (1978), *Ain't Misbehavin'* (1978), and *Sugar Babies* (1979); in the latter, *The Fantasticks* 1960), *You're a Good Man, Charlie Brown* (1967), *Godspell* (1971), *I'm Getting My Act Together and Taking It on the Road* (1978), and *Little Shop of Horrors* (1982). Also in this list is the Off-Broadway revue *Don't Bother Me, I Can't Cope* (1972). All of these shows ran well over one thousand performances. Admittedly, the line between revues and book musicals can often be blurry; what remains clear is the tremendous debt that shows from *Hair* and *The Magic Show* to *A Chorus Line* and *Cats* owe to the revue genre.

2. For further discussion on the evolving relationship between popularity and critical acclaim see Block, "The Broadway Canon," 525–44.

3. Swain, 309–18.

4. Walsh and Gottfried, *More Broadway Musicals Since 1980*. Despite a strong advance sale, Lloyd Webber's *Aspects of Love* (1990) failed at the box office as well as with critics and closed after 377 performances, "the biggest financial loss ($11 million) in Broadway history." Gottfried, *More Broadway Musicals*, 74. Lloyd Webber's latest musical as of this writing, *Sunset Boulevard*, although initially reliant on a big star (Glenn Close), returned the composer to his accustomed win column.

5. If one were to exclude performances on Broadway and in major professional theaters in London, Sondheim may already be enjoying a comparable number of revivals to Lloyd Webber on regional, semiprofessional, and college stages.

6. Sondheim's essays on the development of his own aesthetic and creative process and his analysis of other Broadway writers forms an indispensable starting point to understanding the man, the career, and the ideas behind the work. See especially Sondheim, "Theater Lyrics" and "The Musical Theater." Other valuable Sondheim surveys are Zadan, Gordon, and especially Banfield, the latter billed without understatement by its publisher as "the first in-depth look at the work and career of one of the most important figures in the history of musical theater."

7. Thomas P. Adler, "The Musical Dramas of Stephen Sondheim: Some Critical Approaches," *Journal of Popular Culture* 12 (1978–1979): 513–25; quotation on 523.

8. Eugene K. Bristow and J. Kevin Butler, "*Company*, About Face! The Show That Revolu-

tionized the American Musical," *American Music* 5 (Fall 1987): 241–54; quotation on 253.

9. Considering this absence of song hits, one cannot help but be struck by the frequency and popularity of revues and other retrospectives based on Sondheim songs, from *Side by Side by Sondheim* (1976) to *Putting It Together* (1993).

10. Gordon, 7.

11. Sondheim remarked in an interview that "Moss Hart did a concept musical. His *Thousands Cheer* was a concept musical in 1933. Concept musicals have existed forever." Quoted in Ilson, 195. For an application of the "ideal type" to the Broadway musical see Block, "The Broadway Canon," 537–39 and n. 15.

12. See Hirsch and Ilson.

13. The use of the concept musical on behalf of the integrated ideal is analogous to the practice of classical modernists (for example, Schoenberg) who offered increasingly complex exhibitions of motivic unity to generate new heights in organicism.

14. See Banfield, 20–25, and Sondheim, "Theater Lyrics," 62–63.

15. Babbitt's encyclopedic knowledge of popular music of the 1920s and 1930s and his aborted aspirations to compose popular music in the 1930s are less widely known. For those familiar with the breadth of his interests it is not surprising that in addition to teaching the European classics, Babbitt would also analyze the popular songs of DeSylva, Brown, and Henderson, Kern, Rodgers, and Gershwin "with exactly the same serious tone." See Eugene R. Huber, ed., "A Conversation with Stephen Sondheim" (typescript), quoted in Banfield, 22.

16. Egerman's song is the first in a triptych of songs the titles of which encapsulate the ethos of the characters who sing them: Egerman's "Now," his son Fredrik's "Later," and his wife Anne's "Soon." After their sequential introduction, the characters will sing their songs simultaneously, a dazzling albeit nonetheless appealing display of musical and dramatic ingenuity.

17. Zadan, 147.

18. The lyrics to all four songs, "Marry Me a Little," "Multitudes of Amys," "Happily Ever After," and "Being Alive," are printed in Sondheim, "Theater Lyrics," 92–97. The first and third songs can be heard in *Marry Me a Little* (RCA ABL1–4159), a musical based on songs cut from previous Sondheim shows. The second remains unpublished. See Banfield, 166–73.

19. Prince, 143–57; quotations on 156–57.

20. Ibid., 183.

21. Gottfried, *Sondheim*, 189, and Banfield, 382.

22. Gottfried, *Sondheim*, 151. Banfield considers the critical problems generated by *Merrily's* autobiographical subject matter: "But it would be difficult to fix the audiences's sympathy—and regrets—on Franklin Shepard, for the simple reason that the musical is about the compromise of his talent and we can only measure that talent by transferring it to Sondheim." Banfield, 312.

23. Banfield would call this technique "reflexivity," i.e., "the words describing what the music is doing." Ibid., 42.

24. The populist Sondheim composed two songs for Madonna to sing in the movie *Dick Tracy* (1990), including the Academy Award–winning Best Song of 1991, "Sooner or Later." Within his Broadway work Sondheim has also embraced rock styles in *Company* ("Company" and "Have I Got a Girl for You"), *Pacific Overtures* ("Next"), and *Assassins* ("Unworthy of Your Love").

25. Sondheim, "Musical Theater," 252–253.

26. On the genesis of *Follies* see the following: Ilson, 177–97; Mandelbaum, 66–78; Prince, 158–70; Sondheim, "Musical Theater," 231–32; and Zadan, 135–53.

27. Another post–Rodgers and Hammerstein musical, *Candide*, underwent considerable literary and musical alterations between 1956 and 1989. See Andrew Porter, "*Candide:* An

Introduction," notes to the 1989 recording, conducted by Leonard Bernstein, Deutsche Grammophon 429–73401.

28. The two librettos of *The Girls Upstairs* (from among the alleged thirteen) housed in the Theater Collection of the New York Public Library (Restricted Material #5870 [first draft] and Restricted Material #2624 [second draft]), for the most part substantiate Prince's recollection. Seven of the twenty-two numbers in the 1971 *Follies* (in addition to the "Prologue") can be traced to these pre-*Follies* versions; four of these songs appear in Restricted Material #5870. The New York Public Library also houses two drafts of *Follies*, one dated September 1970 (Restricted Material #2625) and the other January 2, 1971 (NCOF+73–1867).

29. Ilson, 180.

30. Many of the discarded *Follies* songs have been recorded, most comprehensively in *A Collector's Sondheim*, issued in 1985 (RCA CRL4–5359).

31. Sondheim discusses the artistic limitations of "Can That Boy Foxtrot!" in Sondheim, "Theater Lyrics," 87–88.

32. Mandelbaum, 70–71.

33. Zadan, 143.

34. Prince, 163.

35. Lonoff, n.p.

36. In honor of Bernstein's seventieth birthday Sondheim composed the parody "The Saga of Lennie," which, according to a particularly helpful anonymous outside reviewer of this book, "shows a good understanding and sympathy with the original 'Saga of Jenny'."

37. Prior to *Follies* Simon had written the books for *Little Me* (1962), *Sweet Charity* (1966), and *Promises, Promises* (1968) (the latter choreographed by Bennett). After *Follies* Simon would contribute uncredited one-liners in Bennett's *Seesaw* (1973) and *A Chorus Line* (1975) (e.g., Sheila's "Sometimes I'm agressive"). Bennett also played an important role in Simon's work. He assisted (without credit) the direction of *The Good Doctor* (1973) and directed *God's Favorite* (1974). See Mandelbaum, 74, 78, 85–86, 124, 146–47.

38. Ibid., 74.

39. Zadan, 150.

40. Ibid., 148, 150.

41. Ibid., 149–51. Although he acknowledged that "many critics felt that Goldman's book was the weak link in *Follies*, and that it contained unpleasant characters difficult to care about and action that was hard to follow," Sondheim concluded that "these critics were only echoing Bennett's sentiments throughout the tryout." Mandelbaum, 73–74.

42. Zadan, 322.

43. Ibid., 151–52.

44. Ilson also notes that "ironically, when the show was revived in London in 1987, Goldman has them [Ben and Phyllis] stay together. Ilson, 196.

45. Sondheim had earlier contributed lyrics to the successful Broadway revival of *Candide* ("Life Is Happiness Indeed"), another work that had lost money after a short run and had been accused of humorlessness in its original form. See Andrew Porter's insightful remarks on the related reasons behind the various versions of *Candide* and *Madame Butterfly*: "How to Live in Grace," *New Yorker*, 1 November 1982, 152–53, reprinted in *Musical Events: A Chronicle, 1980–1983* (New York: Summit Books, 1987), 329–33; "Clipped Wings," *New Yorker*, 23 July 1984, 96, 101–3, reprinted in *Musical Events: A Chronicle, 1983–1986* (New York: Summit Books, 1989), 175–79.

46. The first movement of Grieg's concerto had also been featured prominently in *Song of Norway* (loosely based on the life of Grieg) and more briefly in Loesser's *How to Succeed in Business Without Really Trying*.

47. As a result of my request to study a copy of the 1987 *Follies* libretto Goldman "turned the matter over to his attorneys" and "notified the Library of Congress that no permission

is to be given for an examination copy." Letter to the author from Barbara Deren, President, Barbara Deren Associates, 5 July 1994. From this letter I have inferred that the librettist favors the 1971 libretto.

48. I am indebted to Larry Starr for making available to me in typescript the penetrating critical overview of *Sunday* he presented at the National Conference of the Sonneck Society for American Music, Nashville, Tennessee, April 1989, "The Broadway Musical as a Critique of Modernist Culture, or Sunday in the Park with Sondheim."

49. See Banfield, 364–79., especially 375–79.

50. See my review of *Assassins* in *American Music* 11 (Winter 1993): 507–9.

SELECT
BIBLIOGRAPHY

Abbott, George. *"Mister Abbott."* New York: Random House, 1963.

Alpert, Hollis. *The Life and Times of "Porgy and Bess": The Story of an American Classic.* New York: Alfred A. Knopf, 1990.

Armitage, Merle, ed. *George Gershwin.* New York: Longmans, Green, 1938.

Banfield, Stephen. *Sondheim's Broadway Musicals.* Ann Arbor: University of Michigan Press, 1993.

Beckerman, Bernard, and Howard Siegman, eds. *On Stage: Selected Theater Reviews from "The New York Times" 1920–1970.* New York: Arno Press, 1973.

Bernstein, Leonard. *Findings.* New York: Simon & Schuster, 1982.

Blitzstein, Marc. "Author of 'The Cradle' Discusses Broadway Hit." *Daily Worker*, 3 January 1938, 7.

———. "The Case for Modern Music." *New Masses* 20/3 (14 July 1936): 27.

———. "The Case for Modern Music, II. Second Generation." *New Masses* 20/4 (21 July 1936): 28–29.

———. "On Writing Music for the Theatre." *Modern Music* 15/2 (January–February 1938): 81–85.

———. *Marc Blitzstein Discusses His Theater Compositions.* Spoken Arts 717 (LP) (1957). Published as "Out of the Cradle," *Opera News* 24/15 (13 February 1960): 10+; reprinted as "As He Remembered It—The Late Composer's Story of How 'The Cradle' Began Rocking." *New York Times*, 12 April 1964, sec. 2, 13+.

Block, Geoffrey. "The Broadway Canon From *Show Boat* to *West Side Story* and the European Operatic Ideal." *Journal of Musicology* 11 (Fall 1993): 525–44.

———. "Frank Loesser's Sketchbooks for *The Most Happy Fella.*" *Musical Quarterly* 73 (1989): 60–78.

———. "Gershwin's Buzzard and Other Mythological Creatures." *Opera Quarterly* 7 (Summer 1990): 74–82.

———. Review-essay on Stephen Banfield's *Sondheim's Broadway Musicals. Journal of the Royal Musical Association* 121/1 (1996): 20–27.

Bordman, Gerald. *American Musical Comedy.* New York: Oxford University Press, 1982.
———. *American Musical Revue.* New York: Oxford University Press, 1985.
———. *American Musical Theatre: A Chronicle.* New York: Oxford University Press, 1986.
———. *American Operetta.* New York: Oxford University Press, 1981.
———. *Jerome Kern: His Life and Music.* New York: Oxford University Press, 1980.
———. *The Oxford Companion to American Theatre.* New York: Oxford University Press, 1992.
Brecht, Bertolt. "The Modern Theatre is the Epic Theatre." In Willett, 33–42.
———. "On Gestic Music." In Willett, 104–6.
———. "On the Use of Music in an Epic Theatre." In Willett, 84–90.
Burrows, Abe. "The Making of *Guys & Dolls.*" *Atlantic Monthly* (January 1980): 40–47, 50–52.
Burton, Humphrey. *Leonard Bernstein.* New York: Doubleday, 1994.
Citron, Stephen. *Noel & Cole.* New York: Oxford University Press, 1993.
———. *The Wordsmiths: Oscar Hammerstein 2nd and Alan Jay Lerner.* New York: Oxford University Press, 1995.
Costello, Donald P. *The Serpent's Eye: Shaw and the Cinema.* Notre Dame, Ind.: University of Notre Dame Press, 1965.
Crawford, Cheryl. *One Naked Individual.* Indianapolis: Bobbs-Merrill, 1977.
Crawford, Richard. *The American Musical Landscape.* Berkeley: University of California Press, 1993.
———. "Gershwin's Reputation: A Note on *Porgy and Bess.*" *Musical Quarterly* 65 (April 1979): 257–64.
———. "It Ain't Necessarily Soul: Gershwin's 'Porgy and Bess' as a Symbol." *Yearbook for Inter-American Musical Research* 8 (1972): 17–38.
Davis, Lee. *Bolton and Wodehouse and Kern: The Men Who Made Musical Comedy.* New York: James H. Heineman, 1993.
Dietz, Robert James. "Marc Blitzstein and the 'Agit-Prop' Theatre of the 1930's." *Yearbook for Inter-American Musical Research* 6 (1970): 51–66.
———. "The Operatic Style of Marc Blitzstein in the American 'Agit-Prop' Era." Ph.D. diss., University of Iowa, 1970.
Drew, David. *Kurt Weill: A Handbook.* Berkeley: University of California Press, 1987.
———. "Kurt Weill and His Critics." *Times Literary Supplement,* 3 October 1975, 1142–44; 10 October 1975, 1198–1200.
———. "Reflections on the Last Years: *Der Kuhhandel* as a Key Work." In Kowalke, ed., *New Orpheus,* 217–67.
———. "Weill, Kurt (Julian)." *The New Grove Dictionary of Music and Musicians.* Edited by Stanley Sadie. London: Macmillan, 1980. Vol. 20, 300–10.
Dudar, Helen. "George Abbott Dusts Off a Broadway Classic." *New York Times,* 6 March 1983, sec 7, 30.
Eells, George. *The Life That Late He Led: A Biography of Cole Porter.* New York: G.P. Putnam's Sons, 1967.
Engel, Lehman. *The American Musical Theater.* New York: Collier, 1967; rev. ed., 1975.
———. *Words With Music: The Broadway Musical Libretto.* New York: Schirmer Books, 1972.
Ewen, David. *George Gershwin: His Journey to Greatness* New York: Ungar, 1970; 2nd enl. ed., 1986.
———. "He Passes the Ammunition for Hits." *Theatre Arts* 40/5 (May 1956): 73–75, 90–91.
———. *New Complete Book of the American Musical Theater.* New York: Holt, Rinehart & Winston, 1970.
———. *Richard Rodgers.* New York: Henry Holt, 1957.
Fordin, Hugh. *Getting to Know Him: A Biography of Oscar Hammerstein II.* New York: Ungar, 1977.
Freedman, Samuel G. "After 50 Years, 'Porgy' Comes to the Met as a Certified Classic." *New York Times,* 3 February 1985, sec. 2, 1+.

Furia, Philip. *Ira Gershwin: The Art of the Lyricist*. New York: Oxford University Press, 1995.

———. *Poets of Tin Pan Alley: A History of America's Great Lyricists*. New York: Oxford University Press, 1990.

Gänzl, Kurt. *Gänzl's Book of the Broadway Musical: 75 Favorite Shows, From "H.M.S. Pinafore" to "Sunset Boulevard."* New York: Schirmer Books, 1995.

Gänzl, Kurt, and Andrew Lamb. *Gänzl's Book of the Musical Theatre*. London: Bodley Head, 1988.

Gates, Henry Louis, Jr. " 'Authenticity,' or the Lesson of Little Tree." *New York Times Book Review*, 24 November 1991, 1+.

Gershwin, George. "Rhapsody in Catfish Row: Mr. Gershwin Tells the Origin and Scheme for His Music in That New Folk Opera Called 'Porgy and Bess'." *New York Times*, 20 October 1935, sec. 10, 1–2; reprinted as "Rhapsody in Catfish Row," in Armitage, ed.

Gershwin, Ira. *Lyrics on Several Occasions*. New York: Alfred A. Knopf, 1959.

Goldberg, Isaac. *George Gershwin: A Study in American Music*. New York: Simon and Schuster, 1931; reprinted with an extended supplement by Edith Garson. New York: Frederick Ungar, 1958.

Goldstein, Malcolm. *The Political Stage: American Drama and Theater of the Great Depression*. New York: Oxford University Press, 1974.

Gordon, Eric A. *Mark the Music: The Life and Work of Marc Blitzstein*. New York: St. Martin's Press, 1989.

Gordon, Joanne. *Art Isn't Easy: The Theatre of Stephen Sondheim*. New York: Da Capo Press, 1992.

Gottfried, Martin. *More Broadway Musicals Since 1980*. New York: Harry N. Abrams, 1991.

———. *Sondheim*. New York: Harry N. Abrams, 1993.

Gottlieb, Jack. "The Music of Leonard Bernstein: A Study of Melodic Manipulations." D.M.A. diss., University of Illinois, 1964.

Gradenwitz, Peter. *Leonard Bernstein: The Infinite Variety of a Musician*. New York: Berg, 1987.

Green, Benny, ed. *A Hymn To Him: The Lyrics of Alan Jay Lerner*. New York: Limelight Editions, 1987.

Green, Stanley. *Broadway Musicals of the 30s*. New York: Da Capo, 1971.

———. *Broadway Musicals Show by Show*. Milwaukee, Wisc.: Hal Leonard Books, 1985.

———. *Encyclopedia of the Musical Film*. New York: Oxford University Press, 1981.

———. *Encyclopedia of the Musical Theatre*. New York: Da Capo, 1980.

———. *The World of Musical Comedy*. San Diego: A. S. Barnes, 1980; 4th ed., rev. and enl., New York: Da Capo, 1986.

———, ed. *Rodgers and Hammerstein Fact Book*. New York: Lynn Farnol Group, 1980.

Guernsey, Otis L., Jr. *Curtain Times: The New York Theater 1965–1987*. New York: Applause Theatre Book Publishers, 1987.

———, ed. *Broadway Song & Story: Playwrights, Lyricists, Composers Discuss Their Hits*. New York: Dodd, Mead, 1985.

———, ed. *Playwrights, Lyricists, Composers on Theatre*. New York: Dodd, Mead, 1974.

Gussow, Mel. " 'West Side Story': The Beginnings Of Something Great." *New York Times*, 21 October 1990, sec. 2, p. 5.

Hamm, Charles. *Music in the New World*. New York: W. W. Norton, 1983.

———. *Putting Popular Music in its Place*. Cambridge: Cambridge University Press, 1995.

———. "The Theatre Guild Production of *Porgy and Bess*." *Journal of the American Musicological Society* 40 (1987): 495–532.

———. *Yesterdays: Popular Song in America*. New York: W. W. Norton, 1979.

Hammerstein, Oscar II. *Lyrics*. Milwaukee, Wisc.: Hal Leonard Books, 1985.

———. "Turns on a Carousel." *New York Times*, 15 April 1945, sec. 2, 1.

Harrison, Rex. *Rex: An Autobiography*. New York: William Morrow, 1974.

Hart, Dorothy, and Robert Kimball, eds. *The Complete Lyrics of Lorenz Hart*. New York: Alfred A. Knopf, 1986.

Hart, Moss. Preface to *Lady in the Dark*. Vocal score. New York: Chappell Music, 1941.

Hirsch, Foster. *Harold Prince and the American Musical Theatre*. Cambridge: Cambridge University Press, 1989.

Hitchcock, H. Wiley. *Music in the United States*. Englewood Cliffs, N.J.: Prentice Hall, 1969; rev. 3rd ed., 1988.

Holden, Stephen. "A Glimpse of Olden Days, Via Cole Porter." *New York Times*, 18 October 1987, sec. 2, 5+.

Horn, David. "From Catfish Row to Granby Street: Contesting Meaning in *Porgy and Bess*." *Popular Music* 13 (1994): 165–74.

Houghton, Norris. "*Romeo and Juliet* and *West Side Story*: An Appreciation." In *Romeo and Juliet/West Side Story*, 7–14. New York: Dell, 1965.

Houseman, John. *Run-Through*. New York: Simon & Schuster, 1972.

Hubler, Richard G. *The Cole Porter Story* (introduction by Arthur Schwartz). Cleveland: World, 1965.

Hummel, David. *The Collector's Guide to the American Musical Theatre*. 2 vols. Metuchen, N.J.: Scarecrow Press, 1984.

Hunter, John O. "Marc Blitzstein's 'The Cradle Will Rock' as a Document of America, 1937." *American Quarterly* 16 (1964): 227–33.

Hyland, William G. *The Song Is Ended: Songwriters and American Music, 1900–1950*. New York: Oxford University Press, 1995.

Ilson, Carol. *Harold Prince: From "Pajama Game" to "Phantom of the Opera."* Ann Arbor, Mich.: UMI Research Press, 1989.

Jablonski, Edward. *Gershwin: A Biography*. New York: Doubleday, 1987.

Johnson, Hall. "*Porgy and Bess*—A Folk Opera." *Opportunity* (January 1936): 24–28.

Kerman, Joseph. *Opera as Drama*. New York: Alfred A. Knopf, 1956; new and rev. ed. Berkeley: University of California Press, 1988.

Kimball, Robert., ed. *The Complete Lyrics of Cole Porter*. New York: Vintage Books, 1984.

———. *The Complete Lyrics of Ira Gershwin*. New York: Alfred A. Knopf, 1993.

———. See also D. Hart.

King, William G. "Music and Musicians. Composer for the Theater—Kurt Weill Talks About 'Practical Music'." *New York Sun*, 3 February 1940.

Kingman, Daniel. *American Music: A Panorama*. New York: Schirmer Books, 1979; Rev. ed, 1990.

Kivy, Peter. *Osmin's Rage: Philosophical Reflections on Opera, Drama, and Text*. Princeton, N.J.: Princeton University Press, 1988.

Kolodin, Irving. " 'Porgy and Bess': American Opera in the Theatre." *Theatre Arts Monthly* 19 (1935): 853–65.

Kowalke, Kim H. "Formerly German: Kurt Weill in America." In Kowalke and Edler, eds., 35–57.

———. *Kurt Weill in Europe*. Ann Arbor, Mich.: UMI Research Press, 1979.

———, ed. *A New Orpheus: Essays on Kurt Weill*. New Haven: Yale University Press, 1986.

Kowalke, Kim H., and Horst Edler, eds. *A Stranger Here Myself: Kurt Weill Studien*. Hildesheim, Ger.: Georg Olms Verlag, 1993.

Krasker, Tommy, and Robert Kimball. *Catalog of the American Musical*. Washington, D.C.: National Institute for Opera and Musical Theater, 1988.

Kreuger, Miles. "*Show Boat*": *The Story of a Classic American Musical*. New York: Oxford University Press, 1977.

———. "Some Words about 'Anything Goes' " and "The Annotated 'Anything Goes'." Notes to EMI/Angel CDC 7–49848–2 (1989), 9–17 and 133–40.

———. "Some Words about 'Show Boat'." Notes to EMI/Angel CDS 7–49108–2 (1988), 13–24.

Ledbetter, Steven, ed. *Sennets & Tuckets: A Bernstein Celebration*. Boston: David R. Godine, 1988.

Lees, Gene. *Inventing Champagne: The Worlds of Lerner and Loewe*. New York: St. Martin's Press, 1990.

Lerner, Alan Jay. *The Street Where I Live*. New York: W. W. Norton, 1970.

Lonoff, Jeffrey. Notes to *A Collector's Sondheim*. RCA CRL4–5359.

Loesser, Frank. "Some Loesser Thoughts on 'The Most Happy Fella'." Imperial Theatre program notes, 1956.

———. "Some Notes on a Musical." Imperial Theatre program notes 1956.

Loesser, Susan. *A Most Remarkable Fella: Frank Loesser and the Guys and Dolls in His Life*. New York: Donald I. Fine, 1993.

mcclung, bruce d. "Life after George: The Genesis of *Lady in the Dark*'s Circus Dream." *Kurt Weill Newsletter* 14/2 (Fall 1996): 4–8.

———. "Psicosi per musica: Re-examining *Lady in the Dark*." In Kowalke and Edler, eds., 235–65.

McGlinn, John. "The Original 'Anything Goes'—A Classic Restored." Notes to EMI/Angel CDC 7–49848–2 (1989), 29–34.

———. "Notes on 'Show Boat'." Notes to EMI/Angel CDS 7–49108–2 (1988), 26–38.

McNally, Terence, Moderator. "West Side Story." In Guernsey, ed., 40–54.

Mandelbaum, Ken. *"A Chorus Line" and the Musicals of Michael Bennett*. New York: St. Martin's Press, 1989.

Mann, Martin Arthur. "The Musicals of Frank Loesser." Ph.D. diss., City University of New York, 1974.

Mast, Gerald. *Can't Help Singin': The American Musical On Stage and Screen*. Woodstock, N.Y.: Overlook Press, 1987.

Mates, Julian. *America's Musical Stage: Two Hundred Years of Musical Theater*. New York: Praeger, 1987.

Mauceri, John. Notes to *On Your Toes*. Polydor 813667–1 Y 1 (1983).

Mellers, Wilfrid. *Music in a New Found Land*. New York: Oxford University Press, 1964; rev. ed., 1987.

Miletich, Leo N. *Broadway's Prize-Winning Musicals: An Annotated Guide for Libraries and Audio Collectors*. New York: Harrington Park Press, 1993.

Mordden, Ethan. *Better Foot Forward: The History of the American Musical Theatre*. New York: Grossman, 1976.

———. *Rodgers & Hammerstein*. New York: Harry N. Abrams, 1992.

———. " 'Show Boat' Crosses Over." *New Yorker*, 3 July 1989, 79–93.

Morison, Patricia, and Miles Kreuger. "Patricia Morison and Miles Kreuger Discuss the Deleted Songs July 5, 1990." In notes to *Kiss Me, Kate*. EMI/Angel CDS 54033–2, 18–20.

New York Theatre Critics' Reviews. New York: Critics' Theatre Reviews, 1940-.

Norton, Elliot. "Broadway's cutting room floor." *Theatre Arts* 36 (April 1952): 80.

Oja, Carol J. "Marc Blitzstein's *The Cradle Will Rock* and Mass-Song Style of the 1930s." *Musical Quarterly* 73 (1989): 445–75.

Osborne, Conrad L. " 'Happy Fella' Yields Up Its Operatic Heart." *New York Times*, 1 September 1991, sec. 2, 5 and 17.

Peyser, Joan. *Bernstein: A Biography*. New York: William Morrow, 1987.

Prince, Harold. *Contradictions: Notes on Twenty-six Years in the Theatre*. New York: Dodd, Mead, 1974.

Redmond, James, ed. *Themes in Drama*. Vol. 3. Cambridge: Cambridge University Press, 1981.

Robinson, Paul. *Opera & Ideas: From Mozart to Strauss*. Ithaca, N.Y.: Cornell University Press, 1985.

Rodgers, Richard. *Musical Stages*. New York: Random House, 1975.

Rosenberg, Deena. *Fascinating Rhythm: The Collaboration of George and Ira Gershwin*. New York: Dutton, 1991.

Sanders, Ronald. *The Days Grow Short: The Life and Music of Kurt Weill.* New York: Holt, Rinehart & Winston, 1980.

Schebera, Jürgen. *Kurt Weill: An Illustrated Life.* New Haven: Yale University Press, 1995.

Schiff, David. "Re-hearing Bernstein." *Atlantic Monthly* (June 1993): 55–76.

Schwartz, Charles. *Gershwin: His Life & Music.* New York: Da Capo, 1979.

Scott, Matthew. "Weill in America: The Problem of Revival." Kowalke, ed., *New Orpheus* 285–95.

Secrest, Meryle. *Leonard Bernstein: A Life.* New York: Alfred A. Knopf, 1994.

Shirley, Wayne. "*Porgy and Bess.*" *Quarterly Journal of the Library of Congress* 31 (1974): 97–107.

———. "Reconciliation on Catfish Row: Bess, Serena, and the Short Score of *Porgy and Bess.*" *Quarterly Journal of the Library of Congress* 38 (1981): 144–65.

Shout, John D. "The Musical Theater of Marc Blitzstein." *American Music* 3 (Winter 1985): 413–28.

Siebert, Lynn Laitman. "Cole Porter: An Analysis of Five Musical Comedies and a Thematic Catalogue of the Complete Works." Ph.D. diss., City University of New York, 1974.

Simon, Robert. "Jerome Kern." *Modern Music* 6/2 (January–February 1929): 20–25.

Smith, June. "Cole Porter in the American Musical Theatre." In Redmond, ed., 47–70.

Sondheim, Stephen. "An Anecdote." In *Bernstein on Broadway,* xi–xii. New York and London: Amberson/G. Schirmer, 1981.

———. "The Musical Theater." In Guernsey, ed., 228–50.

———. "Theater Lyrics." In Guernsey, ed., 61–97.

Spewack, Bella. "How to Write a Musical Comedy." In *"Kiss Me Kate": A Musical Play,* book by Samuel and Bella Spewack, lyrics by Cole Porter. New York: Alfred A. Knopf, 1953.

Starr, Lawrence. "The Broadway Musical As a Critique of Modernist Culture, or Sunday in the Park with Sondheim." Unpublished typescript.

———. "Gershwin's 'Bess, You Is My Woman Now': The Sophistication and Subtlety of a Great Tune." *Musical Quarterly* 72 (1986): 429–48.

———. "Toward a Reevaluation of Gershwin's *Porgy and Bess. American Music* 2 (Summer 1984): 35–37.

Stempel, Larry. "Broadway's Mozartean Moment, or An Amadeus in Amber." In Ledbetter, ed., 39–55.

———. "The Musical Play Expands." *American Music* 10 (1992): 136–69.

———. "*Street Scene* and the Enigma of Broadway Opera." In Kowalke, ed., *New Orpheus,* 321–41.

Suskin, Steven. *Opening Night on Broadway: A Critical Quotebook of the Golden Era of the Musical Theatre, "Oklahoma!" (1943) to "Fiddler on the Roof" (1964).* New York: Schirmer Books, 1990.

Swain, Joseph P. *The Broadway Musical: A Critical and Musical Survey.* New York: Oxford University Press, 1990.

Symonette, Lys and Kim H. Kowalke, eds. and trans. *Speak Low (When You Speak Love): The Letters of Kurt Weill and Lotte Lenya.* Berkeley: University of California Press, 1996.

Thompson, Ezra Bell. "Why Negroes Don't Like 'Porgy and Bess'." *Ebony* 14/12 (October 1959): 51–53.

Thomson, Virgil. "George Gershwin." *Modern Music* 13 (November–December 1935): 13–19; reprinted in *A Virgil Thomson Reader,* 23–27. Boston: Houghton Mifflin, 1981.

———. "In the Theatre." *Modern Music* 15 (January–February 1938): 113.

Walsh, Michael. *Andrew Lloyd Webber: His Life and Works.* New York: Harry N. Abrams, 1989.

Weill, Kurt. Notes for the original cast recording of *Street Scene.* Columbia OL 4139.

———. "Über den gestischen Charakter der Musik." *Die Musik* 21 (March 1929): 419–23; English version in Kowalke, *Kurt Weill,* 491–96.

Welsh, John. From Play to Musical: Comparative Studies of Ferenc Molnar's 'Liliom' with Richard Rodgers' and Oscar Hammerstein II's 'Carousel'; and Sidney Howard's 'They

Knew What They Wanted' with Frank Loesser's 'The Most Happy Fella'. Ph.D. diss., Tulane University, 1967.

Wilder, Alex. *American Popular Song: The Great Innovators 1900–1950*. New York: Oxford University Press, 1972.

Willett, John, ed. and trans. *Brecht on Theatre*. New York: Hill & Wang, 1964.

Woll, Allen. *Black Musical Theatre: From "Coontown" to "Dreamgirls."* Baton Rouge: Louisiana State University Press, 1989.

Zadan, Craig. *Sondheim & Co.* New York: Harper & Row, 1990.

INDEX

This selective index includes page references to the shows featured in this volume along with their songs, literary sources, composers, lyricists, librettists, directors, producers, choreographers, musical borrowings, and interpolations. Titles in bold refer to shows and other major works. Titles in italics refer to songs. Pages in italics refer to musical examples; pages in bold refer to drawings and photographs.